TEXT AND THE CITY

D0907662

ASIA-PACIFIC: CULTURE, POLITICS, AND SOCIETY

Editors: Rey Chow, H. D. Harootunian, and Masao Miyoshi

TEXT AND THE CITY

ESSAYS ON JAPANESE MODERNITY

町 朋

黒 町閭黒東 坂 町 谷 長 目

MAEDA AI

住

Edited and with an Introduction by JAMES A. FUJII

町 間 从 伍人

Duke University Press Durham and London 2004

© 2004 DUKE UNIVERSITY PRESS. All rights reserved.

Printed in the United States of America on acid-free paper ∞

Designed by Amy Ruth Buchanan. Typeset in Carter & Cone Galliard

by Tseng Information Systems, Inc. Library of Congress Cataloging-

in-Publication Data appear on the last printed page of this book.

CONTENTS

ACKNOWLEDGMENTS

This anthology is the fruit of hard work by nine translators, whose own careers had varying intersections with that of Maeda Ai. A few knew only his published work, others had met him in academic venues, and still others had the pleasure of exploring parts of a city with him. That which makes Maeda's scholarship so cross-disciplinary, learned, and imaginative made translation truly daunting work; I remain in awe of the results produced by my fellow translators. Chicago would be the city where the authors of the essays that frame the translations at both ends of this volume, Harry Harootunian, Masao Miyoshi, and Bill Sibley, would invite Maeda for an extended stay that would contribute to the role played by the University of Chicago as the center of critical theory and Japan studies in the late 1970s and 1980s. My debts to all four scholars go well beyond the horizons of this anthology.

Every essay in this volume bears the mark of what can only be called heroic work on the part of Junko Matsuura, who performed with intelligence, resourcefulness, and diligence myriad tasks that extended well beyond the boundaries of remunerated labor. In addition to translating two essays that appear in this volume, my colleague Ted Fowler provided scholarly discernment, guidance, and friendship during the many years that this project took shape. Steve Carter, in his capacity as chair of my department and friend, also found creative ways to loosen up valuable time and support to help realize this anthology; he also helped make sense of a few vexing passages. For clarifying some obscure references and works from the *kinsei* (early modern) era, Masa Higurashi of Hōsei University deserves our sincere thanks. Rey Chow, now of Brown University, encouraged me as interlocutor and friend from the early stages of this project. Among the friends and colleagues not directly involved in translating Maeda's essays but whose support and friendship helped make this work possible are Brett deBary, Norma Field, William Haver, Kamei

Hideo, Komori Yoichi, Vic Koshmann, Frederic J. Kotas, Marti Miyoshi, Tetsuo Najita, Naoki Sakai, Barbara Sato, Kazuki Sato, Seki Reiko, Miriam Silverberg, and Stefan Tanaka.

In addition to producing a beautiful translation of "The Panorama of Enlightenment," Henry Smith was able to arrange for permission from the Santa Barbara Museum of Art to include Kobayashi Kiyochika's *Kaiun Bridge and First National Bank in the Snow* and *Shinbashi Station*, both of which appear in the chapter titled "The Panorama of Enlightenment." Mr. Narahara Makio of Hara Shobō publishers helped provide illustrations of Japanese prisons that appear with their permission in this volume. Staff at the Modern Japanese Literary Archives (Nihon kindai bungakukan), the Tokyo Metropolitan Central Library, and the National Diet Library responded to our queries related to citation both in person and by electronic media with dispatch and thoroughness. Editors at Chikuma Shobō, publishers of *The Collected Works of Maeda Ai*, were as generous with their time as they were in giving permission for use of many of the illustrations that appear in this book. Farrell Graves, Adrienne Hurley, Kota Inoue, Helen Lee, Michele Mason, Junko Matsuura, and Jen Mertens provided perceptive comments in seminars that touched upon some of these essays by Maeda, and Michele also provided timely research assistance. Reynolds Smith of Duke University Press has been steadfast in his support throughout this project, and I owe him and Sharon Torian heartfelt thanks for their hard work and timely responses to uncountable questions. Kate Lothman provided superb editorial help in getting us through the always difficult later stages of production, and Judith Hoover deserves our thanks for her meticulous and skillful copyediting. Thanks also to Amy Ruth Buchanan, whose keen eye is evident in the design of this book. Funding support came from the School of Humanities at the University of California, Irvine, the University of California President's Fellowship, the Office of the Dean of Humanities, and the UCI Humanities Research Center. Some of the release time made possible from an NEH grant for a project focused on railways, I must admit, also migrated over to enable the completion of this one. Pam LaZarre, Dianna Sahhar, Suzy Jung, and Gerry Lopez of the UCI Interlibrary Loan Service and Document Delivery Services were unfailingly helpful in providing their services, including the processing of hundreds of books and articles we sought and received without a hitch. Michael J. Miller at the UCI Multimedia Development Computer Support Instructional Technology Center provided valuable support in helping to create maps and diagrams. We also received timely help from Hisayuki Ishimatsu, librarian at the University of California, Berkeley.

I am grateful to Ellen Radovic, who urged me to undertake this project, read multiple versions of translations, edited passages with a fresh and discerning pair of eyes, and supported me in countless ways that defy cataloguing; oddly enough, her presence added immeasurably to more than one of my many meetings with Mrs. Maeda, even though Ellen does not speak Japanese. If a book that is not really mine can be dedicated, it goes to Mrs. Maeda, who has inspired me as much as her husband did in his capacity as one of my academic mentors. In a conversation wedged into her busy schedule as a full-time clinical social worker with hours of additional weekly volunteer work, with a mixture of diffidence and affirmation, Mineko Maeda recounted to me her first meeting with the young undergraduate who would become her husband—he from Tōdai, she from Ochanomizu Women's College—at rehearsals for a leftist collegiate drama society. This volume celebrates that union of two remarkable individuals. Finally, let me mention our wonderful canine companion of twelve years, Nassi, whose last six years were mostly spent with me as I worked on this anthology, as well as other projects, both at home and at the office.

Maeda Ai in Kuruizawa. Photo by Sayama Tatsuo. Courtesy Shōgakukan P.C.

A Walker in the City:

Maeda Ai and the Mapping of Urban Space

HARRY HAROOTUNIAN

In a life that passed too quickly and ended too abruptly, Maeda Ai was able to live the time of his life more fully and imaginatively than most of us who have been granted the span allotted to us. For those who knew him in what now seems to have been a momentary meeting the effect of his swift passage through our lives has far exceeded the event of an encounter. Many of us in the 1960s and 1970s interested in pursuing the study of Japan's culture, literature, and history, found in Maeda's writings an interpretative propaedeutic far richer and more complex than the simplistic exercises area studies promoted as forms of training—usually little more than extended language study informed by indefensible claims of cultural transparency. In the Japanese scholarly world the interpretative templates were no more helpful. As a result, Maeda occupied an ambiguous position, often reinforced by a disciplined self-marginalization between mindless empiricism, shared by both Marxists and non-Marxists alike, and approaches driven by outrageous conceits of exceptionalism based on the irreducible authority of cultural (read as ethnic) authenticity that not even the most masterful acquisition of language proficiency by a foreigner could ever hope to match.

Maeda was not simply devoted to understanding the spectacle of Japan's capitalist modernization since the nineteenth century; he was also a committed modernist convinced that the singular transformation brought Japan into the world as readily as it brought the world into Japan. This meant that despite, or better yet, because of the necessity of recognizing the inheritance of a specific culture of reference as it mingled with the new, he was able to recognize how much Japan had changed and how the nature of change, as already forecast by the philosopher Tosaka Jun in the 1930s, "linked Japan to a wider world." As the essays in this collection show, time and again, Maeda's work was devoted to demonstrating how the great transformation was simply part of what Frederic Jameson has called a "singular modernity," making Japan's inflection interchangeable with modernizing experiences found elsewhere throughout the globe and thus as accessible as any other instance of the modern to seekers of the meaning of modernity. When I first met Maeda back in the 1970s and described my interest in Tokugawa nativism and thinkers such as Hirata Atsutane, perhaps the most intellectually obdurate exceptionalist thinkers Japan has produced, his response was to protest that he "was allergic to such people" and what they stood for.

Maeda Ai was formed in an intellectual and political culture marked by the immediate postwar years, when he attended university and began his teaching career. These years witnessed the incendiary mass mobilizations from 1960 on that expressed dissatisfaction with Japan's dependent relationship to the United States (now that the military occupation had officially ended). It was inflamed by the new U.S.-Japan Mutual Security Pact, the singular failure of social democratic discourse and its subsequent darkening in the lengthening shadow of a one-party "democracy" supported by the United States, and the explosion of a student movement and its radicalization prompted by both the state's effort to "manage" universities and the recognition that U.S. involvement in Vietnam was becoming a global event. In Japan during the decade of the 1960s and early 1970s, most universities were either periodically closed or campuses and buildings were sporadically seized and occupied on an unscheduled basis by student groups. Frequent confrontations on the streets between students and riot police often defined the educational culture of the times and resembled, in pace and rhythm, carefully orchestrated scenes seemingly inspired by cinematic medieval horse operas (chanbara).

If the conjuncture provided the background noise to Maeda's formation (in an ironic gesture he once confessed to me in a Chicago bar to his own "political cowardice"), the movement of events simply reinforced his perception that the site of modernity and its consequential discords had always been the city—the large urban concentrations that signified for him the moment Japan, with other industrializing societies, changed the received human ecology between countryside and city, provoked by the massive migrations of peasantry into the new urban industrial workplace. It was this fact that constituted for Maeda the singularity of modernity, inasmuch as it manifests the fateful and inevitable alteration of the space-time relationship by privileging the former over the latter and thus necessitated the identification of a new chronotope. With Maeda this privileging of space signaled the importance of the modern city—the massive urban complexes that reached deeply into the surrounding countryside, according to the folklorist Yanagita Kunio, and demanded its sacrifice—transmuted into the space of culture. Yet it is interesting to notice how the city, the expanded urban space, not only incorporated time by ontologizing the present but also absorbed the countryside itself, in his view lost its claim to autonomy promised by an older division of labor between town and country. Concern for the maintenance of the division between city and countryside appeared precisely at the moment the new metropolitan cities embarked on their expansion and colonization of space and when they projected a "universal" self-image of modernity that excluded any other alternative.

Maeda saw the emergence of this new urban space both as the subject of cultural analysis and as the occasion for working a new and appropriate interpretative strategy capable of bringing together history, urban geography and planning, ethnography, material culture, and literature into what now appears as a cultural studies "before the letter."

Although Maeda saw his own method as topographical (and even topological, hinting at mathematical rigor and scientific precision), in keeping with the spatial privilege modernity accords to the city, his primary instrument of analysis was the text of literature produced within the space of the city and that constituted its inscription. Texts needed deciphering as well as reading, and here Maeda turned to the model of the map, the principal template for representing space as such. The map supplied the coordinates organizing space that could provide an optic through which to look at literary texts and ways they signified the cityspace of their production. In this regard, Maeda's earlier work on late Tokugawa fictions, *gesaku*, already disclosed an interest in the city, albeit a premodern Edo that would become Tokyo, and how it supplied the space for literary production and the market of a reading public. It is hardly surprising that this work concentrated on examining writers imbedded in Edo life (Bakin) and its transition to Tokyo in the early Meiji period (Narushima Ryūhoku). But what these fictions and subsequent literary nonliterary texts offered were maps detailing specific spaces and sites, whether the "utopia" of Meiji prisons, the quarters of lower-class Tokyo reported by Yokoyama Gennosuke, or the Shanghai Bund in the late 1920s envisaged by Yokomitsu Riichi. Maeda looked upon literary texts as maps capable of yielding knowledge of a location and delineating the details of organization of streets and sites that filled and shaped the interiority of a city space to make it recognizably a place. But reading as a form of mapping required a committed observer of the scene itself, an urban ethnographer willing to walk the streets of the city and faithfully record, like the great urban ethnographer of Tokyo streets of the 1920s Kon Wajirō, the passing montage.

More than anything else, Maeda was a walker in the city, any and all cities, even though Tokyo was the place he loved most and knew best, a careful observer of its infinite and often overlooked ordinary details that revealed all but forgotten remnants of different histories coexisting in the modern present yet capable of recalling other moments. As much as he was a scholar of literature he was a reporter of urban sites, always maintaining a slight distance from them, like Kon and indeed all those Japanese writers he tracked down who traveled to and wrote from foreign cities. In his principal book, *Toshi kukan no naka no bungaku* (Literature as cityspace), Maeda frequently focused on narratives whose authors were implicated in specific cityspaces: Ōgai's Berlin; Yokomitsu's Shanghai, the quintessential colonial city before the war, with its dangerous mix of foreign imperialists and subject peoples; Higuchi Ichiyō's late Meiji Tokyo, still vibrant with the rhythms of its Edo past mixing with the new in the neighborhood of her late nineteenth-century childhood; and Kafū's historically completed Paris, contrasted to a Tokyo "under reconstruction." As a good geographer and explorer, Maeda would walk these cities and acquire firsthand knowledge of the specific locations that structured stories and novels, always seeking to follow the traces of authors who had come before him to make the space of the city the subject of their texts. When he was in Chicago as a visiting professor he walked its streets tirelessly in search of traces of Japan and went to Kalamazoo to fulfill one stop in Kafū's only American itinerary. An indefatigable traveler, perhaps satisfying one of the unfulfilled ambitions of Tokugawa eccentrics (who were prohibited from traveling abroad) and their desire for difference, Maeda went to Berlin, Shanghai, Paris, and indeed anywhere the writer had preceded him. His most complex map and greatest mastery was the city of Tokyo, which over the years he had carefully deciphered for its multiple and mixed pasts and still surviving signs of other temporalities, however slight and insignificant, now concealed by the massive materiality of the modern city. I remember an exhausting walking tour of parts of Tokyo Maeda had mapped out, especially remaining traces from its Edo past, and that still housed the faintest traces of a forgotten history that he identified and that still bespoke its memory. I even tried once to recuperate this mazelike tour, looking for a restaurant that apparently had originated in the late Edo or early Meiji period, but failed miserably. Maeda recognized how much Tokyo had changed since its modern beginnings, how much the signs of mixed temporalities had been all but destroyed by the succession of earthquake, World War II bombings, and the senseless desecration inflicted by the Olympics and entrepreneurial developers, how important it was to keep vigil on the remains and survivals of earlier times. It was, in fact, this immense sensitivity to the minute reminders of the city's pasts, made indistinct by the image of an endlessly present space, that disclosed how Maeda envisioned the relationship between time and space demanded by modernity, industrialization, and urbanization. And it was precisely this approach that guided him as he sought to read texts for inscription of cityspace.

Maeda was no ordinary flâneur, however. His earlier studies on the verbal fictions of Edo in the late Tokugawa period acquainted him with a kind of premodern urban ethnography, where authors were always looking in on a scene, seeking to "penetrate the hole," as it was put, as well as the whole, in order to grasp its topos, voyeurs, peeping toms, recording things that colonized space, conduct, but always at a distance. Their purpose was to get behind (*ura*) the surface (*omote*) to make proper judgments concerning the style or lack of it in the subjects under observation. In a sense, this talent reflected "taste," "discernment," to constitute a culture of *furyu*, as it is often called, whose principal figures were eccentrics like Hiraga Gennai, marked by their desire for difference (defamiliarizing and even exoticizing everyday life), centered in the city life of merchant quarters. In this regard, Maeda resembled Roland Barthes, on whose method he wrote an informed essay, and shared with him a passion for the ordinary that is habitually overlooked but invariably capable of emitting cultural meanings. Maeda's walking, his incessant threading through the byways of a text's space, following its coordinates to grasp the totality, like Edogawa Rampo's amateur detective Akechi, ultimately fused a premodern ethnography practiced by the eccentric with a modern awareness of how the space of the city has come to constitute the central subject of modern literature.

The essays selected for translation in this volume offer the English reader a first glimpse of this complex but modernist vision, its interpretative accessibility, to those who can claim no special knowledge of Japan but only an interest in the experience of modernity and the ways Maeda went about implementing it. But they also constitute what Claude Roy, referring to the interwar years in France, once described as "a remembrance of things to come" that has now appropriately become our own inheritance.

Refiguring the Modern: Maeda Ai and the City

JAMES A. FUJII

Every major Japanese newspaper reported the unexpected and sudden death of Maeda Ai in the summer of 1987 at the age of 55. One of the most prominent and influential literary and cultural critics of the late twentieth century, as well as a public intellectual who appeared on national educational television, was interviewed in magazines and newspapers, and taught adult education courses, Maeda had approached the study of modern Japanese literature and culture with daring, imagination, and uncommon erudition. A decade or so earlier, at a time when Japan's sensitivity to intellectual currents of Continental Europe would begin to yield Japanese translations of works by Merleau-Ponty, Barthes, Derrida, Kristeva, Foucault, Bachelard, and Deleuze almost as quickly as they appeared in the original French, Maeda was not simply "applying" but rigorously interrogating and practicing semiotic, structuralist, Marxist, and poststructuralist theory, in turn transforming it by bringing it into congress with native cultural achievements.

It may surprise many who are acquainted with Maeda Ai's (1932–1987) studies of modern Japanese society and culture that he was, by training, a student of premodern (*kinsei*) Japanese literature. Maeda often confounded his mostly traditional fellow scholars of Japanese literature by a profound erudition that (to many of them) was maddeningly informed by rigorous engagement with European critical theory. His distinctive practice of studying modernity through the optic of postmodernity spanned the years from the late 1960s to his death. As a contemporary of Foucault, Poulet, Bachelard, Derrida, Kristeva, and Lefebvre, he engaged their works as deeply and deftly as he did that of earlier students of modern society whose sensibilities intersected with his own, such as Benjamin, Marx, the Tartov School critics, Bakhtin, Piranesi, and a legion of others whose work he brought into the compass of his own study of modern Japanese life, especially through articulations of urban space.

If literature centers Maeda's vast corpus, many of these works read more like social history, cultural criticism, advanced texts on semiology, even a mathematical proof.[1] He was an explorer, much like the urban geographers and literary heroes that figure prominently in his "Utopia of the Prison-house" (chapter 1), and he found a way of discovering the space that text and city, map and narrative, would open up in his explorations of infinitely rich, contradictory, vexing, and rewarding phenomena to which these days we give the all-encompassing term "modernity." Maeda took the text and showed us how to visualize its contours as one might make sense of a set of relationships on a map. At the same time, a significant part of his work represents an extended engagement of visual culture, which he traced as a defining characteristic of both Edo (1600–1867) and Meiji (1868–1912) city life. His innovative focus on text and visuality would coalesce into a literary-historical-critical practice that was centered on notions of space, *kūkan*, that became the signature of his scholarship. He unapologetically reveled in the practice of theory, and at the same time, he remained steadfastly a theorist for whom spatiality spelled historical understanding. When linguistics and literary theory showed us the conjuncture and separation of *langue* or system (*seido*) to parole, the enunciative moment was "discovered" as a way to relativize figurations of diachronic representations. Building on the conceptual richness of this enunciative moment where subjects encounter Others and contingency replaces fate or teleology, Maeda explored the space of intersections, of contest, exchange, that is, a dialogics broadly, richly, and finely articulated as speaking and listening, oppressing, resisting, and mobilizing—in short, the *productions in space* as a supplement to Lefebvre's production *of* space. Like Walter Benjamin who turned to the flâneur and his street-level performance as a way to interrogate modern society, Maeda took to the city as an effective avenue for making sense of modernity. What this approach would repeatedly yield was understanding of the *materiality* of *things* (*mono*) that constitute city life. It is as if the self-conferred epithet of "useless man" (*muyō no hito*) by the subject of Maeda's first study, Narushima Ryūhoku (see below, and "Ryūhoku in Paris," chapter 9), would alert him to the blinding dominance of utilitarianism in Meiji society. If a totalizing *instrumentality* seized modern Japan and attempts to study it, Maeda would examine the modern by steadfastly focusing instead on the *materiality* of modern, urban life.

Ultimately, however, what distinguished Maeda's work was the conjuncture of a populist sensibility that led to a rich array of concerns in Japanese literature and society and a determination to subject critical theory to a radically different cultural space. In 1989, just two years following his death, Chikuma Shobō would issue *Selected Works of Maeda Ai* (*Maeda Ai chosaku-shū*)[2] in six thick volumes. Even a cursory look reveals how its editors strained to fit his essays into these thematically ordered books.[3] His studies of mass culture, the underside of modern life, visual media from *manga* (of the 1920s and 1930s) to panoramas and film, women's magazines and female readership, Higuchi Ichiyō, world's fairs and expositions, Meiji-era *kanbun-gesaku* literature (playful fiction written in Sino-Japanese), and the cultural habits of everyday life in the city would effectively change the register of inquiry for students of modern Japanese literature and cultural history. How much greater is the inadequacy, then, of a single-volume anthology of his essays in translation. Against these odds, I have selected works that presciently questioned and explored new dimensions of Japanese modernity and that resonate deeply with the concerns of literary and cultural studies today. Maeda was also a peerless student of textuality when neoformalist theorists (e.g., Greimas, Barthes, and a rediscovered Bakhtin) forced the word beyond its semiotic boundaries and headlong into "discursive realities." Collectively, these essays continue to serve as important models for how to read literature and culture in concert with the political economy which they both reflect and help shape. [4]

Visual Culture and Textuality

This anthology appears at a moment when the study of modernity has come to be identified with visuality as its defining constituent. Maeda was already vigorously exploring this connection in modern Japanese society back in the 1970s and 1980s. His interest in Western theoretical works would help him recognize the visuality that marked his initial specialization, late Edo literature and culture. Gesaku, he notes in "Modern Literature and the World of Printing" (chapter 8), must be viewed as a form of mass-produced urban literature whose textual-visual hybridity was enabled by the technology of woodblock printing. This text-image relationship profoundly shaped the very nature of literature itself, and it would not suddenly cease just because the shogun was replaced by the emperor to inaugurate the modern era. Alongside such visual-literary practices, Maeda convinces us in "From Communal Performance to Solitary Reading" (chapter 7) to consider another Edo-era literary-cultural practice: reading literary works aloud to an audience. The intersection of such "vestigial" practices, with new technologies like movable-type printing and new formations of visuality, he shows, were important determinants that have been overlooked or ignored in received ways of making sense of modern Japanese literature. These essays show Maeda as a revisionist theorist-critic whose legacy informs, rather than has been overtaken by, recent cultural work.

In "The Panorama of Enlightenment" (chapter 2), Roland Barthes's and Roman Jakobson's semiotics and the Marxist critic Henri Lefebvre's theorization of space help Maeda produce stunning new insights regarding the relationship between social space and text. In his reading of Hattori Bushō's *Shin Tōkyō hanjōki* (New tales of Tokyo prosperity), Maeda analyzes the array of *things* displayed along the Ginza Brick District this way:

> The visual image of *things* lined up [catalogued] on display is conveyed directly by a rhetorical succession of nouns, while the parallel phrases of *kanbun* serve as a device to contrast the new and the old. The rather stereotyped listing of phrases beginning with "gold and silver sparkle" serves as a perfect representation of the dazzling fantasy of an overwhelming array of goods on display. Each separate *thing* is no more than an image that flashes on for just an instant, a symbol of consumption that has been emptied of all meaning. The richness of the display stands in odd contrast to the visual monotony of the Brick District itself, with row after row of the same standardized building design along the eight blocks of the Ginza. Constructed in the functional materials of white plaster over brick that excluded all traces of decorative meaning from the buildings themselves, the Brick District denied the possibility of going beyond the immediate perception of the material object itself. What rises before us is a symbol of "civilization and enlightenment" that is merely a myth emptied of meaning." (From Henry Smith's translation of "Panorama," chapter 2)

What virtually all Japan historians and critics read simply as the signifier of modern urban culture—the Ginza Brick District—Maeda unmasks as a harbinger of alienated production. The audience for the earlier *Tales of Edo Prosperity*, Maeda concludes, were busy "at play," be it in the brothels, theaters, or picnic sites, whereas Bushō's guide to the Meiji capital reveals "people who consume *things* as symbols of 'enlightenment' and people who gaze upon the new sights of Tokyo, so that the mode of interaction is rather between people and things."

If, as observed earlier, Maeda brought his own profoundly original sensibilities and training together with Continental high theory to produce literary, social, cultural, and intellectual history in his distinctive way, he was also following the legacy of earlier generations of Japanese intellectuals, from philosophers such as Nishida Kitarō and Watsuji Tetsurō to Marxist thinkers like Nakano Shigeharu and Aono Suekichi. (Western academics remain generally unaware of this decidedly cosmopolitan legacy among Japanese intellectuals that distinguishes the latter from their European counterparts, who typically know nothing of non-European thought, nor the irony of a term like "cosmopolitan" that denotes a parochial Western European continentalism.) Today Maeda's achievements can de discerned in the continuing interest that Japan specialists exhibit for urban ethnographers such as Gonda Yasunosuke, Kon Wajirō, and Matsubara Iwagorō and such Marxist writers and social critics as Ōya Sōichi and Aono. Together with a handful of scholars in allied disciplines, Maeda also helped generate widespread interest in studying mass culture on the one hand and the marginalized sectors of modern Japanese society on the other.[5]

Maeda's essays implicitly challenge the reified separation of text and society, or more specifically, the divide between cultural production and the urban space that it at once belongs to and helps constitute. Most important, this binary served as a means for Maeda to effectively displace what has steadfastly remained the reigning ideology that effectively deformed the study of modern Japanese literature and society since at least the 1880s: the appropriated concept of the modern "self" of Western provenance, or the *kindai jiga*. A short decade or two after Western mercantilism (in the form of Commodore Perry's gunboat diplomacy) pried open Japan into the "new world order" of global capitalism, Japanese government officials, intellectuals, and writers would be seized by the necessity to fashion a "modern Japanese subject" adequate to the times. Their efforts, alas, would collectively help reify the kindai jiga as an ideology consigning Japanese subjectivity to an inferior status relative to its manifestation in the West. Programmed for "failure"— whether we look to the postwar political scientist Maruyama Masao's self-exhortatory criticism of Japanese subjectivity (*shutaisei*) or even more recent exceptionalist affirmations of Japanese identity—ultimately problematic resolutions would be offered over the decades, from Marxist explorations of subjectivity in the 1930s to the advent of postmodern theories in the 1970s and 1980s that would confer on Japanese society a (decentered, fractured, radically contingent) subjectivity a few critics would claim existed in a Tokugawa society that was "already postmodern" before Japan had experienced modern life inflected with specifically Western practices.

Maeda took a different route, problematizing the kindai jiga by combining semiotics with figurations of the body. Semiology provided a way to defamiliarize concerns about forging a modern literary language, while the body (*shintai*), which he explored primarily in relation to urban space, afforded new avenues of displacing the positivist hold of the modern subject that has endured well into the 1970s and continues to this day. When prominent literary critics like Senuma Shigeki and Etō Jun were pursuing ideations of the self in relation to the family, Maeda's work interpellated the subject into the *city* as an alternative, contingent site of mediation that related the subject to the nation-state in more complex ways. The result is work that came to be called *toshi-ron* (critical interventions on the city) and *kūkan-ron* (theorizing space), inaugurating what was an all too rare but still ongoing quest to seek ways of decentering Eurocentric approaches to the study of literature and society without resorting to a reactionary and essentialist affirmation of Japanese culture.[6]

If the study of discourse had become standard in the lexicon of historical investigation of the late 1970s and 1980s in order to help prise the self away from the rigidly given institutional structures of a nation, the horizon of study still tended to remain with discourses that were produced by these very institutions. Maeda explored the body as it negotiated and in turn refigured urban space as a way to find new paths for understanding the relationship between the nation and its subjects, which he would insistently recast in terms of conflict between state power and private desire. Ultimately, however, it was the city, the space that mediated this relationship, that captivated Maeda, and he would use it to challenge the all too familiar paradigm that viewed the individual directly in relation to the social or to state institutions. By examining the body in relation to the city, Maeda would show how subjects participated in the production and reproduction of everyday life. As a way to challenge the given-ness of the modern self, which Maeda himself asserted was something he explicitly sought to critique,[7] he shifted the terms of analysis from "interiority" to an examination of the materiality of the body as a viewing position, an object of the gaze, and as a player in the city, that is, as a subject whose materially conceived agency would allow one to recognize the political and social dimensions and consequences of participation in city life. To this end, he was particularly concerned with technologies of visual manipulation designed to shape the behavior of Japanese who would attend industrial and world expositions, visit panorama halls and movie theaters, explore lands beyond Japan's borders, and negotiate the pathways lined by newly "invented" display cases in department stores designed to stimulate consumption.

Revising the Japanese Modern

A profoundly democratic bent is present in Maeda's work, and his focus on the city and urban life provided a way to distance himself from the hierarchical logic immanent in conventions of literary studies as well as the articulations of state authority that sought to manage the modern nation-state.

In his capable hands, urban space proved to be an effective construct for exploring the crenelations of lived space that exceeded the rule of social hierarchy. His egalitarian impulse underwrites the very focus of "From Communal Performance to Solitary Reading," which addresses the material and social conditions that shaped diverse practices of readership in the Meiji era (instead of resorting to the time-honored practice of reproducing the "author" that Foucault, Barthes, and other theorists had problematized, for example). We see a kindred egalitarian drive underwriting his careful study of women's magazines in "The Development of Popular Fiction in the Late Taishō Era" (chapter 6), where, instead of contributing to the reification of genre conventions, he effectively interrogates them in an essay that affirms what had been a neglected aspect of Japanese literary studies: female readers. The 1980s, when Maeda's work came to focus more emphatically on the city and urban life, was marked by the rise of widespread interest among the Japanese in community-based initiatives of *machi-zukuri* (literally, "town building"), a kind of grassroots alternative to urban planning (*toshi keikaku*) with its centrist, bureaucratic associations.[8] Asakusa, generally viewed simply as the "traditional" entertainment district of the masses, for Maeda is a space of far greater complexity. Here the denizens of *The Crimson Gang of Asakusa* ("Asakusa as Theater," chapter 5) stage their lives much as they perform their onstage roles in the multiply marginalized realm of the profane and the sacred, that uneasy space given to performer-entertainers in Japanese society. Maeda's populist humanism is also evident in the attention he gives to the student radicals of the 1960s in Shinjuku, the 1903 striking workers in Hibiya, and on to the early Meiji writers whose canonization as producers of idealistic political novels was belied by their frequent imprisonment by an oppressive new carceral technology ("Utopia of the Prisonhouse"). Just as Foucault discerned regimes of discipline and punishment in so-called enlightened society, Maeda would recognize new technologies of regimentation and repression in modern Japan. His recasting of the Meiji-era political novel as a testament to the tremendous violence and oppression that lay at the center of modern nationness, and more specifically its identification as fundamentally a literature of incarceration, is sure to revise our received assumptions regarding the Japanese novel (*shōsetsu*).

As if to counter assiduous Meiji government efforts to wipe away the untidiness of pre-*bunmei-kaika* Japan, Maeda takes the eminent historian Amino Yoshihiko's notion of the space of evil (*akubasho* or *akusho*) to discern the profound contradictions and unevenness of Japanese modernity itself, riddled as Meiji urban space was with the very elements of darkness, despair, and vast marginal populations that had marked Tokugawa Japan. In addition to his extended critique of the reified modern subject, Maeda would tacitly part company with widely observed academic convention that placed the origins of Japanese modernity with the Meiji Restoration of 1868. His exploration of spatiality provided a way to challenge the rigid association of temporality to historical understanding, which, coupled with his training in premodern literature, opened the way to implicitly challenge the still widely held view that Japan's modernity was simply the product of concerted, reasoned importation of Western ideas, means of production, and political institutions—views largely promoted by everyone from officials in the Meiji government to postwar modernization scholars.

Even as he ostensibly critiqued the dimensions of modern Japanese subjectivity as it emerged in the Meiji era, Natsume Sōseki did more than any other writer to effectively affirm the modern bourgeois subject in Japan. In "In the Recesses of the High City" (chapter 11), Maeda's discussion of Sōseki's *Mon* (The gate) highlights the emergence of what we today call the urban middle class through the generation of new spatial arrangements in post-Restoration Tokyo. Commuter railways would play a principal role in transforming Tokyo into a different version of what class-based residential separation had maintained between highland samurai and lowland commoners in the Tokugawa era. The Chūō Line running from Shinjuku to Manseibashi, and its electrification in 1910, would help make the latter the busiest transport node of the inner city for a time, even as the center of transit would move steadily west toward Shinjuku, and dramatically so after the Great Kantō Earthquake of 1923. The redrawing of *sakariba* (aptly naming a place where people congregate, whether to simply pass through or to seek out as destinations for pleasure) would be accompanied by redefinitions of newly conceived private space, as we see in Sōseki's description of Hirota Sensei's house in the novel *Sanshirō* (as explored in Maeda's "Recesses"). Maeda's reading graphically reveals the reorganization of urban space that simultaneously involves the westward shift of the "center" of Tokyo and the dramatic transformations of interior household space.

At the same time, Maeda was struck by the modernity of Edo and by the Edo in Tokyo. The cultural practices typically attributed to the Edo period (especially the later years, spanning the 1700s up to the 1868 Restoration) would endure into or be reinvented during the Meiji era and would help give Japan's modern moment not just residual traces of a bygone era, but the vigorous and indeed defining contradictions of modern life. Through a reading of Nagai Kafū's "The Fox" ("Kitsune") in "The Spirits of Abandoned Gardens" (chapter 3), Maeda reveals the unevenness of modern urban life in Japan's capital city that is a patchwork of lit-up streets and residential space marked at the same time by wilderness, wily foxes, and deep dark wells that echo the vestiges of times supposedly long gone. For Maeda, how we create, reformulate, negotiate, and conceive of space were keys to help discern significant aspects of modernity that at once provided analytic acuity without carrying the overdeterminations of West–non-West conceptualizations and their variants. And in those "lived spaces" sedimented by the unevenness generated by capitalism "as it enters societies at different moments and different rates of intensity,"[9] Maeda would locate modernity, especially in cityspace that eluded or exceeded the systematization imposed by the state.

One such space was Asakusa, a diverse place of mass entertainment, which Maeda used to read Kawabata Yasunari's daunting, modernist prose narrative, *The Crimson Gang of Asakusa* (*Asakusa kurenaidan*, 1929–30) in "Asakusa as Theater." Maeda teases out a bewildering "plot" centered around the gender- and identity-bending beautiful androgynous heroine, Yumiko, of Kawabata's critically acclaimed avant-garde novel. Her adventures are depicted in a cinematic parallel-tracking narrative of intrigue, revenge, and adventure that unravels through the maze of a densely textured Asakusa, home to Edo-era amusements and seedy reviews and performance theaters whose very amateurish qualities form part of their allure, as well as panorama halls, an aquarium, and movie houses modeled on their Western counterparts. In "Asakusa as Theater" Maeda masterfully stitches the local lore and mythology of Asakusa and its environs to the labyrinthine story involving Yumiko and a cast of fellow amateur performers, beggars, and gang members, as a way to make the case for Kawabata's arguably most interesting work as a novel about transformation, be it in forms of mass entertainment, questions of personal identity, or Tokyo from a city of waterways to a land-based capital city.[10]

Whereas "The Panorama of Enlightenment" employs a familiar Edo-Tokyo opposition only to deconstruct the binary, perhaps the most conspicuous example of Maeda's historical revisionism can be observed in his work on Narushima Ryūhoku ("Ryūhoku in Paris"). This essay, along with his other works on Ryūhoku, helped establish Maeda early as a scholar willing and eager to displace the time-honored convention of viewing 1868 as the line separating medieval from modern Japan. Ryūhoku would write "modern" literature in the idiom of Tokugawa gesaku, written not in the customary and widely accessible *kana* syllabry associated with gesaku, but in the Sinified Japanese of officialdom, *kanbun*, to produce a distinctively *modern* literature in the 1870s and 1880s, a period that literary histories tend to reduce to a transitional moment for the development of the colloquially based modern (*genbun'itchi*) novel of the late 1880s. Maeda uses Ryūhoku's self-abnegatory epithet, "useless man" (*muyō no hito*) as a trope that contrasts Ryūhoku with the figure of Fukuzawa Yūkichi, an iconic figure of a former samurai leading Japan's transformation into a modern, capitalist nation. Ryūhoku, the Tokugawa family loyalist with an accordingly much lower profile, is noteworthy precisely because his activities as a citizen and writer of Meiji Japan tellingly capture the complex nuances of a modernity inflected with the culturally specific contradictions of Meiji Japan. Maeda's Ryūhoku essays also testify to the centrality of military institutions as a requirement for modern statehood in an imperialist world.

The Space of Play

Whether we look to his studies of late Tokugawa-era merchant culture–based popular culture, his work on Taishō (1912–1926) mass culture, his readings of contemporary urban entertainment guides like *Pia*, or his analyses of urban space in literary texts, Maeda repeatedly identifies "play" as a part of everyday life that serves variously to diminish, confound, and resist the state. A postmodern inflection of the idea of play is evident in his insistent deconstruction of received categories for apprehending Japanese modernity. If we apprehend Meiji society through its new modern institutions and its exhortation to develop a strong army and create a society in the image of civilization and enlightenment, then it will appear predictably Westward-looking. And, as has become de rigueur, if Japanese modernity is symbolized by cinema, dance halls, cafés, beer halls, and a sudden emphasis on youth culture (e.g., *moga*, *mobo*, juvenile magazines), the complexion of the Japanese modern will be similarly monochromatic. But the theoretical force of play urged Maeda to employ it as both method and subject of inquiry, and he would find mass urban society richly striated by a cultural crossbreeding that was no simple echo of Western modernity. Most important, Maeda would find such cultural "contamination" from top to bottom in Japanese society—among the street people in the depths of Tokyo's slums, in the populist mass culture of Asakusa and Ginza, as well as among the intelligentsia of early twentieth-century Japanese society.

The self-declared "useless" Meiji man Narushima Ryūhoku would come to embody a playful subversiveness that would land him in jail, even as he briefly found employment in the new Meiji government. And play would find explicit and extended address in Maeda's arguably most celebrated work of literary analysis, "Their Time as Children: A Study of Higuchi Ichiyō's *Growing Up*" (*Takekurabe*; chapter 4). In his influential reading, the play of children whose parents live off the world of adult play of the licensed pleasure quarters shunted off to the outskirts of Tokyo becomes a way to understand labor, friendship, the working class, monied relations, and, of course, childhood in the new calculus of social relations in Meiji Japan. Here Maeda is at his best as he deploys the many permutations of space—the periphery of the city, agricultural production, main street and backstreet, the countryside—where space as both subject and method coalesce in the material articulations of the city. The deadly serious dimensions of play as they are embodied in each of the children, and especially in Midori, destined to become the ultimate plaything in the world of licensed pleasure in its last years of licensing, also becomes an overlooked yet powerful means of demystifying a modern Japan formulated by the horizons of a West-native binary. Also revealing in this essay is Maeda's adroit identification of the gaze and its permutations in a society that, under the mantle of modernity and Western-style progress, increasingly takes on the functions of surveillance (a topic he would revisit and extend in "Prisonhouse"), even in the world of child's play on the margins of Tokyo. In related fashion, the gaze would figure early and prominently to mark the way space, social class, and gender would help define the parameters of Ōta Toyotarō's conduct in Berlin depicted in Ōgai's "The Dancing Girl" ("Berlin 1888," chapter 10).

Travels of a Ragpicker

We are accustomed to viewing the modern in temporal terms. Maeda recognized the problems of reducing historical understanding to simple chronological formulations. Raymond Williams found the residual as a way to capture the multifarious texture and contradictions of a historical moment; Maeda would use space to "discover" simultaneities as the defining feature of city life in post-Restoration Japan. Japan's move to embrace the institutions of a modern nation-state took place during what we now call the age of (Euro-American) empire, and by the 1890s Japan would claim its membership in the modern world by itself colonizing neighboring countries. By turning his attention to lived space, Maeda was able to interpellate a variety of subjects—social critics, revolutionaries, the working class, and the lumpen proletariat—who, at varying points, would contest such space with officials of the Meiji state who were eager to appropriate, regulate, and manage that space.

Unlike space that is marked off in advance by the state, such lived space takes shape only when contingencies (an event or encounter) in turn give meaning to the space they inhabit. In a short essay written for a general audience entitled "Machi no yomi-kata: Bungaku ni arawareta toshi fūkei" (Reading the city: Urban landscape in literature), Maeda observes that student activities in the late 1960s represented a revolutionary moment that also changed the functions and meanings given to urban space.[11] In the late 1960s, the bus terminal at the west exit of Shinjuku Station was quickly turned into a plaza where youth held frequent antigovernment demonstrations, rallies, and street theater that spread even to the space of shrine compounds. To prevent the performance of such unauthorized events in the future, the government rebuilt the west side into a multilevel driveway for controlled vehicular access that was pointedly unsuited for mass mobilization. Maeda would not live to see the resolution to yet another unwanted "contingency" in the early 1990s, when the homeless built their cardboard village in the lower pedestrian levels of the station's west exit, and the government would eventually "reclaim" this public space, this time by installing a moving pedestrian walkway and planting "decorative" plastic figures into the floors to prevent the homeless from using the space for shelter.

Space that belongs to such events or comes to be "claimed" by the uses put to it by ordinary citizens typically fails to receive institutional recognition. What the phenomenal encounter through walking had once given names, new modes of transport (cars and trains) have reduced to instrumental points on a map or simply eliminated. Thus, maps show the locations of government buildings and list the official names given to monuments, but they do not record what a work like Tayama Katai's *Tokyo no sanjūnen 1885–1915* (Literary life in Tokyo 1885–1915, 1917) is replete with: the name of a hill, a valley, the corner plaza, alleyways, a small pond, a large tree at a bend in the road, an informal gathering spot—in short, the features that have meaning to locals in everyday life. Maeda lamented this phenomenon of lost names as a process of homogenizing urban space and the evacuation of the things that helped give meaning to everyday life. He pointed to such contemporary literary works as Murakami Haruki's *Kaze no uta o kike* (Listen to the song of the wind) and Tatematsu Wahei's "Mitsugetsu" (Honeymoon), wherein place is typically rendered abstract and naming is eschewed entirely even when the stories are clearly set in Tokyo.

Not surprising in a scholar-critic who valued the quiddity of cityspace, Maeda himself would frequently take to the road, traveling both far and close to home to discern the meaning of urban space in a register often ignored or erased, whether by officialdom, new transport, or contemporary literary practice. Walking trips along the avenues, besides landmarks, and in nameless places in the very urban landscapes that inspired much of modern Japanese literature were integral to Maeda's idiosyncratic approach to historical understanding as it was transposed into the key of literature. The gaze, the body in space, and phenomenal experience would come to be not just the subject of his critical practice, but an important component of his "method." Both his interest in the theoretical notion of (sociohistorical) "contingency" and an abiding love of the city would help make the field trip an important part of his scholarly practice.

Meiji-era Japanese literature itself comes marked by travel—within the city and the nation and well beyond its borders—and Maeda retraced the steps of literary characters and authors in such cities as Chicago, Berlin, Shanghai, and Tokyo. His seminal work on modern Japan's preeminent woman writer, Higuchi Ichiyō, set in a neighborhood adjacent to the pleasure quarters, led him to sites for repeated excursions, although in the years Maeda was revisiting these sites, the "pleasure quarters" could be identified only by a remaining five-foot-long segment of the original ditch that separated the quarters from residential neighborhoods and a lone willow tree replanted and memorialized as the tree that Ichiyō's short story "Child's Play" had depicted in its memorable opening scene. Maeda was part scholar of expansive erudition, as evident in the many, often abstruse, forgotten literary works and figures that he revisited, and part ragpicker, or *bataya*, digging through the rich layers of "stuff" or "things" whose very plenitude, even in the deepest slums of Tokyo, epitomized modern urban life (see "Prisonhouse," "Panorama," and "Recesses of the High City"). And as he explored the city at street level, he insistently sought to make modernity something more than a parochial phenomenon confined to any particular cultural or geographic landscape, whether identified with Paris, Berlin, or Tokyo. Maeda's interest in the field trip—to the serpentine alleyways in both the high and low city sections of Tokyo that were integral to his readings of Kawabata, Sōseki, Kafū, the backstreets of Berlin that served as setting for Ōgai's "Dancing Girl," the topography of Shanghai that would inform his reading of Yokomitsu Riichi's novel *Shanghai*—was simultaneously an expression of his theoretical inclinations. His many forays into terrain vaguely mapped by literature or the work of urban ethnographers like Matsubara Iwagorō, the author of *In Darkest Tokyo* (1893), was in large part determined by his interest in the body as both the locus of meaning production and an effective means for his sustained problematization of the enduring ideology of the "modern subject" (kindai jiga). More than just figuratively, for Maeda the city and urban space was the *embodiment* of modern life, and in more than one essay of Tokyo's entertainment district, Asakusa, becomes a gigantic anthropomorphized organic subject that lives by ingesting, digesting, and disgorging ("Prisonhouse").[12]

Whether it is his masterful analysis of Midori on the cusp of becoming the most abject form of plaything-commodity in the world of licensed pleasure quarters or his intense interest in the plenitude of "things" that mark urban life, we might refer back to the ragpicker as a label that nicely fits Maeda, who himself relished this role even as he critiqued the commodification of city dwellers and the accoutrements of urban life. Maeda's familiarity with Benjamin's and Baudelaire's work may suggest the flâneur, which Bruce Mazlish describes this way: "In the middle of the nineteenth century in Western Europe the *flâneur* emerges as a new sort of hero, the product of modernity at the same time as heralding its advent. He is the 'spectator' of the modern world, as it manifests itself in the capitalist metropolises, especially Paris, strolling its streets and lovingly regarding his own image in the glass of the arcades and the new department stores."[13] While sharing these characteristics, Maeda resists the self-insinuation of the flâneur into the spectacle of the streets, adopting instead, the practiced eyes of the bataya, who must discern the artifacts of everyday life, collecting what others deem useless and putting it to the imaginative uses his fertile imagination would confer. At the same time, the bataya does not exactly participate in the creation and perpetuation of commodified life. Such a liminal role undoubtedly appealed to Maeda.

Mapping Culture

To Maeda Ai, for whom the interrogation of "representation" underlay everything from his readings of literary texts to his exploration of space in its many permutations, maps provided a particularly rich medium for exploring their intersection. His analysis of Isoda Kōichi's widely read work, *Shisō to shite no Tokyo* (Tokyo as thought, 1978) is probably his most celebrated, if controversial example of such work.[14] Isoda's discussion of an Edo-period map of Tokyo has become canonical: the vast emptiness of the castle grounds in the center around which waterways spiral out into concentric rings; samurai residences indicated by names written with the top facing the direction of the center from all locations of the city, with all shrines and temples named in reverse with the words facing away from the center. Isoda argued that the placement of the samurai family names reflected homage paid to their feudal lord in the center, whereas the temple and shrine names were written facing away from the central castle to designate their function as guards facing outward to confront evil from without. The word for castle, he noted, was written "upside down" on a map that shows the direction west at the top. The character printed upside down, asserted Isoda, expressed deliberate disrespect to the former head of state, the emperor, residing to the West (in Kyoto).

Maeda would frame the map itself—by repositioning the Edo-era map into its own enunciative moment—leading to rather different attributions of meanings. European maps, he observed, were designed to be viewed hanging on a wall, and accordingly the words appear right-side up from the viewing perspective that is away from the wall. But Japanese maps were placed on tatami mats, with viewers seated surrounding the map on all sides. The names of samurai who resided on these lots were written to accommodate those seated around the map. The person of highest rank would be seated at the top (west) of the map, and though to us the word for castle in the middle looks upside down, it would be right-side up for the occupant of that honored position. Maeda explains the upside-down word for castle (*shiro*) as well as the direction of writing for temple and shrine names by noting that naming was historically viewed as a disrespectful practice requiring some method of mitigating or softening the affront implied in such directness. The characters in *The Tale of Genji* are named only by the rooms or wings they occupy, and in writing the emperor's title the first character was often omitted (*ue no ji o akeru*). Hence, written characters denoting the location of the head of the nation and the names of temples and shrines must have been written to appear upside down or at an angle as a mark of polite indirection. Maeda was careful to affirm Isoda's contention that a map comes inscribed with the ideologies of its time. But he attempted to restore what he felt was missing in Isoda's otherwise impressive reading: the historical context of the map as an artifact reflecting the meanings given to social relations, things, and space that the map would yield most clearly by being repositioned into the semiotics of Edo cartography.

When Roland Barthes came to Japan to walk its streets in the 1970s, Maeda was struck by the conjuncture of text (map) and everyday life (walking) that would result in the production of a narrative reading of the city (*Empire of Signs*), leading him to observe that "the novel is a text/product of the city" ("shōsetsu wa toshi no shomotsu de aru"). It is this confrontation—between text and street, map and user, pedestrian (flâneur?) and place—that Maeda recognized and studied as the site where meaning was produced in everyday life. Accordingly, virtually every essay in this anthology pursues, in one form or another, urban space as the site of productive friction, as he strove "to bring into confrontation the oppositional aspects of the city as an expression of the System (central authorities) and the city as the space of desire."

Having spilt this much ink (or "processed so many words"?) to convey something of the approach and range that characterized Maeda's work, let me end with a simple observation that is perhaps all the reader really needs to know: Maeda read literature, history, cultural practices, maps, and events with a brilliance rarely encountered in his day or ours. His studies are sure to lead the reader to unexpected and welcome "pleasures of the text."

The place of publication for Japanese works, unless otherwise noted, is Tokyo.

1 For a critical look at Maeda's scientific theorizing, see, Joe Murphy's "Maeda Ai: Topology and the Discourse of Complexity in Japanese Literary Criticism," in *Metaphorical Circuit: Negotiations between Literature and Science in 20th Century Japan* (Ithaca, N.Y.: Cornell East Asia Series, 2003), 142–179. Heidegger and Poulet are used by Maeda when he explores the relationship between textuality and space, which keys the way he can relate literature to its largely urban context. The reader must refer to such essays as "The Text of Space, the Space of the Text" ("Kūkan no kekusuto tekusuto no kūkan") and *A Primer for Literary Texts (Bungaku tekusuto nyūmon)*, which also appeared as a book, in volume 1 of his *Selected Works*, Maeda Ai, *Maeda Ai chosakushū* (Chikuma Shobō, 1989–1990).

2 I have sacrificed consistency for a kind of place-specific logic in presenting book titles. For example, Edward Fowler explicitly lays out his rationale for using *Takekurabe* instead of an English translation of the title throughout the essay he has translated as "Their Time as Children." Whenever practical, however, an English-language title is used for the title of literary works, especially when an English-language translation of the work is available, as in *And Then* for Sōseki's *Sorekara*. Nonliterary works, such as *Nihon no kasō kaikyū*, even though well-known, are generally presented with their translated titles—*Japan's Under Class*, in this example. Meant to accommodate non–Japan specialists and specialists alike, I am guessing that the *effect* created by following these procedures will appear far more "natural" and sensible than does this convoluted note seeking to explain them.

3 The six volumes are *Bakumatsu ishin-ki no bungaku: Narushima Ryūhoku* (The literature of the late Tokugawa-Meiji Restoration era: Narushima Ryūhoku), *Kindai dokusha no seiritsu* (The rise of the modern reader), *Higuchi Ichiyō no sekai* (The world of Higuchi Ichiyō), *Genkei no Meiji* (The phantom landscape of Meiji), *Toshi kūkan no naka no bungaku* (Literature of urban space), and *Tekusuto no yūtopia* (The utopia of the text), all published by Chikuma Shobō from 1989 to 1990.

4 Instead of situating Maeda Ai's work in relation to two prominent, recent translations of Japanese literary-critical works, Karatani Kōjin's *The Origins of Modern Japanese Literature* and Kamei Hideo's *Transformations of Sensibility*, I have chosen to outline the contours of his critical range in the form of an abbreviated introduction to the essays selected for inclusion. I refer the reader of this volume to the superb editor's introduction to Kamei's book (by Michael Bourdaghs) and to Kamei's preface for the English translation, which serves as a kind of genealogical tracing of *Transformations* at the same time that it provides a concise intellectual history of what might be called the theory and the politics of subjectivity in mostly recent-postwar Japan. Although Kamei does not mention Maeda by name—he wrote what was on balance a critically supportive review of Maeda's *Toshi kūkan* shortly after its publication (see Kamei Hideo, "Maeda Ai cho: *Toshi kūkan no naka no bungaku*," *Kokugo to kokubungaku* [January 1984]:

67–71)—we can see the divide in sensibilities that marks Kamei's rigorous and steadfast interest in what Bourdaghs identifies as focused concern with addressing Japanese modernity by engaging the linguistic immanence of Japanese literature as opposed to Maeda's equally tenacious exploration of Japanese literature via nonnative Western European theory, particularly as it informs Maeda's own theorizing of culture and native urban space. In this volume, I have let this selection of essays appearing in a wide array of venues spanning a good part of his career give shape to the populist dimensions of Maeda's oeuvre.

5 Along with such contemporaries in kindred fields as Minami Hiroshi, Tsurumi Shunsuke, and Amino Yukihiko, who immediately come to mind.

6 For another effective recent challenge to *jiga*-centered approaches to modern Japanese literature around the same years, see Kamei Hideo's phenomenologically informed studies, including his study recently translated as *Transformations of Sensibility: The Phenomenology of Meiji Literature*, translation edited and with an introduction by Michael Bourdaghs (Ann Arbor: Center for Japanese Studies, University of Michigan, 2002).

7 This intention is affirmed in such essays as "Toshi no kaidoku" (Decoding the city) and in his afterword to *Toshi kūkan no naka no bungaku* (Literature in urban space).

8 See Nakai Norihiro, "*Toshi Keikaku* and *Machi-zukuri*," in *Social Science Japan* (Newsletter of the Institute of Social Science, University of Tokyo) 23 (April 2002): 17–19.

9 Harry Harootunian, *History's Disquiet: Modernity, Cultural Practice, and the Question of Everyday Life* (New York: Columbia University Press, 2000), 32.

10 Kawabata's *Asakusa kurenaidan* is forthcoming in a translation by Alisa Freedman as *The Scarlet Gang of Asakusa* from the University of California Press. An extended discussion of the novel is provided by Seiji Lippit in *Topographies of Japanese Modernism* (New York: Columbia University Press, 2002).

11 *Maeda Ai chosaku-shū*, vol. 5, *Toshi kūkan no naka no bungaku* (Chikuma Shobō, 1989).

12 See his "Toshi o yomu" (Reading the city) and "The Utopia of the Prisonhouse."

13 Bruce Mazlish, "The *Flâneur*: From Spectator to Representation," in *The Flâneur*, ed. Keith Tester (London: Routledge, 1994), 43.

14 "Toshi o kaidoku suru" (Deciphering the city), in *Maeda Ai chosaku-shū*, 5:401–419.

LIGHT CITY, DARK CITY: VISUALIZING THE MODERN

1. Utopia of the Prisonhouse: A Reading of *In Darkest Tokyo*

(Gokusha no yūtopia)

TRANSLATED BY SEIJI M. LIPPIT AND JAMES A. FUJII

"The Utopia of the Prisonhouse" ("Gokusha no yūtopia") originally published in 1981, addresses the intersection of literature, politics, intellectual history, urban planning, and prison reform in both Europe and late Tokugawa (1600–1868) and early Meiji (1868–1912) Japan.[1] Its central theme is the unexpected conjunction between conceptions of the prison and utopia, which recurs in a number of different historical and cultural contexts. Maeda traces the superimposition of a confining material space onto an expansive imaginative space from various philosophical, literary, and artistic figures in eighteenth- and nineteenth-century Europe to the genre of the political novel in the second decade of the Meiji period. Against this narrative of literary and intellectual history, Maeda further situates the interconnections between various efforts at prison reform and urban planning. Ultimately, the contradictory space of confinement and liberation serves as an image underlying the experience and representation of the emergent city of Tokyo in modern times, from government efforts to restructure the city based on conceptions of hygiene and visibility to Matsubara Iwagorō's *In Darkest Tokyo* (*Saiankoku no Tokyo*, 1893), which detailed the dark underside of the city submerged beneath the veneer of civilization and enlightenment. Maeda's essay, in both methodology and content, provides a powerful illustration of the complex and often cryptic trajectories connecting the discursive and material histories of modern Europe and Japan.

1

If utopian literature is the product of an intense vision to materialize human happiness within a closed and organized space, it perhaps maintains, at the deepest level, an analogical relationship to the mechanism of power that is the prison. For both the prison and utopia are nothing other than subspecies born from the matrix of the city. The image of the medieval European city, which constructed a living space in opposition to agricultural nature through the construction of an enclosure, would eventually create—at its positive and negative extremes—both the fantasy of the prison as a device for quarantine and punishment as well as utopia, which promised human freedom and liberation. No doubt, as the centralized nation-state of the modern period took away one after another the special rights and freedoms that had been permitted cities in the past—and thereby accelerated the cities' dissolution and transformation—these two extremes came to be grasped by people's consciousness. Utopia is an urban hallucination of an alternative nation-state, which represents an attempt to escape from the dominance of the real nation-state. The prison, in turn, is an alternative city created by state power through the inversion of the urban and which is inserted into the womb of the city.

The literature of utopia, which enjoyed a resurgence with the advent of the Renaissance, typically begins with an explorer's discovery of an unknown island in the middle of the ocean. This island is surrounded by sturdy walls, within which the splendid sight of an ideal city unfolds. Such an introduction is quite appropriate to the great seafaring age, but is not the golden island itself, isolated in the middle of the sea, a reverse image of the prison or the prison colony? In truth, the El Dorado of the New World, colored with rosy expectations of extreme wealth and romantic adventure, was also a dismal penal colony where serious criminals exiled from the Old World were sent. (Until the Revolutionary War of 1776, the number of prisoners sent from England to the American colonies exceeded a thousand per year.)

However, the indisputable evidence of an underlying connection between the prison and utopia is the fact that utopian literature was frequently conceived by actual prisoners. These writers literally experienced the paradox that the prison as space of confinement was also a space of the imagination. For example, Campanella, the author of *The City of the Sun*, was a patriot who was confined for twenty-seven years in a prison in Napoli, and the Marquis de Sade, who depicted a utopia of eros with the clarity of an encyclopedia, spent the greater part of his life in a state of confinement, from the time he was detained at Vincennes in 1763 at the age of 23 to his death in 1814. Undoubtedly, for both Campanella and Sade, the dismal experience of a life spent in confinement was inscribed within their utopian worlds in the form of a liberated will to power and sexual desire. The blueprint for the "city of the sun," in which the castle towering atop a hill is enclosed by seven circular zones, is itself an image of a prison, and the maxim of the city's citizens whereby "there is no personal affair of the individual that is not a part of the communal whole" calls to mind the organization of the prison managed in an ideal manner. As

Michel Foucault writes, in Sade's case the images of closed spaces, including the "fortress," "solitary cell," "basement," "monastery," and "unapproachable island," were inextricably tied to his utopia, and the machines and devices to increase pleasure are virtually indistinguishable from the tools of torture. The private room where the libertines assault the young girl is itself the picture of a prison.

The eighteenth century, which Foucault referred to as "the age of the great confinement," was a period in which the double image of the prison, alternately expressing the pain of confinement and the pleasure of fancy, was willingly taken as a symbol of self-consciousness. W. B. Carnochan's *Confinement and Flight* (1977), which builds on Georges Poulet's *Metamorphoses of the Circle* and Foucault's *Madness and Civilization*, is a work of intellectual history that attempts to excavate the meanings of such tropes of the prison, primarily in eighteenth-century English literature. The beginning of the second chapter, entitled "Islands of Silence," includes an extremely interesting sketch that clarifies this theme by analyzing two contrasting images of confinement.[2] The first is the well-known "Fifth Walk" from Rousseau's *Reveries of the Solitary Walker* (1782), within which Carnochan focuses on the structure of the closed ring that forms around Rousseau's fulfilled heart as its center. The "Fifth Walk" recounts Rousseau's life of seclusion on the Island of Saint Pierre in the middle of Lake Bienne, where he stayed in the autumn of 1765; it is a beautiful piece of prose in which the tranquil happiness of melting into nature is expressed through picturesque descriptions. Some sections express a philosophical resignation reminiscent of Kamo no Chōmei's *Hōjōki* [An account of my hut, 1212]. Yet it is nothing other than the image of the prison that Rousseau projects onto this place of such scenic beauty: "Because of the forebodings that troubled me, I wanted them to make this refuge a perpetual prison for me, to confine me to it for life, and—removing every possibility and hope of getting off it—to forbid me any kind of communication with the mainland so that being unaware of all that went on in the world I might forget its existence and that it might also forget mine."[3] The distortion of this text, whereby the Island of Saint Pierre—which to Rousseau must have appeared a lost paradise—is transformed into a closed prison, no doubt reveals the form of self-consciousness peculiar to the Romantic human being. It demonstrates the depth of fancy that held Rousseau's soul, or perhaps the sensitivity of his ego. Rousseau withdrew from the slanders and intrigues of the peripheral world of human society and shut himself into a narrow circle. The Island of Saint Pierre, surrounded by Lake Bienne, is precisely such a circle or prison. Yet Rousseau's contracted ego also attempts to recapture a cosmic expansiveness through the inflation of fancy: "I have often thought that in the Bastille—even in a dungeon where no object would strike my sight—I would still have been able to dream pleasurably."[4]

Serving as a distant response to Rousseau's image of a prison is the image of the desert island in Pascal's *Pensées* (1670). Pascal writes of feeling as though he had been brought to a terrifying desert island while sleeping—when he awakes there is no way to ascertain where he is, and all means of escape have been taken from him. He is nothing more than a trifling existence wandering the edges of the universe, and the world around him is enveloped in a deep darkness. Nevertheless, being nothing more than an infinitesimal point in the broad cosmos, he must begin with the self-awareness of his own wretchedness. "Let us, having returned to ourselves, consider what we are, compared to what is in existence, let us see ourselves as lost within this forgotten outpost of nature and let us, from within this little prison cell where we find ourselves, by which I mean the universe, learn to put a correct value on the earth, its kingdoms, its cities, and ourselves."[5]

Pascal's melancholy understanding that the universe is itself a prison and that human knowledge confronts a limitless space without walls establishes a sharp contrast to Rousseau's happy prison, which is fulfilled through fancy. If Pascal's "prison" allows for a glimpse of the mystery of human existence suspended between the infinitely large and the infinitely small, Rousseau's prison offers a restful existence in a hidden house, a place that promises convalescence for a damaged ego. Using the words "Island of Despair" inscribed in the early pages of Robinson Crusoe's diary as a clue, Carnochan reads the meaning of Crusoe's life on the desert island as the transformation of the image of Pascal's desolate island into the image of Rousseau's comfortable prison. Here, I would like to touch on Giovanni Battista Piranesi's etching entitled *Carceri d'invenzione*, which transformed Pascal's prison into an icon.

In a small masterpiece of thematic criticism entitled "Piranèse et les poètes romantiques français," Poulet writes as follows of Piranesi's figures, who appear in identical form at all points on a giant staircase that is intricate like a labyrinth:

> Self-multiplication is an attempt to discover one's self, to project everywhere an image of the self which can never coincide with it. Space and time are not only the primary place where self-multiplication takes place, but appear as the profound reason for the dispersal of the multiplied self within an expansive space-time. Multiplication is fragmentation and dispersal. Worse, no matter where one exists within the expansive spread of the double space-time, it is impossible to establish any relationship between human existence and the surrounding totality. This is the tragic

sentiment already understood by Pascal, the discovery of an absolute separation between the infinity that encompasses us and the finitude of the time and place where we currently stand. Human beings wander within the broad expanse of the universe.[6]

The prison depicted by Piranesi is not the closed space of solitary confinement but instead exists on a massive scale approaching that of a temple or palace (figure 1). The mass of small characters, drawn indistinctly like small points or stains, conversely reinforces the impression of the expanse and distance of this space. Massive columns and gothic arches, the winding staircase that climbs endlessly upward to a limitless blue sky. The borderline between the end of the building and the beginning of the sky is not clearly defined. (In contrast to the second edition of *Carceri d'invenzione*, which emphasizes the strength of the pillars and walls by highlighting the contrast between light and dark, I believe the first edition of the etching, which is drawn with a rougher touch, is more effective in generating the nightmarish effect of the space.) As Poulet points out, Pascal's image of the universe as prison, on whose edges human beings wander as miniscule points, is reproduced here with perfect technique.

In *Carceri d'invenzione*, strange devices and machines that evoke the actual tools of discipline and torture used in eighteenth-century prisons are distributed at strategic points and serve as accents pulling together the picture's composition. At the base of the round pillars are chains and iron rings to bind the prisoners, and from the ceilings dangle pulleys and cables to cause the pain of being suspended in midair. The wheels placed on the floor are perhaps for drawing and quartering. There is even a pommel horse bristling with needles. What one naturally imagines from the sight of these horrific devices, which cast their deep shadows here and there throughout the dungeon, is the hollow time after the rituals of torture have ended. The characters who climb the crowded stairways appear to be attempting a desperate escape from the pain of torture. Yet the winding stairs are ruptured bridges that break off in the middle, and none of the spiral staircases that continue limitlessly leads to any exit. If Piranesi's prison as a whole is a space that condenses the time of a nightmare, then the people on the stairs are perhaps nothing more than passing phantasms produced by the obsession of escape.

The labyrinthine prison created by Piranesi would eventually become a powerful motif that stirred the imagination of Romantic poets. William Beckford's gothic romance *Vathek* (1786) and Thomas De Quincey's *Confessions of an English Opium Eater* (1821), Alfred de Musset's *La Mouche* (1853) and Théophile Gautier's *Mademoiselle Dafné* (1866). In Piranesi's prison, these writers saw the movement of a self-consciousness that is at once tied to a laby-

Figure 1. *Invenzioni Capriedi Carceri*, plate 8. Etching by Giovanni Battista Piranesi. Courtesy Chikuma Shobō, 1982

rinthine world yet that also continually desires flight and escape—in other words, something that touches on the core of the Romantic spirit.

However, Piranesi's original intent in creating *Carceri d'invenzione* was not the expression of Romantic self-consciousness, but the recuperation of baroque grandeur. At the very least, behind the Piranesi who continues a desperate escape along the spiral stairs, there is another, counter-Piranesi hidden in the image of *Carceri d'invenzione*. In the preface to his first published work, the *Prima Parte* (1743), Piranesi writes alternately of being moved by the magnificent scale of Roman architecture and of his despair at the lack of spirit in contemporary architecture. He claims that if no contemporary architecture is able to equal the Amphitheater of Vespasian or the Palace of Nero, then he will at least try to recreate Roman splendor through architectural drawings. Despite their massive scale, the Roman-style buildings and ruins in *Prima Parte* are unable to avoid a realistic narrowness in their details. In the *Carceri d'invenzione* published eight years later, however, standards of perspective and detailed technique are discarded. Instead, the free and uninhibited line, the contrast between light and darkness, create the effect of a fantasy space. What is contained there is the passion of Piranesi, who was drawn to the splendor and magnificence of ancient Rome.[7] As De Quincey says, the picture overflows with an "extraordinary power." Instead of shedding sentimental tears for the imprisoned criminals, Piranesi praises the severe will to power embodied by the prison. Art as an expression of power. What Piranesi placed at the foundation of the world of *Carceri d'invenzione* was precisely such a baroque tradition.

In the second half of the eighteenth century, when the prison reform movement of John Howard led to enterprising architects being entrusted with the design of new prisons, the type of fear created by the space of Piranesi's prison played an important role in determining their outer style. In contrast to the interior of the new prisons, to which hygienic and humanistic considerations were given, their façades were based on various fantastic ideas designed to evoke sensations of terror. For example, at the new prison of Newgate designed in 1769, the opening of the empty and overpowering façade was extremely truncated, creating an effect of severe solemnity, as if the prison were a grave that would entomb its prisoners alive. The Provence prison designed by Claude-Nicholas Ledoux appeared from the outside like a combination fortress and mausoleum, on top of which the heavy porte cochère supported by short columns evoked an image of the gateway to Hell. The modern prison was called on to arm itself in visual signs emphasizing the prestige of the law and the will to merciless punishment.[8]

Yet it was Jeremy Bentham's "Panopticon" that succeeded in translating

the Piranesi-esque space of terror into the *internal* structure of the prison—
in other words, in the opposite direction from Ledoux's prison or the Newgate prison—thereby achieving a mechanism for functional domination. In
its outward appearance, it was a commonplace six-story cylindrical structure
recalling the structure of the Panorama, although the numerous windows cut
into the walls somewhat lessened its overpowering impression. The inmates
are not greeted by a gate mimicking the entrance to Hell, but are drawn inside
through an underground passageway. The internal space is organized around
a central observation tower; a circular building divided into individual cells
surrounds the tower and a courtyard occupies the space between them. One
can think of the observation tower as the observation deck of the Panorama
where spectators are brought, and the Panorama screen viewed from the observation deck is replaced by the donut-shaped ring of cells where inmates
are confined. (The Panorama was invented four years before the Panopticon,
in 1787, by Edinburgh portrait painter Robert Barker, but there is apparently
no direct relationship between the two.) The principle of the Panopticon is
that the guard in the observation tower cannot be seen by the inmates and
is able to observe their every move; it is summed up by the principle of the
superiority of vision (seeing without being seen). Conversely, the inmates are
of course unable to see into the observation tower and are also unable to
make contact with their fellow inmates, who are separated by the walls of the
individual cells. Moreover, the large windows in each cell opening out to the
external world merely highlight the prisoners' silhouettes in backlight, while
the sunlight streaming in from the massive skylight directly above the observation tower covers the tower itself in a curtain of light. At night the lamps
hanging on the outer walls of the tower are illuminated, and mirrors affixed
to these lamps send blinding light directly onto the prisoners. It is the same
principle as the familiar interrogative technique seen in foreign films whereby
the detective shines a blinding light on the suspect. As Foucault writes, the
inmate confined to his cell "is the object of information, never a subject in
communication."[9] He is confined within a cunning trap of light and visibility,
and the deep darkness that had previously shrouded underground dungeons
is here completely eliminated.

The light from lamps and the sun that illuminates the Panopticon's interior is an effective weapon for the inspectors, but from the inmates' standpoint it represents a violence that strips them of the power of vision. This
paradox of darkness within light is precisely a variation on a Piranesi-like
theme. The figures of *Carceri d'invenzione* who attempt a desperate escape up
the stairs are confined not within a limited space, but in a prison of infinite
breadth and distance. It is the trap of proliferating labyrinthine space. The

Panopticon is also an ingenious device that fully deploys the effects of light distribution and the gaze to make a limited space seem infinite. The sight witnessed by the inspector in the observation tower, the panorama of prisoners, materializes the fantasy seen by Piranesi—his own pain multiplied to infinity. "The scene, though a confined one, would be a very various, and therefore, perhaps, not altogether an unamusing one"—this is a passage in which Bentham boasts of the effectiveness of the Panopticon.[10]

2

The second half of the eighteenth century that stretched from Piranesi to the Marquis de Sade is usually interpreted as the age of reason, yet in fact it was also an age in which the theme of the prison took root as a sinister fantasy in the depths of intellectual history. According to Victor Brombert, "The symbolic value attributed to the Bastille and other state prisons viewed as tyrannical constructs, the nightmarish architectural perspectives in the famous 'Prigioni' etchings of Piranesi, the cruel fantasies of the Marquis de Sade conceived in prison and projected into further enclosed spaces, the setting of Gothic novels in dungeons, vaults, and oubliettes—all this can tell us a great deal about the structures of the Romantic imagination, and the favored dialectical tensions between oppression and the dream of freedom, between fate and revolt, between the awareness of the finite and the longing for infinity."[11] If one seeks something corresponding to this "age of the great confinement" in our own country, then it would perhaps be the tumultuous half-century from the end of the Tokugawa period to the beginning of the Meiji period.

For example, there is the following text:

Confined to a one-mat room, day and night I scheme to take possession of the five continents. Everyone laughs at this mad delusion, but those who laugh live in a narrow world, while the world I inhabit is expansive. The severity of our nation's ban on sailing abroad has prevented people from traveling beyond the nation's sixty-six provinces. Therefore, their vision is confined to the sixty-six provinces, and their world is exceedingly small. Yet alone I stand by and watch over all things from past to present, looking across all nations. Therefore I am able to achieve an unknown and unimaginable expanse. This is not due to the superiority of my intelligence over others, but only to the size of my spirit's home.[12]

This is a passage from *Lectures on Mencius* [*Kō-Mō yowa*], the lectures that Yoshida Shōin (1830–1859) had begun delivering to fellow inmates at Noyama prison in Hagi in 1855 (Ansei 2). Shōin, from the base of his "room of confinement" cut off from the real world, deliberately distills his anti-bakufu ideology. In the world of thought, the actual "expanse under heaven" is "narrow," and his small "cell" is reversed into an expansive space opened up to the five continents. Isolationist Japan is a "prison" shutting itself off from the world. Of course, this paradox is not mere wordplay. The wretched failure of his grand plan at Shimoda and the dark reversal of fortune whereby the man who planned to tour the five great continents was chained hand and foot in prison—when this cruel drama experienced by Shōin achieved expression in words, it necessarily took the form of paradox. In this text Shōin says that "everyone laughs at this crazy delusion." Yet it was Shōin himself, more than any other, who clearly realized that his actions were delusional and foolish. Shōin did not attempt to turn his eyes from the negative values of his being a disloyal subject, an unfilial son, and an insane prisoner. The insane must affirm their madness and by becoming self-aware of their borderline status, alienated and marginal, transform their defeat into a conviction of future victory. Stripped of freedom of action, forced into the humiliation of being a convicted criminal, prisoners are precisely those who have already been liberated from the values of the center, from established order and status consciousness; they are a chosen group of people who are able to experience with all of their pain the revelation of change. "We are people placed in adversity, and can therefore only effectively explain conditions of adversity"—these are the words whereby, at the opening of his lectures, Shōin explained the significance of learning in prison.[13] He asserts that those confined to prison, because they are cut off from worldly benefits of fame, wealth, and professional advancement, do not approach learning as a tool for worldly profit and so are able to master its essence. Furthermore, the very fact that they have been cast out from society and placed into adverse circumstances leaves them better able to understand the nation's "adversity"—its situation of crisis after the arrival of Commodore Perry's ships.

The optics of the prison inmate opened up by Shōin's words—the dynamics of liberation and confinement—would be developed by the generation that lived through the quarter century stretching from the turmoil of the Restoration to the Freedom and Popular Rights Movement. Above all, it was something that determined, at the most profound level, the conception of the political novel of the Meiji 10s (1877–1886). Not only was the prison used as an effective metaphor to figure the oppression of the Meiji state, but the authors of political novels themselves had often experienced life in prison. For example, in Suehiro Tetchō's (1849–1896) *Setchūbai* [Plum blossoms in the snow, 1886], the author's experience of confinement in Kajibashi prison, together with Narushima Ryūhoku (1837–1884), for violating libel laws [Zanbōritsu] is reflected in the protagonist Kunino Motoi's prison experience. Tōkai Sanshi's (1852–1922) *Kajin no kigū* [Chance encounters with beautiful women, 1885–97], which begins with a description of the Liberty Bell in Philadelphia's Independence Hall, is broken off at the point of Sanshi's own distress after being thrown into Hiroshima prison for involvement in the Princess Min-bi assassination incident in Korea. Furthermore, Miyazaki Muryū (1855–1889), who suffered an early death, was obsessed with the motif of the prison, from *Kishūshū* [Demon cries, 1884–85], which depicted the underground activity of Russian terrorists, to the late work *Susuki no hitomura* [A clump of silver grass, 1888], into which he projected his own prison experience. This genealogy of "prison literature," which, despite a rather antiquated style, contained the latent heat of political romanticism, led ultimately to Kitamura Tōkoku's *Soshū no shi* [A prisoner's song, 1889] and *Waga rōgoku* [My prison, 1892]. Yet, there is also an undeniable discontinuity between the prison of self-consciousness imagined by Tōkoku and the prison of the political novel, which is depicted as a space of opposition pitting freedom against oppression. What does this continuity and discontinuity signify? And what is the perspective that will allow for the reconsideration of the metaphor of the prison contained in the intellectual history of the turbulent period from Shōin to Tōkoku? Furthermore, what effects did the "age of the great confinement" in Europe generate on the Far Eastern monarchy of Japan? To address such questions, I would like to begin with a consideration of the institution of the modern prison itself, which was introduced during the age of "civilization and enlightenment" in the Meiji era. This introduction was marked by the promulgation of *Prison Regulations* [*Kangokusoku*] in November of Meiji 5 (1872).

The man who in essence enacted *Prison Regulations* was Ohara Shigeya, known as the founder of the modern penal system. Born in 1834 (Tenpō 5), Ohara was a samurai of the Okayama domain; as a youth he was incarcerated in Tenmachō prison for involvement in acts of treason. After the Restoration he was selected as domain representative [*kōshi*] and subsequently served as a judge in the Office of Criminal Law. Due to his miserable experience in Tenmachō prison, Ohara believed strongly in the need for prison reform, and in October 1869 (Meiji 2) he submitted a lengthy written opinion to Minister of Justice Ōgimachisanjō. In this text, Ohara describes in detail the actual conditions of the prisons during the old bakufu regime, based on his own experience. The following year he was granted permission to travel abroad to study the issue of prison reform; from February to August 1871 he accompanied British Vice-Consul John Hall to observe prisons in British colonies such as Hong Kong and Singapore. *Prison Regulations* included the results of this foreign inspection, which were apparently recognized in the report to the Ministry of Justice as follows: "Based on the record of direct observations by Ohara Shigeya and others and of the testimony of the British, the prison systems of various neighboring countries were compared to our nation's regulations; some elements have been drawn from them, taking into consideration custom and human nature."[14]

Prison Regulations by Ohara Shigeya is an unconventional text that deviates widely from conventional laws. Instead of creating a cold and transparent text, Ohara was engrossed with weaving his own fantasy through the vehicle of the law. What he depicts there is precisely the utopia of prison—there is a sense in which the vivid memory of his painful experience in Tenmachō prison is turned inside out. One passage in Ohara's report to the minister of justice reads: "Upon arrest, prisoners are herded together into the pitch darkness of a three-foot high space where they crouch down. Their very breath cut off from the sunlight, their health is excessively damaged." In contrast, *Prison Regulations* continually extols the light of the sun and fresh air, as well as expansive, hygienic spaces. Against the scale of Tenmachō prison—56 by 9 meters—the total area established for the prison in *Regulations* is the broad expanse of more than 20 acres; a cross-shaped prison, with each wing measuring 100 meters, was to be placed within a circular plot measuring approximately 300 meters in diameter. These dimensions are large enough to encompass the majority of government offices related to the law that existed in the Meiji 10s (1877–1886), including the Ministry of Justice, the Grand Court of Judicature, the Tokyo Court, and the Metropolitan Police Department. Furthermore, this large lot was to be filled with flowering plants and herbs to provide ease and comfort to the spirits of the prisoners. "Prisons shall be placed at a remove from cities on empty and elevated ground and be expansive in size. As shown in a diagram, the small paths extending across the various gardens are to be covered with sand and the empty spaces along each side will be planted with medicinal herbs and beautiful flowers and fruit-bearing plants in order to relieve the spirits of the inmates and to bring in fresh air. Moreover, their sale will be a source of profit."[15] Was the Singapore prison that Ohara observed filled with tropical flowers such as bougainvillea or hibiscus? The idea of selecting "empty elevated ground" as the site for prisons may have been informed by John Howard's prison reform proposals; in *The State of the Prisons* (1777), Howard wrote that the preferred place to build prisons was first on a riverbank and second atop a hill.

For the construction of the prison, stone or brick is preferred. In 1872, when *Prison Regulations* was promulgated, Thomas Wartlus's plans for the Ginza "bricktown" were made public. The distinguishing feature of the Ginza bricktown was the straight-line boulevards and the two-story brick structures "painted with white chalk" [*Tokyo shin-hanjōki*]. The structure of the prison called for in *Prison Regulations* was also a two-story stone or brick building, and to maintain light inside the individual cells, the inner walls were required to be painted with white chalk. In addition, the cross-shaped prison evokes the intersection of straight-line boulevards. Through such analogies with the Ginza bricktown, it is not very difficult to discern the "city" hidden within *Prison Regulations*. The prisons were to be supplied with a system of water-works and sewage ("The inside and outside of the prison are to be free of filth. First the height of the land should be measured and waterworks installed to drain rainwater; in each structure the rainwater and excess water for daily use shall be disposed of in a distant location. No ditches to hold stagnant water will be dug, even outside the enclosure"); a clean hospital surrounded by a park ("The prison infirmary is to be situated at the highest point of the grounds. . . . The windows and doors shall be large so as to bring in fresh air, and the infirmary is to be surrounded by a clean garden with flowering plants to ease the sight of the patients"); and a library stocked with a rich collection of books ("An archive shall be placed inside the prison to keep excellent books presented for the inmates' reading").[16] The system that structures this closed space includes the various apparatuses necessary for the modern city—the utopia of prison dreamed by Ohara calls to mind a miniature utopian city. The ideal prison presented in *Prison Regulations* has a beautiful garden adorned with flowering plants and medicinal herbs, and there is even a small collective farm where criminals convicted of lesser offenses are allowed to grow vegetables and where cows, sheep, pigs, and chickens are raised and milk and cheese are also produced. This is an image well-suited to the age of capital production, yet if one eliminates its utilitarian effect it also presages the "garden city" that would be proclaimed by Ebenezer Howard at the end of the century. Ohara, who dedicated himself to sweeping away the dark image accruing to the prisons of the old regime, had ended up depicting, on a level beyond his consciousness, an image of the future of Tokyo, enveloped in the trappings of civilization.

Yet it goes without saying that the modern city, which displayed such a brilliant outer surface, maintained another, unsightly face. If the outer face of the city consisted of the avenues and government buildings transformed into monumental spaces, as well as the public squares and parks enveloped in natural scenery, there was also a dismal space proliferating unceasingly behind this façade. These are the factories as black boxes that organize labor within the framework of training and regulation and the slum areas abandoned to decrepit conditions. The ideal prison conceived by Ohara does not escape this irony of the city. The tranquil scenery of parks and small farms, reminiscent of a garden city, was in fact a hypocritical design within which the prison as a ruthless apparatus of punishment needed to drape itself. Or more precisely, the two conceptions—that of organizing a space for the efficient administration of punishment and that of reforming the dark, unclean spaces (which had also served to shield criminals from the watchful gaze of officials) into a hygienic space of clear vision—are ultimately two sides of the same coin.

The prisons of the old bakufu regime (1600–1868), as is well-known, were managed according to an unwritten, extremely complicated "self-rule system" of prison officials, who ranged from the prison "lord," the assistant officer, first officer, second officer, to the positions known as *sumi no inkyo* ["recluse of the corner"] and *tsume no inkyo* ["recluse of the water-closet"]. It was an antiworld that inverted the secular order existing outside of the prison, and which, as Amino Yoshihiko writes, served as a gruesome *asyl* [sanctuary], drawing on the genealogy of the *muenjo*, or "autonomous places," which guaranteed an inverted freedom in the medieval period. The hierarchy of prisoners who have been cut off from the secular world is determined by the quality of the "performance" of their crimes.[17] However, *Prison Regulations* introduced nothing other than a new class hierarchy to replace the ambiguous standard of the "performance" of crime. It is the standard of aptitude toward regulation and discipline and the "skill" of labor required by industrial society. For example, prisoners are categorized not by the length of their sentences but according to the following five-level hierarchy:

Fifth Class: Those who carry earth and stone, develop wild land, pound rice in a mortar, press oil, and crush stone.

Fourth Class: Those who construct the various official residences, repair streets and restore tile, earthenware, and brick, or work in cultivation and the like.

Third Class: Woodworkers, bamboo craftsmen, rattan workers, metal workers, stone workers, tub and tile workers, cobblers, leatherworkers, weavers and such. Specialization is permitted.

Second Class: The same as third class; however, prisoners will instruct other prisoners in their area of expertise or otherwise use their skills in kitchen work and the like.

First Class: The same as second class; however, when this level is fulfilled, prisoners are to be released.[18]

It is clear that this five-level structure is organized according to a progression from simple manual labor to agricultural work to unskilled labor to skilled labor. As Foucault writes, "The distribution according to ranks or grade has a double role: it marks the gaps, hierarchizes qualities, skills and aptitudes; but it also punishes and rewards."[19]

Moreover, the class to which each prisoner belongs must be clearly marked through an assemblage of bodily signs, such as the presence of shackles or the type of clothing worn. Those who have attempted to escape once are given a light-green sleeve; those who commit the same offense again are given two such sleeves; the third time, half of their hair is shaved off, and so on. The punishments for prisoners who deviate from discipline and training are divided into six types: (1) bar and chain, (2) demotion, (3) steel ball, (4) bearing a heavy weight, (5) darkroom, (6) disciplinary whip. Excluding demotion and darkroom, these disciplinary measures represent bodily punishments organized around visual signs.

Ohara Shigeya, who would later be selected as a commissioner of the art division for the National Industrial Exposition, was apparently possessed of some artistic sensibility; the diagrams attached to *Prison Regulations* include detailed depictions of the prison building, the facilities inside the cells, the instruments of punishment, and work tools. (Among these, the diagrams of rope-making machines and brick-making devices were especially detailed, but did Ohara realize that for the prisoners, these were dismal symbols evoking the state of confinement?) Furthermore, there are also sample statistical tables—such as the "Prison Officials Table," "Prison Expenditures Table," "Prison Revenues Table," and "Prison Accounts Table"—to increase the efficiency of prison management. This set of diagrams and statistical tables is no doubt closely linked to the idea of dividing prisoners by means of visible signs, and it also anticipates the model of rational administrative systems required by industrial society. At the center of *Prison Regulations*, which attempts to extend the function of the gaze to all corners of the prison, is a conception of division and observation that can be termed virtually naturalistic. The key elements of prison design in *Prison Regulations* were focused on just such matters: "The regulations for the guard-house are that a circular room shall be placed at the center of the prison's four corridors so that guards can see everything at a glance without any intervening obstacle. This is a means to reduce the number of guards. Details are provided in the diagram."[20] It is impossible to determine whether Ohara knew of Bentham's existence when he wrote *Prison Regulations*, yet it is precisely the principle of the Panopticon that is here put into play.

In previous histories of Meiji thought, the influence of the utilitarian philosophy of Bentham has been traced through the discourse of enlightenment intellectuals, beginning with Nishi Amane's (1829–1897) "Teachings of the Three Treasures of Life" ["Jinsei sanhō setsu," 1875], yet perhaps the gestalt of the Panopticon cited in the text of *Prison Regulations* offers a glimpse of an alternative thinking that had seeped into the system: to strengthen the function of the gaze from center to periphery, thereby transforming an opaque space into a transparent space, or, through the division and organization of space, to create a mechanism rendering the use of power more efficient. This method of grasping space, appropriately captured by the translation phrase "seeing everything at a glance" [*ichimoku dōshi*], does not stop only at the organizing principle of the prison but shapes a hidden context that extends across all of the institutions created by Japanese modernity. For example, there is the "One-Five-Thousandth Scale Map of Tokyo" created by the General Staff Office of the Army Surveying Section in the second half of the Meiji 10s (1877–1886). This map of Tokyo, considered a masterpiece of modern urban cartography, brilliantly renders the complex topography of the Yamanote plateau (the western "high city" section of Tokyo) through 2-meter-interval contour lines, and it even clearly marks the site of each private home's well and the water pails buried underground. It is made with such detail that it includes eleven different signs designating various enclosures, such as "stone fence," "iron railing," and "bamboo hedge."[21] At the same time, however, following the methodology of Edo-period illustrated maps, the imperial palace at the center of the city is left blank, and there is conscious manipulation whereby the majority of military facilities are removed to nine sheets outside the boundaries of the map. This methodology, which conceals vital areas while depicting other areas in detail, clearly indicates the aim of this map, which was intended for use in street combat, to quell either rebellion among the nobility or uprisings among the people. Yet, in the very fact that a map intended for use in street combat creates the impression of the most beautiful urban map one can read the subtle gap that emerged between the perception of space through the gaze that "sees everything at a glance" and the actual space of the city.

One can also raise the example of the first National Industrial Exposition held in Meiji 10 (1877) in Ueno Park. As the guide to the exhibition prepared by the Secretariat of the Exposition notes, "Observation, when carried out in such detail, brings all things before the human eye, serving as a vehicle for increasing total knowledge and as a tool for spreading information." Here, the effectiveness of observation for expanding knowledge is emphasized. This conception originated in the proposal requesting the construction of a museum, which was submitted to Sanjō Sanetomi by Ōkubo Toshimichi: "In the power of vision resides the ability for the human spirit to touch all matters and to give rise to emotion and discernment. The ancients said that 'seeing something once is better than hearing it a hundred times.' Only in the learn-

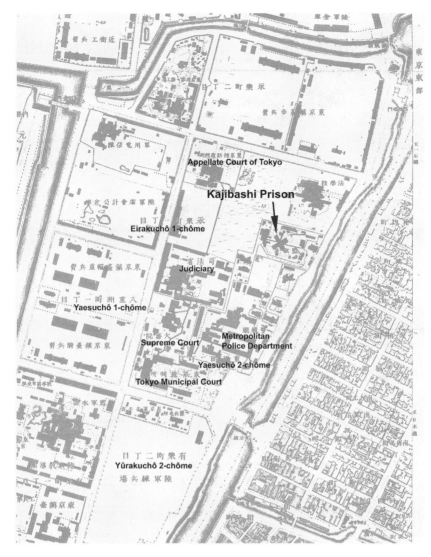

Figure 2. Kajibashi prison. "One-Five-Thousandth Scale Map of Tokyo" by the General Staff Office of the Army Surveying Section, 1883. Courtesy Chikuma Shobō, 1982

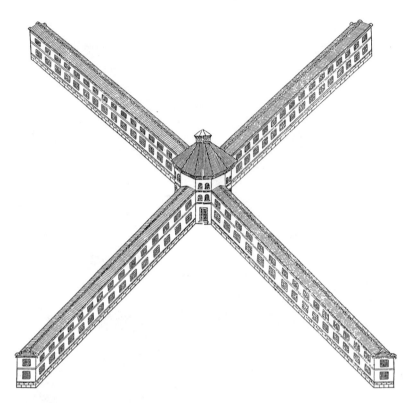

Figure 3. Sketch of a Japanese prison with radiating cells and a central guardhouse. From *Kangokusoku* (Prison regulations) by Ohara Shigeya, 1872. Courtesy Hara Shobō, 1974

ing provided by the eye is there an expedient means for enlightening human knowledge and encouraging the industrial arts." What is apparent here is a naturalist spirit that attempts to grasp the form of things more accurately through vision; "the power of vision" is seen as the most effective means of understanding in the context of civilization and enlightenment and the encouragement of industry. Those who visited the exhibition hall were able to experience a signifying space whereby they could see at a glance the entire Japanese territory on the level of commodities; yet it was the organization of the exhibition space itself that even more strongly illustrated "the power of vision" as "an expedient means for the advancement of the industrial arts." On either side of the front gate were placed such structures as the Hall of Machines, the Horticulture Buildings, and the Hall of Agriculture, which demonstrated policies aimed at promoting industry. If this section can be considered the base of a triangle, the two main buildings displaying the products of each prefecture (the Eastern Main Building and the Western Main Building)

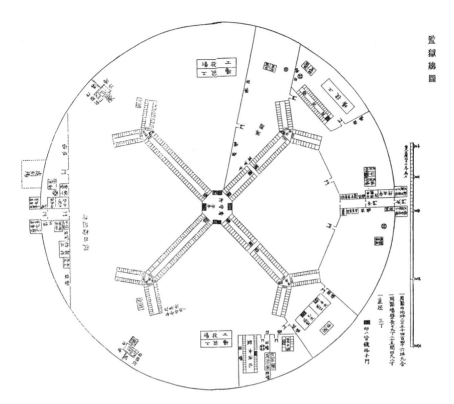

Figure 4. Diagram for a Japanese prison. From *Kangokusoku* (Prison regulations) by Ohara Shigeya, 1872. Courtesy Hara Shobō, 1974

formed each oblique side, and the position corresponding to the triangle's pinnacle is the main structure of the art museum. It goes without saying that the art museum, which is placed at the center as the focal point of the overall space of the exposition, displays the function of art as the essence of "the power of vision."

After less than a year, the *Prison Regulations* established by Ohara were effectively scrapped for budgetary reasons. Yet their conception was materialized, albeit incompletely, in December of Meiji 8 (1875) in the form of Kajibashi prison (figure 2), which was constructed at the northern end of the Metropolitan Police Department. Each wing of the cross-shaped, two-story wooden structure was approximately 20 meters in length, and its grounds covered an area of approximately two acres (figures 3, 4). From the perspective of *Prison Regulations*, its scale was miniaturized to one-tenth.

It was the following year, in February of Meiji 9 (1876), that the *Chōya shimbun*'s Narushima Ryūhoku and Suehiro Tetchō were charged with violating libel law and confined to Kajibashi prison. When he accompanied the head of the Nishi-Honganji temple on a tour of Europe from Meiji 5 to 6 (1872–1873), Ryūhoku had had the opportunity to observe Paris and London jails. In his "Prison Stories" ["Gokunai banashi," translated by Matthew Fraleigh as "Tales from the Slammer"], serialized in the *Chōya shinbun* after his release from prison, it is no surprise to find the following passage, which reveals the essential characteristics of the first Western-style prison in Japan: "Its construction was generally modeled after Western prisons, and it took the shape of a cross. Both the upper and lower levels are divided into eight wards. Each ward contains ten cells, totaling eighty in all. *On both the upper and lower levels, the guards are situated in the center, and watch over all four directions.*" On the other hand, Tetchō used his prison experience as the basis for the passages in *Plum Blossoms in the Snow* in which the protagonist Kunino Motoi is thrown in jail. It is the climax of the work: "Long ago in the West, a man named Bentham came forward and argued that there should be laws and regulations regarding the construction of prisons and the division of prisoners, and each nation's government also used this argument to completely change the style of prisons. I hear that gradually the numbers of criminals decreased, and I hope that Japan too will soon reform its prison system."[22] This is a passage in which Kunino addresses his cell-mates to argue for prison reform, but I wonder whether Tetchō realized that the Kajibashi prison in which he was confined was in fact built on the principle of the Panopticon propounded by that same Bentham. In any case, the gap between the realism of the rulers, who understood so quickly the effectiveness of the Panopticon, and the optimism of the ruled, who wanted to see Bentham as a forerunner of prison reform, is unmistakable. There is a bitter irony here, whereby discursive thinking is betrayed by material thinking.

3

An archetypal example of the attempt to transpose the thinking of the Panopticon onto the level of the city may be Baron Haussmann's reorganization of Paris under the direction of Napoleon III. Haussmann's work, which mercilessly destroyed old winding streets and carved out instead straight-line boulevards offering unobstructed views, was able to materialize Louis Napoleon's dream of "the most beautiful city in the world." It is the perspective of grand boulevards lined with trees and flowers and the monumental spaces of squares adorned with fountains and marble sculptures. However, this vista of reorganized Paris also concealed a strategic intention to defend the capital city from civil strife and uprisings. Not only did the straight-line boulevards allow for rapid deployment of police and military troops, but they also eliminated the blind spots where insurgents could lay in ambush, while also rendering more difficult the construction of barricades; there was thus a calculated strategy to kill two birds with one stone. (The Second Empire had learned a bitter lesson following the Revolution that paving stones could be diverted for use as material for barricades, and had come to use asphalt pavement.)

The substance of Haussmann's design was to reconstruct the center of the city as a strategic point for the flow of traffic. Hence the plan to cut and divide the central portion of the city by way of "the Paris cross" (*la croisée de Paris*) formed by the north-south and east-west boulevards. The Rue de Rivoli (completed in 1855), which runs east-west through the north bank of the Seine, and the Boulevard de Sébastopol (completed in 1860), which intersects it at a right angle—these literally form the skeletal structure of the Paris reconstruction design.[23] Haussmann's plan to transform the function of the "center" from narrow paths that block traffic to a circle linking the entirety of the city recalls the function of the tower at the center of the Panopticon, which casts its watchful gaze at the surrounding cells. At the same time, the tangled mass of workers' homes at the center of the city was relegated to the periphery, and the Parc des Buttes Chaumont, which was created as a resting place for workers, was seen as their compensation. As Taki Kōji writes, "Just as the Panopticon was structured from the standpoint of a gaze that governs space, Haussmann's city was pierced from end to end by the gaze of the observers (the rulers)."[24]

The outline of this reorganization plan of Paris was introduced in Japan as early as *Record of a Tour of the United States and Europe* [*Beiō kairan jikki*, 1878], the public record of the Iwakura delegation, which visited post–Franco-Prussian War France in Meiji 6 (1873). When substantive deliberations on city reorganization began in the second half of the Meiji 10s (1877–1886), this Paris reorganization design was seen as the best model for the future map of Tokyo. At the first meeting of the committee to investigate the reorganization of municipal wards held in February of Meiji 17 (1884), Secretary of Home Affairs Yamazaki Naotane explained the outline of the reform plan and spoke as follows:

> To raise two or three examples with which to compare our proposal for reform: the greatest avenues will be reconstructed in the manner of those "boulevards"; Shiba Park in Asakusa will become a promenade for citizens like the Parc Monceau; Ueno Park will be ceded by the Ministry of Agriculture and Industry to the city of Tokyo and will become, like the Bois du Bologne, a public meeting place for upper-class gentlemen; the

Suitengū Konpira Shrine will be rebuilt in brick and opened to the people, giving benefit to them; cleaning away the slander of idols and shrines for evil deities, it will be transformed into a respected "monument"; several "squares" will be created in densely populated areas such as Nihonbashi Ward or Kyōbashi Ward; . . . those wards that detract from the city will be reformed into wards displaying a Western-style aesthetic.[25]

Yamazaki's plan, which depicted a future image of an imperial capital modeled after the reconstructed Paris and adorned with the aesthetic of a baroque city, was ultimately discarded due to its wide divergence from the original proposal prepared by Yoshikawa Akimasa, who served as both governor of Tokyo and chairman of the screening committee. Nevertheless, although the original proposal was limited to the improvement of roads, rivers, bridges, and harbors, the construction of parks, markets, theaters, business assembly halls, and public exchanges were added to the report.

The city reconstruction plan that was submitted to Minister of Home Affairs Yamagata Aritomo was subsequently shelved for a time following the creation of the Interim Bureau of Construction, over which foreign minister Inoue Kaoru presided; instead, the centralized design for grandiose and baroque government offices submitted by Ende-Böckmann, who had been invited from Germany, was advanced. The Ministry of Home Affairs would regain control over city planning only after Inoue resigned as Foreign Minister in September of 1887 (Meiji 20), taking responsibility for the breakdown in the renegotiations of the unequal treaties. The following year, in 1888 (Meiji 21), the city reorganization plan entrusted to the council of the *genrō-in* [Senate] was scrapped because it was deemed to lean toward the beautification of the city in imitation of the Paris reconstruction. Refusing to submit to these repeated failures, Yamagata resorted to the form of Imperial Ordinance, issuing a proclamation of "Regulations for the Tokyo City Reorganization" on 6 August 1888.

The Tokyo City Reorganization Committee held its first meeting on 5 October of that year to discuss these regulations; prior to the opening of the conference, committee chairman Yoshikawa delivered a speech indicating the overall policy of the reorganization effort. The first essential point was, "Rejecting the argument of focusing only on the central districts of the city, we plan to reorganize all of the municipal districts and determine that the purview of the reorganization shall extend to all areas under the control of the old Edo magistrate." The scope of the municipal reorganization was not limited to the central districts of the city, but rather extended to the "sixteen-mile zone," which included the so-called *shubikinai*, or "Vermillion Line" area.[26]

Furthermore, the main goals of the city reorganization were narrowed to (1) the improvement of traffic, (2) the prevention of fires, (3) the improvement of urban hygiene:

1. Tokyo is the site of the Imperial Palace and the seat of government, the locus of commerce and industry. It is truly the capital of the entire nation. Nevertheless, since the time of its construction it has experienced continual warfare. Therefore, the primary concern has been defense of the city. With some exceptions, the question of city planning has been neglected, as if it were not a concern. For this reason, the streets are narrow and meandering and are inconvenient for the passage of horse-drawn carriages. What was previously regarded as a strategic advantage is now unfavorable and inconvenient.

2. Since the Restoration, firefighting methods have improved. Hand water pumps were replaced by mechanical pumps, which were later replaced by steam pumps. Although these pumps are tremendously effective, regrettably, because of the many narrow roads, four-horse carriages are unable to arrive immediately at the necessary place and are unable to deploy their capability fully.

3. Waterworks and sewer systems are still incomplete. Housing is still built without adequate standards. For these reasons, drinking water is laced with noxious organisms that are harmful to the body, sewage collects and stagnates and a hundred virulent poisons blanket every street. Housing is irregular, with tall residences standing next to low buildings, small houses and large ones stand together, some have tile roofs, others come with wooden shingles. When it comes to the back alleys, sediments of filthy garbage and puddles of rain water fill these spaces that never see the light of day; there is no circulation of air, and not only is there no outlet for these piles of filth, these are the main sites that produce pestilence and epidemics.[27]

Fujimori Terunobu responded to the Tokyo City Reorganization Committee's deliberations with the following critical evaluation: "The level of discussion was disappointing, with hardly any substantive or rigorous inquiry."[28] This assessment was merited, but it should be noted that this keynote speech clearly reflected the perspective of Yoshikawa Akimasa, who was an official of the Ministry of Home Affairs. This is evident in the stated intention to transform an enclosed, fortress-like medieval city into an open, modern city. The narrow, crooked pathways that gave Edo its character were supplemented with concentric swirls of outer moats, anchored at intervals by squares serving as approaches to the castle gates, which in turn broke up these swirls to form a complex line of defense against outside invaders. The gates that enclosed alleyways [*machi*] were also part of this system. One of the earliest signs in the transformation of this web of enclosed spaces was the construction of Tokyo's first stone bridge, Manseibashi, built from rock recovered from dismantling what was then the Sujikaemitsuke guardhouse that overlooked the Kanda River. Manseibashi inaugurated the conversion of Tokyo's wooden bridges to structures of stone and steel, and in 1882 tracks for horse-drawn railway cars were laid on the main highway running from Shinbashi Station to Ueno and Asakusa. Yoshikawa's recognition that "what were once embraced as advantageous and designated conveniences have become drawbacks and inconveniences today," aided by the understanding that Tokyo was changing from a city of waterways to a land-based city, would help give birth to plans calling for a network of main streets ranging from first-class streets [*ittō dōro*] to fifth-class tertiary roads extending out from the city center. Yoshikawa's realism led him to flatly reject the baroque aesthetic celebrated by the urban renewal plans for Paris, even as he had unerringly grasped its strategic virtues. One can discern such designs in his own urban renewal plan, which nonetheless repudiated the overt conception of Edo as a fortress.

Yoshikawa did not hesitate in making the elimination of backstreet shops and slums an explicit target of his city reconstruction project. As long as the establishment of a new system of streets required the removal of residences, it became necessary to somehow recognize and then to assign a negative value to the slums as an integral part of the modern city. What emerges is an awareness of oppositions between hygiene and filth, health and illness, discipline and punishment. Still vivid was the terror of cholera that in 1886 had claimed 9,879 lives and 12,000 hospital patients in Tokyo alone, generating the mythology of a virulent, rotting ether [*kūki*]. The stagnant, filthy atmosphere associated with the backstreets of the city would come to be dreaded as a horrifying symbol of evil, not only from the standpoint of medical science but in the realm of morality. Yoshikawa, and indeed every member of the Tokyo City Reorganization Committee, suffered from the illusion that the same fetid air that one would find trapped inside a prison cell blanketed the backstreets of Tokyo. During the eighth meeting of the Committee, when the chimney of the Koishikawa munitions factory was raised as an issue, Nagayo Sensai (1838–1902), who served as chief of the Health Division of the Ministry of Home Affairs, observed, "Around the globe, many are those who die in prison, and statistically speaking, in prisons of Western nations the death rate is thirty per thousand whereas here under our own jurisdiction in the lower city the rate is over forty per thousand. The poor circulation of air would be one of the reasons behind this. But, were we to probe the causes of these diseases, generally they would be fevers that originate among the lower classes, and if we further investigate the fury of these diseases, we would discover that they attack those above the middle class." This fear of the "evils of toxicity" found in the Tokyo City Reorganization Plan reflects the absence of provisions for waterworks both above and below ground and the lack of cleanup plans for the slums of Tokyo. (The Tokyo cholera epidemic of 1886 had been attributed to an antiquated water system inherited from the Edo period.) Deliberations on large and small parks by the Reorganization Committee did not reflect concern so much for aesthetic considerations as for the effective use of space that would help eliminate the "evils of toxicity" that might spread communicable diseases. I cannot help but detect a disturbing analogical relationship between the alarmist tone that clings to the City Reorganization Plan emphasizing the functional aspects of the city and Ohara Shigeya's utopic, sanitary prisons.

The new (Meiji) era had not only given a new name to the capital city but was effectively putting an end to vestiges of Edo life. The City Reorganization Plan was designed to remake Tokyo into a central, bureaucratic, capital city, but at the same time these efforts helped foreground the negative signs of the modern city such as slums and disorderly backstreet life. In quick succession, journalists began to publish documentaries on the underside of urban life. Sakurada Taiga's *Records of Exploration in the World of Dire Poverty, Hunger, and Suffering* [*Hin tenchi dai kikan kutsū tanken ki*, 1890] and Matsubara Iwagorō's *In Darkest Tokyo* [*Saiankoku no Tokyo*, 1893] deserve mention for pioneering this genre, even as Yokoyama Gennosuke's *Japan's Under Class* [*Nihon no kasō shakai*, 1898] has rightly received the highest critical acclaim for works of this kind. Certainly such figures as Sakurada and Matsubara, who were unable to go beyond their roles as investigators of the depths of poverty, lacked the breadth to consider the lives of the lower classes in the context of larger social structures, and at times they seemed a bit wanting in their sympathies toward their subjects. However, putting aside Sakurada's work, Matsubara's modern-mythic achievement, *In Darkest Tokyo*, which captures Meiji-era Tokyo through the contradictory elements of "civilization" and "darkness," deserves a close look. In exploring the mythology of the negative that marked the urban renewal plan for Tokyo, it leads us into realms that Yokoyama's social scientific study did not.

In Darkest Tokyo, a work that attempts to capture the shady "underworld"[29] of the slums that lay hidden beneath the slick surface of the city, is very likely to have been inspired by accounts of London's East End which appeared from the 1880s and into the 1890s. Together with George Sim's *How the Poor Live and Horrible London* (1889) and Charles Booth's *Life and Labour of the People in London* (1889), it was William Booth's *In Darkest England and the Way Out* (1890) that shocked educated Japanese of the time. Under the stewardship of Tokutomi Sohō, the journal *Peoples' Companion [Kokumin no tomo]* published two articles (on 23 May 1891 and 23 April 1892) that introduced Japanese readers to these works, and in Yokoyama Gennosuke's *Japan's Under Class* we find these words that refer to these British works: "Like those who live in east London as depicted in *In Darkest England*, it is not uncommon to see the ugly, sad plight of the poor here in Japan."[30] Although we lack concrete knowledge about whether or not Matsubara Iwagorō had read through Booth's work, it is quite likely that as a guest lecturer of the Minyū-sha he was familiar with its subject matter. Indeed, the very title of *In Darkest Tokyo* seems to have been taken from Booth's work.

William Booth founded the Salvation Army in 1861 and for the next thirty years vigorously pursued relief work in London's East End. *In Darkest England*, which forwarded a view of this area as a labor colony, was in a sense the culmination of his relief work. The distinctive elevated writing style of this documentary owes in part to the help he received from W. T. Stead (1849–1912), the journalist of the *Pall Mall Gazette*. What is accentuated in this account of the East End is the image of darkness that appears in section 1.

The figure of darkness that Booth used to symbolize the East End seems to have been directly borrowed from Henry M. Stanley's *In Darkest Africa* (1890).[31] The great expedition of seven hundred men that Stanley mounted for his last such venture in the Congo, which lasted from 1887 to 1889 (figure 5), was justified by its mission to rescue Emin Pasha, the mysterious figure who intermittently had engaged in isolated combat against the Maadii Islamic sect who had earlier defeated and killed General Gordon at Khartoum. *In Darkest Africa*, which has as its climax this rescue operation, would garner widespread journalistic attention on the way to becoming a global best-seller. It is reported that the publisher, Sansom and Co., paid £40,000 in royalties to Stanley. Booth would attempt to exploit the popularity of Stanley's work by appropriating the image of darkness to fan public interest in relief efforts directed at the "darkness" of London's East End.

According to Booth, Stanley's depiction of the Congo's endless jungles, the pygmies and cannibals who inhabit them, the avaricious slave traders and ivory hunters who invade native habitats with Enfield guns in hand to steal everything from the natives—these hideous images are directly analogous to the wretched conditions of London's East End: "Darkest England, like Darkest Africa, reeks with malaria. The foul and fetid breath of our slums is almost as poisonous as that of the African swamp."[32] The gist of Booth's first chapter, "Why Darkest England?", addressed the continuing indifference to the

Figure 5. Illustration from Henry M. Stanley, *In Darkest Africa, or the Quest, Rescue, and Retreat of Emin Governor of Equatoria*, 2 vols. (New York: Scribner, 1890)

existence of such primitive darkness in the heart of England's capital, which represented a profound irony in this civilized, Christian nation. On the heels of this scathing indictment, chapter 2 opens with an analysis of the class structure of the East End and moves on to provide a diligent and thoughtful investigation of housing problems, homelessness, and the life of crime.

Prior to its publication as a book, an earlier version of Matsubara Iwagorō's *In Darkest Tokyo* was intermittently serialized from November 1892 to August 1893 in the newspaper *Kokumin shimbun* [The peoples' newspaper]. It was during its serialization that Hakubunkan published Stanley's *In Deepest Africa* in Japanese with the title *Ankoku Ahirika*. Translated by Yabe Shinkichi, it was issued in six volumes, beginning with the first one in March 1893. As mentioned earlier, there is no explicit textual evidence of Matsubara's familiarity with Booth's work, but hints of Stanley's influence appear in *In Darkest Tokyo*, as when Matsubara depicts the underside of Tokyo as unknown territory waiting to be discovered by explorers on an expedition in search of the depths of poverty. (Indeed, the expression "explorers of the slums" [*hinkutsu tankensha*] appears repeatedly in his study.) Matsubara, who lumps together those denizens of the slums eagerly making their way back home after a hard day's work as "these hordes of a mysterious species," uses images reminiscent of those used to characterize the pygmies and cannibals encountered by Stanley's expeditionary forces. So if Matsubara's work was inspired by Booth's association of these African natives to London's East Enders, what was it that relentlessly moved Matsubara in the direction of the image of darkness?

In what is known to be one of Matsubara's earliest works, "Questioning Civilization" ["Bunmei gimon," 1888], a work he never completed, we can see the germination of some of his ideas that would appear in his later works. In short, this was a rather incoherent work that sounded like a muttered curse directed at the Westernization craze of the Rokumeikan era,[33] and on top of that, it affirms the excesses of "civilization" [*bunmei*] that is enlarging rather than reducing the disparity between rich and poor. And yet, oddly, the evolutionary schema of the thesis of survival of the fittest that Katō Hiroyuki had used in his work "Outlines of Truth" ["Shinsei Taii," 1870] to attack the thesis of "natural rights of man" [*tenpu jinken ron*] was used almost verbatim by Matsubara, who argues the futility of eliminating the disparity between rich and poor:

> At any rate, unfailingly the efficacy and good fortune of civilization favors members of society in very skewed fashion, and if we were to switch our concern to the distribution of misfortune, it is inevitable that people will lose their livelihoods to the power of machines, labor power will be exhausted by the power of capital, the number of companies engaged in the same enterprise are reduced as the fire of competition is fanned, and the results of direct and indirect appropriation of profit take away from weaker ones who lose to the stronger in the firm. It has always been the established view of scholars that the advance of civilization facilitates the well-being of people, but in real life that is not the case, and the state of affairs in society as we know it operates under the principles of survival of the fittest.[34]

Matsubara's cynical views on civilization reflected the sense of defeat that came from the reversals suffered by the People's Rights Movement, and at the same time they expressed emotions similar to those felt by those "contemptuous youth" [*reishō seinen*] of the late 1870s and early 1880s who eyed the wave of Westernization with cool defiance. Even though Matsubara's words betray some confusion, in essence his perspective is similar to those thoughts that are rather archly conveyed by Kitamura Tōkoku in such essays as "Feelings from the Current Age" ["Jisei ni kan ari," 1890] and "To Laugh or to Cry" ["Nakan ya warawan ya," 1892], works that are deeply colored by a melancholy that hovers over an era of severe social restrictions. Like Tōkoku in his early years as a writer and thinker, in *Interrogating Civilization* Matsubara was able to address civilization only as the object of a rather vague and diffuse indictment. Not until he was inspired by the works of Booth and Stanley was he able to rationally conceive how "civilization" worked to expunge the image of "darkness" from society and could he make use of the medium of the social documentary [*shakai ruporutaaju*] and go on to attain the status of a man of letters with original contributions of his own to make.

According to Uchida Roan's reminiscences, Futabatei Shimei, whom Matsubara had attentively waited on as his mentor when Futabatei was an employee of the department of the government gazette [*kanpō-kyoku*], would change his appearance to assume the mien of a member of the lower classes: "He would barge in on a gang of craftsmen wearing a crested workman's coat with his fist under the shoulder of his coat in the stock gesture of laborers and gamblers, or on other occasions burst into a drinking establishment wearing Western clothing and a derby hat."[35] Matsubara's notion of slum exploration [*hinkutsu tanken*] is not without the element of romantic adventure that his senior-mentor Futabatei sought, but in Matsubara's case, for good or for bad, he managed to avoid the latter's sentimental humanism and his "somewhat forced illusory, blanket idealization of the poor."[36] As we can observe in Matsubara's words, that "affairs of the poor are what proved to be my baptism,"[37] he was motivated by a vital curiosity that might be called almost totally innocent as he faithfully recorded the minutiae of slum life that appeared before him as a world of unfolding mystery. His approach to capturing this world might be termed cataloguing, whereby he would collect details from observable, surface life as a way of giving shape to the whole. He would enumerate the furnishings and appliances that filled the 9.9-square-meter space[38] of a backstreet shop to vividly convey the living conditions of his subjects. This careful listing of one worthless item after another becomes a long, complete inventory that, through the sheer materiality of *things*, evokes the conditions of lived life. This vast accumulation of objects starts to serve as metonymy, for example, for the Yotsuya Samegahashi slum district, where an astonishing 5,000 people live in 1,370 dwellings squeezed into swampy lowlands measuring no more than one square kilometer.

In Darkest Tokyo subverts common sense, which equates poverty with the absence of things. It is chiefly in the form of countless foods that the fecundity of *things* is expressed in this den of poverty. (Of *In Darkest Tokyo*'s thirty-five chapters, fifteen of them refer to food in some form.) For example, here is the passage on Shiba Shin'amichō:

> They buy the remains of dead animals like tongue, bladder, intestines, liver and other offal, cut them up, and then skewer and cook them as a

stew for sale right out of the pot there on the roadside. A gang of young-sters stakes out an area for this makeshift eatery of the slums, and then satisfied with the food they have seasoned, call out in the idiom of the streets the words they have memorized such as *hoku*, *fuha* [lung], and *shita* [tongue].[39] Carried on the back of an eight-year-old girl is an infant no more than ten months old, so young that its eyes are completely clear, it can utter no words, and is yet toothless, but its mouth holds one of those skewers bought for 2 rin [rin = tenth of a sen] as it cries, nonetheless, as if seeking the sweet teat of its mother. Another band of kids are noisily digging a hole by the toilet pit in the back to bury a dead cat, while yet another group looks like sewer rats, covered from head to toe with the clogged sewage they are trying to discharge.[40]

This picture of viscera and entrails from butchered animals simmering in a kettle immediately evokes images of slum dwellers whose digestive systems are greedily devouring these very organs. The excretory functions of toilets and sewers are also a part of this image of the slums. Children covered with slime who show no signs of letup in their struggle with clogged sewage, the infant who sucks on skewered giblets as if it were breastfeeding, and the burial of a dead cat all seem to overlap into a sad composite scene. We are left with the feeling that a dark energy that can only be called the power of darkness overflows here amid the chaos where the border between humans covetously devouring animals and animals reduced to dead meat, the bound-ary between life and death itself seems to dissolve. While the details contrib-ute a graphic realism, taken as a whole, this picture of humankind's basic desires and functions—the cycle of ingestion, digestion, and excretion—is evocatively expressed more in the register of fantasy and illusion than in a realist genre, even as it produces images of a strong corporeality.

Matsubara, who attempted to capture the vitality of the slums by inun-dating the reader with images of food, extends that image and recasts the whole of Tokyo as one, colossal body: "The capacity of this city of beasts to transport its lifeblood in the course of daily life is remarkable. What might be called its product, namely food, is delivered daily from the central market in hundreds of thousands of cartloads, and blood, which could be thought of as the lifeblood of these people, is shipped off in all directions totaling 60,000 handcart loads daily to every part of the city, as if coursing through the cap-illaries and cells of the body."[41] If the Rokumeikan Hall symbolized the civi-lized veneer of Tokyo, Matsubara had discovered its flip side, the horrors of the "city of beasts," wherein all the varied activities of city life had regressed to a single, naked, primal appetite: "Their rich, complicated everyday lives extended well beyond their own quarters, and as for the hidden reaches of their lungs, the recesses of their stomachs, the disrupted flow of the body's blood, and the complex entanglements of various strands, even the great Doctor[42] has not yet been able to reach an adequate diagnosis, as he is left grasping an empty spoon."[43] Matsubara chose to pry open the far reaches of "darkness" that up to that time writers and journalists had ignored and thus remained concealed within the belly of the "city of beasts." Precisely because these slums, which had been hidden from purview as filthy and disgraceful nether regions, were shadowy places that defied easy description, they helped give shape to the idea of a hidden center of the "city of beasts," and it was the image of ceaselessly proliferating food that would actively contribute to the image of Tokyo as the sign of civilization.

Invoking the concept of communitas that was developed by Victor Turner in *The Ritual Process: Structure and Anti-Structure*,[44] Yamaguchi Masao makes the following point about feelings and emotions that link beings relegated to the periphery of the city: "Those who have been forced to assume a recessive, secondary position in society are likelier to form intense communitarian affiliations almost in inverse proportion to the marginalization they have been forced to endure."[45] Yamaguchi argues that this kind of communitas is abundantly present in scenes of backstreet tenement housing from (Edo) period pieces in Japanese cinema. Indeed, he attributes such feelings to the explorers of urban slums as well as identifying the presence of neighborly warmth and kindheartedness in Edo tenement culture that would in due time become modern urban slums. It was Yokoyama Gennosuke who observed that the slums, commonly viewed as a battlefield and scene of carnage, are in fact a place where the prevailing sentiment calls for the cultivation of "sympathetic feelings among those who care for each other and belong to the same class,"[46] but in *In Deepest Tokyo* Matsubara's enthusiasm for the communitas he observes in the slums effectively romanticizes these communitarian sentiments to a higher pitch:

> No matter what life throws their way, how unfailingly even-tempered are those who toil at the lowest rung of society and how admirable the resolve with which they confront everyday life, entertaining no aspirations beyond giving their all to their work while asking no more than simple compensation in return. . . . An indomitable spirit anchors their daily lives. Such is the way that without wavering, these people live their lives. How pure the blood in their veins must be. Ah, if only I were not encumbered by my own limitations—education being chief among them— I would waste no time in becoming one of them.[47]

These words of self-reflection that grew out of Matsubara's own experiences when he had taken it upon himself to work as an assistant at a *zanpanya*[48] in Yotsuya Samegahashi reveal feelings of guilt suffered by an intellectual who was unable to feel a part of the masses, and they also testify to the profound skepticism that he felt toward a society in which his own life was deeply enmeshed. Matsubara was moved by his own self-reflection as well as by what he saw as the conversion of the merits of state-authorized careerism into real, meaningful value that was to be discovered in the slum as utopia.

However, the author of *In Darkest Tokyo* was also attuned to the double character of what was at once a grim prison-like world and a utopic space. In a chapter entitled "The Beast in the Depths of Darkness" ["Saiankokuri no kaibutsu"], which was based on materials collected in Ikaho Hot Springs in Jōmō,[49] Matsubara explores the furthest reaches of darkness. The town of Ikaho that lies on the hillside of Harunasan [Mt. Haruna] can be divided into layers, with the upper stratum having a Japanese style-inn and restaurant, with a liquor store, caterer, a store selling household goods, and a laundry rounding out the lower level, and finally, an even lower, subterranean level consisting of a cavernous space built into the rock:

> Who are these folks who eat and sleep in these lower regions? All of them are invalids, disabled, either deaf and mute, or blind, and most of them are entertainers who cater to those coming to wash away their aches and pains, musicians who entertain with flute, *shakuhachi*, *koto* and *shamisen*, while still others provide massage, deep abdominal massage, acupuncture, and moxa treatments. Take a look at these misshapen figures here and you will find cripples, the lame, a giant of a man with a lump the size of an Irish potato on his forehead and eyes squashed in like oysters, a little monster with a shaved head, a blind itinerant musician with her face disfigured by smallpox, a paralytic who moves by supporting his weight on his knuckles, a sufferer of elephantiasis, and a dwarf, all living anywhere from five to seven or eight to a single unit. Although the interior is dark and [it is] impossible to distinguish objects, there is no need for lamps since all are blind. Among these inhabitants that number in the hundreds there is a leader, a large, eccentric acupuncturist with a large, bowl-shaped lump on the left side of his forehead who claims a retinue of four women ranging in age from about 25 to 40 who serve as his attendant, wife, and concubine and who wait on him seated in a row from left to right at mealtimes.[50]

I read this passage of grotesque images, not as a reflection of Matsubara's eccentric tastes, but as a metaphor for the dark depths of modern city life. *In Darkest Tokyo'*s abundant details converge to produce this image of a cavern enclosed in darkness. Matsubara does not shrink from taking a close look at these misshapen figures of subterranean life, and he manages to avoid adopting a glib, humanitarian posture toward the physically disabled. For him, the world of the city was not so much a space where the poor are expelled to the margins by the rich and the disabled and sick are relegated to isolation on the periphery, but rather a place that could accommodate all these unfortunate beings together. Or more correctly, precisely because they have been marginalized, they could not help but play an integral part in shaping the world of the city. All the more because, to a person, these cave dwellers work in the world of popular entertainment, the resulting image of this group that appears much like actors in a banquet scene shrouded in darkness is that of a tableau vivant, where each member bears the stigmatized signs of physical impairment on his or her body that together represent in condensed form all the attributes of those who live in the slums. We might also view Matsubara's work as a Meiji-era literary reproduction of the principle followed by landless, patronless [*muenjo*] medieval temples that extended aid to members of the entertainment world who were cut off from mainstream society. More significant, this domain of darkness that is ruled by a gigantic beast most resembles the dreary prison at Tenmachō that was run under the absolute authority of its warden. Why is it that a harsh class structure indistinguishable from prison society of premodern days is reproduced in this sanctuary of darkness that is supposed to render irrelevant the status of the self as determined by society? Matsubara, who warned us that "the traces of these monstrous tyrants encountered here are everywhere, where they can be seen imposing their will on others," could not help but acknowledge that such contradictions cast a shroud of misery even over the slums.[51]

It remains a profound mystery why literary histories have regarded the literature of this era, including such subgenres as the "tragic romance novel" [*hisan shōsetsu*] and the "crisis novel" [*shinkoku shōsetsu*], as being untouched by the images of cosmic darkness spreading throughout Meiji society that works such as *In Darkest Tokyo* discovered and recorded.

4

Among the political novels that flourished during the Meiji era, the writer whose works most insistently addressed the prison as a motif was Miyazaki Muryū (1855–1889). To say that for him the political novel was a literature of the prison is not an overstatement. Muryū, who left Tosa for Tokyo in the spring of 1882 and joined the staff of the *Free Press* [*Jiyū Shimbunsha*], would begin writing *An Account of the French Revolution: The Triumphant*

Battle Cry of Freedom [*Furansu Kakumei-ki Jiyū no kachidoki*, 1882] in August of the same year. Based on Alexandre Dumas's *Ange Pitou*,[52] what Muryū was able to take from Dumas's work was the significance of the Bastille prison, much hated by Parisians as a symbol of oppression. What Muryū emphasized was not so much the facts pertaining to the liberation of the Bastille as the prison's function as an emblem, a battle cry for freedom. In the second decade of the Meiji era, prison came to symbolize such legal instruments as the Libel Law of 1875 [Zanbōritsu], the Press Ordinance of 1875 [Shinbun jōrei], the Public Gatherings Ordinance of April 1880 [Shūkai jōrei], and the Explosives Control Ordinance of 1884 [Bakuhatsubutsu torishimari jōrei] that the government established to ensure the absolute suppression of the Freedom and Popular Rights Movement, and at the same time, prison seemed to be an apt symbol of a people's consciousness that had become resigned to such oppression. Moreover, as the number of Liberal Party activists and journalists who had actually experienced the pain of imprisonment was not insignificant, prison served as a perfect literary symbol that could rouse antiestablishment passions. Muryū seized on the plural images of prison that were engendered by the repressive conditions of the age by using the narrative of the fall of the Bastille to highlight the opposition between liberty and oppression here at home. This was an allegorical strategy widely embraced since Toda Kindō had used it in *Tumultuous Sentiments* [*Jōkai haran*, 1880].

However, as a pall began to shroud the Freedom and Popular Rights Movement, Muryū's prison began to shift away from the confines of allegory and take on a distinctive, idiosyncratic form. Here is his image of the prison that appeared in an article titled "Tears of the Transient World" ["Ukiyo no namida"] serialized from September to December 1883 in the *Jiyū shimbun*:

> Prisons erected one after the other, stand blanketed by the gloom of
> dark clouds,
> The blowing winds carry the unending, chilling reverberations of iron
> chains and the sound of whips,
> Over there stands a mountain of bones, and over here flow waves of
> blood,
> How many thousands have lost their lives to the severe sentence of a
> hundred years,
> Under the indigo evening sky, the phosphorescent will-o'-the-wisp
> scattering every which way, and apparently emanating from nowhere
> the anguished cries of departed souls once innocent victims,
> And all who witness this scene, cannot but be moved and unable to
> stem their tears in indignation.

This ghastly image is a far cry from depictions of prisons found in Suehiro Tetchō's *Plum Blossoms in the Snow* and Tōkai Sanshi's *Chance Encounters with Beautiful Women*. Muryū's prison is a steel tomb where freedom fighters are buried alive and where spirits of those who have sacrificed their lives emit a bluish phosphorescent glow as they fly about in the dark night. Muryū, who held an uncommon interest in Russian revolutionaries, would write *The Whip of Innocence* [*Mujitsu no shimoto*, 1882], in which he introduced the achievements of Vera Zasulich (a Russian revolutionary, 1821–1919), followed by his *Demon Cries* [*Kishūshū*, 1884], a work based on Sergei Stepniak's *Underground Russia* (1882).[53] The tale *Demon Cries* concludes with a scene in which the spirit of an executed member of the Peoples' Will Party wanders along the Neva River in St. Petersburg.[54] In the background of *Demon Cries* lies a noteworthy twin development in world history: the bomb assassination of Czar Alexander II by a member of the People's Will Party, and the development of a potassium chloride-based explosive by radical members of the Liberal Party of Japan, who took their cue from these Russian revolutionaries and who would meet their demise at what would come to be known as the Kabasan Incident of 1884.[55] The Neva River scene in Muryū's work was meant as at once a requiem for the victims of the Kabasan Incident and a memorial address mourning the demise of the all too short Freedom and Popular Rights Movement.

A Clump of Silver Grass [*Susuki no hito mura*], written in 1888, the year before Muryū's death, is an odd work that has a female descendant of Takeda Kōunsai, the samurai of the late Tokugawa era who lived from 1804 to 1865, entangled with a Russian terrorist, but in the work is a scene of Kajibashi prison that draws on Muryū's own earlier imprisonment. In this scene, young Miura, the protagonist, hears the sounds of a military band being performed at an evening concert at the Rokumeikan Hall.[56] We can probably say that by the last year of his life Muryū had reached the point where he could make sense of the late 1880s–early 1890s through its contradictory features of a delightful "civilization" and the "darkness" of prison.

Kitamura Tōkoku mocks the Rokumeikan era in his essay, "The Tenor of These Times" ["Jisei ni kan ari," 1890] that opens with the following sentence: "Unbeknownst to you, people are like fish who live in the dark, lose their way in the dark, live in the cold, and live their lives with little to eat."[57] Tōkoku, who likened the eyes of fish lost in the dark to his own as a way to reflect on the "confused and disordered state of the world," undoubtedly borrowed Muryū's image of the blue meteor lamp will-o'-the-wisps[58] flying about in the darkness that blanketed the steel graves, in solidarity with Muryū's stand as a witness to the unfortunate demise of the Freedom and

Popular Rights Movement. It was in 1892 that Tōkoku wrote in "Three-Day Fantasy" ["Mikka genkyō"], "For these past seven years, I have been in a kind of prison."[59] However, even as the two writers shared the darkness of prison, they arrived at quite different representations of it. In contrast to Muryū, who stuck to the image of the prison as a reflection of the state of society in these times, Tōkoku would employ the metaphor of the prison to begin narrating the drama of a modern self-consciousness pitted against the times. Tōkoku's first work that pursues this exploration of the self was his epic poem, "A Prisoner's Song" ["Soshū no shi"], which he published at his own expense in 1889. As is well-known, this work was inspired by Lord Byron's "Prisoner of Chillon." From the isolated life of a prisoner chained in his cell, his melancholy relieved only by the companionship of moonlight and the call of birds, to the eventual release of the prisoner, Tōkoku's work appropriates the main plot outline of Byron's piece. Furthermore, if we are to believe Tōkoku's words in his preface, it appears that prior to writing "A Prisoner's Song," he had attempted a translation of Byron's epic poem. To trace the outlines of the words of "Prisoner of Chillon" was to confirm the catalytic role given to linguistic expression as sublimation of the darkness that Tōkoku was carrying in his heart. The echoes from "Prisoner of Chillon" that can be picked up in Tōkoku's work have been assiduously explored in earlier studies. Here, let us look at the third stanza:

A Prisoner's Song

The dungeon! In which I wander aimlessly about
Is cut off from the world by double walls
Yet, sunlight seeps through cracks in the wall
Burrowing through holes
And casting a sunbeam that cannot escape
That races about the cell
Where it illuminates my pale arm
And creeping along the wall,
It finds its way to my lap

Prisoner of Chillon, II

There are seven pillars of Gothic mould,
In Chillon's dungeons deep and old,
There are seven columns, massy and grey,
Dim with a dull imprison'd ray
A sunbeam which hath lost its way,

And through the crevice and the cleft,
Of the thick wall is fallen and left;
Creeping o'er the floor so damp,
Like a marsh's meteor lamp:
And in each pillar there is a ring,
And in each ring there is a chain

The lines that read "Yet, sunlight seeps through the cracks in the wall/Burrowing through holes/Casting a sunbeam that cannot escape,/That races about the cell" borrow almost directly from Byron's poem, but taken in its entirety, Tōkoku's prison differs quite markedly from that described by Byron. Compared to the latter's depiction, which conveys the utter massiveness of the subterranean keep, aside from the unschooled description that Tōkoku manages, his prison seems vague and insubstantial, as if it exists in a dream. The underground prison of Chillon Castle that Byron visited in 1816 has been renovated into a monastery today, although its gothic columns remain just as they were. Byron's verse appears rooted in the actual space of the dungeon, even as it reminds one of the painterly images associated with Giovanni Battista Piranesi (1720–1778), the Italian artist and architect. The gigantic gothic columns that can be discerned in the dim light of the prison along with the steel rings and chains attached to them, the sunbeams that seep through cracks in the thick walls, the faint light that streaks like meteor lamps from platforms on cobblestones—such scenes of the subtle dance between light and dark must have permeated every description in Piranesi's *Carceri* (1745) etchings.

Byron, who in *Childe Harold's Pilgrimage* presented a eulogy to William Beckford, the abbot of Fonthill Monastery, capped by a mysterious soaring gothic spire, always kept within reach a copy of Beckford's gothic romance on the Orient, *Vathek* (1786), and indeed it was the author of this work who was among the earliest to introduce the Italy of Piranesi to England. It was during his trip to Italy in 1780 that Beckford, who had visited Venice, had his imagination roused by Piranesian chains and wheels that he encountered in the prisons that were attached to the palace, and he would soon be found with sketching pencils in hand on the Bridge of Sighs overlooking them. He also superimposed the ruins of the Roman Theater in Verona to the images found in Piranesi's etchings.[60] As Poulet observed, the endlessly continuous hallways and maze through which the protagonist of *Vathek* wanders is a nightmarish space engendered by Piranesi's "prison fantasies" in his *Carceri*. H. Walpole, the great master of the gothic novel who preceded Beckford, was also captivated by the power of Piranesi's work, and the well-known scene in *The Castle of Ostranto* (1764), where the son of the castle lord, Conrad, is crushed by a large falling helmet, is thought to be inspired by plate 8 of Piranesi's *Carceri*.[61] In addition to *The Castle of Ostranto*, from early in his writing career Beckford was familiar with gothic literature, including such works as Matthew Gregory Lewis's *The Monk* (1796) and Charles Robert Maturin's *Bertram* (1816). In particular, Byron's epic poem *Manfred*, set in an old castle in the mountains, was a work that owed much to the legacy of gothic novels. If among the motives that drove Byron to undertake his pilgrimage through southern Europe was his yearning for the world of dark, gloomy, and secluded ruins that appealed to his gothic tastes, it is not that implausible to think that Piranesi's fantasy prison, which had spurred the imaginations of Beckford and Walpole, had cast its spell on *Prisoner of Chillon*.

The gothic effects and contrivances that give the prison in *Prisoner of Chillon* its distinctiveness are clearly absent from Tōkoku's "A Prisoner's Song." This is not surprising, for as Tōkoku notes in the author's preface, "Such things as the interior of the prison are undoubtedly inaccurate, since I was not attempting to depict contemporary prison life through this prisoner."[62] Instead, the prison in "A Prisoner's Song," which was a metaphorical expression of the isolated self-consciousness and a darkness concealed within Tōkoku, was much more like the nightmarish space that was invented by Piranesi. Like dream images, this strange space of the prison would alternately expand and contract. For example, three lines beyond the passage already quoted that reads "this prison was spacious and at the same time, empty," we find a quite contradictory description, that he was "confined in a mercilessly cramped cage."[63] And in contrast to part 4, which reads, "The groom and bride are both in jail, the prison is cramped, but within this small space are two worlds," in part 9, wherein the bride and three fellow activists disappear, the "I" is left behind alone in a "large room."[64] There is also something ambiguous in the way Tōkoku describes the position of the "I" who, from some undetermined vantage point, watches his bride and their fellow Freedom and Popular Rights activists confined to a room "separated by four walls." Is the "I" imprisoned along with his four comrades, or is he over here gazing at them occupying four separate cells? It seems futile to map the interior space of the prison through a careful, close reading of the work.

To help us determine the significance of such mutating space in Tōkoku's poem, let us recall Georges Poulet's essay which analyzed Piranesi's *Carceri*. To repeat part of a passage quoted earlier: "The infinite multiplication of the self amounts to torture. It is an endless torture that is devoid of any awareness of failure. Self-multiplication is an attempt to discover one's self, to project everywhere an image of the self that can never coincide with it. Space and time is not only the primary site of self-multiplication, but appear as the profound reason for the dispersal of the multiplied self within an expansive time-space."[65] Did the bride and three companions who appear in "A Prisoner's Song" exist in real life? Were they not phantoms that materialized from his consciousness, or, to borrow Poulet's words, projections of "an image of the self that in pursuing the form of the self, can never become one with it"? If so, the carceral space that repeatedly alternates its expansion and contraction is, in fact, the cause of this illusion to in turn materialize and flicker away. Moreover, for the "I" that must directly confront this dream-like drama, the boundary that separates times of wakefulness from dreams becomes indistinct. Tōkoku depicts the scene where the "I" is roused from his reverie of a time when he had picked flowers with his beloved:

> Violets growing everywhere from the pristine soil,
> Its name, appropriately refined, the forget-me-not
> Gently picking other flowers with them,
> I pin one bunch to my chest
> The other one I present to my love
> Oh, this is a dream
> Look! My bride turns this way
> How sad her figure!
> Ahh, I am here in prison
> A hell on earth. (From part 5)

What awaits the "I" who has just awakened from a reverie of the past is another dream: the nightmare of prison. The hell that confined him was not a subterranean cell filled with instruments of punishment and torture. Rather, it was the hell of having to gaze, endlessly, without sleep. The "I" is able to see the "sad figure of his bride" with his own eyes, but is not permitted either to speak or to be with her. The three fellow activist comrades, with whom he had pledged his life, like his bride, appear only as objects of his gaze.

This nightmarish hell that restricts the protagonist of "A Prisoner's Song" to the horror of an eternal gaze was probably related to the trauma experienced by Tōkoku for having left the Freedom and Popular Rights Movement. Even as he felt an aversion to the aggressive temperament of these revolutionaries, after choosing not to join his sworn friend Ōya Masao, who had asked him to help plan the Korean Revolution, he would continue feeling guilt and a compulsion to atone for his decision.[66] The opening verse of this Chinese-style poem reads, "Once I mistakenly broke the law, and then was arrested as a political prisoner." Despite its appearing to be the self-righteous expression of a political offender, critics have noted a contradictory meaning in these stanzas. Indeed, what remains thinly veiled beneath these words is Tōkoku's desire to atone for his abandonment of Ōya, who was behind bars in Toku-shima at the time as a political prisoner. That the protagonist of "A Prisoner's Song" uses the third-person pronoun "they" instead of "we" in referring to his sworn revolutionary comrades in arms must reflect the reproach Tōkoku directed at himself (the protagonist of Byron's *Prisoner of Chillon*, in contrast, uses "we" in reference to the self and two brothers). The profoundest mean-ing of the "prison" that holds the "I" captive is to be found in this self that has been sundered from the community of the plural pronoun.

In Martin Buber's work, what he calls two primary words—each "word" a combination of two relational terms—denominate the relationship between a person and the world that contains him or her: "When the world becomes the subject of a person's experience, it belongs to the realm of the primary word combination 'I-It.' . . . [But] another primary word combination, 'I-Thou,' produces the world of relationship."[67] Furthermore, Buber asserts that this "I-It," that is, the event that is the foundation of self-centered experience, comes to signify the split between the body [*shintai*] as the knowing subject from the world that encompasses it. The visual torment that separates the "I" from his bride and fellow revolutionaries in "A Prisoner's Song" is based on the drama within Tōkoku, who adopted as a form of self-punishment and atonement an "I-It" relationship representing his own estrangement from the "I-Thou" dyad. This transition from an "I-Thou" to an "I-It" relationship is figuratively expressed as an opposition between "prison cell" and "home" [*kokyō*] in "My Prison" ["Waga rōgoku," 1892], one of the few prose narratives that Tōkoku would write:

> I was not born in this cell. If I am to recognize this place as marking the second period of my life, in retrospect I feel reverence for the first. For in that first period I had freedom in many ways, going where I wanted, staying where I pleased. I have come to understand the vast differences separating these two periods, the first as a world of freedom and the sec-ond as a world of confinement. . . . Here, in this cell, I cannot bring my-self to face the present, but should I do so, I would be reduced to being an infant on the brink of despair. Only by summoning memories of my first period am I able to feel hope. The time I have given the name "first period" was by no means pleasing, but if I can call it my home [kokyō], it is, indeed, my homeland to where all my thoughts go, the source of my aspirations, the place that will harbor me at life's end, and it is indeed this homeland that makes me detest the prison that confines me today.[68]

It hardly requires explanation that the real-life model for Tōkoku's "home-land" was the "phantom realm" [*genkyō*] of Kawaguchi-mura in Santama, a place linked to memories of his comrades with whom he had endured good times and bad—the chivalrous old eccentric, Akiyama Kunisaburō,[69] and Ōya Masao, who "laments current events while stroking the handle of his sword." For Tōkoku, languishing in a prison of his own devices, this modest one-time communitas is literally a utopia, that is, "a place that doesn't exist," nothing more than a "phantom realm." The image of Tōkoku's prison that is split between the two poles of "homeland" as utopia and the "prison" of self-consciousness is, undoubtedly, the archetype of "urban things" that live on within each of us.

Notes

In this volume, notes marked (M) are Maeda'a citations. All other notes belong to the translators.

1 First appearing in *Bunka no genzai 4: Chūshin to shūen* (Iwanami shoten, 1981), the text used for this translation is from Maeda Ai, *Toshi kūkan no naka no bungaku* (Chikuma Shobō, 1982), 164–210.

2 W. B. Carnochan, *Confinement and Flight: An Essay on English Literature of the Eighteenth Century* (Berkeley: University of California Press, 1977), 26–59.

3 Jean-Jacques Rousseau, *The Reveries of the Solitary Walker*, in *The Collected Writings of Rousseau*, ed. Christopher Kelly, trans. and annotated Charles E. Butterworth, Alexandra Cook, and Terence E. Marshall (Hanover, N.H.: University Press of New England, 2000), 8:41.

4 Ibid., 8:47.

5 Blaise Pascal, *Pensées and Other Writings*, trans. Honor Levi (Oxford: Oxford University Press, 1995), 66.

6 Georges Poulet, "Piranèse et let Poetes Français," in *Trois essais de mythologie romantique* (Paris: Librairie José Corti, Saint-Brieuc, 1966), 153–154.

7 Lorenz Eitner, "Cages, Prisons, and Captives in Eighteenth-Century Art," in *Images of Romanticism*, ed. Karl Kroeber and William Walling (New Haven: Yale University Press, 1978), 22–23. (M)

8 Ibid., 27–29. (M)

9 Michel Foucault, *Discipline and Punish: The Birth of the Prison*, trans. Alan Sheridan (New York: Vintage, 1995), 200.

10 Jeremy Bentham, *The Works of Jeremy Bentham*, ed. John Bowring (Edinburgh: William Tait, 1843), 4:45. (M)

11 Victor Brombert, *The Romantic Prison* (Princeton: Princeton University Press, 1978), 3–4. (M)

12 Yoshida Shōin, *Kōmō sakki*, in *Yoshida Shōin zenshū* (Iwanami shoten, 1934), 2:441.

13 Ibid., 2:266.

14 Ogawa Tarō, "Ohara Shigeya," *Keisei* (1970): 1. (M)

15 Ohara Shigeya, *Kangokusoku*, in *Hōrei zensho*, ed. Naikaku Kanhōkyoku (1889; reprint, Hara Shobō, 1974), 5:363.

16 Ibid., 5:363, 366, 379.

17 Amino Yoshihiko, *Muen, kugai, raku: Nihon chūsei no jiyū to heiwa* (Heibonsha, 1978), 28. (M)

18 Ohara, *Kangokusoku*, 369.

19 Foucault, *Discipline and Punish*, 181.

20 Ohara, *Kangokusoku*, 363.

21 Shimizu Yasuo, "Gosenbun no ichi Tokyo zu," in *Chizu* (Nihon Kokusai Chizu Gakkai), 3, no. 1 (1965). (M)

22 Suehiro Tetchō, *Setchūbai*, in *Meiji seiji shōsetsu shū* 2, vol. 6 of *Meiji bungaku zenshū* (Chikuma Shobō, 1967), 131.

23 Anthony Sutcliffe, *The Autumn of Central Paris: The Defeat of Town Planning 1850–1970* (London: Edward Arnold, 1970), 33–36. (M)

24 Taki Kōji, *Me no inyu: Shisen no genshōgaku* (Seidosha, 1982), 122. (M)

25 Fujimori Terunobu, "Meijiki ni okeru toshikeikaku no rekishiteki kenkyū" (Unpublished manuscript, 1979), 76. (M)

26 An area centered on the Edo Castle, extending to Shinagawa Ōkido, Yotsuya Ōkido, Itabashi, Senjū, Honjo, and Fukagawa. In Edo-period maps, this area was designated by a vermillion line.

27 *Tokyo shiku kaisei iinkai gijiroku* (Tokyo City Reorganization Committee proceedings), vol. 1 (1888): 120–121. (M)

28 Fujimori, "Meijiki ni okeru," 102. (M)

29 Maeda uses the English word to denote the criminality and the hiddenness of those consigned to life on the lowest rungs of modern Japanese society.

30 Yokoyama Gennosuke, *Nihon no kasō shakai* (Iwanami bunko, 1988), 375.

31 Henry M. Stanley, *In Darkest Africa, or the Quest, Rescue, and Retreat of Emin Governor of Equatoria*, vols. 1–2 (New York: Scribner, 1890).

32 William Booth, *In Darkest England and the Way Out* (New York: Garrett, 1970), 14.

33 Rokumeikan, literally "Deer Cry Pavilion," was a hall built in 1883 to foster contact of Western diplomats and dignitaries with their Japanese counterparts.

34 Matsubara Iwagorō, *Bunmei gimon joron* (Introductory remarks on doubts regarding civilization), part 1 of 2 (Satō Eizō, 1888), 11.

35 Uchida Roan, "Futabatei Shimei no isshō," in *Uchida Roan zenshū* (Yumani Shobō, 1983), 3:290.

36 Ibid., 3:291.

37 Matsubara Iwagorō, *Saiankoku no Tokyo* (In darkest Tokyo), (1893; reprint, Koten bunko: Gendai shichōsha, 1980), 25.

38 9 shaku = 2.7 meters, depth of 2 ken =3.6 meters, equalling 6 tatami mats, or 9.9 square meters for this 9-shaku-2-ken space.

39 We are indebted to Ted Fowler, who referred us to Nobi Shōji, *Shoku niku no buraku-shi* (A history of outcaste food) (Akashi Shoten, 1998), 70.

40 Matsubara, *Saiankoku*, 61–62.

41 Ibid., 80.

42 The word used here, *daikokushi*, is an appellation accorded one who was particularly skilled in the healing arts.

43 Matsubara, *Saiankoku*, 80.

44 Victor Turner, *The Ritual Process: Structure and Anti-Structure* (Chicago: Aldine, 1969).

45 Yamaguchi Masao, *Bunka to ryōgisei* (The duality of culture) (Iwanami Shoten, 1975), 238.

46 Yokoyama, *Nihon no kasō shakai*, 60.

47 Matsubara, *Saiankoku*, 58–59.

48 *Zanpanya* were establishments that collected leftover food from school cafeterias and army barracks to sell to the poor. See Konishi Shirō, ed., *Meiji hyakunen no rekishi, Meiji hen* (Kōdansha, 1968), 217.

49 In present-day Gunma Prefecture.

50 Matsubara, *Saiankoku*, 115–116.

51 Ibid., 118.

52 Alexandre Dumas, *Ange Pitou*, vols. 1–2 (Boston: Little, Brown, 1894).

53 "Stepniak" was the pen name used by Sergei Mikhailovich Kravchinski (1852–1895), a Russian revolutionary and writer. His *Underground Russia* featured profiles of Russian revolutionaries.

54 The Peoples' Will Party was a militant oppositional offshoot of the populist movement that arose in response to the oppressive actions of Czar Alexander II (1818–1881).

55 Kabasan is the mountain (in present-day Ibaragi Prefecture) to which radical members of the Liberal Party fled and were caught after their plans for bombing key government officials were discovered.

56 Ochiai Haruo, "Meiji seiji shōsetsu shū kaisetsu," in *Meiji seiji shōsetsu shū*, Nihon kindai bungaku taikei series, vol. 2 (Kadokawa Shoten, 1974). (M)

57 Kitamura Tōkoku, *Kitamura Tōkoku shū, Nihon gendai bungaku zenshū*, ed. Itō Sei, Kamei Katsuichirō, Nakamura Mitsuo, Hirano Ken, and Yamamoto Kenkichi (Kōdansha, 1980), 9:23.

58 *Rinka*, or *ignis fatuus*, is defined as "a light that sometimes appears in the night over marshy ground and is often attributable to the combustion of gas from decomposed organic matter" (Webster's New Collegiate Dictionary, 9th ed.).

59 Ibid., 9:61.

60 Kenneth Churchill, *Italy and English Literature 1764–1930* (London: Macmillan, 1980), 13–14. (M)

61 Ibid., 5. (M)

62 Kitamura, *Kitamura Tōkoku shū*, 9:177.

63 Ibid., 9:182.

UTOPIA OF THE PRISONHOUSE 63

64 Ibid., 9:179.

65 Poulet, "Piranèse et les Poetes Français," 153.

66 Ōya Masao, 1863–1928, was a radical activist involved in poor peoples' revolts during this era.

67 The quotes used here seem to distill what appears on pp. 3–11 in Martin Buber's *I and Thou*, 2d ed., trans. Ronald Gregory Smith (New York: Scribner, 1958).

68 Kitamura, *Kitamura Tōkoku shū*, 9:7.

69 Akiyama Kunisaburō (1823–1903) was active in local politics and a strong advocate of the peoples' rights movement.

2. The Panorama of Enlightenment

(Kaika no panorama)

TRANSLATED BY HENRY D. SMITH II

Maeda here focuses his attention on the city of Tokyo in the early years of the Meiji period (1868–1912), the so-called era of civilization and enlightenment (*bunmei kaika*) that reached a peak in the years 1873–77. He takes as an emblematic literary text of this era the best-selling *New Tales of Tokyo Prosperity* (*Tōkyō shinhanjōki*, 1874) by Hattori Bushō, a series of detailed descriptions of the leading new sights and Western-style institutions of the capital city. Maeda argues that the flowery if archaic rhetoric of the literary Chinese style (*kanbun*) in which the text was written served effectively to convey the contemporary fascination with the superficial and material qualities of Western "civilization." While acknowledging Hattori's debt to an earlier work of the 1830s by Terakado Seiken on the "prosperity" of Edo, Maeda emphasizes the diminishment of the sociality that characterized earlier literary gazetteers of the city, which were structured by the cycles of work and play and dwelt on the relaxing moods of the city's waterways. Maeda's own sentiments are clearly on the Edo side of the Edo-Tokyo divide, and he reveals a special sympathy with the woodblock print artist Kiyochika, whose work reveals the survival of Edo into Meiji. In the new Meiji Tokyo, the city of water and shadows that was Edo gives way in Hattori's work to a city of land-based transportation and artificial lighting. Above all, he stresses by his emphatic use of the word, it is a conception of the city rooted purely in material *things*. In terms of rhetorical style, it was effectively conveyed by a reliance on metonymy in a syntagmatic dimension.

1

One of the finest prints in Kobayashi Kiyochika's color woodblock series, *Famous Views of Tokyo* [*Tōkyō meisho zu*, 1876–81], is *Kaiun Bridge* (figure 1), a view of the First National Bank in the snow.[1] The bank building, which in

Figure 1. *Kaiun Bridge and the First National Bank in the Snow (Kaiunbashi Daiichi ginkō setchū)* by Kobayashi Kiyochika. Multicolored woodblock print on paper. Courtesy Santa Barbara Museum of Art, Gift of Mr. and Mrs. Roland A. Way

the print we see looming to the east of Kaiun Bridge, was constructed as a money exchange by Mitsui in July 1872 and then taken over by the new Meiji government. It became one of the popular new sights of Tokyo, endlessly reproduced in color woodblock, copperplate, and lithographic prints of the early Meiji period (figure 1).

The grim countenance of Kiyochika's First National Bank, however, sets it apart from any of the countless other prints in which the building appeared. Against a steel gray sky loom the towering five stories of the Western-style building, half covered in snow, and in the foreground, as though confronting the bank, is shown a woman, seen from the back with umbrella in hand, about to cross the bridge. Providing a sharp accent against the chill and muted colors that dominate the view is the crimson red of the woman's obi sash. Our line of sight as we view the print is seized by this striking red and then climbs upward along the lines of the First National Bank building, whence it is finally drawn into the far right distance by the dark forms of three birds that dart about in the snow-clouded sky. The movement of this line of sight, receding obliquely off into the distance, corresponds perfectly with the overall composition, in which the lower half of the building seems to submerge into the shadows of the bridge while the three-story tower climbs high in the sky.

The First National Bank building was designed by Shimizu Kisuke II, the same builder who completed the Tsukiji Hotel. It was constructed in an eclectic style, in which the lower two stories featured a Western-style veranda with railings and supporting bronze columns, while on top was mounted a three-story tower in the manner of a Japanese castle, embellished with assertive gables. Kiyochika's composition, with its unusually low vantage point, thus relates in subtle ways to the architectural style itself, working to underplay the Western-style lower half of the building while giving special emphasis to the powerful volume of the tower above. What we can read from this is none other than a reflection of Kiyochika's own emotional conflict as he confronted this monument of the early Meiji era of "civilization and enlightenment" [*bunmei kaika*], divided between vague hostility and dark lurking fear. In this way, the line of sight linking the woman under the umbrella with the dark birds in the sky becomes precisely the gaze of Kiyochika himself, looking out on the landscape of "enlightenment" from the standpoint of a former retainer of the Tokugawa bakufu.

The art historian Sakai Tadayasu, noting these hidden motifs in Kiyochika's *Kaiun Bridge*, has commented, "It may be reckless to read the psychology of a former bakufu retainer into this work, but the very grandeur of the First National Bank serves to emphasize the contrast with the world to which it is set in opposition. The bridge is thus a border zone between the two worlds."[2] Elaborating on Sakai's interpretation, we can see how the viewpoint of Kiyochika, born into the old city of Edo, stands resolutely on the near side of the bridge, on the side of the "world set in opposition" to the First National Bank in the distance. Taking as his cue vivid recollections of the spatiality of Edo, Kiyochika attempted to insert a sharp fissure into the landscape of civilization and enlightenment. Sure indications of this anxiety are the black silhouettes of the three birds that pierce the gray sky.

Two years before Kobayashi Kiyochika began his *Famous Views of Tokyo* print series in 1876, an ex-samurai from the provinces had completed writing a series of sketches of Enlightenment Tokyo in a playful style of *kanbun*, the Japanese variant of the classical Chinese written language. His name was Hattori Bushō (1842–1908), and his book was a leading best-seller of early Meiji, *New Tales of Tokyo Prosperity* [*Tōkyō shin-hanjōki*, 1874]. As the son of a Confucian scholar-official from the domain of Nihonmatsu in the Tōhoku region of northern Japan, Bushō was raised in a world in which the written language was that of kanbun. The very idea of capturing the new customs of Enlightenment Tokyo in traditional kanbun was itself anachronistic, but what rather interests us are the ways in which the various *things* [*mono*]³ that served as symbols of the "enlightenment" produced a certain grating against the forms of the classical Chinese language itself. When Bushō mobilized this kanbun style, which Nagai Kafū once referred to as "a strange hybrid form, much like the mythical *nue* beast," what sort of Tokyo landscape was recreated in the pages of his book?⁴ Let us consider his description of the same First National Bank building that we saw in Kiyochika's print:

> The First Bank stands on the eastern side of Kaiun Bridge, in the northern corner of Kabuto-chō. Words cannot express its grandeur of construction, its beauty of design. Taking its model from the West, a Dragon Palace of the Sea has been created on land. Enclosed by stone gate and iron fence, it is the glory of modern building. . . . Seen from afar, it is like a miniature Chinese palace, but as one draws near, it appears as a great Buddhist temple. The stone of the walls is straighter than boards, the iron of the columns smoother than wood. Copper tiles lie in rows like the scales of a fish, and white plaster serves as cosmetic powder: the one blacker than the face of a darkey, the other lighter than the skin of a whitey.⁵ Each story is set off by carved railings, painted in bright colors: missing only are the crimson sleeves of a court lady. Doors and windows are all covered in glass. They shine like drops of falling water, fit for the brocade robe of a celestial maiden. The roof is surmounted by three towers, each topped by a tall pole.⁶

Whereas the First National Bank appears in Kiyochika's *Kaiun Bridge* as a whole, apprehended directly, in Bushō's passage the building is presented in parts, each severed from the whole into contrasting pairs by the use of the parallel phrasing of classical Chinese. The copper tiles are set against the white plaster, and the railings with their carved ornament form a pair with the glazed windows. (In the Kiyochika print, the snow that covers the building tends to soften these same contrasts.) But these paired phrases are chosen with almost no concern at all for the spatial relationships among the separate parts of the building or for the system of meaning that unifies them. Bushō has made no attempt in his prose at a faithful recreation of the structure of the *thing* itself, but has sought to convey the gorgeous external appearance of the bank building only as it directly stimulated his visual senses. The contrasting forms and colors that are offered in such segmented language serve to create for the reader a vivid impression of this new exotic form of architecture, but it offers no information beyond this.

The parallel structure typically used by Bushō consists of the pairing of a *thing* with a metaphor, as in "carved rails" with "court lady" and "glass" with "angel." In each case, the superiority of the various *things* that serve as symbols of "enlightenment" is affirmed by comparison with objects from the past, using an exaggerated form of personification. This is, on the one hand, an innocent expression of the astonishment and admiration of the Japanese of the Enlightenment era when confronted with the strangeness of the West, but at the same time it signifies a strategy whereby the foreign objects that had so relentlessly invaded their field of vision were familiarized by incorporating them into the world of classical kanbun rhetoric. The order of random objects like "stone walls," "iron columns," "copper tiles," and "white plaster," which have no meaning in and of themselves, is enmeshed within an order of metaphor that links them to the associations of such concrete terms as "Dragon Palace," "celestial maiden," "Chinese palace," and "court lady." The one exception is the description of copper as "blacker than the face of a darkey" against plaster "lighter than the skin of a whitey," a clear example of the dissonance produced when Western *things* are subjected to kanbun rhetoric.

Seen in a different light, however, the image of the First National Bank that Bushō has captured with the rhetoric of kanbun style may in fact be remarkably faithful to the eclecticism conveyed by the building itself, of which the bottom two stories were in Western style and the top three in the Japanese manner. If there was indeed a common sense of design to this era, one that encompassed both the eclecticism of the bank building and the "strange hybrid form" of Bushō's prose, it is perhaps epitomized by the carved design on the carriage porch of the Kaichi School in Matsumoto City (figure 2). The designer of the building, Tateishi Kiyoshige, placed in the gable beneath the carriage porch roof a carving of two cupids holding aloft a plaque inscribed "Kaichi School," a motif that was inspired by the nameplate of the woodblock news-sheet series *Tokyo Nichinichi shimbun* created by the *ukiyo-e* artist Ochiai Yoshiiku. Beneath the cupids, in the entablature above the porch, he placed a writhing dragon, with the conventional clouds carved into the railing of the balcony above and into the bracketing of the columns below. This bizarre combination is a three-dimensional visualization of the rhetoric used by Bushō in applying the image of a traditional celestial maiden [*tennyo*] to the beauty of an exotic glass window.

New Tales of Tokyo Prosperity unfolds in successive scenes as a veritable panorama of Enlightenment Japan as reflected in the eyes of one provincial samurai, in which we get a glimpse of multiple aspects of the reality of "civilization and enlightenment" as they are transformed by the language of the kanbun style. Some landscapes are neatly absorbed into the world of kanbun, and others escape its grasp, while conversely, some landscapes end up transforming the kanbun style itself. The stylistic appeal of the work, infused with

Figure 2. Carriage porch, Kaichi School, Matsumoto, Nagano Prefecture, 1876. Designed by Tateishi Kiyoshige. Photo by Jonathan Reynolds. Courtesy Henry D. Smith II

a vital if incoherent energy, derives from these multiple aspects of the drama enacted between words and their referents, and of the first encounter of the world of traditional kanbun and the objects of European civilization. For example, this is how Bushō describes Shinbashi Station, a building designed in the classical style by the American architect R. P. Bridgens: "In the center of the compound is a stone hall. It is known as a 'station.' Stone serves to face the pillars, and polished stone covers the walls. It is refined and beautiful, as though a single great stone had been carved into a multi-storied building."[7] This curt and prosaic description is in clear contrast with the much more embellished account of the First National Bank; the single-minded emphasis on the raw material of *stone* in Bushō's account of Shinbashi Station serves in itself to stress the functional character of the building.

What about Kiyochika's depiction of the same Shinbashi Station (figure 3)? Here the deep gloom of night envelops the huge stone monument of the new era, and the lights of countless lanterns reflecting off the rain-drenched pavement compete with flares of gas lamps gleaming in the windows of the station building. In this case, the object serving as a symbol of

Figure 3. *Shinbashi Station* (*Shinbashi sutenshon*), 1881, by Kobayashi Kiyochika. Multi-colored woodblock print on paper. Courtesy Santa Barbara Museum of Art, Gift of Mr. and Mrs. Roland A. Way

"enlightenment" has been relativized by nature in a manner reminiscent of the spaces of Edo, and thus stripped of its sharp geometrical contours. In Kiyochika's *Famous Views of Tokyo*, the prosaic landscape of Enlightenment Tokyo is bathed in a distinctive poetic atmosphere in which light and shadows subtly play against each other.

No matter which print in Kiyochika's *Famous Views of Tokyo* one selects, it will be full of rich memories of the spaces of Edo, city of water. Of the ninety-five prints included in the series, some thirty works are associated with the Sumida River, at such locales as Hashiba, Mukōjima, Ryōgoku, and Ōkawabata. If one includes views of other waterways, such as the canal at Nihonbashi Bridge and the Kanda River at Ochanomizu, or of Shinobazu Pond at Ueno, then over half of all the views in the series are linked to water. And if you then add snow scenes like *Kaiun Bridge* and *Suruga-chō in the Snow*, plus rain scenes such as *Shinbashi Station* and *Kudan Hill on an Early Summer Night*, Kiyochika's persistent predilection for water becomes unmistakable. Here Kiyochika is heir to the vision of Hiroshige's *One Hundred Famous Views of Edo*, in which the artist freely indulged in such lyrical depictions of the Sumida as *Sudden Shower over Shin-Ōhashi Bridge* and a night view of the *Pine of Success*.[8] In this respect, it is probably of symbolic importance that Kiyochika terminated his Tokyo series with a series of three prints depicting a fire of February 1881 at Ryōgoku, and a final one showing the *Outbreak of Fire Seen from Hisamatsu-chō* a month later.[9] Just as his preoccupation with water was finally brought to an end by fires, so we can see the old world of Kiyochika being pushed aside by the willful advance of a new era.

By contrast, in the scenes of Enlightenment Tokyo described in Bushō's *New Tales of Tokyo Prosperity*, even views of such manmade waterways as moats and canals are eliminated, to say nothing of the areas along the Sumida River. The sole exception is to be found in the sequel published seven years later (1881), in the entry for "boathouses" [*funayado*]. Here for the first time the author described the early Meiji system of water transport centered around the funayado, riverside establishments that rented out boats and provided for entertainment on them. Just as nostalgia for Edo as a city of water runs throughout the *New Chronicle of Yanagibashi* [*Ryūkyō shinshi*, 1874] of Narushima Ryūhoku, who was born in a *daimyo* mansion on the banks of the Sumida at Ōkawabata, so Bushō's *New Tales of Tokyo Prosperity* could not escape the fate of one who was raised inland, in the castle town of Nihonmatsu.

When Bushō described the beautiful sight of the First National Bank as "a Dragon Palace of the Sea created on land," he himself was probably unconscious of how aptly this phrase captures the very essence of *New Tales of Tokyo Prosperity*. What Bushō somewhat prematurely anticipated was the shape of "land-based Tokyo" [*oka no Tōkyō*],[10] which would in the end dismember and eventually eliminate Edo as a city of water. Whereas Kiyochika's landscape prints, rooted in the watery environment of the Sumida River as the basic link to memories of Edo, merely returned the gaze of Tokyo in this new era, Bushō's *New Tales of Tokyo Prosperity* was rather an effort, using the code of traditional kanbun, to decipher the new text of "land-based Tokyo" that was then being woven from the various symbols of the Japanese Enlightenment and working its way into the spaces of Edo.

2

The panorama as a device for replicating the urban landscape on a 360-degree painted surface in realistic perspective was actually invented at the end of the eighteenth century,[11] but it was apparently only from about 1830 that this type of vision was incorporated into literature as a technique of description. Louis Jacques Mandé Daguerre, who would go on to invent the daguerreotype as a pioneering technique of photography, created the diorama in 1822 as an improvement on the panorama.[12] By various techniques of manipulating the way light of various colors fell on the painting, he succeeded in giving an even greater sense of three-dimensional illusion. The illusions of urban space that were enabled by the panorama and diorama stimulated popular authors in France to write a series of works in "panorama style," unveiling various scenes of city life one by one. According to Walter Benjamin, "They consist of isolated sketches, the anecdotal form of which corresponds to the plastic foreground of the panoramas, and their informational base to its painted backdrop."[13]

The style of the "tales of prosperity" [hanjōki] genre that was initiated by Terakado Seiken in his *Tales of Edo Prosperity* [*Edo hanjōki*] of 1832–36 was similar to the French "panorama literature" in the way diverse vignettes of the city were composed by the use of both "anecdotal form" and an "informational base."[14] In Japan, however, the panorama itself was not introduced until the spring of 1890 at the Third Domestic Industrial Exposition in Ueno Park, so the visual mode corresponding to the "tales of prosperity" style must instead be found in the lineage of "lens pictures" [*megane-e*] that were created under the influence of Chinese woodblock prints and Dutch copperplate etchings.[15] These megane-e were first devised by Maruyama Ōkyo in Kyoto in the 1750s for use with lens-equipped viewing devices that in effect reversed the principle of the camera obscura, and were then further developed in Edo by ukiyo-e artists, primarily for use in a peep-show box [*nozoki-karakuri*], in which the picture was placed inside and viewed through a lens fit into the front of the device. These pictures included scenes of the city executed in a simplified version of Western linear perspective. The background receded into the depths, while the people in the foreground appeared to project out toward the viewer.

An early example of a correspondence between such views and literary descriptions of the city is to be found in comparing Shiba Kōkan's hand-colored copperplate etching *View of Ryōgoku Bridge* [*Ryōgokubashi zu*] of 1787 (figure 4) with the description of the plaza at Ryōgoku Bridge that had appeared over two decades earlier in Hiraga Gennai's *Rootless Grass* [*Nenashigusa*, 1763].[16] Gennai's description begins with the reed-covered tea stalls that lined the plaza and the activities of the throngs of people who gathered there, moving on to the skiffs and pleasure boats on the Sumida River. Kōkan's print also shows the crowded activity on the plaza in the lower third of the picture, then a view of the Sumida River in the middle ground, and finally recedes in the distance to a vanishing point around the area where we can see smoke curling up from the tile kilns of Imado. If we consider the genre of Edo guidebooks, beginning with Asai Ryōi's *Chronicle of the Famous Places*

Figure 4. *View of Ryōgoku Bridge* (*Ryōgokubashi zu*) by Shiba Kōkan (1747–1818). Hand-colored copperplate etching, 1787. Courtesy Kobe City Museum

of Edo [*Edo meishoki*] of 1662 and concluding with Saitō Gesshin's massive gazeteer, *Illustrations of the Famous Places of Edo* [*Edo meisho zue*, 20 vols.] of 1834–36, we can detect a spatial conception that grasps the city as a homogeneous whole, corresponding to the kind of bird's-eye vantage point found in large screen paintings of the city of Edo. By contrast, the "tales of prosperity" style that found its precedent in Gennai's depiction of Ryōgoku in *Rootless Grass* developed a method of composition by which urban space was first segmented into diverse elements, each of which was then constituted as a scene combining landscape and figures with the use of linear perspective.

Using André Leroi-Gourhan's classification of space into two types, "intinerant" and "radial,"[17] the Edo guidebook genre would appear to be roughly equivalent to intinerant space, that of movement along an intinerary. Asai Ryōi, in the preface of his *Chronicle of the Famous Places of Edo*, uses the phrase, "If one tours around Edo, with its countless places of note . . . ,"[18] and Saitō Gesshin in *Illustrations of the Famous Places of Edo* described the space of Edo as the "ground" [*chi, ji*] on which the three generations of the Saitō family—Gesshin, his father, and his grandfather—had inscribed the "figure" [*zugara*] of their wanderings about the city. In this way, the image of the city was constituted by the complex traces connecting the countless points of the city's historical memory, in shrines and temples, in places made famous by poetic tradition, and in sites of history and legend. Gesshin thus conceived of the city of Edo as a dense distribution of such symbolic places as shrines, temples, and historical sites; as he wrote in the preface to *Illustrations of the Famous Places of Edo*, "The land of Edo is broad and prosperous, and the deeds of the illustrious figures of the past that illuminate the pages of its history are abundant, while Buddhist temples and sanctuaries stand as dense as the trees in a forest, so that it would be impossible to mention them all."[19]

The preface to *Illustrations of the Famous Places of Edo* continues with the explanation, "Starting with the great castle, I proceed in rotation from the south, completing the course in a total of seven books, each corresponding to one of the stars in the Big Dipper." Starting from Edo Castle, the narrative proceeds to the Kanda and Nihonbashi areas, and then on to Shiba and Shinagawa in a structure that rotates clockwise. Takizawa Bakin complained in *A Draft Miscellany of Strange Tales* [*Ibun zakkō*, ca. 1836] that this structure made it difficult to locate places in the book, but in fact it faithfully reflects the formal "system" of the Edo plan, divided according to the three layers of moats that encircle the castle in a clockwise spiral, a spatial arrangement also seen in maps of Edo, in which roads proceed in circling patterns with Edo Castle at the center, marked by the hollyhock crest of the Tokugawa family. The key motif of *Illustrations of the Famous Places of Edo*, however, was to constantly reread this space of the Edo "system" as the space of myth. It is an immense symbol-space in which countless gods, buddhas, and tutelary spirits extend their protecting arms out to Edo Castle towering in the center. This ideology of *Illustrations of the Famous Places of Edo* was rooted in the mentality of Saitō Gesshin, born in Kanda Kiji-chō into the line of one of the founding headman families of Edo, one who never failed to participate in the formal visit to Edo Castle that was permitted on the third day of the New Year.

Terakado Seiken's *Tales of Edo Prosperity*, which was published in the same Tenpō era of the 1830s as *Illustrations of the Famous Places of Edo*, opens with chapters on "Sumo," "Yoshiwara," and "Theaters." This was not a random order, but rather reflects the assertion in the preface of the first volume, that "nothing more signals the great peace of Edo's prosperity than the four-hour sumo matches, the three theaters, and the brothels of the Five Streets of the Yoshiwara." Putting the sumo to one side, what does it indicate that the theater and brothel districts were known as the *akusho*, or "bad places,"[20] constituting a sort of other world separate from normal urban space? According to Hirosue Tamotsu, the distinctive feature of the early modern city in Japan was the way these "non-everyday" spaces of the theater and brothel were located on the peripheries of the normal world:

> If we may distinguish the "everyday" [*nichijō*] from the "non-everyday" [*hi-nichijō*], then the akusho constituted a non-everyday site. And yet it impinged on the everyday in subtle ways. Just for the price of general admission, you could treat yourself to a kabuki play—maybe not in one of the upper-class boxes, but at least in the pit or the peanut gallery. Or you could slip off to the brothel for a quick nip. . . . In other words, the everyday world and the site of the "non-everyday" were continuous with one another. For this reason, the akusho was somehow different from a one-shot festival, even a festival that came around periodically. It was a non-everyday place that existed in an everyday way. For those who lived in early modern feudal society, especially in its cities, these places were real places. This seems to have been a kind of experience particular to the early modern era.[21]

The pleasure quarters were driven in the early Edo period from the original Yoshiwara that adjoined the downtown area, to the "New" Shin-Yoshiwara in the rice paddies of Asakusa, and the theater districts of Sakai-chō and Fukiya-chō were ordered at the time of the Tenpō Reforms in 1842 to relocate from the city center to a lot near the temple of Sensōji, in the same Asakusa area. This section to the northeast of Edo Castle, in the dangerous "quarter of evil spirits" [*kimon*], was a foreboding zone of the non-everyday, so that the Shin-Yoshiwara was understood as an impure facility, of a class with the Nippori crematorium and Kozukappara execution grounds that lay nearby. The great zone of temples that lay along a belt joining the temples of Kan'eiji at Ueno with Sensōji at Asakusa served as a barrier to protect Edo Castle from this space of ill omen.

The conception of *Tales of Edo Prosperity*, in seeking out the roots of prosperity in places like the Yoshiwara and theater district that had been forced into isolation on the urban fringe, is in direct opposition to the structure of *Illustrations of the Famous Places of Edo* as a symbolic space under the protection of gods and buddhas encircling the central starting point of Edo Castle. What this discloses is a wholly different rhetorical segmentation of urban space, one that inverts the spatial order of "system" and "myth" found in *Illustrations of the Famous Places of Edo*. Using Seiken's terminology, we might describe it as the opposition between the "useful" [*yūyō*] and the "useless" [*muyō*]. The leaders of the "useful" world—samurai, priests, and Confucian scholars—were constantly relativized by the logic of the "useless" world, and thereby served up as the targets of scathing parody.

The world of *Tales of Edo Prosperity*, depicted as a vast space of play with its core in the Yoshiwara and theater district, is laid out spatially around such temples and shrines as Sensōji, Shiba Shinmei, and Ichigaya Hachiman, together with their adjacent centers of entertainment, and at the same time in the local outing spots along seasonal lines of blooming flowers and annual events, such as the cherry blossoms at Ueno and the fireworks at Ryōgoku. At the same time, however, as the "ground" on which these "figures" are drawn, we are provided with minutely detailed descriptions of scenes of daily life, in the backstreet tenements, the public bathhouses, and the barbershops. *Tales of Edo Prosperity* is an epoch-making book that seeks to decipher the overall space of Edo as a complex tapestry of paired meanings: sacred and profane, everyday and non-everyday, prosperity and poverty, city and suburb, main street and back alley. What gives rich meaning to these fragments of the urban landscape that have been snipped out is the activity of the people who gather there, and it is from this sense of the word "prosperity" that we must begin to unravel them.

3

Henri Lefebvre has proposed a three-dimensional model for the structure of the code that is needed to decipher the vast number of messages that are constantly transmitted by urban space. These three dimensions are the *symbolic*, which generally refers to monuments and consequently to ideologies and institutions, both present and past; the *paradigmatic*, which is an ensemble, or a system of oppositions; and the *syntagmatic*, which refers to linkages (the *parcours*, or route).[22] In this model, the concrete markers for the symbolic dimension are "buildings," "style," "historical memory," and "continuity"; for the paradigmatic dimension, they are the oppositions of "city-country," "inner-outer," "center-periphery," and "enclosure-gate"; and for the syntagmatic dimension, they are "transportation system," "road network," and "units of residential land and their connections." Unfortunately, there is no space here to show how Lefebvre has transformed into a three-dimensional scheme the bipolar model of "syntagm" and "system" that Roland Barthes, drawing on the linguistic theories of Saussure and Jakobson, elucidated in *Elements of Semiology* (1964). But I wish here simply to emphasize that this model is extremely useful as a way of understanding the meaning of such "urban texts" as *Illustrations of the Famous Places of Edo*, *Tales of Edo Prosperity*, and *New Tales of Tokyo Prosperity* that appeared from the 1830s on into the Meiji period. Just as the focus of *Illustrations of the Famous Places of Edo* encourages a reading in the symbolic dimension and *Tales of Edo Pros-*

perity one in the paradigmatic dimension, so we might read Hattori Bushō's *New Tales of Tokyo Prosperity* as a book that interprets Enlightenment Tokyo as process, in which syntagmatic elements are brought to the fore, while the symbolic and paradigmatic elements that constituted the space of Edo are relegated to the background.

The fifty-two chapters that constitute the five books of *Tales of Edo Prosperity* can be seen as an aggregation, under the single theme of "prosperity," of various elements that Terakado Seiken has isolated from the urban landscape and city life. We can further detect certain subgroupings within the aggregate that reveal much about the way Seiken read the urban context. There is a category, for example, of temples, shrines, and festivals, which includes chapters on the temple of Sensōji at Asakusa, Shinmei Shrine at Shiba, Mount Atago, Ichigaya Hachiman, the religious "unveilings" known as *kaichō*,[23] periodic shrine fairs, and festival days. Another category might be called "suburbs and outings," including the chapters on the summer fireworks at Ryōgoku, the spring cherry blossoms of Ueno and the Sumida embankment, the Benten shrine on the island of Enoshima, and the Hyakkaen flower garden in Mukōjima.

These two groupings, of religious festivals and suburban outings, together constitute a realm of play and festivity [*hare*] and stand in clear opposition to others that deal rather with the ordinary [*ke*], with daily life, covering categories like food and dress (the old clothes market at Tomizawa-chō, the Nihonbashi fish market, meat restaurants, baked-yam peddlers), items of local community (tenements, the bathhouse, barbers, vaudeville theaters), and fringe areas of the city (Senju, Shinagawa, Fukagawa, Honjo). This opposition of hare and ke may also be seen as one of "front" [*omote*] and "back" [*ura*], a theme that runs through many of the details of *Tales of Edo Prosperity*, such as the chapter on "Senju" in which the prosperity of the eel restaurants and vaudeville theaters is juxtaposed with the grim sight of the execution grounds and crematorium at Kozukappara. The deep structure of the way *Tales of Edo Prosperity* articulates the city is revealed by the insertion of the alternating life rhythms of hare and ke, of play and daily life. The "prosperity" of Edo may be understood as a "gathering" of people who freely move among the sites of hare and ke, and of the accumulation of the lively exchanges by which they constantly make and break communication with one another. As shown by the fact that only a single chapter ("Palanquins and Taxi Skiffs") deals with transportation, a syntax of "gathering" takes precedence over that of "flow."

For Hattori Bushō, who learned the style of "tales of prosperity" from Terakado Seiken, the assembly constituted by *Tales of Edo Prosperity* provided a model that he could not overlook. In fact, eighteen chapters, or half of the total of thirty-six chapters that make up the six books of *New Tales of Tokyo Prosperity*, share themes with chapters of *Tales of Edo Prosperity*. Some of these are virtually the same topics, as in the entries for schools, brothels, and female singers, whereas others are functional substitutes, such as *jinrikisha* in place of palanquins, expositions for medicine fairs, butchers selling beef for wild boar stores, Western-style barbers for traditional topknot salons. These correspondences provide detailed information on customs and serve to highlight the transformation of the city before and after the Meiji Restoration. It is basically a scheme that serves to set the "old evils" [*kyūhei*] of Edo in opposition to the "enlightenment" of Meiji.

But by articulating the city according to the formula of "old evils" versus "enlightenment," *New Tales of Tokyo Prosperity* tends to downgrade and bracket the structural oppositions of *Tales of Edo Prosperity* into "front" versus "back," or play versus daily life. For example, in *Tales of Edo Prosperity*, the chapter on "Palanquins and Taxi Skiffs" incorporates the opposition of land and water as a metaphor for play and life, whereas in *New Tales of Tokyo Prosperity* the comparison between the palanquin and the jinrikisha lies rather in the realm of efficiency: "The power of the old two-man palanquin came from those who ran as if they had no legs and flew without wings. But the power of the new jinrikisha comes from using two legs in place of four, to carry two passengers instead of one. That was like taking the proverbial pilgrimage to Zenkōji temple on an ox; this is like cracking the whip over a tiger to cover a thousand miles through the jungle. These are not similar types of force: it is the direct versus the roundabout, the swift versus the leisurely. This is why the palanquin has disappeared from view, and the jinrikisha is now dominant."[24] The narrative style here, proceeding from a thing (jinrikisha) to its functional value ("direct" versus "roundabout") and on to its meaning ("civilization and enlightenment"), suggests the code by which we can decipher *New Tales of Tokyo Prosperity*. A certain clarity of logic is provided by the parallel phrasing and hyperbolic expression of the kanbun style itself, but the standard of judgment based on efficiency and rationality works to isolate *things* from the multiple levels of meaning that they transmit to people.

This operation, by which the multiple meanings of a *thing* are transformed into a single meaning, as the symbol of "enlightenment," may also be seen in the ways *New Tales of Tokyo Prosperity* transforms the subgroupings of *Tales of Edo Prosperity*. Only a handful of chapters in the Meiji work —such as "Ueno Park," "Special Festivals," "Yasukuni Shrine," and "Zōjōji Temple"—correspond to the older categories of "suburbs and outings" or "shrines, temples, and festivals," and topics dealing with the realm of daily life are almost nonexistent. The three topics that come as a set at the very start of *Tales of Edo Prosperity*—"Sumo," "Yoshiwara," "Theaters"—are separated off and dispersed in *New Tales of Tokyo Prosperity*, thus dissipating the meaning of the "bad places" [*akusho*]. On the other hand, the category dealing with modes of transportation and communication becomes correspondingly larger, in such chapters as "Jinrikisha," "Shinbashi Railroad," "Tsukiji Telegraph Office," "Shiba-Kanasugi Gas Company," "Newspaper Companies," and "Attorneys' Offices." Moreover, leading examples from this category serve as the opening chapters for each of the six volumes of *New Tales of Tokyo Prosperity*, creating a common thread: "Schools" (book 1), "Kyōbashi Brick District" (book 2), "Shinbashi Railroad" (book 3), "Expositions" (book 4), "Tsukiji Telegraph Office" (book 5), and "Shiba-Kanasugi Gas Company" (book 6). The main axis of Tokyo as the capital of this new era, leading from Shinbashi Station to the Ginza Brick District, becomes itself the organizing principle of *New Tales of Tokyo Prosperity*.

In the chapter of book 6 that deals with "Girls' Schools," Bushō writes, "In beginning my account of the 'new' prosperity, I start with schools because the prosperity of the state depends in the first instance on the prosperity of the culture." If we just replace "culture" with "civilization" here, we can see that the sort of "prosperity" he has in mind is vastly different from that of *Tales of Edo Prosperity*, which started rather with the akusho. Whereas Edo appeared to Seiken as a "gathering" of people, Bushō was pursuing a rhetoric of the city that corresponded to the structure of "flow." The resulting landscape, which makes visible the circuits that concentrate and distribute both *things* and information, is precisely that of "land-based Tokyo." And to the extent that *New Tales of Tokyo Prosperity* precisely delineates the various aspects of this "land-based Tokyo," it also neglects the canals and alleys that provided the "flow" of Edo and rich metaphors for the play and daily life of its people.

4

The first impression that we get from the world of *New Tales of Tokyo Prosperity* is the image of a display case packed with *things* that serve as symbols of "civilization and enlightenment." One indicator of the way the figure of "land-based Tokyo" is delineated against the "ground" of Edo space is the density of these very *things*. Among these are built-things [*tate-mono*], like the Ginza Brick District and the First National Bank; things-to-ride [*nori-mono*], like jinrikisha, horse trolleys, and steam locomotives; goods [*shina-mono*], like oil lamps, beer, and soap; and things-to-show [*mise-mono*], like peep shows, expositions, and so forth. When Bushō writes in the chapter on the Kyōbashi Brick District that "to lift the darkness and spread knowledge, there is nothing like showing the actual scene with the real things," he considers it his function to provide the readers with a catalogue of "civilization and enlightenment" as exact copies of the Western world. But this is not to say that he explains all the effects of each and every *thing*. Some, for example, are introduced as elements of the landscape or as curious objects that stimulate the visual imagination. Here, for example, is his depiction of the Ginza Brick District:

> Countless shops of craftsmen and stores of merchants stand in long rows, each prospering in the bustle of the market and lined up one after the next. They rival one another in the arrays of new goods, and compete in the display of strange items that sparkle with gold and silver, and throb with blue and red. The beautiful clothes glitter like stars, their fabrics layered in clouds. Imported textiles stand next to kimono cloth, and buckwheat noodles face off with beef. The beating rag makes a slapping sound as the bookseller dusts his merchandise, while a machine for sewing Western clothes whirrs like a lathe. Dishes and metal objects are on display, while craftsmen assemble jinrikisha and leather shoes.[25]

This same sort of cataloguing technique is used in the chapters on "Bookstores," "Expositions," and "Import Stores." The visual image of *things* lined up on display is conveyed directly by a rhetorical succession of nouns, while the parallel phrases of kanbun serve as a device to contrast the new and the old. The rather stereotyped listing of phrases beginning with "gold and silver sparkle" serves as a perfect representation of the dazzling fantasy of an overwhelming array of goods on display. Each separate *thing* is no more than an image that flashes on for just an instant, a symbol of consumption that has been emptied of all meaning. The richness of the display stands in odd contrast to the visual monotony of the Brick District itself, with row after row of the same standardized building design along the eight blocks of the Ginza. Constructed in the functional materials of white plaster over brick that excluded all traces of decorative meaning from the buildings themselves, the Brick District denied the possibility of going beyond the immediate perception of the material object itself. What rises before us is a symbol of "civilization and enlightenment" that is merely a myth emptied of meaning.

Beginning with the Tsukiji Hotel that burned to the ground in the fire of 1872, there appeared in Enlightenment Tokyo a whole series of buildings in Western or pseudo-Western styles, including the First National Bank, Shinbashi Station, and the Tsukiji Telegraph Office. Making generous use of materials like granite, brick, glass, and iron that stimulated the sense of vision, these buildings became the landmarks that demarcated the territory of this capital of the new age. They were the "new famous places" of the city, the sacred precincts of Civilization and Enlightenment, luring the gaze of the people to the far-off West. The dazzling external appearance and imposing bulk of these buildings served to make them into black boxes, concealing the networks within that worked to link the various functions of the city, and thereby lending them an even greater air of mystery. Bushō, for example, summarizes the appearance of the First National Bank this way: "On the flagpoles left and right, gold arrows on the weathervane indicate the directions, and from the center tower flies a trademark flag. It is like a gold brocade pennant fluttering in the wind, as though it were directing the trade of the entire capital. The leaves and branches of the tree of Enlightenment grow luxuriantly, and the golden flowers of Tokyo are in full bloom."[26] Through this flowery but wholly vacuous rhetoric, Bushō strives to extol the myth of money and the myth of commerce. In the chapter "Tsukiji Foreign Residences," he relates the episode of the country bumpkin who bowed down before the stone-built foreign residences, mistaking them for sacred halls dedicated to Fudō or Benten, thus revealing how the sacred spaces of Edo such as Sensōji or Shiba Shinmei, which functioned both as religious symbols and entertainment districts, had now been replaced by the Ginza Brick District as the sacred space of "land-based Tokyo," its buildings serving as halls for the worship of fetishized commodities. (It might be noted that immediately after its completion, the Ginza Brick District still had many vacancies, and for a brief period served as the venue for such sideshows as wrestling bears and dancing dogs.)

The operation that transforms the horizontal *paradigm* of the city as an assembly of *things* into a vertical *syntagm* is accomplished by the distinctive style of the "tales of prosperity" genre, in which expressive episodes (the horizontal paradigm) are set against a reportorial background (the vertical syntagm). This might alternatively be described as a transposition from the world of nouns to the world of verbs. The various commodities that constitute the landscape of the Brick District are situated within a drama of distribution and consumption that pervades all the conversations and activities of people in the city. For example, in his sketch of the crowd of people, both young and old, male and female, who gather at Hoteiya, the most celebrated silk fabric store on the Ginza at this time, Bushō uses sketches of people to explain such trade-related slang as "chilling" [*hiyakashi*, looking at goods without buying], "pissers" [*shōbenmono*, buyers who agree to a purchase but never return to pick it up], and "drum-stretchers" [*taiko o haru*, seductive women who conspicuously ask the price of clothing in the hope of persuading a smitten customer to buy it for them]. Or in the ensuing depiction of the popular restaurant Matsuda Palace, Bushō provides vignettes of merchants exchanging tips about investing in the breeding of rabbits (a brief but frenzied fad of early Meiji) and of small-time hustlers with big dreams of success in trade. What provides the occasion for these episodes is the Brick District itself, symbol of wealth and of the elemental act of trade.

Hattori Bushō's conscious method was to explicate the networks and structures of the city by interweaving descriptions of both *people* and *things* at the various stages of consumption, distribution, and exchange. His blunt and unambiguous point of view, as revealed in such assertions as "the railroad is nothing more than a road to profit" ("Shinbashi Station") or "as society at large becomes enlightened, so the various modes of commerce will be enlightened, and with the enlightenment of commerce, the flow of cash will be inevitable" ("Attorneys' Offices"), was unrivaled by any of the other contemporary writers of "tales of prosperity." Many of the figures who appear in the foreground of the city landscapes delineated by Bushō compose scenes of consumption or purchasing, and their topics of conversation are limited to information on trade and investing or the naked envy of wealth. The people of *Tales of Edo Prosperity* who gathered in the brothels, theaters, or picnic sites were above all people enjoying themselves, people at play, creating an atmosphere of easy communication between people and people. By contrast, the people of *New Tales of Tokyo Prosperity* are people who consume *things* as symbols of "enlightenment" and people who gaze on the new sights of Tokyo, so that the mode of interaction is rather between people and *things*. Bushō is well aware of the fact that a new type of crowd has made its appearance in Enlightenment Tokyo, of a wholly different order from the crowds who gathered at the shrine and temple fairs of Edo or in the scenic suburbs. Now it is the crowd of traders who shuttle back and forth between Tokyo and Yokohama[27] on the railroad's "road to profit," or the throngs who gather at the Matsuda Palace restaurant on the Ginza:

> The Matsuda Palace is located next to Kyōbashi Bridge. It is a huge palace, with countless rooms, serving rivers of drink and mountains of meat. The fish is fresh and the flavors fine. It even rivals Yaozen, although no one can invite geisha, nor is there any chance for the free exchange of cups among the guests. None of the guests fall into drunken fist games or loud singing: they take a drink and leave, eat their food and are on their way. . . . Banquet rooms are available, holding several hundred at a time. When guests arrive, a waitress hands them a red wooden tag with their name on it, and asks what they would like to order. There is sashimi, salty stew, sweet stew, teriyaki, pan-stewed chicken, vinegar fish salad—each item

no more than about five sen. Some come dressed in formal robes, some in work frocks. From lunch on to dinner, there is a veritable flood tide of customers, jostling shoulder to shoulder and elbow to elbow, seething with laughter as one repartee follows another.[28]

We can probably detect a certain tone of light irony in the odd comparison of the high-class Edo restaurant Yaozen and a place with "each item no more than about five sen." Here throngs of all classes, high and low, gather by the hundreds to satisfy their appetite, driven by the need to purchase a fleeting moment of tipsiness, then leaving in haste. It is the sort of scene one sees regularly in department store restaurants nowadays, but in the days of Edo, places like this were on the borderline of respectability, known by the contemptuous term of "servant teahouses" [yakko-chamise]. With its tawdry exterior covered with stained-glass windows, it was a sight that typified the "prosperity" of the Ginza Brick District. The guests who gathered there were not permitted to exchange drinks with their neighbors, and the drama of partaking of a meal was reduced to a bare minimum.

"Land-based Tokyo" thus created a large number of places where citizens unknown to one another might come together, meeting at random through the mediation of *things*. Compared to the neighborly world of Edo, it was a world of strangers, people who were first cut off and then reunited into an urban space by the networks of information symbolized by newspapers and the telegraph. In the assertion in the chapter on "Newspaper Companies" that "on a single sheet of paper, all the new curiosities of the world are brought together, leaving out not a single item," we can seen an adumbration of the function of the newspaper as a copy of the world. As a service to the readers, *New Tales of Tokyo Prosperity* provided generous amounts of information about sexual services in such chapters as "Restaurant Entertainment," "Geisha Teahouses," "Shinbashi Geisha," "Barley Tea," "Concubines," and "New Hot Springs," but these do not appear as lyrical spaces conveyed by metaphors of suburban nature (as in the romantic novels of Tamenaga Shunsui) or the water of the Sumida River (as in Ryūhoku's *New Chronicle of Yanagibashi*), but rather are organized within a temporal and spatial complex that is abstract and commodified. What emerges transparently is the theme of the exchange of sex for money, as in the explanation in the chapter on "Geisha Teahouses" that "if you have the cash, they'll flirt with you, but when you run out of it, they chase you away; this is what the dancing girls mean by 'enlightenment.'"[29] At the same time, these intimate spaces are made available to a whole range of social classes that made up the citizenry of Tokyo, from government officials to merchants, students, and artisans, revealing the secret hidden ecology of the city as though it were displayed in a peep show. This is the back side of the "prosperity" of "land-based Tokyo," a hidden tuck in the fabric of cityspace, where the function of the old akusho that had been the core of Edo's prosperity was now rendered shadowy and marginal. "The downfall of the old pleasure quarters," Bushō explains in the chapter on "Restaurant Entertainment," "is a mark of the prosperity of the capital."

The "land-based Tokyo" that Bushō structured according to the formula of the agglomeration, distribution, and exchange of *things* is transposed at the rhetorical level to the structure of metonymy. Roman Jakobson, in his classic essay "Two Aspects of Language and Two Types of Linguistic Disturbances," took aphasia as a clue and argued that the distinction between the linguistic acts of combination and selection were related to the semantic poles of metonymy and metaphor.[30] He then further proposed that these two levels could be applied to nonlinguistic sign systems such as painting and cinema. Here the pole of metaphor corresponds to the paradigmatic dimension in Lefebvre's model, and metonymy to the syntagmatic dimension. *New Tales of Tokyo Prosperity*, which uses linked series of metonymy to read Enlightenment Tokyo as a code in the syntagmatic dimension, may well serve as a model for conceptualizing the semiology of the city.

The chapter "Shiba-Kanasugi Gas Company" provides a concrete example that makes it easier to grasp the metonymic method that undergirds the structure of *New Tales of Tokyo Prosperity* (figure 5). Starting with the process of manufacturing the coal gas that provides fuel for street lamps, it explains the supply route via Kyōbashi and Nihonbashi on to Manseibashi. Interspersed with sketches of the lamplighter who appears at dusk in the Ginza Brick District and the streetwalker who is stopped by a policeman under the light of a gas lamp, this chapter hints at the north-south axis running through "land-based Tokyo" and is also probably the first literary attempt to trace the networks of the modern city that are not visible to the naked eye. In the opening lines, "gaslight" is presented as a synecdoche of "civilization and enlightenment," a rhetorical device that is then contrasted with the episode of a blind person (literally, one who "lost the light"), who complains indignantly to street noodle vendors about the culture of "civilization and enlightenment." In this sense, the streetwalker who mumbles to her customer, "For me, looking at a gas lamp is like peering into the mirror of hell" is also a case of synecdoche, and Bushō, while tracing the supply route of the gas from Shiba to Ginza, and from Ginza on to the gas lamps of Nihonbashi, is an example of a "realist" writer who, in Jakobson's words, "is fond of synecdochic details" and who "digresses metonymically from the plot to the atmosphere and from the character to the setting in time and space."[31] What illuminates the itiner-

Figure 5. *National Industrial Exposition Gas Pavilion* (*Naikoku kangyō hakurankai gasukan*) by Kobayashi Kiyochika. Courtesy Chikuma Shobō, 1982

ant noodle vendors setting up shop at the foot of Nihonbashi Bridge is not gaslight, but the flickering light of paper-covered lamps, which is an indication of the way the world of civilization centering on the Ginza Brick District is enveloped in the dark nighttime space of the city that survives from Edo.

The metonymic method of *New Tales of Tokyo Prosperity* uses as its basic framework the style peculiar to the "tales of prosperity" genre in which units of "reportorial background" and "episodic expression" are blended, and the series of metaphors that stand for the process of exchange between people and circulating *things* (commodities) gives a sense of changing appearances, but in the background only a unitary meaning is repeated over and over. It sends forth dazzling images that stimulate the eye, but it is in a relation of equivalence to the agglomeration of commodities that enlivens the Ginza Brick District and its shops, devoid as they are of all but the most shallow meaning.

So it is a rhetorical strategy whereby metonymy takes precedence over metaphor. It is a collection of showy symbols from which all operation of meaning has been removed. The world revealed to us by *New Tales of Tokyo Prosperity* is a thoroughly materialist space in which relations between people are mediated by exchange value and commodity fetishism. To be sure, it is a biting caricature of an Enlightenment Tokyo that took in Western civilization at the level of *things* and was content to worship them in an obsequious way, but the essence that is extracted here also provides an elemental model for the structure of the modern city. In this respect, we must note the paradox that the very anachronism of *New Tales of Tokyo Prosperity*, rooted in the hollow and stereotyped rhetoric of kanbun style, was an effective way of grasping the structure of the modern city, which is transparent but utterly lacking in any depth. But Bushō's effort to provide an overall deciphering of the city as a text signifies at a deeper level a betrayal of literature, so that one of the first tasks of the modern novel was to discover ways to provide some sort of human meaning in urban space. The result is the Tokyo of Tsubouchi Shōyō's *The Character of Modern Students* [*Tōsei shosei katagi*, 1885–86], in which meaning is imparted by the way the students give vent to their desires with an innocent spontaneity, or the Berlin of Mori Ōgai's "Maihime" ["The Dancing Girl," 1890], where the ambition of Ōta Toyotarō gives rise to a perspectival view of boulevards and monuments. In these cases, we see unfolding a truly inhabited space that is the exact opposite of the space of *New Tales of Tokyo Prosperity*, in which all is controlled by *things*.

Notes

1 This essay first appeared in *Tenbō*, October 1977, and was reprinted in *Toshi kūkan no naka no bungaku* (Chikuma shobō, 1982). The text for this translation is from the latter work, pp. 96–117. Kobayashi's series of ninety-five prints did not originally have a series title, which was provided by later commentators. Some of the individual prints as well, including *Kaiun Bridge*, were similarly untitled. For a complete reproduction of the series, see Takahashi Seiichirō, ed., *Kobayashi Kiyochika, "Tōkyō meisho zu"* (Gakushū Kenkyūsha, 1975). For details on the series in English, see Henry D. Smith II, *Kiyochika: Artist of Meiji Japan* (Santa Barbara: Santa Barbara Museum of Art, 1988), 24–27, 32–51.

2 Sakai Tadayasu, commentary on pl. 14 in Takahashi, *Kobayashi Kiyochika, "Tōkyō meisho zu,"* 27. (M)

3 In Maeda's original text, the word *mono*, "thing," is written phonetically with the hiragana syllabary and given emphasis by placing a dot next to each syllable, equivalent to underlining or italics in English, thus serving to accentuate the sense of materiality of "things." Maeda continues to provide this emphasis for almost all of the subsequent twenty-odd usages of *mono*, which emerges as a key theme in his overall argument. In the translation, the emphasis has been indicated by the use of italics in those cases where it seemed most appropriate to convey Maeda's point.

4 The *nue* was said to have the head of a monkey, the body of a raccoon-dog, the tail of a snake, the limbs of a tiger, and the cry of a thrush.

5 The orthography of the racial epithets used here is two-layered: "darkey" is written in kanji as "black slave" and glossed with the conventional epithet *kuronbō*, and "whitey" is written with the characters "white person" and glossed with the neologism *shironbō*.

6 Hattori Bushō, *Tōkyō shin hanjōki*, in Narushima Ryūhoku et al., *Narushima Ryūhoku, Hattori Bushō, Kurimoto Joun shū*, Meiji bungaku zenshū, vol. 4 (Chikuma Shobō, 1969), 214.

7 Ibid., 179.

8 For these two prints, see Henry D. Smith II, *Hiroshige, One Hundred Famous Views of Edo* (New York: George Braziller, 1986), 58, 61.

9 See Smith, *Kiyochika: Artist of Meiji Japan*, 50–51.

10 The phrase is from Ōta Masao [Kinoshita Mokutarō], "Tōkyō no kashi," *Hōsun* 1, no. 4 (April 1907), as cited in Hasegawa Akira, *Toshi kairō* (Sagami Shobō, 1975), 56, 64–70. (M)

11 For the history of the panorama hall, see Ralph Hyde, *Panoramania! The Art and Entertainment of the "All-Embracing" View* (London: Trefoil, 1988).

12 Daguerre's diorama was in fact a wholly new invention with little similarity to the panorama; instead of the fixed and static 360-degree painting of a panorama, the diorama featured a succession of flat transparent canvases, suspended vertically, each with different paintings on either side, and a system for shifting the illumination between front and back so that the image was gradually transformed from one to the other. For details, see ibid., ch. 4.

13 Walter Benjamin, "Paris, Capital of the Nineteenth Century," in *Reflections: Essays, Aphorisms, Autobiographical Writings*, trans. Edmund Jephcott (New York: Schocken, 1978), 149. (M) The "plastic foreground" mentioned by Benjamin refers to the use of mannequins and sculptured props at the base of panorama paintings to increase the illusionistic effect.

14 For a discussion of *Edo hanjōki* and translations of selected passages, see Andrew Marcus, "Terakado Seiken's 'Blossoms along the Sumida,'" *Sino-Japanese Studies* 3, no. 2 (April 1991): 9–29, and "Meat and Potatoes: Two Selections from the *Edo Hanjōki*," *Sino-Japanese Studies* 4, no. 2 (April 1992): 7–26.

15 Prints of this type are usually known in Europe by the French term *vue d'optique*, an optique being the lens-equipped viewing device. For a history of such prints in Japan, see Oka Yasumasa, *Megane-e shinkō: Ukiyo-eshi tachi ga nozoita Seiyō* (Chikuma Shobō, 1992).

16 For an English translation of the passage describing the Ryōgoku Bridge plaza, which appears at the beginning of chapter 4 of *Nenashigusa*, see Haruo Shirane, ed., *Early Modern Japanese Literature: An Anthology, 1600–1900* (New York: Columbia University Press, 2002), 473–476; the translation is by Chris Drake.

17 André Leroi-Gourhan, *Gesture and Speech*, trans. Anna Bostock Berger (Boston: MIT Press, 1993), 325–326; originally published as *Le Geste et la parole*, 1964. According to Leroi-Gourhan, humans perceive the surrounding world in two ways, one dynamically, by movement through space on an "itinerary," and the other in

a "radial" mode of perception, with the observer fixed at one point and reconstituting circles around the self extending to the limits of the horizon.

18 Asai Ryōi, *Edo meisho ki*, in *Edo I*, vol. 3 of *Nihon meisho fūzoku zue*, ed. Asakura Haruhiko (Kadokawa Shoten,1979), 7.

19 Saitō Gesshin, *Edo meisho zue*, in *Edo II*, vol. 4 of *Nihon meisho fūzoku zue*, ed. Asakura Haruhiko (Kadokawa Shoten,1980), 10.

20 I have here changed the term *akubasho* that Maeda uses in his original text to the shorter form *akusho*, which is more familiar and which corresponds to the usage of Hirosue Tamotsu in the subsequent quotation.

21 Hirosue Tamotsu, *Henkai no akusho* (Heibonsha, 1973), 12–13. (M)

22 Henri Lefebvre, *La révolution urbaine* (Paris: Gallimard, 1970), 120. Italics are in the original. (M)

23 For a description in English of *kaichō*, see P. F. Kornicki, "Public Display and Changing Values: Early Meiji Exhibitions and Their Precursors," *Monumenta Nipponica* 49, no. 2 (Summer 1994): 174–181.

24 Hattori, *Tōkyō shin hanjōki*, 150.

25 Ibid., 164.

26 Ibid., 214.

27 Maeda's original text has "Keihan" (that is, "Kyoto and Osaka"), but this must be a slip for "Keihin" ("Tokyo and Yokohama"). The only railroad in Japan at this point was the Shinbashi-Yokohama line.

28 Hattori, *Tōkyō shin hanjōki*, 166.

29 Ibid., 170.

30 Roman Jakobson, "Two Aspects of Language and Two Types of Aphasic Disturbances," in Jakobson and Morris Halle, *Fundamentals of Language* (The Hague: Mouton, 1956), 67–96.

31 Ibid., 92.

3. The Spirits of Abandoned Gardens: On Nagai Kafū's "The Fox"

(Haien no seirei: "Kitsune")

TRANSLATED BY WILLIAM F. SIBLEY

Maeda's main text here is a short story by Nagai Kafū (1879–1959) entitled "Kitsune" (The fox).[1] Written within months of Kafū's return from five years in the United States and France, "The Fox" is cast in the form of a reminiscence about a small but momentous event in the narrator's childhood. First published in the following year, 1909, in its evocation of a past set early in the Meiji era and so, with respect to various lingering customs and beliefs, continuous with the preceding Edo period, "The Fox" resembles in this general way such other Kafū texts of this particularly productive year as *Sumidagawa* (The river Sumida) and *Fukagawa no uta* (A song of Fukagawa), while it stands with these other works in sharp contrast to such other contemporary publications as *Shinkichō nikki* (The diary of a recent repatriate) and *Reishō* (Sneers).

The two last-named works, together with a number of others in a similar vein that followed over the next few years, have generally been considered "typical" of this phase of Kafū's long career for their sharp contemptuous observations of the surfaces of frenetically modernizing Tokyo life: its architectural and sartorial pretensions and eclecticism; the boorish affectations in public manners that his narrators ascribe to, in particular, the burgeoning lower middle class. But amid Kafū's prolific writings of this period, through his discussion of "The Fox" and a few related texts, Maeda has laid bare here contrary roots of a deeply elegiac, though by no means unambivalent, evocation of certain kinds of Japanese pasts, a tone and vision that would come to inform Kafū's finest works in the succeeding decades (chief among them, no doubt, his diary of six or so volumes, depending on the edition, which is one of the greatest achievements of modern Japanese literature).

1

Nagai Kafū (1879–1959), having settled in at his father's house in Ōkubo Yochō-machi after close to five years abroad, wrote about his reactions to being back in Japan in a card sent to his friend Inoue Aa: "As expected, there were no repercussions at home. When I came back I naturally thought about what happened last night. It has left me with a melancholy yearning, and the desire to amble across town tonight and every night. Surrounded by brothers and friends who have made their way in the world, I feel oppressed and ill at ease. Looking out from the verandah, I find the dark trees on this house's grounds frightening, and fear that I am slipping into madness."[2] This postcard is dated 26 July 1908. Reading between the lines, we gather that the pleasant reunion with his old friend Inoue Aa had included a leisurely ramble through the city streets on this weekend night. Perhaps we may also see here a transferal to nocturnal Tokyo of the *déraciné* habits Kafū had acquired abroad, where he would happily lose himself in the slums of Lyon and the lively quarters of Paris. But from his wish to "amble across town" every night it is clear that what Isoda Kōichi has called "the complex web of responsibility imposed upon the eldest son"[3] weighed heavily on his heart. For Kafū, who showed not the slightest sign of seeking to assume the bright public role expected in this era of Japanese recently returned from Europe and America, to while away his days as a kind of uninvited guest under his father's roof can only have led to a state of irritable boredom. The dark, tangled summer grove contemplated from the veranda can be read, then, as an objective correlative of his state of mind.[4]

Behind the Jailhouse [Kangoku-sho no ura] has the same aura of deep resignation and innermost thoughts projected onto exterior objects as that which pervades the note to Inoue Aa. Here, too, we may glimpse an expression of Kafū's renewed astonishment at both the "humid climate" and the dark nights of Japan: "Oh, the darkness of the Japanese night defies description! Darker, colder, lonelier than death or the tomb. A bulwark of darkness, one might say, impenetrable alike to the sharpest sword of despairing anger, the hottest flames of malevolent resentment."[5] In such overwrought passages there is a sentimental undertone of nostalgia for his delicious years of wandering abroad. But they also provide a measure of the acuteness of Kafū's reaction after returning from the pellucid environment of the West to which he had grown so accustomed. It was a culture shock that this sojourner newly returned from abroad had to undergo for a time on leaving behind the lands of broad-leafed deciduous forests and reentering the zone of dark, moist, shiny-leafed evergreens.

What lay in wait for Kafū after his five years as a free agent in America and France were exceedingly unpleasant, oppressive ties of blood. His actual surroundings as his thoughts took flight to the distant blue skies of France were those of the grove in the family garden, ineluctably ordered by the ominous powers of sheer reproductiveness. The onerousness of Japanese family relations and the alien character of the nature around him cast a dark shadow over Kafū's spirit as he went on writing the remaining pieces contained in *Tales from France* [*Furansu monogatari*, 1909]. The problem posed to him, as he put it in "Dentsūin," was this: "Whatever we may do, we are never able to forget the little corner of this everyday world into which we happen to have been born."[6] It was in response to this problem that "The Fox" ["Kitsune"] had to be written, seeking as it does to go back to the distant sources of his own life in the early years spent in Koishikawa Kanatomi-chō.

In 1886 Kafū returned from his Washizu grandparents in Shitaya Take-chō to his parents' house in Kanatomi-chō and in the same year entered the Kuroda elementary school in Kobinata. The boy Kafū appeared in class wearing a stylish sailor suit, though with short pants. This was the height of the "Rokumeikan era," when the middle-class intelligentsia, emulating the upper class, plunged into the fad for the superficial trappings of a Western lifestyle, and Kafū's father, Nagai Kyū'ichirō, a high official in the Home Ministry who had studied abroad, was no exception. He had chairs and a table set up in a ten-mat-size sitting room where, on returning from his office and changing into a smoking jacket, he would puff away leisurely on his large English-style pipe and sink into his reading. Here, too, Kafū's mother would spread a white cloth over the table and present the family-style Western dishes she had learned at the church in Hongō Ikidonozaka which she attended with her mother (the Washizu family now lived in Shitaya). All in all, they led a middle-class lifestyle typical of this high tide of Meiji Europeanization. But all traces of those Westernized trappings that we assume to have been systematically adopted into the Kafū household have been thoroughly expunged from "The Fox," except for the fleeting detail of the father's changing into Western clothes before he goes out to subdue the fox.

The events told in the tale of "The Fox" are posited in the text as having taken place "at a time when the city water flowed openly to Kobinata-chō through dewy grass, like a river crossing a country field."[7] According to *Illustrations of Famous Places in Tokyo, Koishikawa Section* [*Tōkyō meisho zue, Koishikawa no bu*], it was around 1878–79 that the Kanda aqueduct was rechanneled underground.[8] In fact, then, by the time of Kafū's birth in 1879, the Kanda aqueduct no longer existed in the form described in "The Fox." From references in the text we may deduce that the earliest possible time for the events it relates would be "just at the end of the Seinan Rebellion" (1877), and the latest possible at the time when the horse-drawn railroad carriages were put into service, that is, 1882.

In Kafū's strategy of putting the time of "The Fox" back far enough to eradicate the aura of "civilization and enlightenment" [*bunmei kaika*] domesticity, we may find proof that this narrative is intended as something beyond a simple reminiscence. The child's gaze is summoned up from the past to serve as a lens for magnifying the experience that the 30-year-old Kafū now confronted in the gloomy summer grove of his father's house. To discover the meaning of the darkness of the shiny foliage that so oppressed him on his return from abroad, he needed to recall the household in Kanatomi-chō as cloaked in an ominousness far removed from the world of civilization and enlightenment.

As described in "The Fox," the property in Kanatomi-chō is bifurcated into the newly built house atop high ground that shears off abruptly at a kind of precipice and, down below, the dark grove. The landscape at the base of the precipice is dominated by a dense growth of cryptomeria, described as "standing there in silence, summer and winter, utterly black"; by an ancient, half-decayed willow with a hollow trunk; and by a bottomless, disused well in and around which swarmed small snakes and centipedes. It is in particular this old well with its attendant rotting willow that acts as the stagnant, compacted center of the whole grotesque landscape down below and "the object of terror on the part of the entire household, except for my father." The eerie darkness of night that enfolded this landscape inspired the greatest dread in the narrator as a child and set him to trembling, such that, as he reminisces, "for a long time afterward I could not rid myself of the feeling that the night itself came gushing up from the depths of the old well."[9]

"The Fox" tells of how a cruel punishment is carried out against a fox that emerges as the avatar of this ominous dark landscape. This main plot is set in motion when, early one morning before the chill has worn off, the narrator's father, in the midst of vigorous archery practice—his daily exercise before leaving for work—detects amid the overgrown vegetation down below what appears to be a fox. On this day the hunt, for which the student houseboy Tasaki and the coachman Kisuke are mobilized, comes to naught, and it is not until January of the next year that an occasion arises, with the killing of a chicken in the coop, for a major expedition to quell the fox. This is how the narrator presents his sighting of the foxhunters as, with his father in the lead, they return in triumph, "tramping across the snow":

When the orderly file first appeared tramping across the snow on the top of the precipice, my father in the lead, Tasaki and Kisuke shouldering the pole from which their trophy hung upside down, Seigorō and Yasu bringing up the rear, my first reaction was to conjure up pictures of the loyal masterless samurai [*rōnin*] in procession from my illustrated edition of *Chūshingura* (the tale of the forty-seven masterless samurai), and I thought, "How valiant!" But when they drew near and I looked at the fox that Tasaki thrust under my nose, with the remark, couched in his usual pedantic terms, "And so it goes, young master, 'Coarsely meshed though Heaven's net be, none can slip through,'" at the sight of its cranium that had been smashed by an axe and the warm blood dripping onto the snow from its clenched canine teeth, I involuntarily hid my face behind my mother's soft sleeve.[10]

Having initially found the procession of foxhunters led by his father to be valiant, the narrator cannot help retreating then behind his mother's soft sleeve. His ambivalence toward the various attractions of the feminine and masculine worlds that tug him now this way, now that can, indeed, be seen as one approach to comprehending the structure of "The Fox" as a whole. The "I" who averts his face from the dead body of the fox is the child summoned up from the past who was filled with terror by the bottomless well and dark grove below. The refuges he seeks from his fear and trembling over the dank darkness of this world are the bosom of his nurse and the soft sleeves of his mother's robes. But on a deeper level, this very fear and the strength of his reaction against the repellent darkness convey as well the attractions it holds for him. We could of course chalk these up to the normal human curiosity about what horrifies us, but beyond this, there is unmistakably something latent in his mother's gentleness itself, which has encouraged him in his fear of the night. "I wanted to see something frightening," the narrator recalls. "And the fragile buds of knowledge of the world that I was able to acquire with my halting, tentative questions were constantly being cut back by the sharp edge of my nurse's endless superstitions."[11] This role played by his nurse can certainly be ascribed, it would seem, to his mother as well. Although the terrors of the night and the gentleness of the mother appear to define polar opposites, in reality they are closely intermeshed in a manner not immediately apparent. For the narrator, the whole area at the base of the precipice is forbidden territory where he cannot freely set foot unless accompanied by the gardener Yasu, the fireman Seikichi, or some other adult. In particular, he has been forbidden to approach the area around the old well, where, after heavy rains, the ground will always sink a foot or two and the nearby willow tree has been established through his father's threats as a symbol of punishment. It is his mother, though, who denies the narrator his wish to join the fox-quelling expedition on the grounds that he will catch cold. And in general, his recent New Year's reveling in kite flying aside, he presents himself as a frail child who spends his time playing mother's little helper around the house and poring over illustrated booklets for children. Cloistered as he is within the household on high ground, watched over by mother and nurse alike, it is no wonder that for him the world at the foot of the precipice remains terra incognita, the realm of an ominously dark, thoroughly repellent night.

The brooding landscape below recurs in the narrator's dream: "Not only the old well, but the half-decayed willow standing right next to it appeared again and again, as a threatening presence in my dreams, a profound force of nature that was preordained."[12] The invoking of this "force of nature" makes it clear that what the narrator sees in his dream is no simple reappearance of a scene viewed in a wakeful state; rather, it is something inextricably rooted in the substrata of his consciousness. The deep darkness that settles over the sunken ground below, the jet-black stand of cryptomeria, the bottomless well, the hollowed-out trunk of the willow—all of these images are closely interwoven and point us toward signifiers of a primordial eros defined by "the hollow" and "the abysmal." They are symbols of "the maternal" that lie entangled in the depths of the narrator's mind. Indeed, we can construe them as being closely associated with C. G. Jung's maternal archetype, rooted in a collective unconscious memory. In Kawai Hayao's encapsulation of Jung's theory, he explains the dual nature of the "great mother," the two faces of the "good mother" and "terrible mother," as follows: "In a most fundamental way the maternal principle possesses the dual aspects of death and life: an affirmative aspect of giving birth and nurturing and a negative aspect of devouring all and inflicting death. Individual human mothers too have within them both tendencies. The affirmative aspect is self-evident. The negative can be apprehended as a form of psychologically driving children to their death through an excessively strong embrace that stifles their autonomy. We may take both to be subsumed within a single common function but with two aspects, one tied to life, the other to death."[13] So long as the narrator remains enfolded in his mother's soft sleeves, he is truly a child whose autonomy is stifled. The various stern prohibitions that lurk behind his mother's gentleness and protectiveness emerge within his unconscious as the signifiers of the forbidding dark grove and the eerie abandoned well. Although he is not, of course, aware that his mother's kindness is stifling his natural inclinations toward a boyish vitality, he does harbor a secret desire to free himself from her protectiveness and to seek independence. According to Kawai, the traditional fund of images of the "great mother" remains more deeply entrenched in East Asia than in the West. It was necessary for Kafū, then, on his return from abroad as a free agent, to come to terms with the dual significance of the maternal archetype, with both the loving attachment and the revulsion it engenders, as he became enmeshed again in the dense web of the Japanese family.

In this particular context, it is altogether natural that the role of slaughtering the fox, the spirit incarnate of all that is signified by the realm at the base of the precipice, should fall to the father. Unlike the child heroes who appear in Western mythology, the narrator makes no attempt to participate directly in the quelling of the beast. Arrested as he is in the womb of the maternal, any advancement toward autonomy he achieves only vicariously through his father and surrogate, who pursues so tenaciously the killing of the fox.

The father in "The Fox" is in part portrayed as a hero who descends from the high ground to establish order once and for all amid the threatening chaos below. These exploits are foreshadowed as early as the narrator's opening query, murmured with childlike simplicity, as to how it could have been that his "father had no fear of the old tree that howled in the wind, cried aloud in the rain, and wrapped itself around the night"[14]; and then again in the scene where, right beside the old well that is the very core of the whole tangled landscape, the father practices archery as if reenacting the ancient ritual of exorcizing evil spirits by twanging the string of a longbow. With the episode in which snakes and various arthropods that come wriggling out when the rotten well-curb is knocked down are thrown into a blazing fire, the final act where the fox is hunted down is directly foretold.

How many are the memories, full of loathing and foreboding, that have clung to the realm at the foot of the precipice: musty funguses, the writhing white bellies of insects, the "filthy hand towel" left behind by the thief in the night. If we see in all of these images of dread recalled from the past an anticipation of the fox that is to arrive like a sacrificial beast, as if branded for all to see, then the cruel fate visited on this creature takes on the aura of a symbolic drama that enacts a purification of the chaotic space below and results in the establishment of order. The particular details of the ensuing foxhunt directed by the father assume almost comic proportions, with longbows, guns, axes, men shouldering poles, sulphur and niter acquired from an apothecary for smoking the fox out of his hole. This excess is required for the performance of a large festival drama, in which the participation of all males, except for the narrator, as hunters and killers takes precedence over any sensible balance between the quarry and the forces assembled against it. Likewise, there is effective staging in the blanket of snow over the garden which reminds the narrator of *Chūshingura*, and throws into relief the symbolic meaning of the sacrificial blood.

After the curtain comes down on the scene of the foxhunt, a banquet takes place with fresh-killed chickens (fish being unavailable because of the snow along the river) to accompany the wine. The narrator lies in bed, listening to the uproar of the banquet and pondering the meaning of the grown-ups' slaughter of the fox. "Why did they hate the fox so much?" he wonders. "If it was because it killed a chicken, didn't they themselves go and kill two of them after they'd killed the fox?"[15] Stranger that he is as yet to the symbolic drama that surrounds the killing of the fox, the narrator cannot come to terms with its irrationality. But to us the meaning of his lamenting over the fox's death is clear. For all his superficial celebrating of his father's "heroic" triumph, on a deeper level he has not yet disengaged himself from the seductive attractions of the maternal.[16]

2

"Around that time, in a single series of transactions, my father had bought up three of the properties vacated by former Tokugawa bannermen and housemen which had come on the market and, leaving their woods and gardens intact, built a large new house."[17] So begins "The Fox," with an account of the provenance of Kafū's first home, No. 45 Kanatomi-chō, Koishikawa, which his father Kyū'ichirō had constructed around 1875–76 when, after returning from his studies in America, he first took a position with the Ministry of Education. On the illustrated small-scale map of Koishikawa published by Owariya, we can see that the three former samurai residences (occupied "on loan" from the bakufu) that Kyū'ichirō acquired all at once had belonged to Gotō Katsujirō, Ōta Heiuemon, and Tōyama Hikosaburō (figures 1, 2). Along with many other bureaucrats newly employed by the Meiji government, Kyū'ichirō was one of the "conquerors" who swept up large swatches of what had been the property of the Tokugawa retainers. But the windfall deals made available to new officials when the early Meiji government sold off bakufu properties—1,000 *tsubo* at 10 to 25 yen—were already a thing of the past, and in order to raise the capital to buy his 415 tsubo Kyū'ichirō had to appeal to his relatives.[18]

As far as may be determined by consulting the 5,000:1-scale map issued by the Army Surveying Section (General Staff Office), the new Nagai residence was situated on land that slopes downward from the Koishikawa ridge, on a site where the vertical drop from the high ground, on which the house stood, to the overgrown garden at the bottom of the slope would have been as steep as 10 meters or so. In the immediate environs, beyond the sloping road to Kongōji, a considerable expanse of fields planted with vegetables and tea shrubs stretched out southward in the direction of Takehaya-chō, with houses here and there surrounded by hedges.

On the low-lying land that abutted the Nagais' overgrown garden there was a cluster of small cottages, the vestiges of a residential district called Koishikawa Tomizaka-shinchō, where *chōnin* [townsmen] dwellings had been wedged into this predominantly samurai area.[19] Arrayed still higher up on the ridge above their residence were the roofs of the Dentsūin compound, and they looked down at the precincts of Kongōji. Given this panorama surrounding the eerie realm at the foot of the precipice in "Kitsune," we need to explore further the meaning of the story's setting in the historical context of the transition from Tokugawa to Meiji.

Foreign visitors to *bakumatsu* Edo were unstinting in their praise for the scenic beauties presented by the crossweb of rivers and canals in the low-lying Shitamachi quarters of the city, but they found equally arresting the contours of the Yamanote highlands, a capital amid the woods. The English botanist Robert Fortune, for example, describes the scenery of the Yamanote in this passage: "The views which are obtained from the hills . . . are such as may well challenge comparison with those of any other town in Europe or elsewhere. . . . The beautiful valleys, wooded hills, and quiet lanes fringed with noble trees and evergreen hedges, would be difficult to match in any other part of the world."[20] Yet once the Meiji government went about disposing of the samurai residences that encircled the Yamanote, and the whole "system" that was Edo was dissolved, the "Nature" in the midst of the city, which had hitherto been so prudently managed and tamed, abruptly started to regain its original untrammeled vitality. As such central areas of Shitamachi as Ginza and Nihonbashi were rapidly painted over with the new scenes of "civilization and enlightenment," the Yamanote became defined as an effaced urban space [*fu no toshi kūkan*] within which the earthly remains of Edo continued to be on display. Apart from some places refashioned into government offices and military stations, the former samurai residences with their imposing phalanxes of turreted gates and lacquered tile walls gave way to ruined gardens with dilapidated remnants of mansions standing amid a wilderness of grasses and weeds. Moreover, in accordance with a policy devised in 1869 by the governor of Tokyo, Ōki Takatō, aimed at both increasing productivity and giving employment to the poor, many plots of land vacated on the demise of samurai residences were turned over to the cultivation of tea shrubs and mulberry trees, which soon came to blanket whole areas. It is recorded that in Aoyama 159,000 tsubo were converted into farmland, in Koishikawa, 139,000, and in

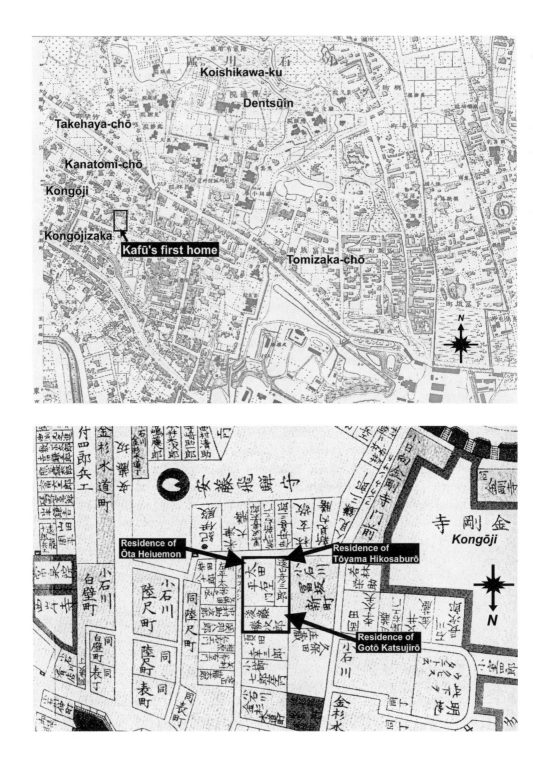

Azabu, 120,000. There is, then, nothing hyperbolic about Narushima Ryū-hoku's lament (in the preface to the second edition of *Ryūkyō shinshi*) that "since the Tokugawa clan went into exile, within the confines of Tokyo many are the mansions with their proud vermilion gates and their powder-white walls, which have been transformed into gardens of tea and mulberry." There is this testimony from Kanbara Ariake (born in 1875):

> Up until 1887 Tokyo continued to be deeply imbued with the atmosphere of late Tokugawa Edo, though with marked signs of decay; and yet the aftermath of the shock sustained at the moment of the Restoration also remained apparent, such that, in contrast with the various establishments of "civilization and enlightenment," there was a conspicuous aura of wilderness all around the city. This was especially true of the Yamanote, where plantations of mulberry had been laid out on the ruins of the residences of the Tokugawa bannermen and their ilk. . . . Indeed, one could say that in this period Tokyo's Yamanote was no different from a stretch of countryside covered with tall grasses. The women and children of Shitamachi said that foxes showed up there all the time, and they would refuse to spend the night in those parts of the city.[21]

The landscape down below in "The Fox" that both enchants and frightens the narrator is not only the maternal archetype, then, but the brooding Nature that pullulates out from the remains of Edo space. We may find analogues for the profound darkness that surrounds the family's pursuit of their "enlightened" lifestyle in Kobayashi Kiyochika's (1847–1915) print series *Illustrations of Famous Places in Edo*, such as his rendering of *Shinbashi Station* [see figure 3 in ch. 2, this volume], in which the huge stone edifices of the new era are enveloped in nocturnal darkness, or his *Kaiunbashi* [figure 1 in ch. 2], where the faux European architecture of the First National Bank is imprisoned under crepuscular, snow-laden clouds. In "The Fox," the memories of the old order latent in the dark remnants of Edo space encircling the seats of the new civilization are conjured up concretely in the form of various traditions centered on the belief that this animal is an emissary of the god Inari:

(Opposite, above) Figure 1. Kafū's childhood home. "One-Five-Thousandth Scale Map of Tokyo" by the General Staff Office of the Army Surveying Section, 1883. Courtesy Chikuma Shobō, 1982

(Below) Figure 2. Kafū's childhood home (former samurai residences). Illustrated small-scale map of Koishikawa, 1957. Courtesy Chikuma Shobō, 1982

O-Etsu the cook, who to begin with was on bad terms with Tasaki, was country-bred and full of superstitions. With a stricken look on her face she warned of the ill fortune that would befall the household if the fox, to which she referred in the most respectful terms, were to be killed. Tasaki rejoined dismissively that it was not for a cook to stick her nose into a matter on which the master had been pleased to issue a firm order. Puffing out her red cheeks, O-Etsu, in concert with the nurse, delivered for my benefit a detailed explanation of such things as fox possession, fox curses, foxes taking on human guise, the miracles wrought by the fox-god enshrined at the Takuzō Inari behind the Dentsūin. I associated all of this with "the marvelous *kokkuri*" [a device akin to a Ouija board] that was all the rage at that time, and part of me was on the side of the stalwart Tasaki, whom I wanted to join in the foxhunt, but part of me wondered if there might not after all be such fantastic things in this world.[22]

In this debate over the appearance of the fox in which they vied to demonstrate their loyalty to the family, the student houseboy Tasaki and the cook O-Etsu represent the opposing but complementary views on this subject held by men and women. All of the men who take part in the foxhunt, Tasaki first and foremost, readily submit to the father's lucid pronouncements. For the civilizing impulse that runs through early Meiji thought, which sought to banish as so much unwanted baggage from the past all manner of popular beliefs, and chief among them those concerning the miraculous powers of the fox, has by now reached the level of the common people. (In Katō Yūichi's "Bunmei kaika," a work that was drawn on by educators as a kind of scriptural source for their sermons, it is set forth that "Henceforth we must all embrace civilization and expose for what they are such notions as those that hold that foxes change themselves into human form.")[23] At the same time, the nurse and the narrator's mother, not to mention the cook O-Etsu, nurture a belief in the fox's supernatural power as part of their philosophy of everyday life. They do so because the traditional fear and awe of the fox has most often been linked to the phenomenon of women's susceptibility to possession by foxes, whose main targets have always been said to be women.

According to the classification of Miyata Noboru, the Edo cult of fox can be divided into five types: fox as an agricultural fertility god; as enshrined within sacred space; as the manifestation of local spirits; as household god; and as a possessing spirit.[24] In the late Edo it was the two last-named types that flourished with new vigor as particularly ambitious men from the lower ranks of samurai installed Inari as their household god in the hopes of securing superhuman intervention in their undertakings, and as small shrines were put up in various places out of gratitude for the dispelling of fox possessions. Had it been under the old order that the fox appeared on the narrator's property, which was after all made up of proper samurai residences, quite possibly it would have led to the installation of Inari as a household god, and indeed his mother and nurse do not neglect to put out the traditional offering of fried tofu after the first sighting. So long as the traditional belief in foxes as the emissaries of Inari held sway, whatever place they showed themselves in became defined as both sacred space and accursed ground and their appearance as a propitious moment for a new enshrining of Inari. Even absent any adherence to such traditions rooted in the Inari cult per se, with its deterministic implications, the ubiquitous shrines to Inari throughout the city of Edo served to mark, in a fragmented, far-flung way, places rendered special by the presence of local spirits, whose protection over the surrounding spaces was deployed through this form of propitiation and hence the old Edo adage "Three things we never lack are shops named Iseya, Inari shrines, and dog shit." These shrines that sought to make palpable the presence of local spirits combined with a great variety of shrines to evil (though often mainly erotic) spirits to create a grid of countless nodes over the whole expanse of Edo. Naturally, with the spread of "civilization and enlightenment" rationalism, the meanings of this grid became ever more attenuated, and the places marked by it gradually changed to undifferentiated secular space.[25]

Formerly regarded as the messenger of local guardian deities, feared and held in awe for its miraculous powers, the fox has here been reduced to a pathetic scapegoat with only the power to mobilize the men who enjoy the father's patronage. The fox's lowly estate is aptly summed up in a pithy comment made by Seigorō of the fire brigade on hearing that a chicken has been devoured: "Lord man has lost his yearly stipend, too—can't get a whiff of that fried tofu anymore, so that's why he's come sniffing around here."[26] The effect of this little sally clearly depends on a subtext involving the image of many former bakufu retainers who, with the loss of their hereditary stipends, have been driven into penury. It contributes to a recurring trope, other instances of which include news of the suicide of one of the slum dwellers down below who had once been a palanquin-bearer and gossip about a former caterer to the Mito household who has gone bankrupt, that can be read in this context as portents of the impending extermination of the fox.

The final hunting down one snowy day in January by the men armed with sulphur and niter is presented as a direct response to, and just retribution for, the fox's devouring of a chicken snatched from the coop. The ambiguous polyvalence of the fox as a creature that inhabits the space below, while the chickens are kept on the high ground, seals its fate as an animal fit for sacrifice. The opposition between domestic and wild animals can be inserted into an array of binarisms that include civilization and nature, Tokyo space and Edo space, masculine sphere and feminine sphere.

Modern techniques of poultry raising were incubated at the close of the Edo period in Owari-han, where there was a concerted movement to encourage the raising of chickens among samurai households. Around 1882–83, which coincides with the time of our story's events, this novel upper-class practice of one form of animal husbandry spread throughout much of the nation, and in Tokyo and Yokohama there was a great vogue for keeping coops of such exotic varieties as Brahma, Cochin, and Leghorn. It is recorded that the first exhibit of such hitherto unknown types of chicken took place in 1884, as part of the seventh annual livestock competition held by the Imperial Japanese Agricultural Society. The "modest chicken coop" that in "The Fox" is located out behind the kitchen next to the new well can be viewed as one of the small fruits of government policies devised by the Home Ministry for stimulating new agricultural productivity. Kafū's father Kyū'ichirō was, of course, both a native of Owari-han and currently a high official in the Nutrition Bureau of the Home Ministry.[27] (Although not mentioned in "The Fox," next to this new well at the house in Kanatomi-chō there was also apparently a large ceramic water filter that had been imported from England.)[28]

Having first seen in the final act of the foxhunt a ritual murder directed against the archetypal "maternal" lurking in the realm below the precipice, we can now view it in a historical perspective as also a symbolic drama in which brooding memories stored up in an Edo space are eradicated by the utilitarianism and rationalism of "civilization and enlightenment." The role assigned to the narrator's father in this drama is to restore order in the world below the precipice, which has loomed up before the son's eyes as a realm of complete chaos enveloped in the dark grove, and in so doing to render one-dimensional what has been full of polyvalent ambiguity. Needless to say, the narrator, who in the story hides his face behind his mother's soft sleeve, signifies Kafū himself, who at the time he wrote "The Fox" had already begun to seek escape from the masculine world of "civilization and enlightenment" that encompassed his father. Here is a prelude to his life-long project of recovering concrete memories of an Edo space suffused with the maternal archetype.[29]

Notes

1 Maeda's essay first appeared in *Yoshida Seiichi hakase koki kinen: Nihon no kindai bungaku sakka to sakuhin* (Kadokawa shoten, 1978). The text for this transla-

tion is from Maeda Ai, *Toshi kūkan no naka no bungaku* (Chikuma Shobō, 1982), 125–140.

2 Nagai Kafū, "Danchōtei sekitoku," in *Kafū zenshū* (Iwanami Shoten, 1965), 25:35.

3 Isoda Kōichi, *Nagai Kafū* (Kōdansha, 1979), 67. (M)

4 Sakagami Hirokazu comments, "One could say that Kafū's brooding thoughts on his return to Japan, when the way before him failed to emerge with any clarity, elicited the dark, frightening images of childhood which are found in 'Kitsune.'" See Sakagami Hirokazu, *Nagai Kafū shū*, in *Nihon kindai bungaku taikei* (Kadokawa Shoten, 1970), supplementary notes. (M)

5 Nagai Kafū, "Kangokusho no ura," in *Nagai Kafū zenshū* (Iwanami Shoten, 1965), 4:59. (M)

6 Nagai Kafū, "Dentsūin," in *Nagai Kafū zenshū* (1963), 5:473.

7 Nagai Kafū, "Kitsune," in *Nagai Kafū zenshū* (1964), 4:94.

8 *Tōkyō meisho zue* (Tōyōdō, 1908; facsimile ed., Mutsumi Shobō, 1968), 11–15. (M)

9 Kafū, "Kitsune," 4:96–98.

10 Ibid., 4:109.

11 Ibid., 4:98.

12 Ibid.

13 Kawai Hayao, *Mukashibanashi no shinsō* (Fukuinkan Shoten, 1977). (M)

14 Kafū, "Kitsune," 4:96.

15 Ibid., 4:110.

16 According to Carl Jung's disciple Erich Neumann, the layers of awareness wherein "consciousness is identified with the figure of the male hero, while the devouring unconscious identified with the figure of the female monster" can be discerned from analyses of symbolism in statuary and art. Erich Neumann, *The Great Mother: An Analysis of the Archetype*, trans. Ralph Manheim (Princeton: Princeton University Press, 1955). (M)

17 Kafū, "Kitsune," 4:94.

18 Akiba Tarō, *Kōshō Nagai Kafū* (Iwanami Shoten, 1966). (M)

19 Koishikawa Kanatomi-chō resulted from the annexation of the formerly detached neighborhood of Koishikawa Suidō-chō, and Koishikawa Tomisaka-shinchō, Kohinata Kongōji-mae, the former estates of the bakufu officials and shogunal retainers across from Tafukuin, and temple property of the area. The current name was given to these lands in the early Meiji period, and the word *kanatomi* was the abbreviated form of the former name for the neighborhood, Kanasugi Tomisaka. From *Tōkyō meisho zue*, section on the Koishikawa district. (M)

20 Robert Fortune, *Yedo and Pekin: A Narrative of a Journey to the Capitals of Japan and China* (London: J. Murray, 1863), 202. (M)

21 Maeda gives no specific citations for his quotations from Narushima Ryūhoku or Kanbara Ariake. But he does add in a footnote the following "impressionistic description of the earthly remains of Edo space" in Natsume Sōseki's *Garasudo no naka*: "And yet when one climbed up the palisade slope, passed by the watchtower of the Sakai residence and arrived on the straight road that runs for some

six hundred meters until it reaches Teramachi, the area would be enshrouded in a sylvan dusk even in the middle of the day, and the skies appeared dark as if permanently clouded over. Along the embankment there stood numerous large trees, each as much as two or three armfuls in circumference, and into every open space among them had grown a formidable thicket of bamboo, such that it seemed unlikely there could be a single moment there when one could see the light of day." See *Natsume Sōseki zenshū* (Iwanami Shoten, 1968), 8:460. (M)

22 Kafū, "Kitsune," 4:100.

23 Katō Yūichi, "Bunmei kaika," in *Meiji bunka zenshū* (Nihon Hyōronsha, 1967), 24:20.

24 Nishiyama Matsunosuke, ed., *Edo chōnin no kenkyū* (Yoshikawa Kobunkan, 1973), 2:254–255. (M)

25 Kafū's father bought the empty lots at the foot of the bluff because it was not possible to build tenement houses for rental on that location. He kept hoping that tract of slum housing in what was formerly Tomisaka shinchō would get cleared away. What we observe here is a very utilitarian and practical logic of containment [*kakoikomu*]. (M)

26 Kafū, "Kitsune," 4:106.

27 According to the research of Sugaya Hiromi on the encyclopedia published by the Ministry of Education in 1876, based on Chambers's encyclopedia, Nagai Kyū'ichirō was responsible for the section on "pigs, rabbits, and edible and pet birds." *Shūji oyobi kabun no kenkyū* (Kyōiku Shuppan Sentaa, 1978). (M)

28 *Kafū zenshū* (1972), 17:33.

29 Isoda Kōichi quotes this comment by the fireman Seigorō: "If we follow the fox's tracks in the snow, they'll take us straight to his Shinoda Woods den" and observes that one subtext in "Kitsune" is the legend of "the white fox of Shinoda Woods" with its maternal symbolism (*Nagai Kafū*, 27–28). If we accept this, it follows that the narrator, with his sympathy for the dead fox, assumes the role of Abe no Seimei (921–1005), who in the legend yearns for the fox. (M) In this legend, usually referred to as "the legend of the Kudzu leaves," his own mother transformed herself into human guise and formed a temporary union of which Abe was the issue.

4. Their Time as Children: A Study of

Higuchi Ichiyō's *Growing Up* (*Takekurabe*)

(Kodomo tachi no jikan)

TRANSLATED BY EDWARD FOWLER

This essay features the novella-length *Takekurabe* (Growing Up, 1895–96), widely regarded as the masterwork of Higuchi Ichiyō (1872–1896) and written near the end of Ichiyō's brief career.[1] The story depicts the lives of several young boys and girls who reside in Daionjimae, a neighborhood right outside the Yoshiwara, the famed licensed quarter. They enter into adolescence against the backdrop of two neighborhood festivals: the Senzoku Shrine summer festival and the Ōtori Shrine Cock's Fair (Tori no Ichi) in early winter. Chōkichi, son of a construction crew fore-man and leader of the "Backstreet Gang," plans to ambush Shōta, the grandson of a moneylender and leader of the "Main Street Gang," on the night of the Sen-zoku Shrine summer festival. His rival never shows, however, and in the fracas that follows, Sangorō, one of Shōta's followers, gets beat up, and Midori, another of Shōta's allies whose family works for Daikokuya, a Yoshiwara brothel, is struck on the forehead by Chōkichi's muddy sandal. Midori quits school the day after the festival. For Midori, who believes that there are no rivals among classmates, the fact that one of them, Nobuyuki, the son of a temple priest whom she looks up to, could be in league with Chōkichi comes as a great shock. The shy, retiring No-buyuki, meanwhile, frustrated by the crass materialism of his parents and sister, is too bashful to cope with the gaze of the flashy, vivacious, and very attractive Midori. Without ever making any real contact, the two go their separate ways: Nobuyuki to a seminary to prepare for the priesthood, Midori to the brothel, to become a courtesan.[2]

1

Sealed within Higuchi Ichiyō's *Takekurabe* (Growing Up) is the realm of children's time, which we adults can never again relive. Under the guidance of Nobuyuki and Midori, we reel in the hours each character spends as a child in the same way that we retrieve lost memories, frame by frame, when pouring over the faded images of an old photo album. Nobuyuki and Midori are not merely children of Meiji; they are the images of our original selves—we who were, of course, also children, once upon a time.

As symbols of unspoiled innocence, and as resisters of a technologized world, children hold manifold significance for contemporary life. We adults, formerly heaping expectations on children as "future adults" and casting an oppressive and vigilant eye on them, are now reexamining our own warped world and attempting to rectify it through a recovery of the child's gaze. This may be taken as a kind of atonement for our having usurped children's places of play, one after another, and thereby stripping children of their life force. In this age of ludic poverty, we adults have taken a more lenient attitude toward the role of play in children's lives. It was Huizinga who in *Homo Ludens* first sought to legitimize the function and mythical significance of play in an effort to de-emphasize the utility and the value of labor—remnants of the nineteenth-century ethos—and to restore the originary richness of life. The recent trend toward greater leniency also indicates an effort to restore the child's worldview [*kodomo no ronri*], which was heretofore wholly shut out by the adult's. In other words, as our freedom to *act* becomes an ever more elusive goal, we have taken to peering into the child's domain, which has come to symbolize the freedom to *escape*. The journey back into children's time, together with the desire to return to nature, forms an illusory axis that propels our detachment from modern industrial society; at the same time, it provides an indispensable vantage point from which we can see through life's barrenness lurking in the shadow of our daily affairs.

This new conception of *Growing Up* as distilled from the above context presents a nice analogy with the two *Alice* books, also products of the late nineteenth century. In *Some Versions of Pastoral*, William Empson argues that "the essential idea behind the books is a shift onto the child . . . of the obscure tradition of pastoral."³ We discern a similarly pastoral theme, *pace* Empson, in the child's world depicted in *Growing Up*. What drew Lewis Carroll into his odd infatuation with little girls, as well as drove him to dissolute fantasies of wanderings about a world on the far side of a mirror and through a wondrous, underground land, was his deep hatred of the prosaic, vulgar bourgeois class, which had become such a pervasive force during the Victorian era. The bourgeoisie's utilitarian worldview was exalted by the Meiji leadership as an "enlightened" philosophy of culture and civilization. Mill's and Spencer's popularity in Japan followed right on the heels of their popularity in England. Samuel Smiles's *Self-Help* is the most typical of those children's books that adapted their message of utilitarianism and pragmatism to the biographical format; from the time it was first published in 1859, six years before *Alice in Wonderland*, until the century's end, it went through forty-nine printings. England's young people, who were allowed to play with Alice in a world of fantasy, would succumb in time to the onslaught of Smiles's pious lectures. The virtues of self-refinement and diligence touted in *Self-Help*, which promised steady success, were the lowest common denominator for the "good children" on whom adults in the Victorian era placed their hopes. *Self-Help* was introduced to Japan in 1870, or the third year of Meiji, through Nakamura Masanao's (Keiu's) celebrated translation *Tales of Success in Western Nations* [*Saikoku risshi hen*] and it became the Meiji period's best-selling book. It is scarcely necessary to mention the impact this book had on the children of Meiji, with its advocacy of *risshin shusse* [personal advancement]. One can discern a parallel between the Alice books and *Takekurabe* in their attempt to retrieve the original world of children at a time when the likes of Smiles were thrusting the role of "future adults" on the children of England and Japan; moreover, if Alice assumes the role of the "child as critic" when she is flung into a nonsensical world that overturned the mores of the Victorian era, then we can say that Midori acts out the role of the "child as merrymaker," who overturns the Meiji ideal of young people diligently struggling to succeed in the world of risshin shusse.

2

One very important cause championed by juvenile literature, beginning with Iwaya Sazanami's *Koganemaru*,[4] was the instilling in children of an awareness of their role as the succeeding generation of the young Meiji state. Thus, *Shōkokumin* [Little citizens], a magazine for primary school-age children first published in 1889, would in its inaugural issue address its readers: "To our young children, who are *the future citizens of Japan*" (emphasis in original). Likewise, Hakubunkan would head the advertisement for its Boys' Literature series, which *Koganemaru* led off in 1891, with the following appeal: "Boys are the flowers of life; and when they bear fruit, they become the bedrock of Japan."[5] It goes without saying that this deliberate act of positioning children beneath the halo of nationalistic consciousness took place at a time when the Meiji state was being established symbolically through the promulgation of the Imperial Constitution and the Imperial Rescript on Education. Juvenile literature of the Meiji 20s (1887–96) thus appeared on the scene as a collaborator fully affirming the state's nationalistic education policies, the course of which was set by Mori Arinori.[6]

Biographies and histories were deemed the most useful genres of early juvenile literature for rearing talented prospects in service to the state. This meant, however, that story content with the kind of literary and emotional substance that developed children's sensibilities and imagination would be all but passed over in silence. Among the thirty-two volumes in the Haku-bunkan Boys' Literature series (1891–96), for example, were eighteen volumes of historical and biographical narratives (both fiction and nonfiction); eleven volumes of boys' fiction; and a mere three volumes of fairy tales, including Sazanami's *Koganemaru*. It was expected that children would extract from histories and biographies the role models needed for making the proper choices in life, and to obtain from them the resources for self-promotion. These adults-in-waiting were necessarily cognizant of the rules governing the real world; to forget themselves in a world of fantasies amounted to a waste of their precious time on the road to growing up. The following words of Kōda Rohan, who contributed two volumes to the Boys' Literature series, *Ninomiya Sontokuō* [The venerable Ninomiya Sontoku, 1891] and *Nichiren Shōnin* (1894), epitomize the stance adopted by all writers who penned histories in this series: "Young men—you who brighten the future with your rising ambitions—do not peruse the likes of *Journey to the West*, a wildly nonsensical story that is but a relic of a dark age in the distant past; read instead books that sport no fantasy, ones about great and wise men whose glorious lives have lit up generation after generation. Ascertain how those ancient men worked to accomplish their goals; study whom they colored with the light of their example. Learn from them and marvel; consider their work and debate their merits. Can such texts possibly be meant only for entertainment?"[7]

The high respect paid to *fact* in histories and biographies unquestionably had a deleterious impact on the domain of the fairy tale. Blatant allegory and shallow moralizing attached a lead weight to flights of the imagination. Sazanami's *Koganemaru*, Ozaki Kōyō's *The Two Men Named Mukusuke* [*Ninin Mukusuke*, 1891], and Kawakami Bizan's *Treasure Mountain* [*Takara no yama*, 1891] were the three texts classified as fairy tales in the Boys' Literature series; *The Two Men Named Mukusuke*, however, was an adaptation of a tale by Hans Christian Andersen,[8] and *Treasure Mountain* was an allegorical tale of ambition. That leaves only *Koganemaru* as a work worthy of the name "original story." And yet, as Sazanami himself confesses, *Koganemaru* takes its plot from Goethe's *Reineke Fuchs* and Bakin's *Hakkenden*.[9] And the weakness of its fictive imagination is unerringly pointed out in a contemporary review, which characterizes the work as follows: "Reading Sazanami's *Koganemaru*, I could see that the author was attempting to put himself in the position of children; but I cannot write my criticism from the same perspective. The work is a straight adaptation of a feudal-period revenge tale into a fable about monkeys and cats."[10] Sazanami, who coined the phrase *shōnen bungaku* [boys' literature] as a translation for *Jugendschrift*, was himself very likely aware of the qualitative difference between that term and *Märchen*.

Early juvenile literature that lured children without prurient interest into the adventure-rich world of fantasy included such late Edo picture books as *The Tale of Princess Shiranui* [*Shiranui monogatari*, 1849–85] and *Jiraiya* (1839–68), Jules Verne's science fiction novels, and political novels such as *Admirable Tales of Statecraft* [*Keikoku bidan*, 1883–84] and *Chance Encounters with Beautiful Women* [*Kajin no kigū*, 1885–97].[11] Children broadened their horizons by snapping up all the adult reading matter within their grasp. Terada Torahiko, for example, who was born in 1878, declared that the illustrated *Journey to the West*, which Rohan had dismissed as a "relic [from] . . . the distant past," made him "yearn for the world of fantasy and supernatural powers," while Verne's *Twenty Thousand Leagues under the Sea* taught him "the astonishing potential that lay in harnessing nature in the real world."[12]

Tanizaki Jun'ichirō, who was born in 1886, devotes a passage in his *Memoir of Early Childhood* [*Yōshō jidai*] to reminiscences about his primary school teacher's recitation of *Admirable Tales of Statecraft*: "This was the very first time our eyes were opened to the world of the West, to lands we had never heard of before. The name of every place and every person seemed strange and wondrous, and we hung on every word the teacher recited with boundless curiosity."[13] Both Terada and Tanizaki were avid readers of the Boys' Literature series as well, but *Keikoku bidan* and the works of Verne provided an entirely different kind of excitement.

Surely there were not a few Meiji juvenile literature writers who, before taking up their pens for the Hakubunkan Boys' Literature series and other anthologies, were absorbed in Yano Ryūkei's *Keikoku bidan* and Verne's science fiction novels, not to mention late Edo picture books, in their youths. Yet rather than spinning their own reading experiences into myriad tales of fantasy and adventure, they were loyal to their mission as transmitters of edifying material to the next generation of children. Books that offered young people guidance and opened the door to the world of adults, rather than ones that provided them with pleasant diversions during their childhood, were chosen as the models for juvenile literature. The most celebrated of these models was Nakamura Masanao's *Saikoku risshihen*.

In 1890, the year before the publication of *Koganemaru*, Kōda Rohan penned a short story for boys entitled "The Forging of Young Tetsuzō" [Tetsuzō tan], the first work of boys' literature by an author with definite opinions about the genre. The story's protagonist, a young boy named Tetsuzō, is reduced to begging in order to survive after his day-laborer father becomes ill. Shamed by the ridicule of his classmates, he lets out a half-crazed groan: "If Providence will not kill me, then let it use me in its service; let it find me work!"[14] An old scholar from the Yanaka district of Tokyo (modeled after Nakamura Masanao) takes pity on him and offers him a copy of Samuel Smiles's *Self-Help* and a few coins, whereupon the boy goes on to greet the New Year having become "a man worthy of the name."[15] The poor young Tetsuzō, motivated by a single book to cultivate his ambitions, is a stereotype that appears repeatedly in Meiji juvenile literature. Kunikida Doppo's "An Extraordinarily Ordinary Man" ["Hiboon naru bonjin," 1903] depicts a youth from a fallen samurai family who, inspired by the Japanese translation of *Self-Help*, goes on to carve out his own life course.[16]

Kaoru, the young protagonist in Hara Hōitsuan's narrative *The New Year* [*Shinnen*, 1892], is the same type as Tetsuzō in "The Forging of Young Tetsuzō." An orphan who supports himself delivering newspapers, Kaoru makes the following New Year's resolution: "Benjamin Franklin, the great inventor and statesman from the United States, wrote and published his own newspaper, and then walked the streets selling it. There is no fundamental difference between occupations. It is the same with the prime minister or myself—we all apply ourselves similarly to our work. I have no reason to feel ashamed. Those lazy fellows who do nothing but play—it is they who ought to be ashamed of themselves!"[17] Having silently conveyed New Year greetings to the nation's police, to his fellow newspaper boys, and to Japanese working abroad, Kaoru buys some rice cakes and is about to celebrate in the traditional manner when a young girl pays him a visit. She has brought a lovely color print she made in payment for a doll that Kaoru gave her the previous year. The girl supports herself by making paint pigments, and Kaoru, moved, hosts a modest, three-person New Year's feast for her and her grandmother. Yet what is notable about this story is the boy's total incomprehension of the meaning of "play," as evidenced by the words "Why do girls want silly things like dolls so much?"[18] He is moved less by the beauty of the girl's print than by the fact that it is the product of her job doing piecework. Lurking in the shadow of his self-reliant spirit is a somewhat vulgar utilitarianism, developed at the cost of a finer sensibility that can appreciate beautiful things and the pleasure of playing.

As unrealistic as this image may have been—that of children who, like

Tetsuzō in "The Forging of Young Tetsuzō" and Kaoru in "The New Year," had their innocent spirits suppressed and were prematurely socialized—it is precisely what the adults in the Meiji state expected. In the sixth episode of *The Character of Contemporary Boys* [*Tōsei shōnen katagi*, 1892], Iwaya Sazanami narrates the story of a young boy who is chosen to deliver a formal response to the recitation of the Imperial Rescript on Education during the New Year's ceremony at school. Despite being dressed in shoddy garb, the boy is confident: "Appearances don't matter, it's what's inside a person that counts. I may be of low status, but I'll be victorious in my studies!"[19] No doubt the following passage from the Imperial Rescript was ringing in the back of Sazanami's head when he wrote this story: "Bear yourselves in modesty and moderation; extend your benevolence to all; pursue learning and cultivate arts, and thereby develop intellectual faculties and perfect moral powers."[20]

This image of the frugal, diligent youth found its historical model, needless to say, in Ninomiya Sontoku. This is how Kōda Rohan begins his *Ninomiya Sontokuō* (1894), which appeared in the Boys' Literature series: "Anyone who gets up at will and sleeps at will, who eats and dresses without purpose, who accomplishes nothing, is not far removed from a beast and by no means worthy of our respect. Admirable is he who studies and cultivates his knowledge. Admirable as well is he who succeeds in his work. More admirable still is he who strives to attain the Way. Most admirable of all is he who possesses sincerity and conducts himself virtuously."[21] Elementary school education in the Meiji period, through songs and visual symbols, did not fail to etch in the hearts of young children the Ninomiya Kinjirō (Sontoku's childhood name) who "studie[d] and cultivate[d] his knowledge" and who "succeed[ed] in his work." This is the image conveyed in the popular song "Ninomiya Sontoku" by Kuwata Shunpū: "Rising early in the morn/he chops wood in the hills/and weaves straw sandals/he is never without his book/late into the night/or while strolling along a path."[22] If one is allowed to replace *Great learning* [*Daigaku*],[23] the book that Kinjirō carries about with him, with Smiles' *Self-Help*, what we have is a most ingenious version of "The Protestant Ethic and the Spirit of Capitalism" Japanese style. In *The Oral Tradition, the Written Word, and the Screen Image*, David Riesman, commenting on the complex connection between Protestantism and print culture, cites the beginning of *The Pilgrim's Progress*. Bunyan's hero, Christian, sets off on a long journey to seek the Kingdom of God looking very much like Kinjirō: "a book in his hand, and a great burden upon his back."[24] The book that Christian carries is, of course, the Bible, and it is a sure sign that he has been chosen by God. Insofar as Smiles's *Self-Help*, in which divine salvation is replaced by worldly success, is imbued with the Protestant tradition, the meaning of this coincidence transcends pure chance. Kinjirō's image, despite its traditional appearance, unquestionably aspires toward modernity at a deeper level. The chopped wood strapped to his back symbolizes the fetters of communal village life, and the book he holds symbolizes the knowledge that promises liberation from these fetters.

The energy that drove Japan's modernization was continually reproduced by the provincial village communities and rechanneled into the major urban centers. Talented young men from the villages would leave their homes, lured by the prospect of personal advancement, and converge on the cities. They were the ones, to borrow Yanagita Kunio's phrase, with "the power to break away from the pack" [*gun o nuku chikara*].[25] Needless to say, the Imperial Rescript on Education (1890) attempted to legitimize this trend through the fiction of "the teaching bequeathed by Our Imperial Ancestors"[26] and through the character of the emperor, brilliantly melding the village community's "pristine morals" [*junpū bizoku*], which formed the base of the imperial state, with the abstemious virtues that promised personal advancement for the chosen few who proceeded to ascend the social ladder from that base to the very apex of the imperial state. Until the end of the war, statues of Ninomiya Kinjirō and detached shrines [*hōanden*, which housed the emperor's portrait and the Imperial Rescript on Education] were erected opposite each other in elementary schoolyards—a configuration that neatly reproduced the symbolic structure illustrated above.

3

The children in *Takekurabe* inhabit a realm that is completely at odds with the one occupied by the frugal, diligent boys in juvenile literature who are modeled after Ninomiya Kinjirō. No child in *Takekurabe* other than Nobuyuki appears devoted to his studies, nor does anyone have the ambition to venture into a life that transcends the diminutive world shaped by the Yoshiwara and Daionjimae (the fictional neighborhood in *Takekurabe* set just outside the licensed quarter). The old, plebeian Shitamachi district lacked from the start any stimuli that fostered dreams of personal advancement for these characters, who, like children before the Restoration, never question the logic of inheriting their families' professions and positions in society. (Note how the characters are labeled by their parents' social status or occupations: "Shōta of the Tanakaya"; "Nobuyuki of Ryūgeji"; "Chōkichi, the Boss's son," etc.) This is how Kaburagi Kiyokata, a native of Tokyo's Tsukiji district, recalls the Shitamachi child's ethos: "Unlike today's children, the children of [early

Meiji] devoted all their energies to play, and the Shitamachi townspeople, who were mostly merchants and craftsmen, didn't care a whit about political goings-on either in the shogun's capital or the emperor's capital. We didn't know anything about the human race. In fact, we didn't know a thing about the Yamanote district across town. You might even go so far as to say we didn't know that the place we lived in was called 'Shitamachi.'"[27] This extremely narrow field of vision is applicable as well to the children in *Takekurabe*.

It is Shōta of the Tanakaya, of all the children in *Takekurabe*, who most desires to enter the world of grown-ups. "I'll be an adult soon, too, you know. I'm going to wear a square-sleeved topcoat like the one that the Kabataya shopkeeper wears. I'll get out the gold watch that Grandma has saved for me, and have a ring made to order, and start smoking cigarettes. As for footwear, let's see now, what would be good? I like sandals better than clogs. Mine would have three-layered soles and satin thongs. Wouldn't I look smashing!"[28] Shōta's all too simple vision of the future immediately earns Midori's sarcasm; yet the image of the young shopkeeper conjured up by this outfit—square-sleeved topcoat, gold watch, ring, cigarettes, sandals—is so self-assured that it is comic. Shōta is indeed naïve; he can envision himself as an adult only by means of this montage of popular images. Yet that very naïveté cruelly exposes his powerlessness and stunted sensibility. We are reminded of the parody-laden verses of "Shoseibushi":

Shosei shosei to	"Houseboy, houseboy"—
Keibetsu suru na	Don't call me that:
Ie e kaereba	When I go home
Waka danna	I'm the "young master."
Kimi boku shikkei de	Don't take your leave
Wakarecha narumai	On such friendly terms—
Waka danna	He's the "young master."[29]

What about the case of Nobuyuki, regarded by his classmates as a "serious student" who is nonetheless "accepted by his peers?"[30] His academic ability does lend him a cachet that is useful in his dealings with the bully Chōkichi. For Nobuyuki, however, whose fate, it has already been determined, is to "enter a certain seminary"[31] as the future head priest of Ryūgeji, academic ability turns out *not* to be the crucial step toward securing personal advancement, as it was commonly thought to be in Meiji times. Moreover, Ichiyō depicts Nobuyuki as a gloomy, introverted boy—a far cry from the ambitious Meiji youth whose virtue was a confident self-reliance. There is of course no possibility that his sister Ohana will wed an adopted husband who would take over the temple in order that he might become independent. Nobuyuki's outstanding performance at school merely testifies to his status as a priest's son and the heir of Ryūgeji.

In the hermetic world of Daionjimae, "Men are no more useful than a mongrel sniffing about a rubbish heap"; here "only the women have any chance of getting ahead."[32] Midori, then, fated as she is to be thrust into the world of prostitution, is the child on whom the neighborhood places its highest expectations. This male-female role reversal is a dark satire directed at the frugal and diligent boys of ambition—the "good children" on whom the Meiji state rested its hopes.

The children in *Takekurabe* are depicted in every aspect of play.[33] One has only to count all the amusements and toys appearing in the story to recognize this fact: *chaban* [skits], *kodomo mikoshi* [children's portable shrine], *gentō* [magic lantern], *tōrō nagashi* [sending Obon lanterns afloat on the river], *nishikie* [color prints], *renge no hana* [wildflower rings], *chie no ita* [tangrams], *jūroku musashi* [a game like Chinese checkers], *kishago hajiki* [a game like marbles, played with periwinkle shells], *anesama ningyō* [bridal dolls]. It is children's pastimes that enliven the forlorn alleyways and the dismal, marshy fields of Daionjimae. Here the children, liberated from schoolwork, spend their free hours. It is precisely because they are shut out from a bright future that they perforce enjoy this brief period of freedom, before being herded off into the adult world.[34]

It need hardly be added that the children's play space falls within the shadow of that notorious playground for adults: the Yoshiwara. Children are infected by the merriment that pervades the licensed quarter; they who one day must live in or live off the brothels instinctively incorporate the ways of the Yoshiwara into their own play through mimicry. *Takekurabe* is the story of the process by which Midori, the "queen among the children"[35] who leads her Daionjimae charges in play, is herself readied for that other playground on the occasion of the Cock's Fair.

If we are to take fresh stock of *Takekurabe* as a text comprising two heterogeneous play spaces, then an entirely different context must be excavated from Ichiyō's minute descriptions of her milieu—descriptions that have been the object of high praise ever since Mori Ōgai's glowing tribute. We begin with the story's celebrated opening:

> It's a long way around to the Yoshiwara main gate, with its wispy "Lookback Willow," if you follow Ohaguro Moat; yet the lamplight flickering in the blackened water below the brothels' third-floor rooms, where guests carouse noisily, seems near enough to touch. The ceaseless flow of rickshaw traffic into the quarter, day and night, speaks of untold riches.

"Daionjimae": the name may reek of the cloth, but this neighborhood is in fact a lively place—or so the people living here say. Once you round the Mishima Shrine on the corner, though, you'll see nary a house worth raving about. Shabby tenements, their eaves atilt, stand ten and twenty in a row; business around here is none too good. Outside the storm windows, all ajar, hang curiously shaped paper slips. Aren't they precious, covered with paint and as colorful as miso-basted daikon on skewers— you can see the sticks on the back. It's not just one or two houses, either, from which you see these slips being hung out to dry at dawn and taken in at dusk. Entire families are absorbed in this line of work. If you ask, "What's going on?" they'll answer: "What, you don't know? These are *kumade* for the Cock's Fair, held in the Frosty Month. Mr. and Mrs. Avaricious will haul them away from the shrine—you know the one—in hopes of raking in good fortune."[36]

It was Okuno Takeo who beheld in this description a "'primitive landscape' of the city": "Each place-name colors the streets with nostalgic hues; the common people, who eke out a living in the shadow of the Yoshiwara Main Gate in the Meiji 20s, come to life in the archaic prose. Here, surely, is a 'primitive landscape' of the city. In it we witness the serene assuredness that results from conceiving of the city as one's birthplace and place of self-development, and as an unchanging living space."[37] From the standpoint of elucidating the loss of a "primitive landscape" in the modern city, Okuno's observation is certainly apt. Yet if we were to shift our focus to the actual period in question, the Meiji 20s (1886–97), we would see that the landscape depicted in the opening passage contains a certain instability that makes one hesitate to call it an "unchanging living space." Why, for instance, are two paradoxes contained in this very first passage?

"It's a long way around . . . yet . . . near enough to touch": this contradictory expression, which is commonly dismissed as mere rhetoric,[38] points to the *distance*—so close, yet so far away—separating the Daionjimae neighborhood from the Yoshiwara brothel proper. And as suggested by the words "It's a long way around to the Yoshiwara main gate . . . if you follow Ohaguro Moat," the Yoshiwara pleasure district was scrupulously isolated on all four sides from the surrounding urban space by water. This physical segregation from the gaudy licensed quarter sets up a vivid contrast with the forlorn streets of Daionjimae. Daionjimae residents were treated to an earful of rickshaw traffic into the Yoshiwara and to an eyeful of the nightless city's flickering lights reflected in the Ohaguro Moat. Isolated from the Yoshiwara's prosperity yet firmly under its control: Daionjimae's existential duality and

Figure 1. *Kumade* (decorative rakes) in the Tori no Ichi festival. Courtesy Edward Fowler, 1984

its duckweed-like unsettledness are brilliantly conveyed by means of this paradoxical syntactic construction. The superficial optimism rooted in the merriment emanating from the Yoshiwara is expressed in the words "'Daionjimae': the name may reek of the cloth, but this neighborhood is in fact a lively place." "Reek of the cloth" works as a metaphor that underscores the bitter reality of daily life in Daionjimae, where it has been established that "business around here is none too good." This metaphor contains a subtle reference, moreover, to Nobuyuki of Ryūgeji, who is introduced at the end of chapter 1 as someone who "already has a pious air about him."[39] Midori, meanwhile, whose character works as a foil for Nobuyuki, is an incarnation of Daionjimae's gaiety and superficial optimism.

The rather humorous description of the *kumade* [decorative rakes; figure 1], manufactured for the Cock's Fair by Daionjimae residents as a side business, reveals of course the neighborhood's parasitic dependence on the Yoshiwara and its money, to which Daionjimae is inextricably tied.[40] A passage that follows the above excerpt ("'All praise to the patron god of the Ōtori Shrine: bless the buyers of these rakes with fabulous luck, that we manufacturers may profit all the more'—so everyone says; *and yet*, oddly, one never hears of any rich folk residing in this neighborhood"; emphasis added)[41] also brilliantly complements the paradox-laden syntactic structure that begins the narrative.

The same Daionjimae that is controlled by the Yoshiwara's money and merriment, however, has another, hidden face. Take, for example, the passage in chapter 6 in which Midori, who has just completed a morning pilgrimage to the Tarō Inari Shrine, runs into Shōta on one of the paths that bisect the Yoshiwara rice paddies. Elsewhere, Chōkichi takes the Backstreet Gang kids to swim in a small body of water called Benten-bori, located in an out-of-the-way section of Daionjimae. The athletic meet held by the private elementary school that Nobuyuki and Midori attend takes place in a field called Mizunoya-no-hara. Red dragonflies dart about as the Niwaka festival, held in autumn, comes to an end;[42] and the cries of quail can be heard in the ditch that cuts across Chayamachi Street. What exactly did Ichiyō intend by these pastoral scenes, which dot the text of *Takekurabe*?

Slaves though we are to the notion that *Takekurabe* is a story typifying Shitamachi life in the Meiji period, the Daionjimae of the Meiji 20s was in fact a peripheral space located where the edge of the city met the agricultural areas beyond. Semirural landscapes were still common here. According to *Tōkyōfu shiryō*, a well-known statistical survey of Tokyo Prefecture's population and commercial industries published in the early years of Meiji, Ryūsenji-mura, the predecessor of Ryūsenji-chō (which would include the fictional Daionjimae), contained 105 households and 364 people. Wet rice paddies covered 6.86 acres of land; dry fields, 20.58 acres. Sakamoto-mura, situated to the west of Ryūsenji-mura, had wet rice paddies covering 39.7 acres and dry fields covering 21.56 acres. Senzoku-mura, to the south, had wet rice paddies covering 88.96 acres and dry fields covering 18.38 acres. The produce of Ryūsenji-mura, as recorded in *Tōkyōfu shiryō*, included 614.4 bushels of rice, 10,000 bundles of shiso, 40,000 goldfish, 20,000 red carp, 4,765 gallons of saké, 1,430 gallons of *shōchū*, and 12,000 bundles of paper hair cords.[43] From this list of produce we can surmise that Ryūsenji-mura comprised a heterogeneous population of farmers, lower-class urban dwellers, and fish breeders. *A Section of a Tokyo City Map*, published in Meiji 13 (1880; see figure 2), confirms this supposition. Asakusa, Ueno, Kanasugi, Minowa, and the Yoshiwara form a horseshoe-shaped triangle facing north, in the middle of which were situated many paddies and fields. The Yoshiwara licensed quarter sticks out like a peninsula into this agricultural area, and the streets of Daionjimae seemingly form a narrow bridge across that area between the Yoshiwara and Kanasugi.

Let us examine a second map, published in Meiji 42 (1909; see figure 3). The tracks of the Jōban Line can now be seen running east and west between

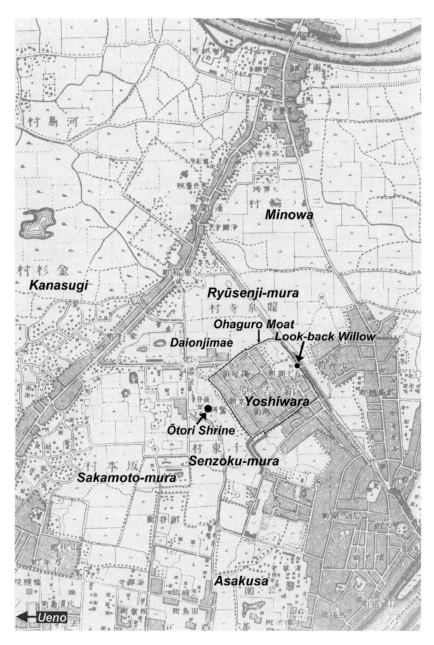

Figure 2. Ryūsenji-mura and surrounding neighborhood, 1880. Courtesy Chikuma Shobō, 1982

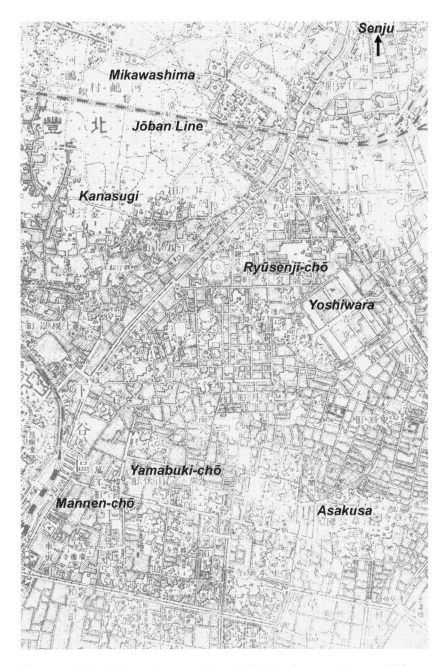

Figure 3. Ryūsenji-chō and surrounding neighborhood, 1909. Courtesy Chikuma Shobō, 1982

Senju and Mikawashima, and the agricultural area inside the horseshoe has been completely urbanized. Ponds of various sizes that still dot the cityscape are undoubtedly vestiges of the earlier rice paddies. Meiji 26 (1893), the year that the Ichiyō family began a sundries shop in Ryūsenji-chō, comes roughly in between the publication dates of the two maps, which, taken together, reveal the process of rapid urban expansion that occurred at this time. It was an unstable time, when the semirural landscape of Ryūsenji-chō and its environs were gradually disappearing.

The Senzoku Shrine summer festival, featured in the first scene of *Take-kurabe*, symbolizes the traces of rural life that persisted in Daionjimae. The two gods celebrated were Susanoō (the brother of the Sun Goddess, who once destroyed rice paddies in a fit of rage) and Uganomitama, god of the five abundant grains. According to Ueshima Kintarō's *Higuchi Ichiyō to sono shū-hen*, an exhaustive study of Daionjimae in the Meiji 20s, the poles used to lift the portable shrines in the Senzoku festival were attached in pairs lengthwise only, making it easier for the shrine bearers to negotiate the narrow paths in between the rice paddies. This arrangement was of course a vestige of the era when the paddies were still plentiful. The book further notes that the festival was held a month late in some years (on 20 September), and that in those years "the head priest could be seen on horseback riding behind the portable shrine as it was transported through the pale yellow plumes of early-ripening rice."[44]

Senzoku Shrine, which originally served as the guardian of the entire Senzoku district, was demoted after the Meiji Restoration to a village shrine, its jurisdiction limited solely to Ryūsenji, and yielded its former grandeur to the neighboring Ōtori Shrine, which is situated adjacent to the Yoshiwara. Dedicated as it was to an agricultural god, it became increasingly removed from the sensibilities of the Daionjimae residents, who were growing more and more urbanized. And yet this festival, held once every summer, was the one opportunity for an agricultural god in decline to express resistance against the control of the Yoshiwara and to perform its role in the face of waning fortunes: "On the twentieth of the Eighth Month, the men of each block vied for attention, dragging their floats and dancing platforms right up the embankment and practically into the quarter itself."[45] On this festive day, Daionjimae residents—liberated from the spell of Ōtori Shrine, which reigned as the guardian deity of the Yoshiwara and as the god of money—resurrected the memory of village life.

4

In the opening scene of *Takekurabe*, Chōkichi the Boss's son, scorned by Daionjimae adults as the "neighborhood bully,"[46] enlists Nobuyuki's aid for the upcoming festival. Chōkichi's eloquent appeal to the logic of territorial bonds takes Nobuyuki aback at first, but it works on him subconsciously. The malice that Chōkichi bears Shōta, leader of the Main Street Gang who commutes to a more prestigious public school (unlike the other children, all of whom attend the local private school), is part of that appeal. "Shōta brags about his school song being the best," Chōkichi tells Nobuyuki. "Well, I say, let him have it. Won't you help? It may be me he's calling a pea-brained private-schooler, but remember, he might as well be saying it to you."[47] These are not merely the resentful words of a student who must attend a private school that cannot even afford to install an organ. Shōta has betrayed his peers by becoming the only child in the community to attend a public school— *this* is what rankles Chōkichi. Kubota Mantarō, who entered Asakusa Public Primary School on Umamichi boulevard in 1895, the year *Takekurabe* began publication, offers a testimonial to the ties between private schools and Shitamachi society: "I didn't attend Ogawa [Primary School]. I went instead to the school on Umamichi boulevard. Yet I always viewed the goings-on at the private school with envy, because of the freedom that students obviously enjoyed there. . . . The friends I played with when I came home were all students at Ogawa. Sometimes it made me feel ashamed."[48] One would do well to superimpose on this recollection Kubota's play, *Ōdera gakkō*, which is an elegy to the old Shitamachi private schools. The principal of Ōdera Primary School proudly explains to a new instructor the territorial bonds that are the special characteristic of these institutions: "The children attending this school are long-time residents of the area. In fact, a lot of them have parents who knew me when they attended. That's the way it is around here."[49]

Nobuyuki, heir to Ryūgeji, the community's other central institution along with Senzoku Shrine, is ultimately persuaded by the logic of territorial bonds. As far as he is concerned, Chōkichi is someone "from the community, born right outside the temple gate."[50]

If the logic of territorial bonds seals the odd alliance between Chōkichi and Nobuyuki, then Shōta, the target of their attack, is the one child who turns his back on that logic. Unlike the others, who are all dressed at festival time in coats made of Mōka cotton decorated with stylized street names, Shōta has prepared a set of livery with his own unique design: "*Standing apart from the crowd*, Shōta of Tanakaya wears a red-striped happi coat decorated with the shop's emblems. The navy-blue waistcoat underneath contrasts boldly with the pale-colored skin at his neck. This, indeed, is a most unusual outfit. But that is not all. Take a look at the tightly drawn waistband, made of the finest light-blue crepe, and look at the shop emblems that adorn his collar—not to mention the headband, tied in back, with a spray of paper flowers attached! You can hear his leather-thonged sandals tapping to the beat, *but he refuses to join the music-makers who are striking up a silly tune.*"[51] The outfit being described is the kind worn by one of those wiry young firemen who would be leading the chanting during a Yoshiwara geisha parade. Unlike the other children of Daionjimae, who run about *barefoot* or in *split-toed socks* and wear *twisted* headbands, Shōta shows off his grown-up attire of "leather-thonged sandals" and a headband "tied in back." It is, of course, a proud display by the heir to the neighborhood's richest shop; at the same time, however, given that a village festival is an occasion for communal solidarity, it signifies an unforgivable betrayal. As Yasunaga Toshinobu writes, "Identical clothing is an essential ingredient of the festival. Tattoos are a most unusual example of this, but there are also banners, family crests, headbands, and today's uniforms and badges. The identical clothing that people wear, as well as the food they eat in common and the songs they sing, are all external means of promoting communal life."[52]

Shōta's grown-up manner has to do with the fact that he is an orphan raised by his grandmother, as well as with the adult work imposed on him, namely, collecting daily interest payments on loans to clients. If rumors of "many large brothels in the quarter being heavily in debt"[53] to the Tanakaya are indeed true, then Shōta is a child who has all too quickly formed inextricable financial ties to the Yoshiwara. The meaning of the fight scene, which brings the first half of *Takekurabe* to a climax, must be extracted from Shōta's role in the neighborhood. It is not a question of gang violence, nor is it a rite in which poor children simply avenge themselves on children of the rich.

In his *Festivals and Society* [*Sairei to seken*, 1922], Yanagita Kunio introduces a sacred ritual known as "Zattona," which is performed at the Shiogama Shrine (in northern Japan):

> You know, the deity enshrined in Shiogama was the strictest enforcer of conformity among its parishioners I have ever come across, rewarding believers and punishing stray sheep. . . . If you take a look at *The New Almanac of Mutsu Province* [*Shinsen Mutsu fudoki*, 1913] you'll find that until just a few decades ago a very severe ritual, commonly known as "Zattona," was performed under the auspices of this deity on the night of 15 January. It wasn't connected with any festival, but people say that it sprang from

the deity's heart, so you can call it a ritual. A kind of faith psychology, in other words.[54]

The most notable thing about this ritual was that the participants were all young children. They wandered about the streets on this particular evening and, as it says in *The New Almanac*, "They would come round to the back door of the house where the person who had perpetrated some wrongful deed lived, viciously denounce in one voice the infamous deed, and then drift away from the house. One child would announce their visit with these words: 'Well, now, well, now [*zatto na, zatto na*], have we something to tell you!' And when the accused replied, 'What is it?' they would respond with a torrent of abuse. Thus the ritual's name."[55]

Yanagita Kunio hears the distant voice of the deity in these "voices of little people." Zattona being the voice of a divine spirit that has lodged itself in the mouths of children, the adults on whom the abuse is being heaped have no choice but to accept their ill luck. The ritual is also a sacred game; the children empathize with the deity and cheer it on by raising a ruckus.

The significance of Chōkichi and the Backstreet Gang's festival night raid on the paper shop, where the Main Street Gang is assembled, is analogous to that of the Zattona ritual. Chōkichi defends his actions to Nobuyuki after the summer festival has ended: "Once we started swinging our lanterns, I couldn't very well turn around and go home. I got caught up in the heat of the moment and made a mess of things."[56] Yet these second thoughts are the kind that could occur only after the excitement of festival day has completely dissipated. The lanterns, moreover, symbols that they are of the festival, are essential in promoting a sense of complicity among the children of the Backstreet Gang, who are thereby encouraged to "raise a general ruckus."[57] Indeed, the lanterns served the same function as the rowdy portable shrines [*abaremikoshi*] whose task it was to mete out divine punishment against those who have betrayed the community. The gang's fighting was a form of sacred play allowed only on festival days; the logic of the festival, which permitted ordinarily pent-up energies to flow out unchecked, takes full control over the gang members. According to this logic, sanctions most certainly have to be meted out, in the name of the guardian spirit, against Shōta's arrogance, which has violated the festival's communality.

Shōta, the target of Chōkichi's violence, goes unharmed, it turns out; in his place, Midori and Sangorō are made the victims. There is an inevitability about Shōta's absence and Midori's and Sangorō's victimization, however, that transcends mere plot machinations.

Midori, who was born in Kishū, is the lone outsider among the children in *Takekurabe*. Her origins are left vague.[58] Strictly speaking, Midori is not under the protection of Senzoku Shrine, nor does her family belong to the Ryūgeji temple parish. This is, after all, the Midori who utters defiantly: "So what if [Nobuyuki] is the young master of Ryūgeji. I, Midori of Daikokuya, owe him nothing—not one slip of paper!" Quite unlike Chōkichi, who was born just outside the temple gate, or Sangorō, who lives on "land owned by Ryūgeji, in a house owned by Chōkichi's father," Midori is exempt from the territorial bonds that entangle the other children of Daionjimae.[59] Her role model is supplied by her sister Ōmaki, who is at the height of her popularity in the licensed quarter and who counts the likes of stockbrokers and bank managers among her regular clients.

A scene in *Takekurabe*, chapter 8, depicts groups of street entertainers, including jugglers, acrobats, puppeteers, and various kinds of dancers, who make the trek to the Yoshiwara from Mannen-chō and Yamabuki-chō in Shitaya.[60] Midori, who astounds the grown-ups by convincing a lovely female chanter to sing a verse from the *shinnai* ballad "Akegarasu," dreams of fraternizing on a grand scale: "I'd just love to gather all the entertainers passing through here into one big group. I'd make them dance and sing and strum their samisens and blow their flutes and beat their drums. I want to try things that people wouldn't ordinarily do." This episode does more than merely reveal her magnanimity; at a deeper level, is it not also evidence of a tacit blood bond between Midori and these performers? Mannen-chō and Yamabuki-chō, along with Shin'ami-chō in Shiba Ward and Samegahashi in Yotsuya Ward, were the most notorious of Tokyo's Meiji-period slums; the wag Sangorō is tagged with the nickname "Mannen-chō" when he helps pull a float during the Yoshiwara Niwaka. Midori is not under the sway of such prejudice; like the street entertainers, she is in effect an outsider who *passes right through* Daionjimae on her way to the Yoshiwara. Perhaps Shōta, who is scandalized by Midori's sudden whim ("'That's not for *me*,' he exclaims, surprised and dismayed"), senses that Midori shares something in common with these performers.[61]

Midori the newcomer is teased at first by the Daionjimae neighborhood girls about her country ways, but eventually she comes to rule her world of play as the "queen among the children." What makes her reincarnation possible is the fabulous sum of pocket money she receives from the Daikokuya:

> Her coin purse is heavy for a child's, and no wonder—it is all thanks to her sister's standing in the house. Every one of her sister's associates, from the young assistant courtesans to the old attendants, makes it a habit of offering her something in order to stay in her sister's good graces. "Mii-chan,

here's something to buy a doll with," or "This isn't much, but use it to buy a rubber ball." The giver is not patronizing, and the receiver not particularly grateful. But how she tosses her coins about! Once she bought matching rubber balls for all twenty girls in her class. She even purchased every last shopworn trinket in the paper shop she frequents, much to the joy of the shopkeeper! No one her age and in her position can approach her extravagance, which continues unceasingly day and night. Now what do you suppose the future holds for her?[62]

The narrative harbors a subtle irony: Midori's largesse is underwritten by the world of the licensed quarter, which will one day usurp her freedom. Midori, who is the very embodiment of play, enlivens the neighborhood and the children's amusements with her immoderate lifestyle; yet her magnanimity is also a display of immodest behavior, breaking the rules of play that Daionjimae children have grown up with and upsetting the fixed hierarchy of skills that demarcate the social order. Midori's role is in stark contrast to that of Daionjimae adults, who are completely under the sway of Yoshiwara money. In a contemporary roundtable discussion of *Takekurabe*, one critic makes the following remark: "What kind of neighborhood is Daionjimae? It is, of course, that most vulgar of places: an area whose residents aren't ashamed of receiving money from people who are engaged in selling sex."[63] The brazen obsequiousness of adults is reflected in the way their children settle on their activities for festival night, fawning all the while over Midori. Children, after all, are "quicker than adults to avail themselves of an opportunity, knowing that it may never come again."[64]

Midori, whose fate is to become a Yoshiwara courtesan, is, on the one hand, the object of envy for Daionjimae residents, who acknowledge, "Only the women have any chance of getting ahead." Yet, on the other hand, she is a girl whom men await the chance to abduct, however much money it may cost. Even "'Lamppost' from the dumpling shop," the most despised member of the Main Street Gang, states unequivocally to Shōta, "Next year I'm going to open my own little shop that sells seasonal goods and make some money, and when I do I'll go buy her for the night."[65]

The only outsider among the children of Daionjimae, Midori is both a child who flings money about in limitless quantities and a girl who inherits the destiny of being sullied by the world of prostitution. These attributes, which set her apart from the Daionjimae children's world, are doubtless the source of her appeal, but they also make her an easy mark for sacrifice come festival time. Shōta possesses nothing that corresponds to Midori's duality, which makes her at once the object of respect and disdain.

Swinging his lantern and descending on the paper shop, Chōkichi hurls a muddy sandal at Midori's forehead and berates her: "What—you're nothing but a whore, a lowly, groveling beggar, just like your sister. This here is all you deserve!"[66] Contained in this abusive language is the resentment that has built up among the Daionjimae residents, who suffer the domination of the Yoshiwara on a daily basis. Stripped of her role as "queen among the children," her identity as a "lowly beggar" laid bare, Midori is easily the most appropriate sacrifice for Chōkichi's Backstreet Gang.

5

The scene in front of the Daikokuya owner's house, in which a rain-dampened strip of crimson Yūzen cloth symbolizes Midori's faint yearning for Nobuyuki, begins: "One half expects a latter-day Azechi widow telling her rosary beads to be inside, and a young Murasaki, her hair clipped short as in the days of old, to come bounding out." This is clearly an allusion to *The Tale of Genji*.[67] Quite unlike Hikaru Genji, however, who catches a glimpse of the maidenly Murasaki on his way home from a retreat in the hills north of the capital where he has undergone spells and incantations for an illness, Nobuyuki himself is exposed to Midori's gaze from behind.

> Realizing that he is in front of the Daikokuya house, Nobuyuki is *filled with dread*. He marches forward resolutely, glancing neither left nor right. But this unlucky rain! This unlucky wind! His sandal strap broken, he has no choice now but to stop at the gate and twist some paper into a new one, feeling overwhelmed all the while by his misfortunes. And to top it off, here come footsteps along the stone walkway, their sound *like cold water splashing on his back*. He doesn't turn around; he knows it is she. He trembles violently and his face changes color. *He turns his back to her* and pretends to be lost in the task of repairing his strap, but he is beside himself, and can only lament, "How long will it take to wear this geta (clogs) again!"[68]

It is doubtless true that we witness in Nobuyuki's anxiety, prompted as it is by Midori's sharp gaze, the "faint emotional tremors that occur between a boy and a girl at the point they are turning into man and woman."[69] However, I prefer at this juncture to focus on the gaze itself—that is, on Nobuyuki's predicament of being viewed from behind by Midori in this scene as well as in the rainy-night scene at the paper shop that precedes it. Nobuyuki's receding figure in the latter scene, as he moves away from under the paper shop eaves, reveals his position at the margins of the play space occupied by Midori and Shōta.

Nobuyuki's father, the head priest of Ryūgeji, is depicted as a vigorous old man who washes down skewers of grilled eel with strong liquor. His mother, a parishioner's widow who becomes the priest's wife, quickly adjusts to her husband's worldly ways and thinks nothing of hawking ornamental hairpins at the Cock's Fair herself. His sister, meanwhile, runs a tea shop, thanks to the intercessions of their father, who capitalizes on his daughter's charms. Nobuyuki believes that the members of his family are "all misguided in their ways,"[70] and it is he, of all the characters in *Takekurabe*, who clashes head-on with the Yoshiwara's spirit of merriment and financial clout, which hold sway over Daionjimae. For him, the qualities of the licensed quarter that Midori exhibits so innocently are an object of dread, the Daikokuya owner's house a forbidden, taboo space.

Midori's yearning for Nobuyuki, on the other hand, represents a departure from her appointed role as the incarnation of play. Although she can entertain—and manipulate—her playmate Shōta at will, she completely loses this power before Nobuyuki. Her very attraction to him, in other words, has provided her with a glimpse of her own liberation from the spell of the Yoshiwara and allows her to grasp an entirely new possibility for growing into an adult. The children of Daionjimae, however, are permitted no escape from their assigned roles. That the lattice gate separating Midori and Nobuyuki never opens must be considered in this light.

In the contemporary review of *Takekurabe* quoted above, Mori Ōgai notes in reference to the scene in front of the Daikokuya owner's house, "The scene obviously has its precedents: one recalls the episode of Oshichi removing the splinter in Kichisaburō's hand with tweezers, or the one of Umegawa mending Magoemon's geta strap."[71] When we recall that Ichiyō was an avid reader of Saikaku in her last years, we realize just how penetrating Ōgai's insight is. It seems hardly necessary to cite the relevant passage in *Five Women Who Loved Love*, in which the greengrocer's daughter Oshichi and the temple acolyte Kichisaburō clasp hands while she removes a splinter from his finger. What interests us here are the comparable roles that Midori's mother and Oshichi's mother play in the two stories. Note the passage, again in *Five Women Who Loved Love*: "The young man becomes carried away and squeezes the girl's hand tightly. She is in no mood to part with him, but, *sensing the gaze of her mother*, reluctantly takes her leave."[72] If the composition of silver tweezers and the couple's joined hands foreshadow their sexual union, then the mother's gaze that Oshichi feels on her back suggests the taboo nature of that union. Later, Oshichi steals into Kichisaburō's bed, and this time the couple trembles in fear of the "temple elder's" gaze. The erotic drama in this meeting between Oshichi and Kichisaburō is built on the complications caused by the anxiety of those under the scrutiny of the gaze, and by the rebellion against that gaze, which represents a taboo.

Midori, who regards Nobuyuki from behind, is herself being scrutinized from behind by her mother. She feels her mother's sharp, penetrating gaze at her back just as poignantly as Nobuyuki feels Midori's on his back. When she recognizes the figure facing away from her as Nobuyuki, Midori "makes her way toward the gate, her body trembling, her head turned—is anyone watching?"—and recoils "each and every time she hears her mother calling out." Her mother hails her, moreover, just when Midori is hiding herself beneath the lattice gate and trying to assess the scene before her. "Just what do you think you're doing?" her mother says. "Don't be getting into any mischief out there when it's raining!"[73]

In his *Asobi to Nihonjin*, Tada Michitarō, amplifying Roger Caillois's theory of the hierarchical order of sacred–profane–play, clearly elucidates the way the world of play is constantly exposed to the vulgar gaze: "Play is always under a watchful eye. Whose watchful eye? That of the 'profane.' Put more precisely, play is monitored by the vulgar order. It can be likened to a detainee under constant surveillance. 'Play' is dogged by the sharp, penetrating gaze of the 'profane.'"[74] This definition certainly applies to the scene in front of the Daiyokuya owner's house. We recall the review of *Takekurabe* in "Sannin jōgo": Daionjimae is "that most vulgar of places: an area whose residents are not ashamed of receiving money from people who are engaged in selling sex." Midori's family, who are entrusted with managing the Daikokuya owner's house, are the most blatant examples of parasites on the Yoshiwara. (Midori's father works as an accountant, and her mother does piece work as a seamstress for the courtesans.) Midori's mother's gaze is none other than the moral order of the Yoshiwara itself, casting its panoptic eye on the activities of the prostitutes.

Filling the eye of Midori as she absorbs the shooting gaze of her mother is a "rude lattice gate" that separates her from Nobuyuki. For her, it is "a gate which she cannot bring herself to open."[75] That is because both the Yoshiwara main gate and the individual brothels' lattice windows are superimposed on it.[76] The gate's true significance is underscored by Chōkichi, who offers Nobuyuki a helping hand after Midori exits the scene. Chōkichi, who has earlier berated Midori ("What—you're nothing but a whore, a lowly, groveling beggar, just like your sister"), appears on the scene on his way home, it turns out, from a night in the Yoshiwara. We are made to see in Chōkichi's entrance an indication of the future that awaits Midori, who will herself one day become the object of some man's lust through the power of money. Put another way, Midori, unable to transcend the barrier of the lattice gate, has been torn away from the play space of children and corralled in the play space of adults. The very moment she catches a glimpse beyond the lattice gate of the one person who can liberate her from the Yoshiwara's spell, she is recaptured by the world of the brothel. The lyrical mood of the rain-soaked crimson Yūzen cloth notwithstanding, this scene in front of the Daikokuya owner's house, as we have ascertained from the episode's composition, becomes a most somber parody indeed of "Young Murasaki" in *The Tale of Genji* and of "The Greengrocer's Daughter" in *Five Women Who Loved Love*.

6

After opening with the Senzoku Shrine summer festival, the *Takekurabe* narrative reaches another climax against the lively backdrop of the Cock's Fair. The fair's principal deity, the Ōtori Daimyōjin, is the patron god of money. With no established parish, it bestows its divine favor equally among the city dwellers. Even the Yoshiwara, notwithstanding its strict segregation from ordinary urban space owing to its status as a brothel district, throws open its gates on festival day. In contrast to the Senzoku Shrine summer festival, which is a festival of the village and of the Daionjimae neighborhood, the Cock's Fair is a festival of the city, and of the Yoshiwara. The fact that these two festivals are out of phase has a ripple effect on the children's lives. The Main Street Gang and Backstreet Gang, which raised their standards in heated rivalry on the night of the summer festival, disband on the night of the Cock's Fair and drift apart, turning their energies instead to setting up makeshift stalls in anticipation of the big crowds and in high hopes of earning pocket money. Examples of these impromptu ventures include Sangorō's steamed potato stall and Lamppost's *shiruko* stall.

Shōta of the Tanakaya, who takes the day off from his collection duties, learns from Lamppost while making his rounds of the Main Street Gang stalls that Midori's "big day" has arrived. The depth of his shock, which he somehow manages to hide from Lamppost, makes itself apparent in the verse from a *sosoribushi* that slips unwittingly from his lips. The passage in question reads: "'She grew up playing/with flowers and butterflies/until she was sweet sixteen . . .' Shōta intones the lines from a song that is popular in these parts in a strangely unsteady voice. 'Now she does nothing/but work, work, work. . . .'

He mouths the lyrics over and over to himself."[77] Let us examine the lyrics as reproduced in Fujisawa Morihiko's history of popular songs in the Meiji period:

> Until I was sweet sixteen
> I was raised by Mummy and Daddy
> Among flowers and butterflies;
> Then I was sold to a brothel.
> They go by the book there,
> Examining me three times a month.
> My screams rival the cuckoo's ceaseless cries;
> It's more terrible than coughing up blood.
> Now I've grown accustomed to the work:
> I make my wealthy patrons spend good money
> And reward them in bed, I'm ashamed to say,
> With all my womanly charms.[78]

The lewd images conjured up by the lyrics, which recall the gaudy colors of those old glass paintings popular in the late Edo period, are completely at odds with the image of Midori that Shōta has nurtured from early on. Whereas Lamppost dreams of opening a shop to earn money for a liaison with Midori in the brothel, Shōta can only whisper, "She should never become a courtesan."[79] For him, Midori is not someone to be violated.

Shōta's house is the richest in the neighborhood, a pawnshop rumored to have "many large brothels in the quarter . . . heavily in [its] debt." That being the case, the relations between Shōta and Midori would in the final analysis be even colder than the dealings between a prostitute and her customer. The fetters tying him and Midori together would be the lump-sum advance that yokes the prostitute to her profession and the daily interest payments on that sum. Here is an example of a written contract exchanged between a Meiji-period brothel and a prostitute:

Memorandum of Agreement
Yen 90. Bearing interest at the rate of 1% (one per cent) per month.

With respect to the above, owing to unavoidable circumstances, I agree, with the consent of my relatives, to practise the profession of a courtesan in your establishment. In this connection I have borrowed from you the sum of money herein-above-written, the due receipt of which I hereby acknowledge. In consideration of the premises, and with the intention of repaying the loan to you from my earnings, I hereby agree to the following clauses of this contract: —

1. My fee for each guest is fixed at 25 *sen*. Out of each fee 12½ *sen* will appertain to myself, 3 *sen* being kept for my personal pocket-money while 9½ *sen* will be applied to the reduction of the principal and interest of my debt. You will please deduct the (latter) amount from the total of my daily earnings when the accounts are made up.[80]

The typically maudlin sentiment in the popular ditty that Shōta hums to himself is in stark contrast to the callous contractual language that is condensed into this "Memorandum of Agreement." Shōta, of course, can hardly overlook the cruel fate the memorandum will bestow on Midori; that fate, moreover, is a blank in the story that Ichiyō was unable to fill in. For Shōta, however, *becoming an adult* was none other than entering into the sort of inhumane bonds that were formed by money.

After parting with Lamppost, Shōta happens on Midori in a corner of the Yoshiwara compound, accompanied by an attendant of the Daikokuya. In Shōta's eyes, Midori, in her "freshly done Shimada hairdo," looks for all the world "like a colorful *Kyoto doll*." Shōta, however, who nags her petulantly, "*Why won't you play* today?," is clueless about the meaning of her transformation.[81] This brilliant scene reveals in a flash the brutal contrast between the Midori who has been ushered into the world of adults, and the Shōta who remains left behind in the world of children.

Midori has her first menstrual period on the day of the Yoshiwara festival. That the calamities befalling her both take place on festival days[82] is surely no mere afterthought by Ichiyō; they reveal the author's meticulous planning. Midori's first period is both a testament to her status as a blood offering to the Ōtori Shrine's principal deity and a symbol of the polluting and sinful burden of sex and money that Midori must bear on her transfer to the licensed quarter: "'If only I could spend my days alone doing as I pleased in a dimly lit room from morning to night, speaking with no one and keeping my face completely out of view. As long as I didn't have people's prying eyes to worry about, I wouldn't get so upset about things, even if I were in poor spirits. How happy I'd be if I could play house forever with all my dolls — oh, I hate it, I hate it! I hate growing up. I don't want to add any more years to my life! Why can't I go back — seven months, ten months, a whole year, if possible!' Absorbed in thoughts far beyond her years, Midori quite forgets that Shōta is by her side."[83] Lying in her "dimly lit room" and oblivious to the bustle of the Cock's Fair outside, Midori is keenly aware that the girl once living inside her is now *dead*. For her to be reborn as a woman who plays with men, the life of the girl who once played as a child must come to an end.

When the realm of children's time, to which Midori formerly had free access, is sealed off, it must be closed to the rest of the Daionjimae children as well.[84] Thus Sangorō: "If there's no fight tonight, then there'll never be one."[85] As for Shōta, no more gay tunes will escape from his lips. And Nobuyuki, who leaves Midori a paper narcissus as a keepsake—what awaits him at the destination of his journey? And Midori? If the true identity of the invisible force that totally obliterates the world of children in Daionjimae can be said to be "modernity," then for us who have just completed our own journey back into the realm of children's time under the guidance of *Takekurabe*, that force is, decidedly, our own original sin.

Notes

1 Originally published in *Tenbō*, June 1975; the text used for this translation is from Maeda Ai, *Toshi kūkan no naka no bungaku* (Chikuma Shobō, 1982), 278–311. The translator wishes to acknowledge the help of Abe Shūjirō, of the Kindai Bungakukan, with numerous archival matters, and the expert assistance of Matsuura Junko in tracking down the essay's more arcane references and meticulously checking a draft of this translation. Some minor errors in the essay (e.g., dates of publication) have been corrected.

   Takekurabe has been translated variously as *Growing Up* and *Child's Play* (see n. 28). A more literal translation might be "Comparing heights."

2 This summary is an adaptation of the introduction to *Takekurabe* which Maeda wrote for another essay on the story ("Higuchi Ichiyō *Takekurabe*: Yoshiwara, Ryūsenji-chō") and that appears in his *Gen'ei no machi: Bungaku no toshi o aruku* (Shōgakukan, 1986), 34.

3 William Empson, *Some Versions of Pastoral* (London: Chatto and Windus, 1935), 253–254. (M). Published in the United States as *English Pastoral Poetry* (New York: Norton, Inc., 1938).

4 Koganemaru is the name of one of the story's characters, all of which are animals.

5 The ad appeared in *Kokumin no tomo*, no. 104 (23 December 1890). (M)

6 Mori Arinori (1847–1889), the Meiji government's first minister of education (1885–89).

7 Kōda Rohan, preface to *Shinsaiyūki* (True journey to the west), in *Kōda Rohan zenshū*, vol. 10, 11 (1949–58; reprint, Iwanami Shoten, 1978), 115. (M)

8 Ozaki Kōyō, *Ninin Mukusuke*, in *Kōyō zenshū* (Iwanami Shoten, 1994), 2:379–423. First appeared in 1891 as volume 2 of the Hakubunkan *Shōnen bungaku* series, 32 volumes (Hakubunkan, 1891–96). (M) [The tale in question is "Little Claus and Big Claus," 1835, in Hans Christian Andersen, *The Complete Fairy Tales and Stories*, trans. Erik Christian Haugaard (Garden City, N.Y.: Doubleday, 1974), 8–19. See Ozaki, *Kōyō zenshū*, 2:461.

9 J.W. von Goethe, *The Story of Reynard the Fox*, trans. Thomas James Arnold

(New York: Heritage Press, 1954); originally published as *Reineke Fuchs*, 1794. Goethe's work is itself an adaptation of a centuries-old German text. Takizawa Bakin (1767–1848), *Hakkenden*, more properly, *Nansō Satomi hakkenden* (The eight dogs of the house of Satomi, 1813–41).

10 Anonymous review of *Koganemaru* in *Nihon hyōron*, no. 21 (1891): 252.

11 *Shiranui monogatari*, at ninety volumes the longest *gōkan* (set of bound-together volumes) ever written, is a revenge tale of a samurai woman facing the downfall of her family. *Jiraiya* (more formally, *Jiraiya gōketsu monogatari*), another gōkan, borrows from the Chinese legend and relates the exploits of a martial arts expert. *Keikoku bidan* (by Yano Ryūkei) chronicles the struggle of Thebes and other city-states to overthrow Sparta's rule in the Peloponnesian War, and was thus an inspiration for Japan's citizens' rights movement. *Kajin no kigū* (by Tōkai Sanshi) depicts the encounter by the author's persona with two beautiful European women, who describe the travails of their loved ones in the struggle to gain independence for their countries. All the above narratives are among the most representative of their times.

12 Terada Torahiko, "Dokusho no konjaku," 1932, in *Terada Torahiko zenshū* (Iwanami Shoten, 1997), 3:251. (M)

13 Tanizaki Jun'ichirō, *Yōshō jidai* (Childhood years), in *Tanizaki Jun'ichirō zenshū* (1968; reprint, Chūō Kōronsha, 1974), 17:222. A translation is available in English, under the title *Childhood Years: A Memoir*, trans. Paul McCarthy (Kodansha International, 1988). Tanizaki describes *Keikoku bidan* in some detail. See pp. 154–157.

14 Rohan, "Tetsuzō tan," in *Kōda Rohan zenshū*, 10:232. (M)

15 Ibid., 10:233. In the story's first edition, the scholar gives the boy a copy of *Hōtokuki* (an informal biography of Ninomiya Sontoku) rather than *Self-Help*, but the meaning of this variation is not clear. (M)

16 Kunikida Doppo, *Teihon Kunikida Doppo zenshū* (Gakushū Kenkyūsha, 1995), 3:127–141. [This story is included in *River Mist and Other Stories*, by Kunikida Doppo, trans. David G. Chibbett (Kōdansha International, 1982), 113–121, under the title "The Self-Made Man."

17 Hara Hōitsuan, *Shinnen*, in *Meiji shōnen bungaku shū*, vol. 95 of *Meiji bungaku zenshū*, ed. Fukuda Kiyoto (Chikuma Shobō, 1970), 114. (M)

18 Ibid., 118. (M)

19 Iwaya Sazanami, *Tōsei shōnen katagi*, in *Meiji shōnen bungaku shū*, vol. 95 of *Meiji bungaku zenshū*, ed. Fukuda Kiyoto (Chikuma Shobō, 1970), 17. (M)

20 Quoted from the official translation, reproduced in Hugh Borton, *Japan's Modern Century* (New York: Ronald Press, 1955), 178.

21 Rohan, *Kōda Rohan zenshū*, 11:5. (M) The version appearing in the *Zenshū* is retitled *Ninomiya Sontoku*. The English translation reinstates one sentence that Maeda has dropped.

22 "Ninomiya Sontoku," lyrics by Kuwata Shunpū. Source unclear.

23 *Great Learning* belongs to the second of two canonical groupings of Chinese

Confucian texts, the Five Classics and the Four Books, which date from pre-Han times.

24 John Bunyan, *The Pilgrim's Progress*, quoted in David Riesman, *The Oral Tradition, the Printed Word, and the Screen Image* (Yellow Springs, Ohio: Antioch Press, 1956), 14. (M)

25 See chapter 14 (entitled "Gun o nuku chikara") of Yanagita's essay, "Meiji Taishō shi sesō hen," in 24:393–408. *Teihon Yanagita Kunio shū* (Chikuma Shobō, 1963).

26 Quoted from the official translation, reproduced in Borton, *Japan's Modern Century*, 178.

27 Kaburagi Kiyokata, *Koshikata no ki*, in *Kiyokata zuihitsu senshū* (Sōgabō, 1944), 5–6. (M) Kaburagi Kiyokata (1878–1972) was a well-known illustrator.

28 Higuchi Ichiyō, *Takekurabe*, in *Higuchi Ichiyō zenshū*, vol. 1 (chapter 11), ed. Shioda Ryōhei, Wada Yoshie, and Higuchi Etsu (Chikuma Shobō, 1989), 433. (M) All English renderings are by the translator. For a complete translation, see *Child's Play*, trans. Robert Lyons Danly, in Danly, *In the Shade of Spring Leaves: The Life and Writings of Higuchi Ichiyō, a Woman of Letters in Meiji Japan* (New Haven: Yale University Press, 1981), 254–287; or *Growing Up*, trans. Edward Seidensticker, in *Modern Japanese Literature: An Anthology*, ed. Donald Keene (New York: Grove, 1956), 70–110.

29 The "Shoseibushi" was an immensely popular song that flourished in the early years of Meiji. *Shosei*, a word that first came into general currency around 1870, means male student, in particular a live-in student who works as a house servant while attending school. The lyrics changed with time, the verses' lead lines ("'Houseboy, houseboy'/Don't call me that") being followed by different punch lines. The above verses are variations on the original verse (which also had slightly differing versions): "'Houseboy, Houseboy'/Don't call me that/Some day I'll be working in the Premier's Cabinet."

30 Ichiyō, *Takekurabe*, 404.

31 Ibid., 446

32 Ibid., 422–423.

33 The utilitarian manner in which play is conceived in the boys' literature of Iwaya Sazanami and others is most plainly revealed in the principal's speech that opens Sazanami's narrative *Summer Holiday* (*Shochū kyūka*, 1892):

> Children, you have all borne the heat well and studied hard up to now. As a reward, I am giving you a summer holiday and you can play all you want! Just remember, though, that you shouldn't be spending your playtime idly, because if you do, then all the things you've absorbed here in school will pass right through you before school begins again. "Time flies like an arrow," you know—just as it says in your readers. Once gone, it will never come back. Your time as children will never return again. That is why you must devote your precious time as children to study. Now, who is it that you study for? Is it for your teacher? For your father? No, not for them, but for you yourselves. You

study in order to become wise and respected, to work for your country, and to do your part as a human being. (Iwaya Sazanami, *Shochū kyūka*, in *Nihon jidō bungaku taikei*, vol. 1: *Iwaya Sazanami* [Horupu Shuppan, 1977], 53)

In a perfect match with the principal's speech, the summer pastimes introduced in this book—swimming, boating, excursions, travel—are all intended to develop body and mind and are new as of the Meiji period. And in contrast to *Takekurabe*, the pastimes that Sazanami depicts here bespeak the life of the middle- and upper-middle-class Yamanote district, not of plebeian Shitamachi. (M)

34 Donald Keene makes the following observation in reference to the children in *Takekurabe*: "Both now and in the past, Japan has been a paradise for children. In the West, there has been only a weak conception of childhood until the twentieth century; the children in Alcott's *Little Women*, as the title indicates, were not children but young adults. In the literature of the West, the theme of growing up raises expectations of first love in the reader, but in Japanese literature it is the child's loss of innocence, more than young love, that takes precedence." Donald Keene, *Nihon bungaku o yomu* (Shinchōsha [Shinchō sensho], 1977), 22. Many foreigners who visited Japan during the Meiji period came away with the same impression. A comment by Lafcadio Hearn is typical: "Not merely up to the age of school-life . . . but considerably beyond it, a Japanese child enjoys a degree of liberty far greater than is allowed to Occidental children." Lafcadio Hearn, *Japan: An Attempt at Interpretation* (New York: Macmillan, 1904), 4. (M)

35 Ichiyō, *Takekurabe*, 409.

36 Ibid., 402

37 Okuno Takeo, *Bungaku ni okeru genfūkei: Harappa, dōkutsu no gensō* (Shūeisha, 1972), 12. (M)

38 The word *nagakeredo* functions as a polysemic "pivot word" (*kakekotoba*), a common rhetorical tool in the classical idiom. Here *nagai* ("long") refers both to the length of the trailing willow branches and to the substantial distance from Daionjimae, which borders the Yoshiwara on its back side, to Ōmon, the quarter's main entrance.

39 Ichiyō, *Takekurabe*, 404.

40 An article in the "Shitaya" section of a special issue of *Fūzoku gahō* entitled "Shinsen Tōkyō meisho zue" (The new illustrated guide to Tokyo's famous locations) describes the manufacture of the decorative rake-shaped charms (*kumade*) used in the Cock's Fair as follows:

— Papier-mâché [*harinuki*]: Until the fifth or sixth year of Meiji (1872–73), "bear-claw toys" [*kumade no omocha*] with decorative symbols, the seven lucky gods, and other ornaments, all made of papier-mâché, were a monopoly of the Masudaya, the toy wholesaler in Asakusa's Kurofune-chō, which did business with hundreds of kumade shops throughout Tokyo Prefecture and which, of course, grew very prosperous. The small shopkeepers who dealt in seasonal trinkets, being unable to make these complex items themselves, came to depend entirely on the Masudaya.

— Cut-outs [*kirinuki*]: An old man by the name of Kamata Kichibei who lived in Minowa, however, began fashioning paper cut-outs into [kumade] charms. Over the years, the papier-mâché variety lost their popularity and were almost completely replaced by paper cut-outs. Making cut-outs was the easiest thing to do: using a stencil brush or pencil, one simply traced around a pattern with a fixed design onto paper and then cut it with scissors. The pattern was made of neither wood nor metal; all one needed was a piece of paper. This method was so convenient that people no longer placed orders with Masudaya; everyone made them at home.

Shinsen Tōkyō meisho zue, ed., *Fūzoku gahō* (Tōkyōdō, 1897), reprinted as *Tōkyō meisho zue*, 21 vols (vol. 11: Shitaya-ku; vol. 12: Asakusa-ku; vol. 13: Asakusa Kōen), ed. Miyao Shigeo (Mutsu shobō, 1968–69), 84. The original "papier-mâché" way of making ornaments for kumade—pasting layers of *washi* paper onto a wooden pattern and then removing the pattern once the paste had dried—required a high level of skill and resulted in a single toy wholesaler in Asakusa Kurofune-chō taking in all orders for their manufacture. In the Meiji period, however, the "paper cut-out" method of making kumade out of cardboard was devised, and it turned kumade manufacturing into a cottage industry. The side business of the Daionjimae residents is the fruit of this modern industrial technology: namely, cardboard. In this connection, the first person to succeed in manufacturing cardboard in this country was Sakuma Teiichi, the founding publisher of Shūeisha. Sakuma, with the encouragement of Nakamura Masano, author of *Saikoku risshihen*, thought up a way to manufacture the cardboard used in books bound in the Western style, and his entry in the First Domestic Industrial Exhibition (Daiikkai Naikoku Kangyō Hakurankai), in 1877, was awarded a medal. See *Nanajūgonen no ayumi: Dai Nippon Insatsu Kabushikigaisha shi* (Dai Nippon Insatsu Kabushikigaisha, 1952), 14–15. (M)

41 Ichiyō, *Takekurabe*, 402–403.

42 The early autumn Niwaka, a carnival that included dancing, parades, and skits, was one of the three great festivals held in the Yoshiwara along with the nighttime cherry blossom festival (Yozakura) and the lantern festival (Tamagiku-dōrō), which were held in spring and late summer.

43 Tosei Shiryōkari, *Tōkyō-fu shiryō*, (1961), 5:41–43. (M) The units of measure in this paragraph (acres, bushels, and gallons) are converted from the traditional Japanese units used in Maeda's text.

44 Ueshima Kintarō, *Higuchi Ichiyō to sono shūhen: Daionjimae no kōsō* (Kazama Shoin, 1969), 85. (M)

45 Ichiyō, *Takekurabe*, 405.

46 Ibid.

47 Ibid., 406.

48 Kubota Mantarō, "Asakusa Tawaramachi," in *Kubota Mantarō zenshū* (Chūō Kō-ronsha, 1967), 10:76. (M)

49 Kubota Mantarō, *Ōdera gakkō*, in *Kubota Mantarō zenshū* (Chūō Kōronsha, 1967), 6:87. (M)

50 Ichiyō, *Takekurabe*, 407.

51 Ibid., 410; emphasis added.

52 Yasunaga Toshinobu, "Matsuri no imi," in *Zōho denshō no ronri: Nihon no etosu no kōzō* (Miraisha, 1971), 350. (M)

53 Ichiyō, *Takekurabe*, 412.

54 The term "faith psychology" is a translation of the phrase *shinkō shinrigaku*, an uncommon word which may be a variant of *shinsō shinrigaku*, the standard Japanese rendering of "depth psychology."

55 Yanagita Kunio, *Sairei to seken*, 1922, in *Teihon Yanagita Kunio shū* (Chikuma Shobō, 1962), 10:402. (M)

56 Ichiyō, *Takekurabe*, 429.

57 Ibid., 414.

58 Ichiyō's own distant memories may be reflected in her casting of Midori as an outsider. Ichiyō's father, Higuchi Noriyoshi, left the place of his birth, Nakahagi-wara in Kōshū Province (Yamanashi Prefecture), with his wife Ayame for Edo. There, he served first as an attendant at the Bansho Shirabe-sho [Institute for the Study of Barbarian Books], and later became a patrolman in Hatchōbori. He was, in short, a refugee from the provinces who abandoned his peasant status. After the Meiji Restoration, Noriyoshi, who had become a junior official in the Tokyo prefectural government, changed his family temple from Manpukuji in his old home of Nakahagiwara to Tsukiji Honganji, in the new capital. Thus he denied himself the means of returning to his birthplace even after he died. In the seventeen years between Ichiyō's birth in 1872 and his own death in 1889, moreover, Noriyoshi, who prided himself on his skill at managing the family business, ended up moving a total of nine times. The moves ranged over six wards: Kōjimachi, Shitaya, Azabu, Hongō, Shiba, and Kanda. (M)

59 Ichiyō, *Takekurabe*, 411–412, 421.

60 Shitaya Ward bordered Asakusa Ward on the west. Ryūsenji-chō (the setting of *Takekurabe*) was located on its northeastern fringe.

61 Ichiyō, *Takekurabe*, 411, 425.

62 Ibid., 408.

63 Mori Ōgai et al., "Sannin jogo," in *Ōgai zenshū* (Iwanami Shoten, 1973), 23:488; originally published in *Mezamashigusa*, April 1896. (M) The three critics are Mori Ōgai, Kōda Rohan, and Saitō Ryokuu, all of whom use several aliases in the course of the discussion.

64 Ichiyō, *Takekurabe*, 409.

65 Ibid., 440. "Seitaka" (lit. "tall person"), translated here as "Lamppost," appears as "Donkey" in the Danly translation and as "Moose" in the Seidensticker translation.

66 Ichiyō, *Takekurabe*, 414.

67 Ibid., 434. The reference is to chapter 5, "Wakamurasaki" (Young Murasaki; "Lavender" in the Seidensticker translation), in which the hero first spies the girl who will eventually become one of his wives. Murasaki Shikibu, *The Tale of Genji*, trans. Edward G. Seidensticker, 2 vols (New York: Knopf, 1976).

68 Ichiyō, *Takekurabe*, 436–437; emphasis added.

69 Nakamura Mitsuo, *Nihon no kindai shōsetsu*, revised ed. (1954; Iwanami Shoten, 1968), 83. (M)

70 Ichiyō, *Takekurabe*, 428.

71 Mori et al., "Sannin jōgo," 23:489. (M) The first reference is to the story of the greengrocer's daughter Oshichi, based on an actual incident and popularized in the fourth tale ("Koigusa karageshi yaoya monogatari") of Ihara Saikaku's *Kōshoku gonin onna* (Five women who loved love), first published in 1686. The second reference is to the Chikamatsu *jōruri* play *The Courier for Hell* (*Meido no hikyaku*), first staged in 1711, which depicts the tragic affair between the courtesan Umegawa and her lover Chūbei. (Magoemon is Chūbei's father.) Both are well-known texts in the classical canon. Although Maeda identifies Mori Ōgai as the subject of this utterance, the subject is in fact somewhat ambiguous, given the use of several different aliases in the text by all three critics. See Chikamatsu Monzaemon, *The Courier for Hell*, in *Major Plays of Chikamatsu* trans. Donald Keene (New York: Columbia University Press, 1961).

72 Ihara Saikaku, *Kōshoku gonin onna*, in *Ihara Saikaku shū*, vol. 1, ed. Teruoka Yasutaka and Higashi Akimasa, *Nihon koten bungaku zenshū*, vol. 36 (Shōgakkan, 1971), 384; emphasis added. (M)

73 Ichiyō, *Takekurabe*, 436, 437.

74 Tada Michitarō, *Asobi to Nihonjin* (Chikuma Shobō, 1978), 17. (M)

75 Ichiyō, *Takekurabe*, 434, 437.

76 This observation is indebted to Seki Ryōichi, "Takekurabe no sekai," in *Higuchi Ichiyō: kōshō to shiron* (Yūseidō Shuppan, 1970), 273. (M)

77 Ichiyō, *Takekurabe*, 440–441.

78 Fujisawa Morihiko, *Meiji ryūkōka shi* (Shun'yōdō, 1929), 447. (M) A *sosoribushi* is a song typically sung by men as they walk through a brothel district.

79 Ichiyō, *Takekurabe*, 440.

80 J. E. De Becker, *The Nightless City, or the History of the Yoshiwara Yūkaku*, with a new foreword by Terence Barrow, 5th ed., revised (1899; Rutland, Vt.: Charles E. Tuttle, 1971), 305. (M) (The Japanese original appears on pp. 303–304. Maeda leaves the monetary figures blank; they have been reinstated here. The contract in question is taken not from the Yoshiwara but from Suzaki, a brothel district in Fukagawa, in southeast Tokyo.

81 Ichiyō, *Takekurabe*, 441–442; emphasis added.

82 Maeda refers to the attack on Midori by the Backstreet Gang during the Senzoku Shrine festival, and to her initiation into the world of the Yoshiwara during the Cock's Fair.

83 Ichiyō, *Takekurabe*, 443.

84 The ending to *Takekurabe* can be understood as anticipating the role that children would play in the literature of the Romantic school. It certainly has elements in common with a poem entitled "Kadobe no kodomo" [Children at the gate, 1897] by Kunikida Doppo, which was written in the style of Wordsworth:

> Whenever I see children
> Playing merrily by the gate,
> Though they be caked in by the city's grime
> And buffeted by the winds of this fragile life,
>
> I think to myself:
> How sad for you children
> To be born into this sorrowful, scheming world
> Only to rush, alas, into a vale of tears!
>
> How pitiful, I think,
> Gazing at the clouds scudding across the sky:
> There is no limit to the distance they travel—
> Nor to the depth of emotion I feel.

Kunikida Doppo, *Teihon Kunikida Doppo zenshū* (Gakushū Kenkyūsha, 1995), 1:30–31. (M)

85 Ichiyō, *Takekurabe*, 445.

5. Asakusa as Theater:

Kawabata Yasunari's *The Crimson Gang of Asakusa*

(Gekijō to shite no Asakusa)

TRANSLATED BY EDWARD FOWLER

The Crimson Gang of Asakusa (*Asakusa Kurenaidan*, 1929–30), a major work of Kawabata Yasunari's (1899–1972) early period, centers on a group of teenage delinquents who call themselves the Crimson Gang, a troupe of would-be actors who wander about Asakusa, home of Tokyo's most famous temple and the site of an urban park created shortly after the Meiji Restoration. The anonymous, first-person narrator takes a keen interest in Yumiko, one of the troupe's members, who is as sharp and brittle as a well-honed knife. The boyish Yumiko has a peculiar hobby: masquerading. The narrator first encounters her playing the piano in the entranceway of a row house, bob-haired and barefoot and wearing a bright red, Western-style dress. At other times she appears as a boy riding on a bicycle, as a ticket taker at the theater, or as a stage player. The pig-tailed young girl in the audience of the Suizokukan Theater is also Yumiko; she awaits Akagi, the man who raped her sister years ago on the night of the Great Earthquake. Later, wearing a pure white overcoat, she lures him to a boat moored on the Sumida riverbank near Asakusa and kisses him, a lethal dose of arsenic pills in her mouth, thus avenging the crime against her sister. At that very moment, the narrator is atop the Subway Station Restaurant tower building with Haruko, a "real woman" who wears a kimono overcoat made out of synthetic fabric. Some of Yumiko's cohorts, who are also atop the building, are observing the boat through binoculars, and the narrator hears them shout: "The sleeve on her white coat is red. It's blood!" Several months later, Japan is in recession and Asakusa overflows with jobless men, prostitutes, and foreigners. One day, the narrator finds Yumiko on the Sumida River ferry bound for Asakusa. Once again she is in costume, dressed this time as an oil peddler. She is looking for someone, she tells him. "You are always looking for someone," he replies.[1]

1

Pass through Niōmon, the gate leading to Sensōji's Kannon Hall, make a left around the new Five-Storied Pagoda, and you will come to a small, sparsely wooded park.² Completely ignored by the good men and women who patronize the temple, this tiny plot is a pitiful remnant of Okuyama, Asakusa's seedy entertainment district, which flourished during the last years of the Tokugawa period (1600–1868) and the early years of Meiji (1868–1912). Here colorful shows and exhibits [*misemono*] abounded, including displays of life-size dolls and the top-spinning tricks of Matsui Gensui.³

Flitting about the litter-strewn park are flocks of pigeons. In the park's most visible spot is a memorial, the figure of Nonki na tōsan ["carefree dad"] carved in relief on top, dedicated to the comedic sensation Soganoya Go-kurō; it is nestled back to back with a statue of Uryū Iwako, whose seated figure faces the Kannon Hall.⁴ Nearby is another monument dedicated to the appearance of the Kannon Goddess and a five-tiered stupa erected in honor of Toda Mosui.⁵ These and other items stand cheek by jowl in wild disarray. What should we call the scene before us: a communal graveyard of monu-ments—a dustbin for the memories that Asakusa has nurtured during her long history?

Immediately adjacent to the park is the Okuyama Teashop, a Japanese-style restaurant. Next to it, separated by an alleyway, is Mokubakan, a theater whose sole form of entertainment until four or five years ago was *yasugibu-shi*.⁶ Today, the theater has two sections: Mokubatei, on the ground floor, which is Japan's only permanent vaudeville stage devoted entirely to *nani-wabushi*; and Mokubakan, located on the third-floor level and accessed by a steep flight of stairs, which presents sentimental historical plays that fea-ture much swordfighting.⁷ Around 3:30 or so, when the Mokubakan daytime show ends, the street in front, known as Pagoda Lane, momentarily takes on a somewhat forlorn liveliness. The entire cast, still in costume, greets as one the audience (mostly older men and women) that spills forth through the ban-ners and wreaths. Even the child actors, dressed in their period-piece wigs, call out in shrill voices.

To talk about *The Crimson Gang of Asakusa* (original book cover, figure 1) is to recall quite naturally the Casino Folies; the Suizokukan ["aquarium"], which housed it, was located right next to the Mokubakan, which is to say the site of the aforementioned Okuyama Teashop. This is also where the Tenryūza (Soganoya's troupe) and then the Okuyama Theater [Okuyama Gekijō], a Kansai-style striptease, held forth after the war.

Billed as "Japan's first revue," the Casino Folies hoisted its banner for the

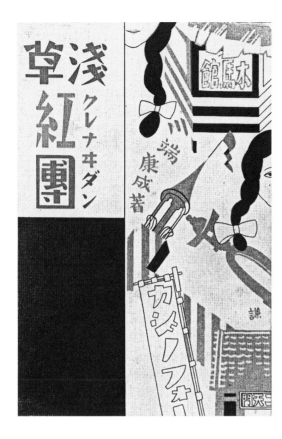

Figure 1. Cover of *Asakusa kurenaidan* by Kawabata Yasunari, in *Senshinsha* (December 1930). Courtesy Nihon kindai bungakukan

first time on the Suizokukan's second-floor stage a half century ago, one July day in the fourth year of Shōwa (1929). The aquarium, which first opened in the thirty-second year of Meiji (1899), remodeled the upstairs floor as a theater in the Taishō period and featured the young dancers of the Nomura Girls' Opera Troupe [Nomura Shōjo Kageki Dan], but failed to win an audience. Sakurai Gen'ichirō, its manager, was at a loss what to do when his brother-in-law, Utsumi Masanari, an artist who had just returned from France, provided inspiration with the knowledge of vaudeville and variety shows he had picked up while abroad. It was Utsumi who suggested the idea of producing a show that combined one of the revues that had taken Gay Paris by storm with a slapstick comedy by Mack Sennett, Chaplin's mentor.[8]

The first program featured two numbers: a revue entitled "Youth on Parade" ["Seishun kōshinkyoku"] and a variety show, "Aquarium" ["Suizokukan"]. The second program, which began on 25 July, featured Enomoto Ken'ichi (known by all as "Enoken"), who had moved to the Casino Folies from the Kinryūkan Opera, where he worked as a chorus boy, and gave a rousing performance in the review "Hit Parade" ["Daikōshin"] to rather sparse audiences, it is reported.[9] Every imaginable means was employed to lure customers, from price discounting (from 40 to 30 sen) to a change of venue (including a trial-run "sand dune review" on a Kamakura beach), but to no avail; the first Casino Folies closed down after just over two months. "Every woman on stage had gone to seed. One might as well have gazed at wrinkled dumplings." These are the biting words of the writer Satō Hachirō.[10]

The second Casino Folies kicked off later that year with young dancers still in their teens, such as Hanajima Kiyoko, who became Enoken's wife, and Umezono Ryūko, a favorite of Kawabata Yasunari's. Business at the Folies finally took off at year's end, thanks to rumors that the dancing girls would be dropping their drawers on Fridays, and to the widespread popularity among students and the intelligentsia of *The Crimson Gang of Asakusa*, which began serialization in the *Asahi* on 12 December. This is how Kawabata, in chapter 10, introduces the Folies stage, which breathed new life into post-Earthquake Asakusa in the tradition of Soganoya's theater and the Asakusa Opera:[11]

> The Insect Museum [Konchūkan] and Aquarium are tucked away in the park's Fourth District, monuments to Asakusa's bygone days.[12] The Casino Folies dancing girls head backstage, making their way past the fish swimming in the tank and cutting in front of a model of the Ryūgū Palace.[13] The noted artist Fujita Tsuguji, just returned from Paris, is here to take in the revue, accompanied by his "Parisienne" wife Yukiko.
>
> If the wild rhythms of the "Japanese-style jazz band revue" characterize the Asakusa of 1929, then the Casino Folies, Tokyo's only "modern," Western-style revue, may very well characterize the Asakusa of 1930, along with the subway station's tower restaurant.
>
> It is all here: eroticism, nonsense, speed, political satire, jazz singing, bare legs. . . . Still, there are not so many guests in the third-floor seats that the conversation between Yumiko and her male companion can be overheard.[14]

The irony of a cutting-edge dance revue—the epitome of 1920s avant garde—springing forth from Okuyama, in Asakusa's backwater Fourth District, is not lost on Kawabata. Nor is the contrast between the lively stage and the quiet house. In this unique spot, with its blend of the old and new Asakusa, might well lie the key to decoding the kaleidoscopic work that is *The Crimson Gang*.

The giant play space of Asakusa has two centers (figure 2). One is the temple itself, Sensōji, along with the shops of Nakamise that line its main

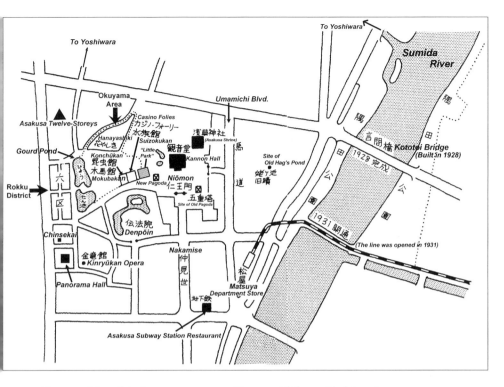

Figure 2. Map of Asakusa area, ca. 1930. Courtesy Chikuma Shobō, 1982

approach; the other is the entertainment district known as Rokku. When Asakusa was first redesigned as a public park in early Meiji, the many stalls housing various exhibits and shows [*misemono-goya*] that once dotted Oku-yama were moved to the Sixth District, which rose up from reclaimed rice paddies. The area eventually became the Rokku ["District No. 6"] Entertainment District, with the dual landmarks of the Jūnikai [Twelve Stories] and Panoramakan [Panorama Hall] standing at its northern and southern ends.[15] The contrast between Asakusa's "front door" (Sensōji) and its "back door" (Okuyama) was replaced by a new polar opposition between the sacred space of the temple and the play space of Rokku. The densely wooded Okuyama, along with Hyōtan'ike [Gourd Pond], became a nebulous area removed from both Sensōji and Rokku—an ominous, liminal space where the sacred was transformed into the playful, the playful into the sacred. In my "Pictorial Map of Asakusa," produced in 1939, the concentration of symbols designating such criminal elements as racketeers, pickpockets, streetwalkers, and vagrants in the Fourth District, stretching from Okuyama to the pond, is the highest of any area in the park.[16]

To the north of the Fourth District lies the Fifth District, which includes Hanayashiki, that most unusual Meiji playground: a combination of amusement park, arboretum, and zoo. The *Gazetteer of Famous Tokyo Sights* [*Tokyo meisho zue*; 1908 edition] lists the following animals kept by the zoo: "a guinea fowl, a brown bear, deer, monkey, tiger, a Korean eagle, field hawk, night heron, crested eagle, a fox."[17]

In his celebrated study, Asakura Musei divides misemono shows and exhibits into three general categories: performances, including dancing, magic tricks, tumbling, acrobatics, and other circus acts; natural oddities, including humans with deformities as well as unusual birds and animals; and artistic handiwork, such as mechanical gadgets, life-size dolls, and glasswork.[18] The shows and exhibits stationed in Okuyama that I said were moved to the Rokku Entertainment District belonged to Musei's first category ("performances"); the birds and beasts, belonging to the second category, were transplanted to Hanayashiki. Given this history, it is easy to see why an insect museum (the forerunner of Mokubakan) and an aquarium were built in Okuyama. Fish and insects supplemented the flora and fauna of Hanayashiki, thus taking their place in the catalogue of items from the natural world that were to be put on display.

From early on, Asakusa as an amusement quarter was unusually fixated on various "worlds." The Jūnikai [the Twelve Stories], for example, was in fact a clumsy copy of the hugely popular Eiffel Tower that was built for the Paris Exhibition, and the Panorama Hall, which opened in the same year (1890), displayed phantom-like scenes from the Battle of Gettysburg to the accompaniment of a music box. From the Chinsekai ["strange world"], a theater erected next to the Panorama Hall, to the Shinsekai ["new world"], an utterly tasteless clump of box-shaped buildings thrown up after the war on the site of Gourd Pond, Asakusa has seemed preoccupied with building models of worlds or universes. Needless to say, this preoccupation has been the wellspring of Asakusa's appeal.

If, among Asakusa's worlds, the Fourth District of Okuyama and the Fifth District of Hanayashiki formed the boundaries of a "nature" that was gently ordered, then we can say that the area around the Suizokukan, where the Casino Folies hoisted its banner, was a sinister periphery, a dark corner where the sun never shone. It is said that the public toilet across the street from the Suizokukan—still the largest in the Park—assailed the Folies' audience with its foul smell. The Suizokukan building itself was the most amorphous of structures: the basement housed an inexpensive eatery and a one-thousand-liter seawater tank; the first floor, the aquarium; the second and third floors, a theater. It was, in short, a hodgepodge. The first-floor aquarium contained sixteen water tanks fronted by a ten-foot glass panel. They housed the likes of saltwater catfish, groupers, gurnards, sea robins, and other fairly undistinguished marine fish. The gloomy atmosphere evoked by the dimly lit aquarium, in which only the sound of bubbles circulating in the tanks could be heard, was something straight out of Edogawa Rampo.[19] As for the theater upstairs with its minuscule audience, Hori Tatsuo provides us with a sketch from his short story "Suizokukan" [Aquarium]:

> I ascend the dusty stairs, trying not to make too much of a clatter with my *geta*. Suddenly I hear music coming from the direction beyond people's heads (the rows of seats right in front of the standing audience are virtually empty, but no one is sitting down), and I can make out girls dancing on the stage. First-time visitors often try sitting on the empty seats in back, but the seats either start wobbling dangerously, or the straw stuffing pours out of the gaping holes in the upholstery; worried about soiling their clothes, they immediately rise again to their feet. The entire auditorium is altogether small, holding a mere two hundred on the second floor and no more than another hundred upstairs on the third-floor balcony.[20]

Hori Tatsuo goes on to write that he at first pushed his way into the second-floor seats nearest the stage so that he could look up the dancing girls' legs, but he eventually tired of the dust rising from the stage with each step and retreated to the third-floor balcony.

Next door to the Suizokukan, the Mokubakan, too, with its merry-go-round was a most forlorn amusement spot. Children straddled wooden horses that were missing a tail or an ear, while their parents, seated on benches, encouraged their broods by waving little flags as the carousel started up to the tune of a small band.[21] And yet this spot's very disrepute, which caused it to be shunned by the rest of Asakusa, offered a most favorable environment for the birth of a new style of performing arts. That is because the ideas of complete amateurs, striking in their originality and nothing like those conjured up by the professional entertainers working out of Rokku, came to life here. Take, for instance, Utsumi Yukitaka, the brother of Utsumi Masanari, who financed the Casino Folies' second phase. Yukitaka sang in the chorus while studying at Hōsei University, but he was a total novice when it came to the theater. Kita Hideo, of the *Shiseiki* group, Yamada Toshio, from Okada Yoshiko's troupe, and Mizumori Saburō, a follower of Takeda Rintarō and a student at Waseda University, gathered around Yukitaka and other young writers and leftist activists and proceeded to come up with one biting satire and crazy gag after the next. Even the actors, excepting the likes of Enoken and Nakamura Zekō, were amateurs. One story has been passed down of a still very young Mochizuki Yūko bringing box lunches to the actors backstage and declaring her desire to become a dancer. Enoken commented favorably on her legs, and she appeared on stage the very next day. Umezono Ryūko was one of the Folies' two stars, along with Hanajima Kiyoko, but her formal artistic education consisted solely of lessons from her grandmother in traditional Japanese dance. The girls' male costumes, which set off their amateurish acting and dancing, and a host of simple gags—such as moving the telephone poles and cars painted on the backdrops to make it appear as though the actors were racing by—actually helped increase the Folies' popularity.

In the chapter of *The Crimson Gang* entitled "Suizokukan" [The aquarium], Kawabata writes: "When there are only a few people in the hall, the walls, chairs, and floor all emit an odor that has, over time, permeated the wood and fabric. It is the smell of beggars. My dear readers: this is no figure of speech. Beggars and vagrants have been part of the audience since the Suizokukan first hosted its dance revue. Beggars and vagrants taking in the naked dancers, their faces made up in the modern style—this bizarre scene, too, is right out of Asakusa."[22] We need only cite a parallel example of Kara Jūrō's troupe holding forth in the Hanazono Shrine grounds east of Shinjuku in the 1960s to demonstrate that the sordid scene depicted by Kawabata in fact represents theater in its most original, primitive form.

The delinquent teenage boys and girls appearing in *The Crimson Gang* have formed a troupe of their own, the Kurenaiza, and they dream of striking the world dumb with their antic performances. The first-person narrator has been charged with providing the script for a play that features the troupe. Yumiko, Umekō, and Haruko, who flit in and out of the narrative at will, are Kawabata's own dream of another, fictional Casino Folies that the author has spun from the stage figures of Hanajima Kiyoko and Umezono Ryūko. The stage on which this script is acted, however, extends well beyond the Suizokukan's second floor, from Asakusa all the way to the Yoshiwara and the Sumida River. *The Crimson Gang* is the tale of Asakusa as theater, and of the urban theater of TOKIO in 1930.

2

The Crimson Gang's most vividly drawn character is Yumiko, the delinquent teenager who introduces the narrator to the behind-the-scenes Asakusa and who enacts a dangerous play of revenge. A most attractive girl, Yumiko makes one imagine how it would be if one of the lead dancers romping about the Casino Folies stage, a Hanajima Kiyoko or Umezono Ryūko, were to appear among the crowds in the park.

The first place we encounter Yumiko, through the narrator's intervention, is at a row house hidden in "a certain alleyway" near the Yoshiwara embankment.[23] The young, fresh-looking Yumiko, dressed in a bright red semiformal evening dress, her white feet bare, is playing the piano with her back turned to the entrance gate. The narrator notes traces of a thin layer of powder at the collar line of her boyish, closely cropped hair. This subtle depiction of a girl in a boy's haircut is in fact an important hint; the reader who takes note will not be fooled by the sudden change of scene that follows in which a youth, who is the spitting image of the piano-playing girl, darts out of an alleyway on a bicycle.

In fact, it is quite difficult to keep track of the repeated, alternating appearances of Yumiko and Akikō, the boy on the bicycle. Even Isoda Kōichi, that most perspicacious of critics, is guilty of a slip of the pen when he wrote, "The narrator, who harbors sanguine dreams about Asakusa, is shown a more realistic side by Yumiko's younger brother [sic]."[24] (It is possible, of course, that Isoda simply chose to conceal the plot, in the manner of a mystery novel commentator.)

Yumiko, who first appears as a piano player in a back alley, assumes a new guise in each successive scene: a young boy on a bike, a ticket taker at Mokubakan, a pigtailed girl crouched in a Suizokukan theater seat, a player in the Tamakiza troupe wearing thread-bare cotton, a proper young girl in a white coat, a peddler of Ōshima hair oil. Having learned during the course of the narrative about the existence of a masquerader in the middle of Asakusa who deals in rental clothing, we the readers are prone to take at face value Yumiko's comment: "You might say I'm the mannequin girl for this shop."[25] Yumiko's manifold disguises, however, are not so much representative of the period as they are a metaphor of Asakusa the place: "a district of many shadows," as the narrator puts it.[26] At the same time, the real source of the confusion created by Yumiko's masquerading lies in her status as an androgynous figure. There is something boyish about Yumiko when she appears as a woman, and a girlish gentleness pervades the gestures and words of Yumiko when she dresses as Akikō.

The face of Akikō this morning—it was he whom I'd lost sight of at Kototoi Bridge—was free of its earlier grime and was now as white as that of a young chorus boy on stage. He walked quickly with hands behind his neck, fingers locked, and his cheeks buried in his elbows, as if to conceal the smoothness of his skin. An object resembling a bag for carrying sandals was suspended from one elbow.

"What's in that thing—your lunch?"

"No, my makeup."[27]

In this scene, the narrator, under Akikō's guidance, is having a look at the vagrants who gather in the park of an early morning. The off-beat eroticism of Akikō viewed from the back, with neck painted white and carrying a toilet kit, is rendered with perfect pitch.

The crucial element of Yumiko's quick-change artistry, moreover, which gives the story a dazzlingly kaleidoscopic illusoriness, lies in the very form of narrative that Kawabata Yasunari has chosen for *The Crimson Gang*. The storyteller, ordinarily a guide who orders the narrative flow and resolves the intricacies of plot, turns out in Kawabata's text to be a most perverse character whose role is apparently to disrupt the plot and divert the reader from the narrative flow. For example, once having learned the whereabouts of the piano-playing girl's residence ("in a certain alleyway"), we readers must sift through a series of images that flicker before us over the space of several pages: the decorative votive slips [*senjafuda*] that the Crimson Gang members carry with them wherever they go; the giant who devours the carp food floating on Gourd Pond, and so forth. After having thus led us astray and continually tried our patience, the narrator at last returns to the story at hand: "I say 'in a certain alleyway'; but I happened upon this 'certain alleyway' not out of some eccentric journalistic whim, but because I had business there— my own private business. And the lovely, bob-haired girl I found in that cul-de-sac, playing the piano, was my reward."[28]

What is required of *The Crimson Gang* readers is a light-footed stance with which to parry all this leg pulling and textual play. For the "square" reader, the text is like a treacherous, pebble-strewn path waiting to trip him up. I first read *The Crimson Gang* in the popular edition published by Kawade Shobō[29] early in my university days, and I remember being so annoyed by the text's incoherent rambling—it was as if my toy box had been upended—that I never made it to the end. Yet I realize now that the narrative's very desultoriness, which has a way of putting off readers just when they think they've grown accustomed to it, is in fact a device that enhances the motif of transformation; moreover, it is a completely novel form of storytelling that incorporates the syncopation of jazz and the rapid-fire scene changes featured at the Casino Folies variety shows. The willful narrative obfuscation that removes the story's binding elements goes hand in hand, moreover, with the lure of the androgynous character played by Yumiko.

The graffiti that appears in the tower room of the Asakusa Subway Station Restaurant epitomizes Yumiko's ambiguity and duality. Yumiko's message is written in a clear, competent hand in the manner of a penmanship lesson:

Haze appears light in the morning, dense in the evening;
Mist appears dense in the morning, light in the evening.
A mirage fades, and it grows light;
Lightning fades, and it grows dark.
Leaves turn color from the peaks;
Flowers bloom from the foothills.
Brooks flow quietly by day, noisily by night;
Waves ripple noisily by day, quietly by night.
Blossoms on trees open in the morning;
Flowers on shrubs open in the evening.[30]

Yumiko's much more feminine companion Haruko declares this message to be an unsolvable riddle that defies comprehension; Yumiko similarly hurls questions without answers at the reader. It is enough for us simply to recognize that her questions swing back and forth continually between two poles.

At the time of the Great Earthquake, Yumiko's older sister, Ochiyo, was raped by one Akagi, a gangster who calls Asakusa his turf. She never recovers from the shock and spends her days henceforth wandering aimlessly about the park. She is known as the "dressed-up madwoman." (Older readers will recognize this nickname from Honda Bizen's famous romance of the same name.)[31] Yumiko, determined to avenge her sister, encounters her sworn enemy at the Mokubakan and lures him to the *Benimaru* [S.S. *Crimson*], a boat docked on the riverbank near Asakusa. Akagi takes a fancy to this girl in a white coat and follows her, whereupon she takes her revenge in the form of a deadly kiss laced with a lethal portion of tiny arsenic pills.

This revenge play, which brings the first half of *The Crimson Gang* to a colorful climax, recalls one of those illustrated Edo-period fairy tales, but it is of course modeled after the ancient "stone pillow" legend of the Old Hag's Pond [Ubaga'ike] near Asakusa. (A large votive plaque by Ichiyūsai Kuniyoshi depicting this legend still hangs high up the walls of the Kannon Hall.)[32]

Legend has it that a "cruel old hag," who lived in an isolated hut on Asaji Moor,[33] a flatland stretching west from the Sumida River, would lure a traveler into her lair, have him rest his head on a stone pillow, and offer her daughter as a bedtime companion. She would then wait until the traveler was fast asleep, drop another stone suspended from the ceiling, and strip away the clothes of the man whose head had been crushed. Thus were 999 men killed, one after the other. The thousandth visitor, however, was the Goddess Kannon incarnated as a young boy. The old hag's daughter, smitten with love for the beautiful boy, lets herself be killed in his place. This is the story line of the stone pillow legend, as transcribed in *Kaikoku zakki*,[34] but there are of course many variations. "I am reminded of this legend by the fact that Yumiko might very well bed down with someone on a slab of concrete, or on a boat deck."[35] So writes Kawabata, who clearly tries to incorporate the legend into his own portrayal of Yumiko's heart-rending despair: she mutters to herself that she would have swallowed the arsenic pills herself and died were she to have fallen in love with Akagi as her sister did. I believe that this portrayal of Yumiko's ambivalent emotions—a compelling attraction *and* a mounting hatred for Akagi—is a dualistic transformation of the old hag's murderous intent and the daughter's sacrificial love. Moreover, if we trace Yumiko's transformation back to the legend of Kannon's reincarnation as a young man, we can say that *The Crimson Gang*, commonly thought to be a cutting-edge depiction of 1920s urban life, presents in fact a far more complex literary universe, one that harbors a folkloric element within its depths as well.

Yumiko and Akagi's rather melancholy interaction on the boat is thoroughly rent by Yumiko's theatrical line: "I am the earthquake's child."[36] Her words, delivered with utter confidence, bursts forth like a lightning bolt. When her sister was raped by Akagi amid the earthquake's chaotic aftermath, Yumiko, a mere fifth-grade elementary school student at the time, made a pledge: to abandon her sex and transform herself into a man. Yumiko may have seen that an opportunity for retrieving the womanhood locked inside her lay in the love she felt for Akagi, who symbolizes the old-generation Asakusa, but her dangerous gamble ends in Akagi's death. If, at its deepest level, the desire for gender transformation signifies the enacting of a death that leads to resurrection, then Yumiko, who has closed off all avenues to rebirth, will surely continue to live as "the earthquake's child," harboring in her breast the shock of widespread destruction. "The new Tokyo was ushered in by that earthquake. Asakusa, too, was born anew."[37] Kawabata's words are both a metaphor for Yumiko's barren love and a prophecy of the decline Asakusa would soon witness.

Yumiko—the beautiful young girl who bears the aura of androgynous sanctity. And her compatriots—all of whom share her predilection for disguise. Add to these the beggars, the pimps, the roguish gangs, the flocks of streetwalkers. *The Crimson Gang of Asakusa*, a world of pure anomie in which such groups, shunned by proper society, run rampant, offers us, it seems to me, a photographic negative of Tokyo in the 1920s, a city upended first by a natural disaster and later in the decade by a manmade one: the worldwide stock market crash. If I may be forgiven a somewhat rash pronouncement, we can discern in the rebellious activities of the underground world that Kawabata glimpses a vision of a very traditional kind of violent popular reformation [*yonaoshi*], one quite different from the blueprint of Marxist revolution we find depicted in proletarian literature. One can of course dismiss this vision with Akagi's own comment—"They are the idle words of a fairy-tale princess"[38]—yet we can grasp the stifling conditions of the 1920s era from the very fact that Kawabata, who occupied a position far removed from the proletarian camp, felt compelled to harbor such a vision at all.

However, Kawabata's scheme of a "fairy-tale" reformation must eventually be abandoned midway through his story. "The earthquake's child" yields the stage to Haruko, a character who is delineated in much sharper outline than Yumiko. The latter, a voluptuous woman who prides herself on her computational skills, possesses none of Yumiko's ambiguity or duality.

At the very same moment that Akagi is being lured onto the *Benimaru*, the narrator is accompanied by Haruko, who is wearing "a gaudy blue synthetic half-coat,"[39] to the tower room of the Asakusa Subway Station Restaurant in a sequence that recalls the parallel editing of the cinema. In the tower room await four men, who, on instructions from the Crimson troupe to gather in Hanakawado, are observing the *Benimaru* through binoculars.[40] (The inspiration for this scene may be Edogawa Rampo's short story "The Traveler with the Pasted Rag Picture," which is about a man who peers from atop the Twelve Stories through his binoculars at a picture made from layers of cloth—he had thought it to be a real woman—housed in a roofless peep show booth.)[41] The light-hearted kisses that Haruko exchanges with each of the four men are in marked contrast indeed to the kiss of death Yumiko delivers to Akagi. Haruko's performance is the Asakusa version of Jean Cocteau's *The Eiffel Tower Wedding Party* (1921).[42]

The forty-meter-tall Subway Station Restaurant building was completed in the fall of 1929, not two years after Tokyo's first underground railway line opened. It became Asakusa's new landmark, replacing the red-brick Twelve Stories, which crumbled in the 1923 Earthquake, and its whitewashed concrete tower easily caught the eye. And yet, the unobstructed view it afforded of Kototoi Bridge would last only a year or so; the Asakusa branch of the Matsuya Department Store opened in November 1931.

What is the meaning of Kawabata's conceit, which blended the whitewashed Subway Station Restaurant building and the *Benimaru*, plying its way up the Sumida River, into a single composition? It is the spatial expression of the subtle power relationships working between the myth of water that Asakusa has nourished since the time of Narihira, the myth of machines that emerge from the flames of the earthquake, and the myth of steel and concrete.

Kawabata, after citing the poem that the Yoshiwara courtesan Zuiun offers to a shrine dedicated to Hitomaro[43] in a further allusion to the "stone pillow" legend, goes on to depict Yumiko, who has lured Akagi into the boat cabin, as an androgynous river prostitute worthy of the protean Undine, a water spirit prepared to "bed down with someone . . . on a boat deck." Haruko, meanwhile, who is cast as the "Eiffel Tower bride," views the Sumida River from the concrete Subway Station Restaurant tower building and quenches her thirst with water tasting of concrete. The showdown between these two rivals is a scene that never materializes in *The Crimson Gang of Asakusa*, but there is no question who the victor would be. For we are witnesses to an Asakusa in which the hidden currents that nourished the water myth have nearly dried up. The best view to be had in Asakusa nowadays is probably from the Space Rocket in Hanayashiki, but even there it is nearly impossible to catch a glimpse of the Sumida.

Notes

1 First published in *Hon no mado*, March and May 1982. The current translation comes from "Gekijō to shite no Asakusa," in Maeda Ai, *Toshi kūkan no naka no bungaku* (Chikuma Shobō, 1982), 402–416. The translator wishes to acknowledge the very capable assistance of Junko Matsuura in the form of source checking and manuscript double-checking; the further assistance of Abe Shūjirō of the Kindai Bungakukan, Kozuka Mitsuhiro and Shirota Teruhiko of the Asakusa Bunko, Ogiso Toshiko (formerly of the Asakusa Bunko), and Yoshimura Heikichi, all of whom provided materials and/or guidance that greatly aided this translation; and finally the Revs. Amino Yoshihiro (of Konzōin), and Shimizu Eijun (of Enmei'in), both attending priests in the Sensōji compound, who generously facilitated the translator's research on Asakusa. The summary is an adaptation of an introductory paragraph written by Maeda for this same essay when it was anthologized in his *Gen'ei no machi: bungaku no toshi o aruku*, under the title "Kawabata Yasunari *Asakusa kurenaidan*: Asakusa" (Shōgakkan, 1986), 146.

2 Maeda uses the park's official name: Shōkōen (lit. "Little Park"). Sensōji is the common name for Kinryūzan Sensōji, the Asakusa compound's major temple, and the Kannon Hall is its principal building. Niōmon, the gate directly in front of Kannon hall, no longer exists. Burnt down in the great Tokyo air raid of 9–10 March 1945 (which also destroyed the Kannon Hall, rebuilt in 1958, and the pagoda, rebuilt in 1973), it was replaced by the Hōzōmon in 1964. This error on Maeda's part may have been a slip of the tongue or, quite possibly, an act of protest; not a few people still refer to the gate as Niōmon, which was a highly regarded landmark.

3 Matsui Gensui was the name of a hereditary line of performers (at least seventeen

generations) who performed in Edo from the early Tokugawa period until well into this century. See Paul Waley, *Tokyo Now and Then: An Explorer's Guide* (New York: Weatherhill, 1984), esp. 180–181, for a general description of Okuyama's amusements.

4   This is no longer the case. In 1994, the park underwent a major cleanup and re-organization. These two monuments now stand at opposite ends of the park. So-ganoya Gokurō (1876–1940) was a brilliant actor and producer who flourished at several Asakusa theaters before and after the Great Kantō Earthquake and whose trademark role was Nonki na tōsan, the name of a character in a newspaper comic strip later transposed to the stage. Uryū Iwako (also Iwa, 1829–1897), a beloved social worker, devoted her life to charitable work in her native Fukushima and in Tokyo after being widowed at an early age.

5   Sensōji is home to a small golden image of the Kannon Goddess, which legend says was discovered by fishermen in the nearby Sumida River in the seventh century. Toda Mosui (1629–1706) was a well-known poet and literary scholar who lived his entire adult life in Asakusa and is buried in this park. The stupa in question was erected while Toda was still alive.

6   *Yasugibushi* (or *yasukibushi*) is a form of comic dance that originated in Shimane Prefecture (western Honshu) and gained great popularity in Asakusa during the Taishō period.

7   *Naniwabushi* (or *rōkyoku*) is a form of oral narrative in which well-known stories are chanted to the accompaniment of a samisen. The Mokubakan began its run as a variety theater in 1977. For more on this theater (Mokubakan Taishū Gekijō), see Mino Hyōgo, *Asakusa Mokubakan nikki* (Chikuma Shobō, 1996); Marilyn Ivy, "Theatrical Crossings, Capitalist Dreams," in *Discourses of the Vanishing* (Chicago: University of Chicago Press, 1995), 192–239.

8   Mukai Sōya, *Nippon minshū engeki shi* (Nippon Hōsō Shuppan Kyōkai, 1977), 162. Mack Sennett's Keystone Studios was the home of many comedic actors, including Charlie Chaplin and Buster Keaton, during their early careers. (M)

9   Enomoto Ken'ichi (1904–1970), one of Japan's most beloved stage and screen actors, was renowned for his kaleidoscopic facial expressions and astonishing acrobatics.

10 Ushijima Hidehiko, *Asakusa no tomoshibi Enoken* (Mainichi Shimbunsha, 1979), 90–91. (M)

11 Asakusa Opera: a generic name for the opera, laced with wit and satire, that took off during the Taishō period after foundering in other parts of the city in previous years. Flourishing in such Asakusa theaters as the Tokiwa and Kinryūkan, it went into decline after the Great Kantō Earthquake.

12 In 1884 the Asakusa temple precincts and environs, which had been designated one of Tokyo's five public parks in 1873, were divided into seven districts.

13 Ryūgū Palace: the underwater home of Urashima Tarō, who, in the eponymous folk tale, returns to his original home on dry land to find that he has aged à la Rip van Winkle.

14 Kawabata Yasunari, *Asakusa kurenaidan*, in *Kawabata Yasunari zenshū* (Shinchō-sha, 1981), 4:75–76. (M)

15 The Asakusa Jūnikai, officially Ryōunkaku (cloud-piercing pavilion), got its nick-name from the twelve stories (ten of brick topped by two more of wood) it com-prised. The Panoramakan housed large, specially lit murals of battle scenes, in-cluding ones from the American Civil War. Both structures were built in 1890. The Panoramakan was torn down in 1910, giving way to the cinema; the Jūnikai, in 1923, after being severely damaged in the Great Earthquake.

16 The map in question is *Asakusa ezu* (1939); reprinted by Asakusa no Kai, 1953. (M)

17 Shinsen Tōkyō meisho zue, ed. *Fūzoku gahō* (Tōkyōdō, 1897); reprinted as *Tōkyō (to) meisho zue*, 21 vols. (vol. 11: Shitaya-ku; vol. 12: Asakusa-ku; vol. 13: Asakusa Kōen), ed. Miyao Shigeo (Mutsu Shobō, 1968–69), 82. (M)

18 Asakura Musei, *Misemono kenkyū* (Shun'yōdō, 1928; reprinted, Kyoto: Shibun-kaku Shuppan, 1977). See the table of contents. (M)

19 Edogawa Rampo (1894–1965), Japan's most celebrated mystery writer, took his penname from Edgar Allan Poe and is famed for his atmospheric tales.

20 Hori Tatsuo, "Suizokukan," in *Hori Tatsuo zenshū* (Chikuma Shobō, 1977), 1:58. (M)

21 See Ichinose Naoyuki, *Zuihitsu Asakusa* (Sekai Bunko, 1966), 113. In his fine short story "Mokuba wa mawaru" [The carousel goes round, 1926], Edogawa Rampo depicts the unspoken fancy of an old bugler, who works at this same Mokubakan, for the young girl who sells tickets, *Edogawa Rampo zenshū* (Kōdansha, 1969), 3:9–17. (M)

22 Kawabata, *Crimson Gang*, 81.

23 Ibid., 52.

24 Isoda Kōichi, "Kaisetsu," in Kawabata Yasunari, *Asakusa Kurenaidan* (Chūō Kō-ronsha, 1981), 272. [Amino Yoshihiro notes that readers of the original version serialized in the *Asahi shimbun* would have less difficulty discerning Yumiko's habit of cross-dressing, because she is depicted in one of the illustrations donning the garb of a youth with his bicycle—in short, as Akikō. See Amino Yoshihiro, "Asakusa kurenaidan nōto," in *Kafū bungaku to sono shūhen* (Kanrin Shobō, 1993), 244 n. 3. The illustration in question is reproduced on p. 227. (M)

25 Kawabata, *Crimson Gang*, 94.

26 Ibid., 93.

27 Ibid., 66.

28 Ibid., 55.

29 Kawabata Yasunari, *Asakusa Kurenaidan* (Kawade Shobō Shimin Bunko, 1951).

30 Kawabata, *Crimson Gang*, 143.

31 Honda Bizen, *Oshare kyōjo* (originally serialized 1922–23), 3 vols (Kōdansha, 1924–25). (M)

32 The plaque of painted wood known as an *ema* hangs there no longer. This and other ema were all moved to an exhibit hall in the basement of the pagoda in 1988.

Kuniyoshi (family name: Utagawa; Ichiyūsai is one of the artist's pseudonyms) was a well-known ukiyoe artist (1797–1861).

33 Asajigahara: in the present-day Hashiba, located along the Sumida River about a mile northeast of Asakusa. Ubaga'ike, the pond in which the old hag is said to have drowned herself after realizing the evil of her ways, was located just east of Asakusa in Hanakawado.

34 Kaikoku zakki, in *Shinkō gunsho ruijū*, 24:195. (M)

35 Kawabata, *Crimson Gang*, 119.

36 Ibid., 106.

37 Ibid., 104.

38 Ibid., 99.

39 Ibid., 122.

40 Ibid., 121.

41 Edogawa Rampo, "Oshie to tabi suru otoko," 1929, in *Edogawa Rampo zenshū* (Kōdansha, 1969), 4:49–64. (M) The English title is taken from the translation by James B. Harris in Edogawa Rampo, *Japanese Tales of Mystery and Imagination* (Tokyo: Charles E. Tuttle, 1956), 195–222.

42 Jean Cocteau's play *Les Mariés de la tour Eiffel* (1921) was translated into Japanese by Horiguchi Daigaku in 1927 as *Efferu tō no hanayome hanamuko*, in *Horiguchi Daigaku zenshū hokan 3* (Ozawa Shoten, 1985). (M) Maeda, however, translates the title as *Efferu tō no hanayome* (Eiffel Tower bride).

43 Kawabata, *Crimson Gang*, 118. The poem, attributed to Hitomaru but whose author is in fact unknown, originally appeared in the *Kokinshū* (905):

> Honobono to Akashi no ura no asagiri ni
> Shimagakureyuku fune wo shi zo omofu.

> My thoughts trail after the boat as it disappears behind the isle,
> Dimly, dimly into the morning mists of Akashi Bay.

6. The Development of Popular Fiction in the

Late Taishō Era: Increasing Readership of Women's Magazines

(Taishō kōki tsūzoku shōsetsu no tenkai: Fujin zasshi no dokusha-sō)

TRANSLATED BY REBECCA COPELAND

In this essay Maeda Ai attributes the rise of popular literature to the confluence in the early 1920s of three separate phenomena: the establishment of a middle class; the rise in education levels for women; and the preponderance of journals aimed at a female readership. Journals for women were not new to the 1920s. *Jogaku zasshi* (Woman's education magazine), established in 1885, is generally considered the first mass-circulated journal to address a female audience. This journal and its immediate successors were largely devoted to educating and enlightening female members of the new Japanese state and as such were aimed primarily at a small elite readership. But as education for women increased across class lines and as the expendable income of the middle class grew, so too did the audience for women's journals. By the 1920s there was a staggering array of journals for women, as Maeda notes, and for women from a variety of life paths and backgrounds. When competition for readership grew severe among these journals, serialized fiction presented itself as an effective market strategy for attracting readership. And so emerged a symbiotic relationship between magazines for women and popular fiction. As one prospered, so did the other.

Scholars of gender, modernity, and journalism have noted that the combination of women, popular culture, and middle-class consumption is frequently positioned in binaries of negativity. "Mass culture" and the "lowbrow" are situated alongside "pure literature" and "high art," with the female consumer as the party responsible for allowing the former to overcome the latter. Maeda's essay provides instances of a similar prejudice, citing critics who held women's magazines accountable for "eroding" the *bundan* and encouraging "hack works" that "dulled the stylistic perfection" of pure literature. But Maeda pushes beyond the standard clichés by removing "popular literature" from the onus of corrupter and reading it as a legitimate literary response to a multiplicity of social and historical contexts. Most important, he acknowledges women's magazines as offering male writers space for artistic creativity and social commentary. And he allows women readers an active role in the development of popular fiction.[1]

1

On 15 December 1926, as the nation braced for the transition from the Taishō (1912–1926) to the Shōwa (1926–1989) reign years, Ōya Sōichi published his first work of literary criticism, "The Era of the Dissolution of the Bundan Guild" ["Bundan girudo no kaitaiki"] in the journal *Shinchō*.[2] This essay, written just as the era of the so-called one-yen books [*enpon*] was dawning, dealt in equal measure with both the newly emergent proletarian movement and the popularization of literature. In so doing, Ōya predicted the death of the Taishō *bundan* [literary guild]. He enumerated the characteristics of the Taishō bundan, which he decreed to be a system of apprenticeship [*toteiseido*].[3] Moreover, he counted the growing appeal of women's magazines as one of the primary factors leading to the demise of these guilds:

> The wave of prosperity that flooded the world after the sudden outbreak of war in Europe enabled many to strike it rich while at the same time it helped those in the middle and lower classes. The expanding markets had an impact on journalism in our country. The most spectacular phenomenon was the increase in readership among women, which influenced journalism with a force similar to the discovery of a new frontier. Thus, the sudden rise in women's magazines has had an effect on the bundan in our country, just as significantly as the growth of the spinning industry—with its appeal to consumers in China—has affected our financial markets. Moreover, the rise in the income of popular writers is proportionate to the expansion of women's magazines.[4]

The improved livelihoods of trendy writers abetted by "the expansion of women's magazines" encouraged the mass production of "hack works" [*daraketa sakuhin*] and dulled the stylistic perfection of the *shishōsetsu* [I-fiction] and *shinkyō shōsetsu* [mental-state novel].[5] The pervasiveness of these "hack works" followed the pattern of "modernism," also seen in the move from teahouses and geisha to cafés and waitresses, and from poem card games and *shōgi* to mahjongg, billiards, and baseball. This aspect of Ōya's observation of the bundan is consistent with Satō Haruo's discussion of the popularization of printing in his essay "On the Livelihood of the Writer" ["Bungeika no seikatsu o ronzu"] in *Shinchō* (September 1926).[6] But what I would like to stress here is the fact that Ōya attributed the phenomenon of the popularization of literature in the late Taishō period to the expansion of women's magazines.

Historically, 1926 was an important year for popular literature [*taishū bungaku*]. The first issue of *Taishū bungei* [Literary arts for the masses] was launched with Shirai Kyōji as its advocate by the *Nijū-ichinichi-kai* [the 21st club].[7] In July, *Chūō kōron* devised a special issue devoted to articles on popular literature. In August, Osaragi Jirō began serializing *Sunny Days, Cloudy Days* [*Teruhi, kumoru hi*] in the *Osaka Asahi Shimbun* and Yoshikawa Eiji began his serialization of *The Secret Naruto Notebooks* [*Naruto hichō*] in the *Osaka Mainichi*.[8] Shirai Kyōji's *Shadows over Mt. Fuji* [*Fuji ni tatsu kage*] and Yada Sōun's *Records of Toyotomi Hideyoshi* [*Taikōki*] were each appearing in the *Hōchi News*.[9] Thus, 1926 saw the simultaneous appearance of all the great preliminary works of popular literature. That this popular literature attracted a wide audience is indisputable, but this was not a bundan issue, as these readers did not overlap with the bundan readership. Yet, bundan members tended to publish their short shinkyō shōsetsu in general interest magazines [*sōgō zasshi*] or in literary journals, while they contributed longer, popular novels [*tsūzoku chōhen*] to newspapers and women's magazines—that was their modus operandi. They may have written popular serial novels, but almost never did this extend to one of those formulaic period-piece novels [*magemono*] set in the samurai days of old Edo. Ōya Sōichi's discussion of the bundan, in which he scrutinizes women's magazines, reflects on the guilt bundan members felt over the fact that they could not avoid this double allegiance.

One and a half years prior to Ōya Sōichi's article, Aono Suekichi had referred to the increase in female readership in his essay "What Women Want in Literature" ["Josei no bungakuteki yōkyū"], which appeared in June 1925 in an unidentified publication and then was reissued in February 1927 in *Literature at the Turning Point* [*Tenkanki no bungaku*].[10] Aono states, "The scope of readers familiar with literature has grown so large that we seem to be living in quite a different world." Yet the fact of the matter was that "the increase in women readers was so remarkable" that now it would seem that "women's magazines and domestic interest magazines [*katei zasshi*] are the main outlets for literature."[11]

A short time after Aono's essay appeared, Katagami Noboru analyzed the differences between readers of pure literature [*jun bungaku*] and those of popular fiction, and discovered that of the readers of popular fiction "the majority were women and significantly they were of the intelligentsia."[12] Aono, Katagami, and Ōya—acting in unison—focused on the phenomenon of the popularization of literature. It is not mere coincidence that they each referred to the increase in female readership as the primary factor controlling the trend in the Taishō bundan, for these were men who sought to introduce into their literary criticism a so-called outsider perspective. It is presumed, for example, that in 1926 Aono represented the front guard for advancing a proletarian literary theory. Moreover, he stated in his own critique of Katagami's "Literary Criticism": "In order to observe literature as a social phenomenon and thoroughly investigate its social implications, we cannot overlook the presence of the reader as an element in the composition of literature. The social class of the reader plays a particularly large role in the deterioration of literary arts and in an age like the present one, this problem is especially significant. Surely the importance of this problem is obvious. Yet no one has dealt with the issue as concretely as Katagami."[13]

Katagami and Aono were both writing at the end of the Taishō era. One was a veteran critic, the other just beginning his career. And yet it seems that each influenced the other. Ōya Sōichi took the work of both these men as his starting point in his rather journalistic "Dissolution of the Literary Guilds." In so doing, he was able to further the discussion by introducing the matter of female readership.

By focusing on the way the Taishō bundan and the increase in female readers influenced one another, these critics contributed to the debate between Kume Masao and Nakamura Murao on shinkyō shōsetsu and *honkaku shōsetsu* [true novel].[14] Although the division between writing pure and writing popular fiction was easy, the debate between Kume and Nakamura, which failed to consider the reader's consciousness, left room for much deliberation. To describe the situation in very general terms, the late Taishō debates between Kume and Nakamura polarized Aono, Katagami, and Ōya against Satō Haruo. Whereas the former brandished their theories of readership and the bundan, the latter responded with "On the Livelihood of the Writer," which focused on the subjectivity of the writer.

2

What factors prompted Ōya Sōichi to write his essay "The Sudden Rise in Women's Magazines" ["Fujin zasshi no kyūgeki naru hatten"]? I shall attempt a rough outline. The most influential women's magazines to emerge in the late Taishō era are listed in Table 1.

Hashimoto Motomu relates that around 1924, when he was the editor of *Woman's Club* [*Fujin kurabu*], *Housewife's Friend* [*Shufu no tomo*] was the preeminent woman's magazine, printing up to 240,000 copies an issue. *Woman's Sphere* [*Fujokai*] followed with 220,000 an issue, and *Woman's World* [*Fu-*

Table 1

Magazine Title (English translation)	Founding Date	Publisher
Jogaku sekai (Woman's education world)	1901	Hakubunkan
Fujin gahō (Woman's pictorial)	1905	Tokyosha; later, Fujin gahōsha
Fujin sekai (Woman's world)	1906	Jitsugyō no Nihonsha
Fujin no tomo (Woman's friend)	1908	Fujin no tomosha
Fujokai (Woman's sphere)	1910	Dōbunkan; later, Fujokaisha
Shukujo gahō (Lady's illustrated)	1912	Hakubunkan
Katei zasshi (Family journal)	1915	Hakubunkan
Fujin kōron (Woman's review)	1916	Chūō kōronsha
Shufu no tomo (Housewife's friend)	1917	Tokyo kaseikai; later. Shufu no tomosha
Fujin kurabu (The woman's club)	1920	Dai Nihon Yūbenkai Kōdansha
Josei (Woman)	1922	Puratonsha
Josei kaizō (Woman's reconstruction)	1922	Kaizōsha
Reijokai (Lady's world)	1922	Takara bunkan
Wakakusa (Young grass)	1925	Takara bunkan

jin sekai] with 180,000.[15] The total number of copies printed for the New Year's issues of women's magazines in 1925 was roughly 1,200,000.[16] In 1919, when *Chūō kōron* was printing 120,000 copies per issue, *Woman's Review* [*Fujin kōron*] was printing 70,000.[17] *Woman's Sphere* had a printing of a mere 13,000 in 1913 but by the fall of 1926 had reached 250,000 copies per issue.[18] *Woman's Club* had a printing of 40,000 when it was inaugurated in October 1920. By its New Year's issue in 1927 it had reached 150,000 copies.[19] Moreover, to celebrate its twentieth anniversary, *Woman's World* printed a staggering 600,000 copies of its May issue in 1927.[20] From the above data we can infer that five of the largest-circulating women's magazines in the late Taishō era—that is to say, *Housewife's Friend*, *Woman's Sphere*, *Woman's World*, *Woman's Review*, and *Woman's Club*—had printing figures in the six digits.

The consumption of this massive amount of women's magazines would seem to be tied directly to the new middle class that grew dramatically in the mid-Taishō era. Minami Hiroshi in his study *Taishō bunka* [Taishō culture] identified three contributing factors that led to the emergence of the new middle class in the Taishō period.[21] First, based on estimates of the actual number of taxpayers in the third-class income bracket, the percentage of total households identified as "middle class," with an annual income of 500–5,000 yen in 1903, was not more than 2.38 percent. However, this number increased steadily hereafter and reached 5 percent in 1917. The favorable economic conditions following WWI meant that between 1917 and 1918, the number of middle-class households increased to about 250,000, and by 1925 the number of households with a yearly income of 800–5,000 yen—identified as "middle class"—had risen to 11.5 percent. In this year, the total number of taxpaying households was approximately 12,000,000.[22] The number of middle-class households would have been 1,400,000. This figure roughly corresponds with the number of New Year's issues of women's magazines printed that year: 1,200,000. Moreover, we can draw a direct line between fixed subscriptions of these magazines and the amount of annual income—roughly 800 yen at the lower end—that would support such an expense. Statistics provided by the Public Sector of the Tokyo Office of Internal Affairs, based on the 1922 Survey of Middle-Class Households,[23] which examined those with monthly incomes between 60 yen and 250 yen, showed that:

1. Government employees with incomes of 60–80 yen had monthly expenditures of roughly 2 yen 20 sen on "self-cultivation" [*shūyō*].
2. Public servants spent 1 yen 40 sen.
3. Police officers, 2 yen 55 sen.
4. Elementary/middle school teachers, 2 yen 37 sen.
5. Bank employees/company employees, 1 yen 47 sen.
6. Streetcar workers, 2 yen 10 sen.
7. Factory workers, 1 yen 47 sen.

For those with income less than 60 yen, the average spent by a policeman's household was 46 sen and 56 sen for streetcar workers. This would just barely cover the subscription to a newspaper. Articles in women's magazines on the management of household budgets help bolster this supposition. In the December 1925 issue of *Woman's World*, we find an article entitled "Household Budgets for Families with Monthly Incomes in the 70-Yen Bracket." The article offers four sample budgets. The first describes the household of an office worker in Yonezawa whose monthly income is 72 yen 25 sen. The budget provides 2 yen 91 sen for "self-cultivation" and "entertainment" expenses.

The rationale for this expense is: "Newspaper subscriptions are 80 sen . . . and then there are costs for *Woman's World* and books—which are about the only forms of entertainment available, as the family lives in a rural area." Then there is a schoolteacher in Shimane Prefecture with a monthly income of 72 yen. His budget allows 7 yen for books and other reading material. This includes 1 yen 20 sen for newspapers; two magazines for the husband, one for the wife, and one for the children, totaling 1 yen 80 sen; and another 1 yen 50 sen for books. Next, the article provides a budget for a company employee in Yamaguchi Prefecture with a monthly income of 71 yen. His family budgets 3 yen for reading material: a regional newspaper, two magazines for the husband, and self-cultivation [shūyō] books and *Woman's World* for the wife. The household of a member of the military service in Chiba Prefecture with an income of 63 yen has 3 yen budgeted for self-cultivation publications. The breakdown: one newspaper and three magazines.

This article on household budgets coupled with the Tokyo survey of incomes are particularly useful in determining interest in periodicals among those with middle-class incomes in the late Taishō period (early 1920s). Although it is important to take into account differences in the years during which this information was compiled (one in 1922, the other in 1925) and differences in the locales of the surveys (one focused on Tokyo and the other on rural areas), nevertheless, this information reveals that in the late Taishō era, middle-class families with annual incomes of roughly 800 yen were able to afford, in addition to newspapers and magazines for the husband, subscriptions to women's magazines for the wife.

The fact that more girls were completing their middle school education in the late Taishō era, combined with the increase of the new middle class, largely explained the rise of women's magazines. The favorable economic conditions that developed in the aftermath of the First World War saw both the improvement in the standard of living in Japan and a demand for advanced education. This in turn precipitated the demand for the expansion of middle and higher schools (see Table 2).

Ordinances for education at the middle, higher, and university levels were revised and amended between 1918 and 1919. Middle schools, which are equivalent to our contemporary high schools, aimed to provide a complete education under the charter of the Agency for Standard Education at the Higher Level, and came to bear the main responsibility for the education of the middle class in correspondence to the expansion of that class.[24] The increase in schools and in the numbers of students was particularly remarkable among higher schools [kōtō jogakkō] for girls. Between 1918 and 1926, the number of schools increased by 2.5 and the number of students by 3.2. (During the same

Table 2. Number of Higher Schools for Girls, Students and Graduates, during the Taishō Period

	Number of Schools	Number of Students	Number of Graduates (Regular course only)
1913	213	68,367	10,163
1914	214	72,139	13,992
1915	223	75,832	15,042
1916	229	80,767	15,896
1917	238	86,431	16,759
1918	257	94,525	18,457
1919	274	103,498	19,984
1920	336	125,588	24,030
1921	417	154,470	27,985
1922	468	185,025	32,635
1923	529	216,624	37,096
1924	576	246,938	42,466
1925	618	275,823	52,845
1926	663	296,935	59,169
1927	697	315,765	64,206

time period, the number of middle schools increased by 1.5 and the number of students by 1.2.) In 1925, the number of women who graduated from higher schools was greater than 10 percent of the total population of young women in that age group. Consequently, the special October issues of women's magazines, which typically featured weddings, were challenged by March and April issues focusing on "the new graduate." This kind of strategy was a clever ploy to tap into the markets offered by an increase in new readership.

The ground on which the so-called New Woman [*atarashii onna*] found her footing in the Taishō era consisted of new middle-class women who had been blessed with the opportunity to pursue a secondary education. These women had their doubts about the erstwhile culture of domesticity that had earlier supported the values of the "good wife/wise mother" and the patriarchal family system. They began to seek greater social engagement. They also began demanding the "rehabilitation" of the women's sphere in Japan that had heretofore been subordinated to that of men.[25] Needless to say, *Woman's Review* [*Fujin kōron*] became an opinion leader in this enterprise, resuming the argument that women be freed from the home, allowed to advance socially, and permitted to enjoy political rights, such as suffrage.

After WWI, the acceleration of women entering the marketplace was a worldwide phenomenon. Unlike the situation in Western countries, however, women in Japan had not taken over the jobs that men had vacated to go to war. Nevertheless, during the war and just after it, new jobs for women began to open up. Among these new jobs were those of typist and bus conductor, and there was a notable increase in the demand for café and restaurant waitresses, who created new categories in the entertainment industry and thus replaced the geisha.

The appearance of women in the marketplace became such a social phenomenon that journals like *Woman's Review* and even those like *Housewife's Friend*—that is, magazines that clearly targeted the housewife—carried special issues in March 1918 on "Women in the Marketplace." One such article in this special issue of *Housewife's Friend*, "A Guide to Female Occupations," listed twenty-seven jobs that were considered appropriate for women. Among the jobs listed were doctor, dentist, pharmacist, railroad office worker, typist, journalist, stenographer, chauffeur, and model. Women's presence in fields traditionally considered appropriately feminine, such as teaching and nursing, grew dramatically. For example, in 1914 there were 14,547 female nurses in Japan. That figure rose to 35,581 in 1919 and to 42,367 in 1924.[26] The percentage of female elementary school teachers in 1912 was 37.5; but in 1917, it rose to 41.5 and in 1922 to 47.5.[27] In 1923, there were approximately 15,000 female office workers in Tokyo City, 8,500 telephone operators, 4,500 store clerks, 1,774 typists, 1,598 elementary school teachers, and 847 secondary school teachers. Additionally, there were 5,000 women employed as waitresses and 1,500 employed in theater and performance-related professions. And, although the numbers are hardly notable, there were also women working as screen actresses, chauffeurs, photographers, guides, reporters, stenographers, detectives, conductors, and other such new professions.[28] What was the dissemination rate of women's magazines among this kind of working woman?

"A Survey of Working Women," conducted by the Public Sector of the Tokyo Municipal Office in 1924, targeted teachers, typists, office workers, store clerks, nurses, telephone operators, and so on. In the section on reading material, among the 900 respondents, 800 indicated that they subscribed to a newspaper and 747 to a magazine. In the section on magazines, among the 1,184 respondents who indicated that they subscribed to a magazine, 841 stated that the magazine was a woman's magazine.[29] When not controlled for multiple subscriptions, this amounts to a very high subscription rate of nearly 93 percent. (In a similar survey of 1,324 female factory workers, 544, or about 41 percent, indicated that they read women's magazines.) As for the level of education among the respondents, 26.5 percent of the teachers finished middle school; 38.5 percent of the typists; 21.6 percent of office workers; and 17.9 percent of store clerks. In his above-cited study, Aono noted the increase in women's magazine readership:

> In the remaining sector of women's society (i.e., all those not iden-
> tified as belonging to either the upper or the lower classes) are women
> in households belonging to the middle-income bracket . . . the so-called
> petit bourgeoisie. The increase in women of this bracket has led to growth
> in readers of women's and domestic-issue magazines. Simultaneously, we
> have found an expansion in the number of people who claim to espouse
> an interest in literature. Contributing to this increase is the growth of
> the number of housewives associated with middle-income households.
> However, we also need to include in this category women associated with
> such female-identified occupations as teaching, office work, and typing.
> Strictly speaking, these women are not categorized among the middle
> class. But whether because of birth or education, many of them espouse
> the spirit of the petit bourgeoisie. In this sense, their intellectual habits
> and emotional needs are consistent with this social group.[30]

Aono's observation suggests that the increase in readership of women's magazines is in direct correlation to the increase in education for women and to
an elevation of social consciousness among women.

3

The newly emerging middle class, which grew rapidly after the First
World War, formed the nucleus of women's magazine readership. This readership soon surpassed 1,000,000. Women's and domestic-interest magazines,
competing for possession of this newly discovered "frontier," as Ōya Sōichi
had termed it, numbered close to twenty or more around the time of the
Great Kantō Earthquake in 1923. Each magazine battled the other for a share
of the market. This ever-escalating competition resembled that among newspapers. In 1923 the *Asahi* and the *Mainichi*, both of Osaka, began trying to
tap markets in the Tokyo area. Their incursions met with similar strategies
on the part of Tokyo-based newspapers, such as the *Hōchi* and *Jiji*, which
tried to press into Osaka markets. Women's magazines, however, were ahead
of the game when it came to marketing campaigns.[31] Moreover, competition
between these magazines was so extreme that when *Women's Reconstruction*
[*Josei kaizō*], for example, was inaugurated by Kaizōsha in October 1922, it
received such intensive competition from *Woman's Review* [*Fujin kōron*] that
it was forced out of business by November 1924.

It was around this time that we see the sudden increase in copies published by *Housewife's Friend* under the direction of Ishikawa Takeyoshi. He employed various techniques to organize and increase readership.[32] Following the New Year's issue of 1922, for example, he experimented with bimonthly issues. When this strategy proved unsuccessful, he created a new division in the magazine known as the "cultural division" [*bunka jitsugyōbu*] in March of the same year. Stopping short of describing this innovation as a "cultural movement" [*bunka undō*], he announced the creation of this new division in the April issue as follows: "We have embarked on a new strategy with this 'Cultural Division' because we wish to usher in a reform of the way we lead our lives on a practical level, while at the same time we hope to develop new avenues of thought [*shisō*]. . . . We propose the convening of numerous lectures and concerts that will accommodate upwards of 500 people. All arrangements for the venue of these events are the responsibility of the convenors."

The first lecture was held that year on 7 March in Yokohama. The next was in Kōfu, then Kyoto and Osaka. Among the names of the lecturers were Kagawa Toyohiko and Miyake Yasuko.[33] Actually, this kind of strategy to organize readership through a lecture series had been used earlier by *Woman's Sphere* under the title Greater Japan Women's Association for Self-Cultivation [Dai Nippon fujin shūyōkai]. *Housewife's Friend* took the word "self-cultivation" [shūyō], which was redolent of the past, and replaced it with "culture" [*bunka*], suggestive of a new era. This was Ishikawa's means of tapping into the demands of the age. Similarly, it was his idea to offer culture-oriented lectures and concerts in combination with exhibits of more practical value. The first of these exhibits, which featured handicrafts for the home, was held in April 1924 in the Ikenohata Annex of the Matsuzakaya Department Store. The exhibit then traveled to Shizuoka, Hokkaido, Kyoto, and Osaka. In Hokkaido and the Kansai region, the exhibit also included knitting demonstrations and explanations as well as lectures and concerts. Among the lecturers were Tagawa Daikichirō, Kubushiro Ochimi, Miyake Yasuko, and Ichikawa Fusae.[34] The concert included Sogabe Shizue and Seki Akiko. The strategy of combining music, lecture, and practical skills in forums for those readers outside Tokyo, together with the editor's policy of targeting readers below the middle class, resulted in a multiplying of sales. The 10,000 copies per issue that the magazine had sold when it first hit the stands grew to 200,000 in a mere seven or eight years.

Housewife's Friend's strategy of organizing its readership stimulated similar strategies among its competitors *Woman's Sphere* and *Woman's Club*. For example, around 1924 *Woman's Sphere* initiated a column called "Interviews with Our Favorite Readers." In this column, readers would sit down with the editors in a roundtable forum [*zadankai*] and exchange ideas. This feature was devised in an effort to encourage readership in rural areas. *Woman's Review* was comparatively late in trying out similar strategies. Editor Shimanaka Yūsaku waited until April 1931 before he began touring the countryside by automobile to host lectures and roundtables with Hosoda Genkichi and Miyake Yasuko.[35]

Of course, it hardly bears mentioning that magazine editors gave serious consideration to expanding the fiction columns in their efforts to attract readership and increased sales. This is especially true of *Woman's Sphere*, which succeeded in signing on two of the most popular writers of the day, Kikuchi Kan[36] and Kume Masao. This strategy paid off and opened an entirely different path from the one *Housewife's Friend* had taken. In "Interview with Our Favorite Readers," Kikuchi Kan's *New Gems* [Niitama], which was being serialized at the time, was frequently a topic of discussion.[37] Even chief editor Togawa Ryū noticed the power of the text to increase sales when he stated, "Thanks to the reviews of *New Gems*, sales of our magazine have increased with every issue. In an effort to express even a fraction of our gratitude, we have increased the contribution rate (meaning the amount paid the author for his manuscript)."[38]

The rise in compensation for writers of fiction most tellingly reflected this tendency to value their contribution to these magazines. Sasaki Kuni's fee for the serialization of his translation of a work by the British humorist Simms, which he began in March 1918, was 1 yen per page.[39] Kikuchi Kan's short story "My Elder Sister's Memoir" ["Ane no oboegaki"], which he published in the inaugural issue of *Woman's Club*, October 1920, earned him 30 yen for eighteen pages.[40] Still, we cannot conclude that the remuneration by women's magazines was unusually high. The going rate for stories published in *Chūō kōron* around 1919, for example, was from 1 yen to 1 yen 50 sen per page (at this time, these rates were not exactly high), compared to the 2 yen per page that *Woman's Sphere* paid Yanagawa Shun'yō and Oguri Fūyō.[41] This represents the high end of the scale in the early Taishō period. Around the time of the 1923 earthquake, manuscript fees increased markedly. Kume Masao's contracted fee for *Shipwreck* [*Hasen*], which he serialized from January to December of 1922 in *Housewife's Friend*, was 10,000 yen.[42] *Shipwreck* came to about 720 pages, which means that Kume received just under 14 yen per page. Kosugi Tengai received 600 yen each time an installment of his *Katakana Festival* [*Katakana matsuri*] appeared in *Woman's World*, and it was serialized from January 1923 to June 1924.[43] Kikuchi Kan, it is estimated, earned between 30 yen and 40 yen per page for his manuscript, *Flowers of Suffering* [*Ju'nan-bana*], which was serialized from March 1925 to December 1926 in *Woman's Sphere*.[44] Kasai Zenzō received 88 yen for his eleven-page work, *Coughing Blood* [*Chi o haku*], which he published in the 1925 New Year's issue of *Chūō kōron*, indicating that by the end of the Taishō era, women's magazines paid manuscript fees that were four to five times greater than those provided by general-interest magazines [*sōgō zasshi*].[45] And, of course, the fees provided by the literary journals, such as *Shinchō*, were lower still. The increase in manuscript fees followed the increase in publications of issue numbers, but on the other hand, this also proves that the editors of women's magazines put a great deal of stock in the ability to mobilize or manipulate the readership of popular serialized novels.

4

Senuma Shigeki (1904–1988) has stated that there was an epoch-making change in the category of domestic fiction [*katei shōsetsu*][46] around the time Kume Masao's *Firefly Grass* [*Hotarugusa*] appeared in *Jiji shimpō* (March–June 1918) and Kikuchi Kan's *Madame Pearl* [*Shinju fujin*] was serialized in the *Osaka Mainichi* and *Tokyo Nichi-nichi* (June–December 1920). He argued that, historically, this change was stimulated by improvements in women's social circumstances, wherein women were finding more opportunities to move beyond their feudalistic family roles and into more socially engaged ones.[47] These long novels by Kume and Kikuchi did not strictly conform to contemporary critics' criteria for domestic fiction and were more in keeping with the classification for "popular fiction" [*tsūzoku shōsetsu*] or popular literature [*tsūzoku bungaku*].[48] According to Miyajima Shinsaburō, for example (see his *Fourteen Lectures on Taishō Literature* [*Taishō bungaku jūyon kō*]), their works were seen as different from those of such domestic fiction writers as Yanagawa Shun'yō and Kikuchi Yūhō.[49] Furthermore, it appears that by early Shōwa, the view that such works as *Firefly Grass* and *Madame Pearl* were the inaugural works of the "new popular fiction" was already well established.[50]

However, while women's magazines were forums for long works of popular fiction, as were newspapers, the former were by nature more conservative. Around 1919 or 1920, when *Firefly Grass* and *Madame Pearl* ushered in a new phase for newspapers, the fiction column in women's magazines had become the private domain of a select roster of established writers. For example, in 1920, the works that appeared in the fiction columns of the five leading women's magazines were as follows:

Woman's Review [Fujin kōron]
> Okamoto Kidō (1872–1939), *The Princess Osakabe or Shōsakabe*
> [*Osakabe or Shōsakabe hime*], April–December
> Kume Masao, *Flowers of Emptiness [Kūka]*, January–December

Woman's Sphere [Fujokai]
> Takeda Gyōtenshi (1854–1926), *The Old Woman Muraoka [Rōjo*
> *Muraoka]*, January–December
> Ōkura Tōrō (1879–1944), *A Marriageable Age [Totsugukoro]*,
> January–December
> Oguri Fūyō (1875–1926), *Beloved Wife [Omoizuma]*, January–
> December 1921

Housewife's Friend [Shufu no tomo]
> Watanabe Katei (1864–1926), *The Gilt Fan [Kinsen]*, January–
> December
> Sasaki Kuni (1883–1964), *Chintarō's Diary [Chintarō nikki]*,
> January–December
> Okamoto Kidō, *Good-luck Grass [Kichijōsō]*, January–December

Woman's Club [Fujin kurabu]
> Nakarai Tōsui (1860–1926), *Fair-weather Revenge [Hare no adauchi]*,
> October–May 1921
> Chikamatsu Shūkō (1876–1944), *Departing Clouds [Yukugumo]*,
> October–January 1921
> Okamoto Kidō, *Last Revenge [Saigo no fukushū]*, October–December

Woman's World [Fujin sekai]
> Kosugi Tengai (1865–1952), *Hell in Three Generations [Sandai jigoku]*,
> January–December 1921
> Kamitsukasa Shōken (1874–1947), *Jewel [Hōgyoku]*, January–
> December

In addition, there were works being serialized in other women's magazines. For example, Tokuda Shūsei's (1871–1943) *Flowers of the Dark [Yami no hana]* appeared in *Woman's Friend*, and Kikuchi Yūhō's *The Woman Who Betrayed Love [Koi o uragiru onna]* was serialized in *Woman's Pictorial [Fujin gahō]*. Takeda Gyōtenshi was the oldest writer of this group at age 67 and Kume Masao, at 30, was the youngest (according to the Japanese style of reckoning years). The others, in descending order of age, were Nakarai Tōsui (61), Watanabe Katei (57), Kosugi Tengai (56), Kikuchi Yūhō (51), Tokuda Shūsei (50), Okamoto Kidō (49), Kamitsukasa Shōken (47), Oguri Fūyō (46), Chikamatsu Shūkō (45), Ōkura Tōrō (42), and Sasaki Kuni (38). Of course, Gyōtenshi, Tōsui, Katei, Tengai, Yūhō, and Fūyō were veteran writers who had begun their careers as newspaper novelists back in the late 1880s, and only Kume Masao and Sasaki Kuni were defined as Taishō writers. Thus, we might describe the situation as "antique" in outlook. However, a mere six years later, the table of contents for these magazines was markedly different:

Woman's Review [*Fujin kōron*]
> Satomi Ton (1888–1983), *Great Gateless Path* [*Taidō mumon*], January–December
> Shirai Kyōji (1889–1980), *Gold Brocade Wars* [*Kinransen*], January–December
> Uno Chiyo (1897–1996), *Madame Ama* [*Ama fujin*], January–March
> Maedakō Hiroichirō (1888–1957), *An Unforgettable Man* [*Wasurenu otoko*], April–June
> Katō Takeo (1888–1956), *Sound of the Waves* [*Tōsei*], July–September
> Sōma Taizō (1885–1952), *Until One Becomes a Stranger* [*Tanin ni narikiru made*], October–December

Woman's Sphere [*Fujokai*]
> Kikuchi Kan, *Flowers of Suffering* [*Ju'nan-bana*], March 1925–December 1926
> Kume Masao, *Heaven and Earth* [*Ten to chi to*], March 1925–December 1926
> Mikami Otokichi (1891–1944), *Charms for Wedded Bliss* [*Oshidori jumon*], January–July 1927
> Hosoda Tamiki (1892–1972), *Lovers* [*Aijin*], September–December 1927

Housewife's Friend [*Shufu no tomo*]
> Ide Karoku, *Maiden at the Crossroads* [*Jūjiro no otome*], January–March 1927
> Tanizaki Jun'ichirō (1886–1965), *The Account of Tomoda and Matsunaga* [*Tomoda to Matsunaga no hanashi*], January–May
> Ōkura Tōrō (1879–1944), *Dancing Sleeves in Autumn Rain* [*Maisode shigure*], January–June
> Sasaki Kuni, *Comedy at Culture Village* [*Bunkamura no kigeki*], June–December
> Ikuta Chōsuke (1889–1976), *Burning the Sacred Fire* [*Seika moyu*], August–December 1927

Woman's Club [*Fujin kurabu*]

    Sasaki Kuni, *Sovereignty and a Wifely Rights* [*Shuken, saiken*], October 1925–September 1926

    Yamanaka Minetarō (1885–1966), *Mutual Love/Mutual Hate* [*Sōshi-on*], October 1925–April 1926

    Baba Kochō (1869–1940), *Bramble Path* [*Ibara no michi*], January–April

    Nakamura Murao, *Good Looks* [*Bibō*], January–December

    Katō Takeo, *Dyed with Love Grass* [*Aizomegusa*], January–February 1927

    Yoshiya Nobuko (1896–1973), *The People of Paradise Lost* [*Shitsuraku no hitobito*], April–November

    Azuma Kenji, *Laughter Farm* [*Warai no nōen)*], October–July 1927

Woman's World [*Fujin sekai*]

    Katō Takeo, *Rhapsody* [*Kyōsōkyoku)*], January-December

    Kitaōji Haruo, *A Dream of Kōro* [*Kōro no yūme*], January–May 1927

    Motoura Naokazu (prize-winning work), *Chapter on Domestic Bliss* [*Katei enman no maki*], January–May

    Ōizumi Kokuseki (1894–1957), *Princess Katsura* [*Katsurahime*], July–December

    Hashizume Ken (1900–1964), *Beauty and Pain* [*Bi'nan*], September–December

In 1926 the great veterans of popular fiction, Takeda Gyōtenshi, Nakarai Tōsui, Watanabe Katei, and Oguri Fūyō, died one after the other. In 1923, Kikuchi Yūhō, using the publication of his fifteen-volume collected works by Kokumin Tosho Kaisha as his opportunity, resigned from his thirty-year tenure with *Osaka Mainichi*. Kosugi Tengai had by this time become a "has-been" in the popular literature arena. In the six years surrounding the Great Earthquake of 1923 (that is to say, 1920–26), the literary realm saw a rapid advance from old to new. Kikuchi Kan and Kume Masao replaced Katei and Yūhō, wresting from them their positions as the top writers. Nakamura Murao and Katō Takeo, surpassing Kikuchi and Kume in production, made their presence felt in the world of popular literature from around 1923. The magemono storytelling style of the samurai tales, such as that popularized by Tōsui and Gyōtenshi, receded swiftly, and the fresh pieces of popular fiction characterized by Shirai Kyōji and Mikami Otokichi took center stage.[51] Shirai's *Gold Brocade Wars* [*Kinran sen*] is set in the spinning mills, which had been exposed by the study *The Sad History of Female Factory Workers* [*Jokōaishi*]; Mikami's *Charms for Wedded Bliss* [*Oshidori jumon*] is purportedly based on a late Edo-era romance involving the problems between society and individuals in love. Both works represent a new direction in popular fiction and in the advancement of women's magazines.

It is also important to observe that works by women writers also began to appear in women's magazines at this time. Clearly, the magazines sought to employ women writers, such as Uno Chiyo, Yoshiya Nobuko, Miyake Yasuko, and Yamada Junko, in a market strategy aimed at attracting greater female readership.[52]

Satomi Ton and Tanizaki Jun'ichirō, on the other hand, were writers of immense creative talent who felt hemmed in by the rigid demands of the literary journals and general interest magazines that advocated a preponderance of short works. Taking advantage of the system of serialization that women's magazines offered, they used them as an outlet for the publication of their own brand of midsize and long pieces of pure literature [*jun bungaku*] (which were typically short works),[53] as evidenced by Satomi's *Great Gateless Path* [*Daidō mumon*] and Tanizaki's *Tomoda and Matsunaga* [*Tomoda to Matsunaga no hanashi*].

This shift from old to new guard and the subsequent advancement of the new into the bundan, accompanied by the pluralization of journalism and the expansion of creative fiction columns, led Aono Suekichi to conclude, "Today we have reached the point where women's magazines and domestic interest magazines offer the main outlet for literary publication."[54] In the second half of the Taishō era, there was a heightened interaction and influence between the bundan and print journalism. To what extent did this affect the transformation of popular fiction itself? I will herewith consider the trajectory of this shift from pure to popular literature by focusing on Kikuchi Kan's activities and the way he successively initiated new directions in popular literature.

5

As I have already suggested, 1920 was an epochal year in which Kikuchi Kan's *Madame Pearl* achieved stunning success as a new kind of newspaper novel at the same time the literary columns in women's magazines still retained the inertia of the old established writers. The content of their works continued to conform to existing stereotypes. If they were period pieces, for example, they were the formulaic samurai-period piece [magemono] in the traditional historical narrative style [kōdan]. Works with contemporary settings followed the pattern of domestic fiction, such as *One's Own Sin* [*Ono ga tsumi*] and *Incompatible* [*Nasanu naka*]. The editors of women's magazines were completely wedded to the ease of signing on an older writer who had already established a reputation as a newspaper novelist and whose writing was thereby predictable.

Let us consider the example of Kosugi Tengai, who began serializing *Hell in Three Generations* [*Sandai jigoku*] in *Woman's World* this year. The theme of this story, as we can ascertain from the title, is how a particular fate is passed through a family for three generations. For Tengai, who advocated Zolaism and subscribed to the importance of heredity, this was undoubtedly a well-polished theme. The story is predictably convoluted as it unfolds around the Kajimura family, wealthy farmers of Maruko Tamagawa on the southern fringe of Tokyo.[55] That which we might consider the main story line revolves around the relationship between Namiko and Makiyama Toshirō. Namiko is the sole daughter of Osumi, the family patriarch Zentarō's mistress, and Toshirō is a university student. However, the love between the two proves impossible when it is revealed that Namiko and Toshirō are actually siblings. Distraught, Namiko leaves for Kyoto. As the story ends, she has taken the tonsure and entered Buddhist orders. The scene in which Namiko sets out in a rickshaw on her way to the Sengakuji temple for a secret tryst with Toshirō is redolent with the flavor of past ages, as are the scenes where the grandfather, Ginzō, who has deprived her of the property she had been bequeathed, meets his own untimely death when the rice-pounding pestle falls on him, or when Namiko's mother, Osumi, having confessed to adultery, goes insane. These grim scenes make it transparently clear that we are dealing with the retribution of karma: cause and effect. In short, they leave us feeling mired in a very old-fashioned tale. The plot structure, where a secret tryst leads to an illegitimate child, relies on one of the hackneyed motifs of so-called domestic fiction, the kind made popular by *One's Own Sin* and *Foster Sisters* [*Chikyōdai*]. In these scenarios, the heroine's life is governed by her irreversible fate. In *One's Own Sin*, the danger for the Sakurado couple appears when they are presented with an opportunity to confess their illegitimate child. Their reconciliation is made possible only by the death of this child. The heroine of *Foster Sisters* suffers misfortune because of her parents' secret marriage and is sacrificed to their conspiracy. The heroine is powerless to resolve the problems stemming from the secret of her birth and therefore becomes a victim of fate. This kind of situation must have elicited the sympathies of female readers who would have identified with the heroine.

Kikuchi Yūhō's *The Keepsake* [*Wasuregatami*], which was serialized in *Woman's Pictorial* from 1918 to 1919, also used a similar motif and is responsible for establishing the prototype for this style. The heroine of *The Keepsake*, Hatsuyo, is a teacher in a kindergarten and is taking care of her elder sister's "keepsake," or daughter, Tomi. When Hayama Shinnosuke goes to the Yanaka

Cemetery to visit his elder brother's grave, he chances to meet Hatsuyo and notices that she is the very image of his brother's lover. Gradually, he falls in love with her. With the dead as their guide and with the child Tomi as their go-between, they are gradually able to fulfill their love—after many twists and turns in the plot. The story concludes on an optimistic note as Hatsuyo's "mother love" is transformed into a happy marriage.

The Keepsake and *Hell in Three Generations* have different conclusions—one is bright, the other dark. But the female protagonist in both the stories is typical of domestic fiction. This type of woman, always a sacrificial victim, trembles before the fate her birth has imposed on her and struggles earnestly to preserve the feminine virtue of submissiveness. Nevertheless, or as a consequence, she is trifled with by men who staunchly support the family system and who prove extremely insensitive to the women in it. The motherliness and maidenly virtue of the women in these stories invite the sympathy of their readers. Katō Takeo[56] enumerates the important features that domestic fiction must not omit: "a faithful observance of commonsense morality; no interest in leaping ahead to present-day or future morality; no sense of adventure; an overall wholesomeness."[57] The lives of the female protagonists in domestic fiction served as a mirror for their female audience. Female readers found a measure of comfort in identifying with these heroines. Yet, at the same time, these stories served to reinforce the discipline imposed on women by the family system.

I should like to note here, however, that newspaper novels contributed to a significant degree in overturning this formula by helping to promote a new type of female protagonist. This new heroine did not conform to the old stereotypes. Kikuchi Yūhō's Tamiko in *A Woman's Life* [*Onna no seimei*], serialized in the *Osaka Mainichi* and the *Tokyo Nichi-nichi* from November 1918, was one such character. Kume Masao's Yurie (Ayako) in *Phoenix* [*Fushi-chō*], which he serialized in *Jiji shimpō* from November 1919, offers another example. Although these works did not eschew the unnatural exaggeration and ornamentation so typical of popular fiction, the female protagonists nevertheless broke free of the mother-maiden mold. In turn, the prostitute type was established as the new direction for literary experimentation. For example, in *Phoenix*, Yurie is a popular stage actress who takes on the role of Ophelia. For her birthday, she invites six of her admirers to a celebration. After the dinner is over, she throws her gold ring into the hearth where the dinner fire yet burns. She plans to acclaim whoever retrieves the fiery red ring as "the winner of her love." Yurie's character, with her reckless wantonness, is little more than a second-rate imitation of Zola's *Nana*. In the tragic closure to the novel, Yurie, having sunken to the level of an itinerant entertainer, grasps the hands of her lover on her death bed, a scene clearly derived from *Nana*.

Tamiko in *A Woman's Life* is a single woman who has just returned from travels abroad made possible by a 250,000 yen inheritance. She marries a prominent politician, Count Katano. Nevertheless, she refuses to share his bed because she is secretly in love with Katano's secretary, the youth Aoyama. Here she finds herself in competition with Katano's niece, Shizuko, who also loves Aoyama. When Tamiko is spurned by Aoyama, she kills herself out of wounded pride. Tamiko's character, an aggressive, whorish type, is thus drawn in contrast to the passive and maidenly Shizuko. We have, in a word, the bad versus the good. Shizuko succeeds in securing the promise of a happy marriage and the balance of commonsense morality is preserved. The same is true of *Phoenix*, in which the determined Yurie is paired against a shy Katsuko.

Ruriko of *Madame Pearl* is cast in the same mold as Tamiko and Yurie.[58] However, in *Madame Pearl* we do not find the maiden-versus-the-whore pattern that we had in the other two stories. Rather, *Madame Pearl* foregrounds the single Ruriko and focuses on her individualism. As the story begins, Ruriko seems to be little more than a beauty with a pure love for the young, aristocratic Sugino Naoya. The first turning point in our perception of Ruriko comes when she vows revenge on the corrupt shipping magnate, Shōta Katsuhei, who, with his evil machinations, drew her father, Baron Karazawa, into a tragic predicament. With this vow of vengeance, Ruriko evolves from a passive victim into an aggressor. She becomes Katsuhei's wife, in name at least, and teases the old man with merciless disregard for his health. Katsuhei plans to take her to his resort house and rape her. However, his imbecile son, who is in love with Ruriko, shows up and fights Katsuhei. In the struggle, Katsuhei suffers a heart attack and dies. Now, with her revenge complete, we discover a new turning point in Ruriko's character. As the widow of a shipping magnate, Ruriko has inherited a substantial amount of money. She establishes a salon and here assembles a number of men who are reputed to be playboys. Her intent is to take revenge against these men on behalf of the women they have hurt. However, among her admirers in the salon is a young man named Aoyama, with whom, she discovers, her stepdaughter, Minako, is in love. Ruriko spurns Aoyama's advances on behalf of her stepdaughter, and in so doing awakens to her responsibilities as a mother. She begins to pray for her stepdaughter's happiness. This marks the third turning point in the novel. Because Aoyama misunderstands Ruriko's intentions, he stabs her in a fit of madness and then drowns himself. Ruriko, who has been mortally wounded, is attended to by her former lover, Sugino. When she breathes her last, he discovers that she had sewn his photograph into her under kimono. As the story reaches its conclusion, the narrator reveals the following: "Even while she had played the role of the beautiful enchantress, flirting with countless men, deep in her heart she had preserved her first pure love. She had protected it there and had polished it until it glowed with the luster of an unsullied pearl."[59] Thus the author plays his trump card, clueing us into Ruriko's true nature.

Beautiful maiden, vengeful daughter, arrogant widow-turned-seductress, protective stepmother—Ruriko took to the stage, transforming herself from one role to the next. Compared to the one-dimensional characters of the earlier domestic fiction who were either good or bad, Ruriko is complex. However, she is not a unified character. Each turning point in the story necessitated unnatural leaps in Ruriko's psychology. This, we can say, was a miscalculation in the construction of the story. We are left with the impression, not of a unified plot, but of a stringing together of several discrete stories. Thus, we lack the sense of unfolding discovery that we would expect in a longer work. This may be because Kikuchi Kan had been primarily a short story writer before trying his hand at these longer pieces. This drawback did not escape the attention of contemporary critics. Hashizume Ken notes in his essay on Kikuchi that "*Madame Pearl* stands as an important debut.[60] The rich material is treated with eager energy. But the peaks and valleys in the piece are traversed by too many narrative tricks. The story is more appropriate as a melodrama on the *shimpa* stage. We lack here the composure of *Flowers of Suffering* [*Ju'nan-bana*]." Kikuchi himself, it seems, was not satisfied with the construction of this, his first long piece.[61]

Yet, even with this fatal flaw in the plotting of *Madame Pearl*, the work was without argument epoch-making as popular fiction in that it destroyed the framework of the existing domestic fiction. Madame Pearl was a woman who was released from the fetters of her complicated blood relations. Tamiko's incorrigible nature and tragic fate in *A Woman's Life* were predicted by her unfortunate birth into a circus. But in *Madame Pearl* we can assume that "there are no lingering regrets" for Ruriko's death. Kikuchi Kan creates a character whose tragedy is the result of her own actions and willful decisions and is not just the product of fate. He sought to create a woman who was liberated from the dark dampness inherent in the family system. Baron Karazawa reproves his daughter when she reveals her plan to marry Shōta Katsuhei: "In order to save the parent from hardship, the son sacrifices himself, and a daughter will sell herself. Aren't these the morals of an ancient and feudal past?" While her father pays lip service to a denial of feudal morality, he cannot think beyond the structure of the family system. Ruriko responds, "The opponent whom I must battle is not the individual Shōta Katsuhei but the evil in the present social situation that he represents, the evil in an entire society that would allow injustice and unfairness, and would do so all for the power of money!"[62] The source of social evil that Ruriko has vowed to battle is found in "the power of money" and "the system of male supremacy."

"I will stake my life on fighting this misbegotten, male-centered morality that renders it just for men to dally with women while it condemns women who dally with men. In our present age, even our nation, even our national laws, and yes, even the various organizations in our society contribute to this corrupt system of thought."[63] Thus we have Ruriko's protest. The recipient of this diatribe is Atsumi, who serves as the *waki* [secondary actor] throughout the story and stands in as the representative for male readers of *Madame Pearl*. The motivation for the revenge against all men, which Shōta Katsuhei inspires, surpasses both the individual and the family system itself and in the end evolves to challenge the evils of society at large. Thus, *Madame Pearl* becomes, in its fresh modernity, a Taishō version of *The Demon Gold* [*Konjiki yasha*]. However, with nothing to accompany her inner voice, the story ends with the illusion that the problem of the family system has been eliminated. Ideologically, this is ill founded. Moreover, as was the tendency for stories in the domestic fiction genre, Ruriko ends as both "mother" and "virgin," consequently diluting and even countervailing the foregoing message. Kikuchi Kan himself, it would appear, was not entirely liberated from the deeply rooted spell of domestic fiction (figure 1).

6

Once Kikuchi Kan established the footing for writers of popular fiction with *Madame Pearl*, which had been serialized in the *Osaka Mainichi* and the *Tokyo Nichi-nichi* from June to December 1920, Togawa Ryū, the chief editor of the *Fujokai* publishers, invited him to write for *Mother's Friend* [*Haha no tomo*], a sister publication of *Woman's Sphere*. Kikuchi answered with *Little Birds of Mercy* [*Jihi shinchō*] which he began serializing in May 1921. From March of the following year, he published once again in the *Osaka Mainichi* and the *Tokyo Nichi-nichi*, serializing the work *Flames of Flowers* [*Hibana*].

Little Birds of Mercy revolves around the complications that ensue between a woman and the two men who pursue her. Opening the story with reference to the legend of Ikuta River, the author introduces us once again to the theme of revenge, which he had tested previously in *Madame Pearl*. In so doing, he attempts to resuscitate the old legend in a modern version. In the original Ikuta legend, the Ashiya Maiden, tormented by offers of courtship that she receives from two young ruffians, throws herself into the Ikuta River.

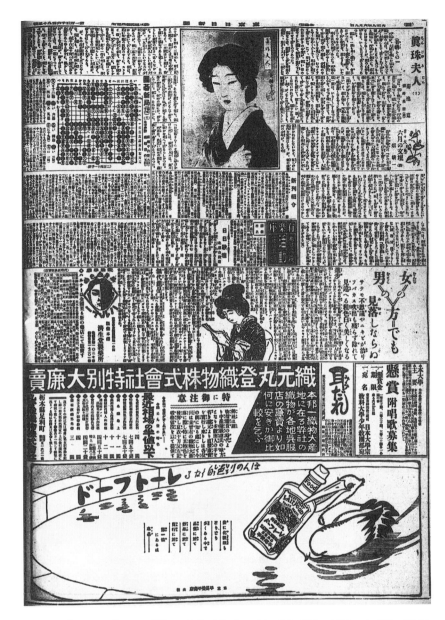

Figure 1. First installment of *Shinju fujin* (Madame Pearl) by Kikuchi Kan, in *Tokyo Nichi-nichi shimbun* (9 July 1920). Courtesy Nihon kindai bungakukan

The modern version, in turn, creates the protagonist Shizuko, who is likewise victimized by her lack of a strong sense of self. The turning point in the story comes when she is visited by the former rival for her love, now a prosecuting attorney, who calls on her after her husband's career has been ruined by a bribery charge. Rather than killing herself, however, Shizuko's eyes are opened to the importance of human life when she is given the responsibility of mothering an orphan.

Little Birds of Mercy was mired in controversy, however, as it was averred that the story was ghost-written by someone other than Kikuchi Kan.[64] Kojima Masajirō (1894–1994), a recipient of Kikuchi Kan's patronage, attests that Kawabata Yasunari, then a fledgling writer, wrote the rough draft of the story.[65] Regardless of the veracity of this claim, it is impossible to deny that the establishment of the mother-type female in *Little Birds of Mercy* is a reversion to patterns fixed in earlier domestic fiction, especially when compared to *Madame Pearl*, which reveals an intentional attempt to create a new female image. Because this was the first long work of fiction that he wrote for a woman's magazine, it could be that Kikuchi Kan was too self-conscious in his attempt to appeal to his female readers. Perhaps at the time, he regarded the medium of newspapers as a more serious publication venue than that of women's magazines. At any rate, the import of his ambitions as a writer of popular fiction is revealed in his third work, *Flames of Flowers*.

Flames of Flowers is also a pioneering work in that it opened a new direction for popular fiction, leading the way to the social novel [*shakai shōsetsu*]. The characters in this work are released from the spell of domestic fiction. Stepping free of their dark interiors, they begin their journey toward the bright streets with a yet unsteady gait. The hero of *Flames of Flowers* is not a handsome young noble. He is not even wealthy. Rather, he is merely a factory worker. Even the "fortune-blessed maid" rescued by the young hero in a Cinderella sequence so much a staple of domestic fiction makes little more than a cursory appearance in this story. Instead of the spoiled aristocrat stuck on his good name and family lineage, the role of the villain is assigned to a cruel capitalist. The motif of revenge, at which this author so clearly excelled, is tied up with the hatred the factory worker harbors for the capitalist.

The hero of *Flames of Flowers*, Kawamura Tetsuzō, works as a bathhouse custodian at a country inn called Gamagōri. One day, Mitsuko, the daughter of the president of the Nanjō Manufacturing Corporation, who has come to the inn to relax and rejuvenate, insults Tetsuzō. He resolves to get revenge. To do so, he travels to Tokyo and secures employment in the Nanjō machine factory. While on the job, however, he gets tangled in a machine belt and loses his arm. The company pays him a mere pittance of 70 yen in compensation and throws him out on the streets. Enraged, he rushes to the Nanjō mansion and demands immediate attention. By a twist of fate, Mitsuko meets him in the reception room and bestows a diamond ring on him. Thus, he must endure humiliation at her hands once again. Almost simultaneous with Tetsuzō losing his job, the skilled worker Saburi and three of his friends, having recently "awoken to the evils of capitalism," are unfairly fired from their jobs with Nanjō. Saburi organizes a strike and Tetsuzō joins the cause. The factory leaders resort to the extreme measure of instituting a lockout to oppose the strike. The workers, in their agitation, press Tetsuzō into marching with them to the Nanjō mansion and demanding the restoration of their jobs. Saburi, who feels betrayed by his comrades, sets fire to the Nanjō estate and threatens Mitsuko with a sword. Tetsuzō overpowers Saburi and, enfolding Mitsuko in a one-armed embrace, leaps with her from the second story as it is engulfed in flames. Mitsuko is saved. Tetsuzō, who shielded her from the fall with his body, perishes.

As this plot summary reveals, *Flames of Flowers* is not exempt from the exaggeration and distortion that typified the popular novel. The workers who are distraught over the lockout are drawn merely as a mass of ignorant riff-raff. Moreover, once Saburi, who had been described as "wise and reliable as the ground beneath one's feet," is betrayed by them, he is transformed into an even more despicable madman. Tetsuzō, who has vowed revenge on the bourgeoisie, is smitten by Mitsuko's charms and cajoled by her kind treatment of him as an employee. He thus displays the kind of cheap heroism we see here. At the conclusion to the story, while two lovers are in flight to Hokkaido, they have the following conversation: "That fellow Saburi is really to be pitied. He's a martyr to the new age." "And, that one-armed man, he's the modern-day hero, isn't he."[66] This exchange reveals the true nature of the "sociality" in *Flames of Flowers* as being detached and superficial.

In *Flames of Flowers*, even while Saburi and Tetsuzō voice their abhorrence of the "evils of capitalism" and profess their hatred of the bourgeoisie, they are depicted as isolated from the main group and as defiant failures. Thus, the story ends up revealing itself as safe, harmless reading material. The system is not threatened but preserved. In place of the realities of Taishō society, this story offers fantasies in which lower-class workers are merely impersonal masses, and in which we have the possibility for betrayal and heroism and a romance between a laborer and a lady. Moreover, these fantasies become the new direction in popular fiction to be adopted by countless imitators.

For example, in Kume Masao's *City of Cries* [*Nageki no ichi*], which he serialized in *Housewife's Friend* from January 1923, we have the daughter of a wealthy but now bankrupt family who attends what will be her last dance party. Demented by grief, she falls in love with a laborer whom she has invited to be her partner. The story concludes with the Cinderella motif in reverse. Nakamura Murao's *The Blind Populace* [*Gunmō*], which he serialized in *Yomiuri* from September 1923, was derived from vivid memories of the recent Kantō Earthquake. He describes a group of workers who go insane and set fires that end up burning down Yokohama. Also, in the opening paragraph of Mikami Otokichi's *White Devil* [*Shiro oni*], which he began serializing in *Jiji shimpō* in 1924, we have a phony hero of the "betrayed" variety who, shaking his fist in the air, urges on a strike of a publishing house.

Leaving aside the quality of *Flames of Flowers*, it is nonetheless to his credit that Kikuchi Kan, a bourgeois writer, remained dispassionate in the maelstrom of proletarian literature's rising influence, even as he was provoked by the great debates of 1920 and 1921 to fully incorporate labor issues into popular literature. His essay affirming the value of "actuality," "Bungei sakuhin no naiyō-teki kachi" [The content value of literary works], contains many of the ideas that would be incorporated into *Flames of Flowers*, which was written at about the same time.[67]

Nearly half a year after the serialization of *Flames of Flowers*, Chiba Kameo (1878–1935) published "The Line between High-class Art and the Popular Novel" ["Kōkyū geijutsu to tsūzoku shōsetsu tono issen"] in *Shinchō* (March 1923). In this essay he raises questions about so-called serious (high) literature [*junbungaku*], noting that it was "nothing more than a high-class psychological game," even though it is averred that "artistry requires skill" and that "capturing attention requires subtlety." In contrast, he expressed high expectations for the popular novel [tsūzoku shōsetsu], which he characterized as being "far more widely and deeply a part of the people and society." That the popular novel attracts a wider audience than pure literature, he continued, is not at all because "the populace's artistic taste is inferior." It was this talented editor, Chiba Kameo, who brought *Firefly Grass* [*Hotarugusa*] to the pages of *Jiji shimpō* and who effectively brought about the transformation of Kume Masao from writer of serious literature to popular fiction writer. In the long run, Chiba Kameo's views would help establish the genealogy for the so-called discourse on popular art, while in the short run, it profoundly influenced Kikuchi Kan's essay "The Content Value of Literary Arts," published nearly simultaneously with *Flames of Flowers*, in which he exalted "actuality." Kikuchi Kan prescribed subject matter derived from actuality as an antidote to the supremacy of "artistic expression," and he sought this actuality in a wholesome appreciation of life that he ascribed to (mass) readers. And it was Chiba who recast this opposition between art for art's sake and art rooted in the materiality of everyday life in the context of the debate pitting "pure literature" against popular literature. The main thread in the great literary debates of the Taishō era, therefore, ran from Arishima Takeo's *One Manifesto* [*Sengen hitotsu*] through Kikuchi Kan's argument for the value of content to Hirotsu Kazuo's argument for the artistry of prose. The discussion of whether or not to respect popular literature was a tangential argument that formed a branch off the main trunk of these debates. Within this divergent branch, we find Nakamura Murao's complaint: "There is no true novel truer than the mental-state novel [*shinkyō shōsetsu*]. Thus, for one such as myself who has great concern for the 'true novel,' I find this current state in a literary world that is most unliterary to be particularly lamentable."[68] Katagami Noburu expressed his lamentation differently, noting that the mental-state novel had deteriorated over time. As he points out in "Sakusha to dokusha" [Writer and Reader], "That the popular novel has been compared to works of 'pure literature' (including the mental-state novel) at all, results in part from the fact that people are tired of this 'pure' or serious literature."[69] At the same time that Kikuchi's *Flames of Flowers* appeared, Kamitsukasa Shōken (1874–1947) published his volume on labor in his multivolume study *Tokyo* (1922) and Nakamura Murao came out with *The Blind Populace* [*Gunmō*], each revealing the trend in popular literature around the time of the 1923 earthquake to take on characteristics of the social novel. Additionally, this ushered in a heightening of interest in "actual events" as subject matter and led to an increased appreciation of the value of popular literature. The deterioration of the mental-state novel and the "socialization" of the popular novel presented two sides of the same coin in the Taishō *bundan*:

> Since the first of the year, the popular novel has suddenly become the subject of discussion. Many writers are now trying their hand at popular fiction, and we have thus reached a stage where the popular novel should become the subject of research . . . . In comparison with artistic [pure] literature the popular novel reflects the trends of the times . . . . In our present age, the most remarkable social phenomenon is the dissemination of economic considerations. Consequently, we have seen the birth of a new class consciousness, accompanied by distrust in both capital and labor. It is this kind of social awareness that has become the main subject matter in popular novels today, a phenomenon clearly represented by Kikuchi Kan's *Flames of Flowers* and Nakamura Murao's *The Blind Populace* and Kume Masao's *Cold Fire* [*Reika*].[70]

In a move to counter the ratification of popular literature that came from within the *bundan*, Maedakō Hiroichirō and Katō Kazuo began advocating a proletarian popular literature. Maedakō, who had brought attention to Kikuchi Kan with "The Superfluous Kikuchi Kan" ["Kikuchi Kan muyō ron"] in the inaugural issue of *Bungei shunjū*, called for writers to move in the direction of popular fiction. He urged them to break away from those "literary creations" that are nothing more than "the playful dalliances of intellectuals," and to instead adopt the "popular" novel that "possesses the ideological power to move a million men."[71] Furthermore, Katō noted that "proletarian authors are needed to study the current social, economic, and political climates. They must present in their art conditions that normal, everyday people might not notice, and they must voice their criticism in a clear, easy-to-understand way." By so doing they will create a popular novel "imbued with the sentiments of our new age" and will thereby "thrust out the worthless popular novels that we now have."[72]

It was in 1925 when Maedakō and Katō staked their claim on the other side of the river from the then existing bundan by advocating a proletarian popular literature. They thus planted the seeds for the popularization of art. At the same time, Kikuchi Kan abandoned the direction toward the social novel that he had courted in *Flames of Flowers* and threw himself into his production of *Flowers of Suffering*, in which he skillfully depicted the vagaries of married life among the bourgeoisie. To borrow Aono Suekichi's words, "Kikuchi Kan returned to the private materialistic base of the individual he had earlier abandoned," and he completely lost sight of the potential for "encouraging an investigation of the materialistic base of society."[73] Kikuchi Kan would henceforth devote his attention to "popular portraits of the vagaries in the world of love and hate."

7

Kikuchi Kan serialized five other popular novels after *Flames of Flowers*: *New Gems [Niitama]* in *Woman's Sphere*, beginning in April 1923; *Mermaid on Land [Riku no ningyo]* in the *Osaka Mainichi* and the *Tokyo Nichi-nichi*, from March 1924; *Flowers of Suffering [Ju'nan-bana]*, from March 1925 in *Woman's Sphere*; *The Second Kiss [Dai ni no seppun]* in the *Tokyo Asahi* and the *Osaka Asahi* beginning in July 1925; and *The Red Swan [Akai hakuchō]* from January 1926 in *Kingu*. Among these works he was particularly pleased with *Flowers of Suffering*, writing of it in his *Half Autobiography [Han-jijoden]*, "Of my early works, this one was especially good. Even when I read back over it today it causes me no embarrassment." Kobayashi Hideo asserted in his reminiscence of the writer, *Kikuchi Kan ron*, "*Flowers of Suffering* is a splendid piece, by far better than *On the Conduct of Lord Tadanao [Tadanao kyōgyōjōki]*."

In *Flowers of Suffering* we do not have a heroine with the kind of strong individualism that we saw in *Madame Pearl*'s Ruriko. Nor are we treated to the class-inspired revenge quest that Tetsuzō displayed in *Flames of Flowers*. Rather, the characters who take the stage are for the most part ordinary bourgeois women. However, as Kobayashi Hideo noted in *Kikuchi Kan ron*, the formal composition of this story is distinctive. In portraying the love lives of three different couples, Kikuchi uses the cinematic technique of cutting from one couple to the other, blending their stories as he proceeds with a film-like tempo. All the while he achieves fine results by his sure hand in accurately conveying social customs. With *Flowers of Suffering* Kikuchi Kan reveals his complete mastery of popular fiction, making it the quintessential full-length popular novel representative of the early Shōwa era (mid-1920s) up through World War II.

In *Half Autobiography Continued* [*Zoku Han jijoden*], Kikuchi Kan describes his inspiration for writing *Flowers of Suffering* as follows: "When the story opens, several schoolgirls are preparing for their graduation. They promise each other that should one of them marry, she will exchange a report on married life with the others in a year's time. I borrowed this idea from a bawdy English novel that I had read. In the novel, three young maidens promise each other just as they are preparing for their weddings, that they will meet in a year and compare notes about married life. A year goes by and they keep their word. When they meet they swap stories about their sex lives."[74] Kikuchi Kan does not mention it here, but having a plot structured around the lives of three women and the difficulties that they encounter in love was surely something that he adapted from his earlier novel *New Gems*. The plot of *New Gems*, in which a lascivious aristocrat seduces three sisters one after the other, seems to lead logically to that of *Flowers of Suffering*, in which he describes the trials and reconciliations in three marriages.

In the introduction to *Flowers of Suffering*, Kikuchi portrays the love complications that haunt these women before their marriages. Teruko was once secretly married to a man who suddenly dies while traveling overseas. Sumiko has had a relationship with a married man who eventually abandons her. When Teruko remarries, therefore, she has to contend with her secret past, and Sumiko has to deal with her own infidelity and with the disparity between her husband's level of education and her own. Then there is Keiko, who has to struggle with her husband's debauchery and his secret past. These love complications create the underplot of the story. During the course of the story, the three couples are able to circumvent their difficulties and obtain a resolution to their problems in various ways. Teruko seeks the intervention of a mediator; Sumiko learns to accept the ordinariness of married love; and Keiko experiences childbirth. Ōya Sōichi had characterized Mikami Otokichi's popular novels as a "potpourri of the modern family," with the plot consisting of the permutations and combinations of the aristocrat, the capitalist, and the poor. Similarly, *Flowers of Suffering* can be viewed as a work expressing the variety of conditions and situations found in married life.[75] Of course, in his case, Kikuchi Kan thought that he could reinforce this novel as guide with his thesis on the utility of the literary arts. In his *Literary Arts and Life* [*Bungei no jinsei*, January 1926] he notes:

> What can we rely on when we are faced with the task of selecting that one special person who will be our mate in weal and woe? Women don't know what kind of man will make a good husband, and men don't know what to look for in a wife; and so they set themselves up for disappointment in life and disaster in marriage. But do they teach how to choose a mate in school? If a man wants to learn the truth of human life, he can't very well go out and conduct research on women; and women can't draw too close to men unless they want to invite trouble. But if it is through literature, one can come to know countless men and women, proper love, and all about married life. And it's all so very simple to do. Moreover, absolutely no danger is involved. Put another way, literature is life's laboratory—a completely risk-free guide to the facts of life.[76]

Buried in Kikuchi Kan's clever turn of phrase "a risk-free guide to the facts of life" we note a contradiction. Although this extraordinarily straightforward writer was a master of vivid descriptions, his portraits of "the facts" are, after all, portraits. And though he "guides" us in our appreciation of life, his life is not "real life." Yet, he was determined that in his capacity as a popular novelist, he would offer his stories to inexperienced youths as "risk-free guides." In that regard, *Flowers of Suffering* serves as a splendid example of the "usefulness of literature."

In his essay, "Kikuchi Kan ron," published in the August 1934 issue of *Waseda Literature* [*Waseda bungaku*], Nakatani Hiroshi discusses *Flowers of Suffering* and *Madame Muyūge* [*Muyūge fujin*], which he considers the representative piece of the Shōwa period. In his analysis of these two works, he notes that the denunciation of the aristocratic life articulated in *Madame Muyūge* is reversed in *Flowers of Suffering* through an affirmation of bourgeois life. Of the three women in *Flowers of Suffering*, the portrait of Sumiko best reflects the author's vision of "bourgeois life." Her husband, Hayashi, is the spoiled son of a capitalist who, having confused arrogance for pride, dropped out of Keio University before completing his degree in economics. Forced into a marriage that she does not want and embarrassed by her husband's in-complete education, Sumiko runs back to her former lover, a married man. By the end of the story, however, she has wisely warded off the catastrophe that threatened her marriage and declares, "To marry the man you love is the greatest happiness life can offer. But to destroy life itself when that is not pos-sible is a great shame indeed. There *is* life beyond love. So long as there is life—there is joy, no matter where one goes."[77]

Reverberating in Sumiko's words are the author's own opinions, as voiced in his statement that the value of literature should be found first in life and second in art. Moreover, by placing love and life as two alternatives to be chosen between, he resolves that life must be the preferred choice. And the "life" that he presents here is a "bourgeois life," or, stated another way, a "cul-tured life" [*bunka seikatsu*]. He charts this life through a variety of scenes that shift among the Imperial Theater, the Mitsukoshi Department Store, the Im-perial Hotel, and the chic cafés along the Ginza. In this cultured life, couples are freed from the clutches of mothers-in-law and have the financial where-withal to lead comfortable, independent lives. The scene thus depicted stands in stark contrast to the world of *Madame Pearl*, where love is accorded a value surpassing all else. But what kind of fate awaits characters who dare to defy the disciplined order of the comfortable bourgeois life and cast their lot with love?

Kitagawa, the hero of *Mermaid on Land* [*Riku no ningyo*], refuses to be roped into a marriage of political convenience and sets out on a honeymoon with Reiko, who is suffering from tuberculosis, knowing full well that "death and disaster must surely await." Murakawa, the protagonist in "The Second Kiss ["Dai ni no seppun"], who mistakenly causes his philistine rival in love to drown, attempts to commit a love suicide in the waters of Ashinoko [Ashino Lake] with Shizuko. Their death journey is depicted as an idealized protest against a vulgar society that would impede and destroy the fulfillment of their love. However, on the other hand, the scene underscores the punishment of dangerous passions that threaten everyday morality and social order.

Stories with two-sided messages such as these became common in the late Taishō period, perhaps in response to the prominent love suicides at the time, such as that by Arishima Takeo and Hatano Akiko.[78] These events were both eulogized and reviled in contemporary journalism.[79]

Whereas the resolutions depicted in *Flowers of Suffering* differed diametri-cally from those in *Mermaid on Land* and *The Second Kiss*, at the basis of each was "the bourgeois life." The following quotation from a study on stories serialized in American women's magazines from the 1920s to the 1930s sheds light on the import of these two different approaches:

The heroine in *Home Journal* possesses typical plain and subdued middle-class feminine virtues (loyalty, chastity, modesty, etc.). Success in love is represented as a reward for her feminine virtue. In *True Story*, however, those who defy standard morality are shown to suffer. On the one hand, we have a positive image of virtue rewarded. On the other, we have the negative consequence of vice duly punished. It was the latter portrait that was preferred. The difference in the two portraits was profoundly important to middle-class readers as it reflects their anxiety over losing social status as well as their anxiety over being placed in the realm of the lower-classes and exposed to the dangers inherent therein. While they represented differing symbolic representations, they shared the same value.[80]

In *Flowers of Suffering*, Sumiko represents "good sense" by sacrificing herself to the happiness of the family and by abandoning her quest for fulfillment in love for the sake of the family's serenity and harmony. On the other hand, the lovers in *Mermaid on Land* and "The Second Kiss," who give themselves to a dangerous passion in defiance of this "good sense," must be punished by society. Again, this offers members of the new middle class an opportunity to indulge in the illusion of the comfortable "cultured life" and to fantasize about the "safe family life." And it assures them that those harmful sentiments that would threaten to destroy this illusion will be contained.

Among Kikuchi Kan's Taishō-era popular novels, the three I have discussed were particularly significant in developing models for future works of popular fiction. *Madame Pearl* introduced ideas concerning women's liberation into the popular novel. *Flames of Flowers*, which could not rise above the level of a quasi-social novel, even as it attempted the incorporation of actual events, and *Flowers of Suffering* propagandized enthusiastically for the disciplined order of the comfortable bourgeois life. With his extraordinary skill, Kikuchi Kan charted a new course for popular literature in the late Taishō era. But to what extent was the development of Kikuchi Kan's fiction intertwined with the rise of the new middle class and the expansion of female readership? Our focus returns to the reader in pursuing this matter in the following section.

8

Novels that adhere to the domestic fiction formula, such as Kikuchi Yūhō's *One's Own Sin* [*Ono ga tsumi*] and *Foster Sisters* [*Chikyōdai*], inevitably describe the turmoil that confronts women embroiled in the intricate complications of the family system. Tragedy necessarily ensues because these women are made to endure a man's selfish seductions while clinging to their own chastity. Readers were moved to tears by these stories, as if they were witnessing events within their own realm of experience and not those involving fictional characters. Indeed, the tragic circumstances that beset the characters in these stories were little more than exaggerations of the trials and heartbreaks that these readers themselves endured day in and day out. Living vicariously through these stories thus allowed readers the opportunity to find—in their sympathy and pity for the characters—a slight sense of superiority over them. The characters in the stories were elite, high-class ladies, the kind of woman the reader would normally admire and jealously aspire to be. But in these stories, even these women were trapped by a fate that they could not escape on their own. What these readers expected, indeed demanded from these novels was a momentary psychological release from the fetters of the "family," an "emotional catharsis" [*jōcho katarushisu*].

However, the new popular novel, beginning with *Madame Pearl*, invited a revolution in the way these works were received. These new novels ushered in a means of experiencing literature that provided "vicarious compensation" [*daishō kōi*]. If, in real life, women readers were trapped in the patriarchic family, in the realm of literature they could taste a freedom imbued with the fantasy of women's liberation. Aono Suekichi, who stipulated that the majority of women's magazine readership consisted of "the petit bourgeois woman," stated in *What Women Demand in Literature* that women had turned to the popular novel serialized in women's magazines to have their social demands met. Aono explains his assertion as follows:[81]

> For example, even if the patriarchal family system were destroyed along with the customs that govern male-female relationships and the institutionalized, conventional restrictions that women face in society, nothing would change. We can destroy the exterior restrictions, but we cannot change the system. This is because the system is dependent on customs and mores that have incredible binding power and cannot easily be undercut. It is the petit bourgeois woman who is most susceptible to this binding power. And it is she who must strive to block this power by engaging in courageous face-to-face combat with these restrictions. Many difficulties lie before these women. Even so there are women who eagerly await the opportunity to sacrifice themselves to this battle. Regardless of the difficulties, the sacrifices, all they see are the realities of their demands and they push bravely ahead. Not surprisingly there are, in fact, more and more women like this.
>
> Even so, ordinary women do not possess this kind of courage. Nor

do they often find themselves in situations where they can safely display such courage. For the most part these women have no other choice but to seek the satisfaction of their innermost desires without ever challenging this binding power. They take the path of least resistance. This mentality is generally attributed to the petit bourgeoisie. Women from other classes offer stark contrasts. But for the petit bourgeoisie, the desire to satisfy one's innermost needs by taking the path of least resistance is the fundamental motive spurring these women on to a love of reading. *In fact, it is through literature that these women are able to manage the needs in their lives.*

The literature that this class of women prefers is now in the process of integrating with the literature of today's bundan. This assertion can be corroborated by the fact that whereas one aspect of this literature caters to the usual sentiments of this class of woman, another aspect endeavors to portray a world of freedom by destroying the social restrictions that have held these women in the home. Nevertheless, this destructive zeal, the criticism of the system, and even the creation of this world of freedom itself must not be tinted with any hint of radical politics. Rather, the works need to adhere to sentimental tastes and aspire to moderation in both what it presents and how it is presented, aiming for softened, poeticized [*shika*] presentation. To cite an old adage: "The playwright who portrays a conflagration on stage must not set a real fire." This clearly illustrates the unique way the petit bourgeois, and particularly the women of the class, find their needs met in art.[82]

In spite of the growing demands for women's liberation at the time, Aono observed that the social restrictions that hindered this liberation were very firmly rooted in society. The featured issues in contemporary women's magazines directly reflected the gap between ideal and reality. For example, in *Women's Review* [*Fujin kōron*] for the year 1920, we find a number of issues devoted to women and society: "Comments on the Three Greatest Confessions in the World" was the focus of the issue for January; "What If Women Were Allowed in Politics?" characterized the February issue; in April, the journal was devoted to "On Reforming Humankind"; in August, "The Unavoidable Need for Contraception and Our Nation"; "Bad Wife, Dumb Mother" in October; and "Advocating the Socialization of Women's Education" in November. In this way, the journal took up themes that promoted greater social advancement for women and advocated freedom from the home. Moreover, these articles reflected the variety of social concerns then confronting Taishō society. For example, the theme of the January issue, "The Three Greatest Confessions," was inspired by Shimazaki Tōson's confessional, social-issue novel *New Life* [*Shinsei*], which had just concluded its serialization in October of the previous year. February's "What If Women Were Allowed in Politics?" was motivated by the Movement for Women's Suffrage, which was part of the New Women's Society [Shinfujinkyōkai] that was to be convened by Hiratsuka Raichō, Ichikawa Fusae, and Oku Mumeo in March.[83] And the focus on contraception in the August issue was a response to Margaret Sanger's visit to Japan that March.

By contrast, that same year *Housewife's Friend* ran articles that dealt exclusively with domestic concerns such as marriage, divorce, child rearing, education, and health. In January the feature articles were "Reclaiming One's Destiny: A Tale of Diligence" and "What Maidens Expect in Marriage." In February, we have "Words of Advice for Parents: How to Ensure Your Child Enters the Best Middle School or Girls School," "Women Who Cry for Men Share Their Confessions," and "How I Cured My Rheumatism." Then in March the feature articles were "Reorganizing a Wedding Ceremony and Banquet" and "Experiences with Miscarriage." Moreover, we should note the personal, communicative style of the articles, many of which were written as confessions, memorandums, or firsthand accounts. For readers who were housewives, shut away with little opportunity for personal communication, this style must have seemed familiar and comforting. The mode here is very close to that of the personal advice columns.

With the exception of *Women's Review*, all the other general interest magazines for women shared these themes with the *Housewife's Friend*. Absorbing themselves in articles such as "How I Was Seduced by a Man," "Successfully Educating a Stepchild," "Confessions of Young Women Worried over Betrothals," "Memories of a Mother Who Aborted Her Illegitimate Child," the readers of these magazines felt profound sympathy for the women in the articles. Surely there is a connection between this sympathy and the reaction readers had to the female protagonists in domestic fiction. The fictional world of the novel allowed readers to experience once again the sense of enjoying a secret communication with those who had sacrificed themselves to the home [*ie*] and who were now asking readers to share in their confessions. The story line of domestic fiction was little more than an artistic reshaping of the situations already described in the women's journals, as if the two entities had entered a craftsman's bargain for sharing skills.

The gap that thus appeared between *Woman's Review* and *Housewife's Friend* represented the rupture between the contributors to the former and the general readership of the latter and other women's journals like it. For example, the October 1920 issue of *Woman's Review*, "Bad Wife, Dumb

Mother," featured Katakami Noboru's "The Significance of a Liberal Arts Education," Yamakawa Kikue's[84] "Wives and Mothers of a Liberal Society," "Good Wife, Wise Mother versus Bad Wife, Dumb Mother," by Hoashi Riichirō, and Hiratsuka Raichō's "Women, Reclaim Yourselves," among others. Each of these articles challenged the validity of the "good wife, wise mother" dictum by arguing for the importance of freedom in love, advancement in women's social standing, and liberation from household labor. These articles were met by columns in *Housewife's Friend* such as "Living with Elder Brother's Wife" that solicited entries from readers. Articles of this sort introduced readers to the secret enmity clinging to the underside of the family system, especially as revealed in old, established households. Seven out of nine of the women whose responses were featured indicated a profound level of animosity between sisters-in-law and sought the readers' sympathies by recording their own personal experiences. For example, a typical entry would have opened: "My elder brother's wife is the devil incarnate. Please listen carefully to my tale of woe." And then, without exception, each writer expressed a desire for separate living quarters, and they also revealed a sense of complete and utter despair over the present family system. Thus, the antidote that Yamakawa Kikue, Hiratsuka Raichō, and others prescribed to combat the miserable realities of the family system was just too idealistic and removed from the oppressive realities of the households within which the typical reader lived.

The role Kikuchi Kan played as a writer of popular fiction was to open new ground with his novels that engaged readers of both *Housewife's Friend* and *Woman's Review*. His novels served as a bridge that spanned the gap between the realities that held the Taishō woman in her place and the dreams of liberation that she secretly harbored. How was it that he accomplished this task? To borrow Aono Suekichi's words, "to portray a world of freedom" Kikuchi Kan offered nothing more than "a conflagration on stage" and not a real fire. But precisely because his portrait was one of fantasy, he was able to promise his new middle-class female readership a compensatory satisfaction. Moreover, the more acutely aware women became of the disparity between their real lives and their desires and the more the new middle class's sense of unease and self-consciousness intensified, the more successful he became. Thus, when Kikuchi Kan first published *Madame Pearl* in 1920, he was writing for those readers who could see only the possibility of the story in their own lives.[85] But, by the end of the Taishō period, he could actually address a female readership belonging to an expanding new middle class.

9

The subtle shift in depicting female characters, from *Madame Pearl's* Ruriko, who wages war on "male-centered morality," to Sumiko in *Flowers of Suffering*, who chooses happiness in marriage over personal love, is surely related
to changes in the way women viewed life during the years before and after
the Great Kantō Earthquake of 1923.[86] The move from a "problem novel"
[*mondai shōsetsu*] like *Madame Pearl*, to a genre story [*fūzoku shōsetsu*] like
Flowers of Suffering suggests that Kikuchi Kan was sensitive to the literary
expectations of the new middle-class female reader. Sensing that his readers
yearned to discover the New Age Woman [*shinjidai no josei*] in the world of
the popular novel, Kikuchi created a heroine, Ranko, in *New Gems* who was
capable of toying with a lascivious aristocrat. In *Mermaid on Land*, a work set
in the fashionable Karuizawa summer resort, he offered readers just a glimpse
of this New Age Woman. Even so, it was not until *Flowers of Suffering* that
she would be etched in sharp relief through the character of Sumiko. Influenced by the portraits that Kikuchi Kan had pioneered, Kume Masao, Katō
Takeo, and Nakamura Murao each turned toward this kind of heroine in their
own popular fiction. As Fujimori Junzō notes, "It would not be an overstatement to claim that Kikuchi Kan surpasses Kume Masao in depicting the
delicate nuances of the relations between men and women. To illustrate let
me note that after the young couples in *Flowers of Suffering* squabble, they
kiss to make up. We cannot conclude that this would never have happened in
the past. But in Kikuchi Kan's hands these scenes are tinged with a sense of
fresh modernity. By way of comparison, Kume Masao treats these relationships in a conservative, moralistic light."[87] The term New Age Woman was
popular in Japanese journalism not long after the earthquake, between 1924
and 1925, and would become much more widely used after it was replaced
by the foreign "loan word" *modan gāru*.[88] In *Flowers of Suffering*, Sumiko's
modern character can be described in the first half of the novel as a New Age
Woman, and by the second half as a modan gāru. The shift between the two
is a logical response to the climate of the times.

In April 1925, *Woman's Review* published Nii Itaru's "Profile of the Modan
Gāru," and in the July issue of that same year *Shinchō* carried a special collection of articles on "Considering the So-called New Age Woman." For a time,
therefore, both terms were employed simultaneously. Yet, it was not long before the awkward expression New Age Woman, which lacked trendiness, was
replaced by the more appealing modan gāru. This New Age Woman–cum–
modan gāru was, needless to say, a different being from the "new woman"
who had emerged from the pages of *Seitō* in the late Meiji period and was then

dubbed the New Woman [*atarashii onna*]. If *Madame Pearl* was the conduit for introducing the New Woman into the world of the popular novel, *Flowers of Suffering* was the work that heralded the modan gāru. The main axis for the development of the popular novel in the later Taishō era was expressed in this evolution from New Woman to modan gāru.

"A Survey of Working Women," conducted by the Public Sector of the Tokyo Municipal Office in 1924 and referred to earlier in this essay, provides a rich source of data in helping us determine the mindset of the pre-earthquake Taishō woman. This is particularly true of the section concerning reading material in which the titles in Table 3 were listed under the category "most important literary work."

Why is it that, with the exception of Kume Masao's *Shipwreck* [*Hasen*], so few "popular novels" made the list? Consider the responses to the section on magazine subscriptions. Of the 1,184 respondents, 196 indicated that they carried a subscription to *Woman's Review*, 181 to *Woman's Sphere*, 144 to *Housewife's Friend*, 86 to *Woman's World* [*Fujin sekai*], 49 to *Woman's Education World* [*Jogaku sekai*], 32 to *Woman's Club*, 32 to *Woman*, and 20 to *Woman's Friend*. Because these figures indicate that subscriptions to women's magazines were relatively high, it is extremely likely that these women were able to read a variety of popular novels. Yet at this time, only a few of the popular novels serialized in newspapers and women's magazines were re-issued as single-volume books. Thus, it is quite probable that once these novels were read, they were discarded.

Let us consider some examples. Shun'yōdō published Kume Masao's first long popular novel *Firefly Grass* as a single volume in November 1918. By March 1920, it had gone through eight print runs. The first half of *Shipwreck* was brought out in book form in July 1922 and by October had gone through ten print runs. The second volume of Kikuchi Kan's novel in two volumes, *New Gems*, was first printed in November 1924 (Shun'yōdō) and by April of the following year it had gone through thirteen print runs. One factor propelling the works of Kikuchi Kan and Kume Masao into best-seller status was the connection these popular novels had with the new medium of film, which had become popular in the late 20s and early 1930s. (*Flowers of Suffering*, for example, which was first published as a single volume in December 1926 by *Bungei shunjū*, had already gone into twenty-five print runs by the end of January the following year.)

Now let us consider the "religious literature" of writers such as Kurata Hyakuzō, Kagawa Toyohiko, Ishimaru Gohei, and Ehara Koyata, whose works were cited far more frequently than those of Kikuchi Kan or Kume Masao in the survey; they accumulated much higher print runs as well. For

Table 3

Author	Title	Number of respondents who listed this title
Kurata Hyakuzō[1] 1891–1943	*Shukke to sono deshi* (The priest and his disciple)	28
	Chichi no shinpai (My father's concern)	17
	Utawanu hito (The person who does not sing)	8
	Ai to ninshiki [to] no shuppatsu (The start of love and knowledge)	7
	Seishi (Meditation)	5
	Fuse Taishi no nyūzan (Prince Fuse enters the mountains)	5
	Shitta Taishi no nyūzan (Prince Shitta enters the mountains)	4
Kagawa Toyohiko 1888–1960	*Shisen o koete* (Crossing the boundary of death)	16
	Taiyō o iru mono (That which pierces the sun)	3
Ishimaru Gohei 1886–1969	*Ningen Shinran* (Shinran, the human)	16
Ōizumi Kokuseki 1894–1957	*Rōshi* (Lao-tse)	5
Tanizaki Jun'ichirō	*Aisureba koso* (Precisely for love)	5
Arishima Takeo	*Sengen* (Declaration)	4
	Seiza (Constellation)	2
Ehara Koyata 1882–1978	*Shin'yaku* (New testament)	3
Natsume Sōseki	*Higan sugimade* (Through the spring equinox and beyond)	4
	Kōjin (The wayfarer)	1
Kume Masao	*Hasen* (Shipwreck)	5
Kikuchi Kan	*Jihi shinchō* (Little birds of mercy)	1

Table 3. Continued

Author	Title	Number of respondents who listed this title
Shimazaki Tōson	*Shinsei* (New life)	1
Shimada Seijirō 1899–1930	*Chijō* (Above earth)	1
Romain Roland	*Jean Christophe*	4
Henryk Sienkiewicz	*Quo Vadis*	3
Henrik Ibsen	*A Doll's House*	3
Emile Zola	*Nana*	3
Fyodor Dostoevsky	*The Brothers Karamazov*	2
Gustave Flaubert	*Madame Bovary*	2
Victor Hugo	*Les Misérables*	2

NB: Among the 900 women who responded to this section, 510 subscribed to a publication. Of these, 223 were literary works. (M)

[1] Kurata Hyakuzō (1891–1943), playwright and critic now regarded as the representative "religious writer." *Shukke to sono deshi* was serialized in *Seimei no kawa* [River of life], a satellite journal of *Shirakaba* in 1916 and published by Iwanami shoten the following year.

example, *The Priest and His Disciple* [*Shukke to sono deshi*], which was first published in June 1917, had gone into 151 printings by January 1922. *The Person Who Does Not Sing* [*Utawanu hito*], which was first published in June 1920, had reached 41 print runs by August of the following year. Sales of *My Father's Concern* [*Chichi no shinpai*], which first appeared in March 1922, had exceeded 50,000 copies by as early as September of that same year. Ehara Koyata's *Old Testament* [*Kyūyaku*] had gone into its sixtieth printing by December 1921, two months after its initial publication.

The high level of support for religious literature that this survey revealed, particularly for the works by Kurata Hyakuzō (representing over a third of the works appearing in the survey), surely indicates a connection between the quest for self-cultivation and these women's attitudes toward life. In response to the question concerning "preparation for marriage," the majority of respondents unanimously insisted that self-cultivation was the mark of a complete individual (25 out of 48 respondents). The typical response was as follows: "Reading new publications prevents the brain from deteriorating and thus takes precedence over material preparations." As this statement frankly reveals, economic requirements were largely peripheral to other concerns, at least at a superficial level.

This survey, which was conducted in 1923, corresponded to the boom in self-cultivation that had begun in the late Meiji and was by this time drawing to a close. The boom had begun in the forty-fourth year of Meiji (1911) with the first printing of Nitobe Inazō's best-seller *Self-Cultivation* [*Shūyō*] and had gained momentum when Noma Seiji (1878–1938) inaugurated *Story-telling Club* [*Kōdan kurabu*] with the intention of offering the formula for self-cultivation to the masses through the medium of kōdan [historical narrative oral performance]. Kōda Rohan followed with his self-cultivation pieces *Essay on Endeavor* [*Doryokuron*] in 1912 and *Self-Cultivation and Reflection* [*Shū-shōron*] in 1914. We might well consider the period extending from the late Meiji to the start of Taishō as the era when the pursuit of self-cultivation reached its height. Throughout the Meiji era, desire for *risshin shusse* [*self-establishment and success*] had percolated down to the lowest social classes, while at the same time, the possibility of ever achieving risshin shusse kept shrinking proportionately. As a result, the virtues of self-denial, motivation, and self-reflection, which had been vigorously promoted as stepping stones to risshin shusse, became recognized as valid personal goals in themselves— in place of an unattainable risshin shusse. Self-cultivation thus emerged as the illegitimate child of a failed Meiji-era risshin shusse. (Needless to say, inherent in this quest for self-cultivation was the danger of being beaten down by the demands of survival in a vulgar world.)

Following WWI and the favorable economic conditions that it precipitated, the self-cultivation that had been dyed with the elements of personal character [*jinkaku*] and cultural refinement [*kyōyō*] characteristic of the Taishō era would be gradually replaced by the affirmation of egoism and the expansion of personal desires. In the context of a society that restricted opportunities for engagement with the real world, self-cultivation tended to express itself in self-aborbed rumination over private liberties that were cut off from society.[89] The following statements from the survey bear this out:

"As one way of realizing fulfillment in life as well as in love, I am looking to marriage." (typist)

"Because marriage is the most important feature of human life, people should select their spouses in accordance with their own free will and should be conscious of the fact that they are creating a new household. I am working hard to realize this." (shop clerk)

On the other hand, in the following response we can imagine the awakened new woman who is self-aware and conscious of herself as a working person with a role to play in society:

"Even if a woman tries to realize her dreams, her fortune is completely in the hands of heaven because our present society will deem her aspirations impossible. Since I am taking the path women are expected to take, I am suffering day and night." (clerical worker)

Indeed, in statements such as this one we can hear the painful sighs of a woman who, desirous of liberation, nevertheless encounters in the real world a thick wall that obstructs her goal from her. Thus, these women turned away from reality and retreated into interior worlds where they sought solace in religion. To wit: "I have experienced all there is of family life, and I endeavor to cultivate my spiritual self through the Bible" (clerical worker).

One might say that this ethos of self-cultivation that appeared among these surveyed working women contained two disparate fantasies: to release the inner self that religion promised was present, and the establishment or affirmation of the socially engaged self in the world of lived reality. Kurata Hyakuzō's *The Priest and His Disciple* brilliantly resolved this dialectic between free love and religious salvation as represented in such lives: "Sacred love requires loving your partner as you love your neighbor, you must love him with compassion, and look upon him as the Buddha looks upon all living things." Kurata's *The Priest and His Disciple* and Kikuchi Kan's *Madame Pearl* took the same approach in presenting the fantasy of women's liberation, but the "poeticization" of religious sentiment (i.e., what female readers demanded in literature) found in *The Priest and His Disciple* made it a much more influential work.

The earthquake exacerbated the dissolution of self-cultivation, which had earlier captivated Taishō-era women. Ishikawa Takeyoshi, editor of *Housewife's Friend*, taking advantage of this decline, offered the concept of culture [bunka] in place of the earlier self-cultivation [shūyō]. The success of his gambit is revealed in the fact that the readership of his magazine increased. Likewise, *Woman's Sphere*, which had earlier established an organization among its readers known as the Greater Japan Women's Association for Self-Cultivation [Dai-Nippon fujin shūyō kai], took advantage of the turmoil following the Great Kantō Earthquake and discontinued their practice of devoting each October issue to "Female Self-Cultivation." This change in policy clearly indicated that the trend in women's journals had shifted away from old ideas of self-cultivation.

The catalyst behind the dissolution of self-cultivation was twofold. On the one hand, there was the emergence of the new *shakai fujin*,[90] or social woman who was less interested in self-cultivation and more interested in self-determination, as is best characterized by the following statement: "We endeavor to lead lives determined by fully awakened selves, lives as liberated as possible. In order to achieve this we must first leave the home and seek work so as to establish ourselves as economically independent."[91] Yet, on the other hand, the large majority of women in the new middle class were not of this variety but were instead enamored of "culture" as the measure of their lives.

In the following I shall describe two typical representations of "culture" as a general concept among the Japanese populace in the late Taishō and early Shōwa period (mid-1920s through the early 1930s).

Consider representation A:

> To enjoy a healthy, happy life by discovering pleasure and entertainment in the common realities of everyday quotidian existence—this is the aim of the *Sandei mainichi*. This journal does not in any way accommodate that element of society that would frivolously seek happiness and pleasure. Rather, both writers and readers of this journal shall mutually endeavor to achieve a seriously cultured life by seeking science and art along the beaten tracks of their daily lives.
>
> The *Sandei mainichi* is devoted to the family. It is devoted to the pursuit of a happy life.[92]

Next there is B:

> To be well versed in world literature is the duty of those who, in the morning, make use of the trains and trolleys and in the evening enjoy radio shows. Without an antenna on their roofs or a complete book series in their studies, they are painfully chagrined. Consequently, the production of this complete series is an excellent barometer for gauging the cultural level of the Japanese mass audience. Indeed, every country and every age is distinguished by its own representative masterpiece. Behold the exuberance of the Japanese populace standing before the public broadcast system as this great news is announced to the nation. See how each household tosses out 1 yen coins. What better evidence can there be of the immense success of these multivolume collections?[93]

Example A was taken from the editorial page of the *Sandei mainichi*, whereas B was an advertisement for Shinchōsha's *Multivolume Collected Works of World Literature*. Needless to say, the weekly magazines and the 1 yen books [enpon] played significant roles in the advent of popular culture at the end of the Taishō and early Shōwa eras. By combining these two statements, we can create an outline of the essential features of this new "cultured life" as follows:

1. In statement A we have reference to the common realities of "everyday life." And in B there is mention of those who "in the morning, make use of the trains and trolleys and in the evening enjoy radio shows." Thus, we can deduce that those who sought "culture" were members of the new middle class.
2. They advocated a petit bourgeois "my-home-ism," a fact we can infer from the statement "The *Sandei mainichi* is devoted to the family."
3. They were consumers, seeking entertainment and pursuing hobbies. This we can conclude from the above references to (A) "a healthy, happy life" and (B) the enjoyment of "radio shows" in the evening.
4. Finally, it is clear that this new "cultured life" was influenced by the development of journalism and the advancement of audiovisual media such as film and radio. This fact is particularly supported by the statement in B about "the exuberance of the Japanese populace standing before the public broadcast system" and the frenzied way in which "each household tosses out 1 yen coins."

For the new middle class, the so-called "culture homes" [*bunka jūtaku*] on the outskirts of the city became an ideal serving as a receptacle for precious culture. Sasaki Kuni gently ridicules this "cultured life" in *Comedy at Culture Village* [*Bunka mura no kigeki*, 1926]. He describes the way "everyday people race straight home from work on the weekdays and how they then speed off to their writing, painting, or curio appreciation classes on the holidays." The people who live in his "culture village" are for the most part "company employees, teachers, government officials, and newspaper journalists and further down the line, the literati and members of the so-called employed-propertyless class."[94]

A culture home consisted of a nuclear family anchored by a husband and wife, who lived the idyllic "simple life," unencumbered by the conflicts created by life with a mother-in-law. The hero of Tanizaki's *A Fool's Love* [*Chijin no ai*] exalts this simple life when he brings his Mary Pickford–lookalike girlfriend Naomi to live with him in the culture home he rents in Ōmori on the outskirts of Tokyo: "In Japanese homes today the chests, braziers, cushions — everything have their place and no deviation is allowed. The husband, the wife, the maid each have separate roles. One must constantly interact with one's neighbors, relatives, and friends and this always incurs considerable expense. There's no way to easily extricate oneself from these arrangements and it's terribly oppressive. For a young man on a salary a life such as this is hardly pleasant. No, not a good thing at all. So, I convinced myself that my plan was rather ingenious."[95]

Beneath the "red slate roof" of his Ōmori home, the artificially crafted Naomi is nothing less than the "Eve of the Future," who hatches the fantasy of the cultured life. Personifying the transition for the New Age Woman to the modan gāru and preempting the self-obsession that accompanied it, she was fully invested with all that entitled her to serve as the model for the new middle-class woman.[96] Moreover, the fact that she resembled a famous foreign film actress symbolically points to one of the most important qualifications that the female literary image required in order to win the admiration of Taishō women readers. The end of the Taishō period saw a remarkable interchange between literature and film. The powerful images produced by the combination of ever-increasing literary works and alluring film stars created a fresh sensation that was unprecedented. When "The Second Kiss" and *Flowers of Suffering* were adapted for the screen and the roles of Kyōko and Sumiko were played by Tsukuba Yukiko and Kurishima Sumiko, respectively, familiarity with these works increased dramatically. The new medium of film allowed viewers the ability to escape from reality and indulge in fantasies even during the day and as such was much more effective than the novel in seducing its audience. The fact that the New Age Woman was highly susceptible to the fantasy proffered by popular novels and the daydreams spun out by the contemporary movies is bolstered by Horiguchi Daigaku (1892–1981), who commented on this element of Japanese womanhood on his return from Europe in 1925: "What struck me most about these women was their romanticism—their desires and dreams. . . . If a man of yesteryear beheld these women, he would be struck by their insatiable optimism. They are incorrigibly cheerful and bright. They possess a kind of poetic sentiment, like a fluttering butterfly. And it goes without saying that they turn to their fantasies as a means to escape this world of painful reality. Clearly, it is romanticism that is at the core of their inner lives, which are thoroughly literary."[97]

The ideals of political and social liberation that the New Woman had expressed earlier had given way to the dream of the cultured life, a life limited to two—a man and a woman—who had slipped the bonds of the real world. Attention was now devoted to new styles and personal fashion. Hiratsuka Raichō, Yamakawa Kikue, and the earlier celebrities of the women's magazines had been replaced by the film stars Yamada Junko and Kurishima Sumiko. Readers of women's magazines now reserved their applause for the cinematic performance of reality and no longer harbored desires for actual liberation. They were satisfied to be "beguiled by a world of dreams."

In its October 1926 issue, *Woman's Sphere* ran an article entitled "Mental Test of the Modern Girl" that was designed to understand her perception of everyday life. Sixty-seven women belonging to nine different categories were surveyed: students [*jogakusei*], young ladies [*reijō*], typists, trolley conductors, shop clerks, film actresses, sportswomen, café waitresses, and nurses. In response to a query about their "favorite actresses," they overwhelmingly cited Hollywood film stars such as Lillian Gish, Mary Pickford, and Gloria Swanson, while Okada Yoshiko topped their pick for a Japanese actress. Their favorite sports were tennis, swimming, ping-pong, and nearly half the respondents offered dance. Compare these responses to those in the 1924 "Survey of Working Women," in which women listed tea ceremony, flower arranging, embroidery, needlepoint, and listening to records—all activities pursued in the home—as their favorite pastimes. Here we see that women in 1926 were far more interested in stepping outside the home and enjoying their activities in public.

When questioned about their ideal married life, almost unanimously the women in the later survey indicated that they wanted to live with a sympathetic husband as an independent couple. For example, a student responded, "I want a marriage without a mother-in-law." One young lady replied, "I want my mother-in-law to live in a separate residence." Another noted, "I don't want my husband to be the center of our marriage. Rather, I would want us to respect each other, like friends." A typist offered, "I want to live a Western-style life as far removed as possible from the complicated family system." "I just want us to understand each other," a trolley conductor answered. A movie actress indicated that she wanted to live a "cultured life for two," and a café waitress hoped for a life as "a couple without a mother-in-law in the house." Two out of three women indicated that they would socialize with their husband before marriage, and most suggested that they would prefer their husband's monthly salary to be between 100 and 300 yen. In short, they aspired to the cultured life of the petit bourgeoisie.

Under the heading of favorite authors, they listed, in order of preference, Kikuchi Kan (11), Kume Masao (6), Arishima Takeo (5), Natsume Sōseki (4), Shimazaki Tōson (4), Kurata Hyakuzō (3), Akutagawa Ryūnosuke (3), Mushanokōji Saneatsu (3), Ishikawa Takuboku (3), Yoshida Genjirō (3), and Tanizaki Jun'ichirō (2). In the 1924 survey, the preference had been for Kurata, indicating readers' interest at the time in self-cultivation. Yet within two years, Kikuchi Kan's popularity had increased dramatically, along with the popularity of his novels—novels that, not incidentally, described the fantasy of women who broke free of their extended families and happily enjoyed their petit bourgeois cultured life, independently alongside their husband.

The three couples depicted in *Flowers of Suffering* thus brilliantly capture the modan-gāru style of life readers so desired.

Kume Masao serialized *Blue Brows* [*Seibi*] in the *Yomiuri* from June 1927. In this story, a writer, who has come by seeking employment, evaluates the heroine Saeko like this: "In the past, women were modern in mind only. They were called 'Bluestockings.' But now women are modern in the flesh as well, and so I have given it my own twist and call them blue brows. In the past they merely slipped into blue stockings and did nothing but reason or argue. But now women paint their brows blue and assert their modernity with their bodies. Surely, you, too, are such a woman."[98]

Madame Pearl introduced the trope of the New Woman into popular fiction. Even so, Ruriko, the widowed heroine, required a large inheritance to protect her freedom. Saeko of *Blue Brows* negotiates her way as a working woman, through the many layers in the male domain, averting danger with both her beauty and her own wits. Kume Masao, having taken his cue from Kikuchi Kan, thus depicts the uneasiness and danger that a heroine—independent and liberated from the fetters of the family—would encounter in the real world. Saeko is thus a new type of heroine, of the same lineage as Mikami Otokichi's Tomeko in *Nichirin* (*Tokyo Nichi-nichi*, January 1926). But both are nothing more than phantom images merely reflecting the illusory life quest of the new middle-class woman in the late Taishō–early Shōwa period. What, then, was the true picture? As an example, let me offer the bored but amicable couple in *Kami-fūsen* [Paper balloon], who, envious of the neat little houses in the Mejiro Culture Village, trade with one another stories of their dreams for a cultured life.[99]

Notes

1 First appearing in *Bungaku* June and July 1968, this is a translation of "Taishō kōki tsūzoku shōsetsu no tenkai: Fujin zasshi no dokusha-sō," in *Maeda Ai Chosaku Shū 2, Kindai Dokusha no Seiritsu* (Chikuma Shobō, 1989), 151–198. For more information on women's magazines in the 1920s, readers should consult *Gender and Modernity: Rereading Japanese Women's Magazines*, ed. Ulrike Wöhr, Barbara Hamill Sato, and Suzuki Sadami (Kyoto: International Research Center for Japanese Studies, 1998).

2 Ōya Sōichi (1900–1970), prominent literary critic. Grew up in the midst of local antigovernment sentiment, poverty, and rice riots. Ōya leaned toward left-wing thinking and had interests in anarchist, Marxist, and communist movements as well as in Christianity, though he never vocally agitated for any particular school of thought. Nevertheless, in his debut work of literary criticism *Bungakuteki sen-*

jutsu ron, he indicated that literature could and should be used as a tool for political agitation.

3   In his preface to his article, "On Literary Activism" ["Bungakuteki senjutsu ron," May 1927], Ōya Sōichi states that he was the first to refer to the post-Ken'yūsha bundan as a "guild," and he cites his article "The Era of the Dissolution of the Bundan Guild" as his source. However, Shiroyanagi Shūko (1884–1950) actually used the term first in his essay "A Bundan Adapted to Commercialism" ["Shōgyō shugi ni dōka shita bundan"], which was published in the July 1926 issue of *Shinchō.* He uses the expression as follows: "According to *Bungei shunjū* and *Fudōchō,* [the bundan] was built on the foundation of a medieval-era guild system." (M)

4   Ōya Sōichi, "Bundan girudo no kaitaiki," in *Bungakuteki senjutsu ron* (Chūō Kōronsha, 1930), 303–304.

5   *Shishōsetsu:* personal fiction. A mode of writing that admits no distinction among the narrated subject, the narrator, and the author. *Shinkyō shōsetsu:* mental-state novels. Often used interchangeably with shishōsetsu, the mental-state novel, in focusing on the narrator/narrated's mental state, is the ultimate shishōsetsu. Some critics contend that the shishōsetsu is a novel of discord that exposes the narrator/narrated's darkest, most humiliating moments, whereas the shinkyō shōsetsu is a literature of emotional harmony wherein the narrator/narrated finds peace and communes with his environment and those who inhabit it. The latter is typified by Shiga Naoya, the former by Kasai Zenzō. See Edward Fowler, *The Rhetoric of Confession: Shishōsetsu in Early Twentieth-Century Japanese Fiction* (Berkeley: University of California Press, 1988), 45.

6   Satō Haruo (1892–1964), poet, novelist, critic. Journal names generally appear in romanized Japanese, as in the case of *Shinchō* in this sentence, but note that for those magazines and journals that are the explicit topic of discussion later in this issue, English translations are used. For a note on the use of English- and Japanese-language titles of novels and other Japanese works, see note 2 in the introduction to this volume.

7   Shirai Kyōji (1889–1980), novelist lauded as one of the pillars of popular (*taishū*) literature in Japan. Helped found the journal *Taishū bungei,* which was the first publication in Japan specifically for the masses. Shirai is responsible for naming the journal and for appending the word taishū to this particular brand of literature. Earlier, the word had been used exclusively in a Buddhist context but henceforth came to refer to "the masses," "the populace," "the everyday." *Shadows over Mt. Fuji,* which is generally credited with opening the doors to the popular movement in literature, was serialized from 20 July 1924 to 2 July 1927. When it was finally published in book form, it spanned eight volumes.

8   Osaragi Jirō (1897–1973), novelist. Educated at Tokyo Imperial University, he was a literary dilettante who took an interest in Marxism and socialism. *Teruhi, kumori hi* (Sunny days, cloudy days) established him as a popular novelist. Although he was adept at creating contemporary stories, he was known for his "period-piece" novels. These novels often concerned *rōnin* who were invested

with wisdom, eccentric individuality, and a modern awareness of themselves as "outsiders." Yoshikawa Eiji (1892–1962), novelist. Best known in the West as the author of *Miyamoto Musashi*, which has been translated into English. His *Secret Notebooks of Naruto* was serialized in the *Osaka Mainichi* newspaper from 11 August 1926 to 14 October 1927.

9 Yada Sōun (1882–1961), novelist, haiku poet. His *Records of Toyotomi Hideyoshi* was serialized in *Hōchi Newspaper* from 15 October 1925 to 30 December 1934. It totaled twelve volumes when published in book form.

10 Aono Suekichi (1890–1961), literary critic and leading theorist in the proletarian literary movement.

11 Aono Suekichi, "Josei no bungakuteki yōkyū," in *Tenkanki no bungaku*, Kindai bungei hyōron zōsho series (Nihon Tosho Sentaa, 1990), 1:312, 313.

12 "Writers and Readers" ("Sakusha to dokusha"), *Shinchō* (March 1926). (M) *Jun bungaku*: pure literature, art for art's sake. In the Taishō era, jun bungaku referred to the shishōsetsu and distinguished it from "popular literature," which was typified by "literature for the masses" (*taishū bungaku*) and "common, colloquial, lowbrow literature" (*tsuzoku bungaku*). Katagami Noboru (1884–1928), literary critic and scholar of Russian literature.

13 Aono Suekichi, "On Mr. Katagami's 'Literary Criticism,'" in *Tenkanki no bungaku*, Kindai bungei hyōron zōsho series (Nihon Tosho Sentaa, 1990), 1:51. (M)

14 Kume Masao (1891–1952), literary critic, novelist, playwright. Writer of both shishōsetsu and popular fiction. Nakamura Murao (1886–1949), author, publisher, critic. Nakamura established the first debate on the shishōsetsu by positioning it against what he termed the *honkaku shōsetsu* or "true novel." *Anna Karenina* is an example of a honkaku shōsetsu, or a novel wherein the author creates a fictional yet realistic world whose characters and events are not identified with the author's personal experiences.

15 Hashimoto Motomu, *Kōdansha o ayunda gojūnen: Meiji, Taishō hen* (Fifty years with Kōdansha: The Meiji, Taishō volume), (Kōdansha, 1959), 609. (M)

16 Nakamura Kōya, *Noma Seiji den* (A biography of Noma Seiji), (Noma Seiji Hensankai, 1944). (M)

17 Kisaki Masaru, *Kisaki nikki* (The Kisaki diary) (Tosho Shimbunsha, 1965), 16. (M)

18 Togawa Ryū, "'Bungeika no seikatsu o ronzu' o yomite" (On reading "The livelihood of the writer"), *Shinchō* (October 1926). (M)

19 Hashimoto, *Kōdansha o ayunda gojūnen*, 470. (M)

20 As reported in the *Asahi Shimbun*, 14 April 1927. (M)

21 Estimating from census statistics in 1920, those identified as the "new middle class" amounted to 5–7 percent of the total number of employed people. Judging from statistics compiled by the Ministry of Education, the percentage of children receiving middle school education was 5–7. Minami Hiroshi, *Taishō bunka* [Taishō culture] (Keisō Shobō, 1965), 183. (M)

22 According to the Second National Census (conducted in 1925) the population of the country was 59,736,822; the total number of households was 11,999,609. (M)

23 This survey targeted:

A. Residents living within Tokyo city proper and contiguous towns.

B. Families with at least two members but with no more than eight.

C. Families with monthly income of between 60 and 250 yen.

D. Families with the main source of income provided by either a white- or blue-collar worker.

E. Families without live-in boarders.

This survey was distributed to 5,000 such families, of which 1,027 responses were received. (M)

24 *Gendai kyōikugaku*, 5, *Nihon kindai kyōikushi* (Iwanami Shoten, 1962), 170. (M)

25 Minami Hiroshi, *Taishō bunka*, 255. (M)

26 From *Teikoku tōkei nenkan* (Statistical yearbook of the [Japanese] empire). (M)

27 From *Mombushō nenpyō* (Annual report of the Ministry of Education). (M)

28 "A Survey of Working Women," conducted by the Public Sector of the Tokyo Municipal Office, 1924, 16. (M)

29 The items in the survey are listed in Table 4. (M)

Table 4

	NEWSPAPERS			MAGAZINES		
	Read	Don't read	Total	Read	Don't read	Total
Teachers	131	1	132	125	7	132
Typists	25	1	26	25	1	26
Office worker	258	34	292	239	53	292
Shop clerk	145	23	168	122	46	168
Nurses	28	12	40	32	8	40
Operator	213	29	242	204	38	242
Total	800	100	900	747	153	900

30 Aono, "Josei no bungakuteki yōkyū," 317–318.

31 *Housewife's Friend*, for example, inserted a free kimono collar in its July 1921 issue. But the Tokyo Magazine Federation, comprising Fujokaisha, which published *Woman's Sphere* [*Fujokai*], and Jitsugyō no Nihonsha, which published *Woman's World* [*Fujin sekai*], determined that *Housewife's Friend* [*Shufu no tomo*] was in

violation of its bylaws and the magazine was forced to pay a 500 yen penalty. ("Shijō kurabu," *Housewife's Friend*, September 1921.) (M)

32 *Fifty Years of Shufu no tomosha* (Shufu no Tomosha, 1967), 91. (M)

33 Kagawa Toyohiko (1888–1960), educator, Christian minister, social reformer, labor and co-op leader. From 1914 to 1916 he studied for a bachelor of divinity degree at Princeton University, taking the opportunity to travel and lecture in the United States. Back in Japan he advocated for the creation of co-op establishments and created a number of his own, from chicken-raising co-ops to medical co-ops. Author of more than one hundred books, pamphlets, and articles, he is best known for his autobiographical novel, *Crossing the Boundary of Death* (*Shisen o koete*, 1920). Miyake Yasuko (1890–1932), novelist and critic. She was known for her shishōsetsu, but she also wrote essays on contemporary social conditions and women's lives.

34 Tagawa Daikichirō (1869–1947), a politician. As a young man he worked for *Hōchi shimbun* covering the Russo-Japanese War. A fervent Christian, he was also an elected member of the Diet. Kubushiro Ochimi (1882–1972), a graduate of Joshi Gakuin, traveled to the United States, where she worked on behalf of Japanese immigrant women, many who had become embroiled in prostitution. Upon returning to Japan, she joined the Christian Women's Temperance Association and campaigned to abolish prostitution. In this effort she was joined by Ichikawa Fusae (1893–1981), a feminist and politician who campaigned for social equality. Ichikawa founded the Fusen Kakutoku Dōmei (Women's Suffrage League) along with other women in 1924.

35 "Fifty Years of *Fujin kōron*" (Chūō Kōronsha, 1965), 126. (M) Hosoda Genkichi (1891–1974), novelist. After working as an editor for Shun'yōdō publishers, where he was responsible for *Shinshōsetsu* and *Chūō bungaku*, he resigned in 1918 to become a full-time writer. He made his debut with largely autobiographical pieces and was eventually identified with the proletarian movement.

36 Kikuchi Kan (1888–1948), novelist, playwright, and early devotee of *junbungaku* (pure literature). Also referred to as Hiroshi, Kikuchi is renowned for his popular fiction and long newspaper serials. Responsible for creating the Akutagawa and Naoki Prizes in literature, there is also a literary prize in his name. From his debut as a popular novelist with *Madame Pearl*, Kikuchi went on to author more than fifty popular novels.

37 For example, during the roundtable with fans in Tokushima, when the reporter asked what readers read first when they opened the magazine, 13 out of 30 replied *New Gems* [*Fujokai*, June 1924]. (M)

38 Togawa Ryū, "Bungeika." (M)

39 "Fifty Years of *Shufu no tomosha*," 67. (M)

40 "Fifty Years with Kōdansha: Meiji, Taishō," 467. (M)

41 Kisaki, *Kisaki Diary* 27. Togawa, "Bungeika," 27. (M) Yanagawa Shun'yō (1877–1918), novelist. A disciple of Ozaki Kōyō, Shun'yō later joined Shun'yōdō as an editor for the journal *Shinshōsetsu*. Distinguished for the quiet nuances of his writ-

ing while under Kōyō's tutelage, Shun'yō became a prominent writer of domestic fiction, best known for *Incompatible* (*Nasanu naka*, 1912–13).

42 "Kume Masao shi to no ichimon ittō" (One question/one answer with Mr. Kume Masao), *Shinchō* (October 1924). (M)

43 Kosugi Tengai, *Nikki* (Diary). Unpublished manuscript, held in Kindai bungaku-kan [Archives of Modern Japanese Literature]. (M) [Kosugi Tengai (1865–1952), novelist. He began his career under the influence of political novels. Inspired by Emile Zola to create "narrative objectivity," Tengai was a pioneer in laying the foundations for naturalism in Japan.

44 Togawa, "Bungeika," and Satō Haruo, "Bungeika no seikatsu o ronzu" [On the livelihood of writers], in Shinchō (July 1926). (M)

45 Kisaki, *Kisaki Diary*, 449.

46 *Katei shōsetsu*: "domestic fiction." A subgenre of popular literature, the katei shō-setsu described situations in the home. When the genre first became popular in the late nineteenth century, it generally depicted wholesome scenes of family life. After the Sino-Japanese War in 1896, the novels began to feature domestic trage-dies, particularly as they related to women struggling against the injustices of the feudal family system. Tokutomi Roka's *Hototogisu*, published in *Kokumin shim-bun* from 1899 to 1900, was the first of its kind, and it inspired many others, such as Kikuchi Yūhō's *One's Own Sin* (*Ono ga tsumi*), which is known today as the quintessential katei shōsetsu. Many of these stories, melodramatic to begin with, became the basis for contemporary Shimpa plays. Around 1908 the katei shōsetsu was displaced by naturalism, only to metamorphose several years later into the popular novels of Kikuchi Kan and Kume Masao.

47 Senuma Shigeki, "Katei shōsetsu no tenkai" (The evolution of domestic fiction), *Bungakukai* (December 1957). (M)

48 It is not known when the term "popular fiction" [*tsūzoku shōsetsu*] was first used. However, Satō Kōroku (1874–1949) notes in his article "The So-Called Popular Novel" ["Iwayuru tsūzoku shōsetsu"] in *Different Harmonies* [*Fudōchō*, August 1926] that "this term was used by Sōma Gyofū (1883–1950) prior to 1923." (M)

49 Kikuchi Yūhō (1870–1947), novelist and a writer for the *Osaka Mainichi shim-bun*. Yūhō helped establish the literary column for the paper (then in competition with *Osaka Asahi shimbun*). Many of his works were adaptations (as opposed to translations) of foreign-language works. Known for his katei shōsetsu (domestic fiction), of which *Ono ga tsumi* is representative.

50 Nakamura Murao states, "Once Kume Masao wrote *Firefly Grass* and Kikuchi Kan, *Madame Pearl*, Katō Takeo, Mikami Otokichi, and others began to write popular fiction. The genre flourished. At the same time, women's magazines and entertainment magazines began to develop at a remarkable rate from the perspec-tive of journalistic and commercial interests. Thus, while popular literature exerts great influence today, it continues to achieve success." From "A Study of Popu-lar Fiction" ["Tsūzoku shōsetsu kenkyū"], in *Lectures on Japanese Literature: The*

Popular Literature Volume [*Nihon bungaku kōza: Taishū bungaku hen*] (Kaizōsha, 1933). (M)

51 Shirai Kyōji (1889–1980), novelist. Known for elaborately plotted popular novels like *Shinsengumi*. Mikami Otokichi (1891–1944), novelist. Noted for his "period pieces," such as *Oshidori jumon*, he was famous for injecting them with modern psychology and writing them in the contemporary *desu/masu* style (polite ending form). Mikami married Hasegawa Shigure, the coeditor of the women's literary journal *Nyonin geijutsu*, which she established with money Mikami donated.

52 Uno Chiyo (1897–1996), novelist, magazine editor, kimono designer. An original *modan gāru* (modern girl), Uno entertained the literary world early in her career with the largely autobiographical accounts of her many romantic adventures. Yoshiya Nobuko (1896–1973), novelist. Known as a writer of stories for girls, she was tremendously popular with adult readers as well. She wrote numerous short stories but is recognized for her long newspaper/journal serials. Yamada Junko (1901–1961), novelist. Author of numerous shishōsetsu, mostly based on her failed marriage, Yamada is perhaps best known as the model for and inspiration behind several stories by Tokuda Shūsei (1871–1943), with whom she was romantically involved.

53 In this instance, we cannot overlook the existence of the woman's magazine *Woman* [*Josei*], which strongly identified with other pure literature magazines with its publications of Tanizaki's *A Fool's Love* [*Chijin no ai*] and Nagai Kafū's investigative essays [*kōshō zuihitsu*]. (M)

54 Aono, "Josei no bungakuteki yōkyū," 313.

55 This convolutedness is typical of Tengai's long narratives. (M)

56 Katō Takeo (1888–1956), novelist, editor of *Bunshō kurabu* and *Bungaku jidai* (under the auspices of Shinchōsha). Also known for his popular domestic fiction.

57 Katō Takeo, "Katei shōsetsu kenkyū" (A study of domestic fiction), in *Nihon bungaku kōza: Taishū bungaku hen* (Lectures on Japanese literature: The popular literature volume), vol. 14 (Kaizōsha, 1933). (M)

58 Yurie of *Phoenix* assembles a salon of men to test the depth of love each man professes. Tamiko of *A Woman's Life* keeps her bedroom separate from that of her husband's, the aging Count Katano. Ruriko in *Madame Pearl* seeks to avenge her father's death by marrying the man she holds responsible. In each of these stories, the heroine is aggressive and uses her sex to gain advantage over the men in the stories, most of whom are represented as corrupt. (M)

59 Kikuchi Kan, "Shinju fujin," in *Kikuchi Kan zenshū* (Bungei Shunjū, 1994), 299.

60 *Shinshōsetsu*, February 1926. (M)

61 In the preface to the Kaizōsha edition of the *Kikuchi Kan zenshū* (The collected works of Kikuchi Kan) we have, "The author himself was rather pleased with his long works such as *New Gems* [*Niitama*], *Flowers of Suffering* and such." There is no mention of *Madame Pearl*. (M)

62 Kikuchi, "Shinju fujin," 99, 101.

63 Ibid., 213.

64 Suzuki Akira in *Kikuchi Kan den* (Biography of Kikuchi Kan) (Jitsugyō no Nihon sha, 1937) refers to the following passage from Kikuchi's letters to Togawa Ryū: "The other day a reporter from a certain women's magazine came to my friend Kume's house and angered me by referring to my work in *Haha no tomo* as being 'ghost written'" (326). (M)

65 Kojima Masajiro, *Ganchū no hitobito* (People in my view), *Shinchō* (June 1967). (M)

66 Kikuchi Kan, "Hibana," in *Kikuchi Kan zenshū* (Bungei Shunjū, 1994), 5:728, 787.

67 Kikuchi Kan, "Bungei sakuhin no naiyō teki kachi," in *Kikuchi Kan zenshū*, vol. 22 (Bungei Shunjū, 1995).

68 Nakamura Murao, "Honkaku shōsetsu to shinkyō shōsetsu to," in *Kindai bungaku hyōron taikei* (Kadokawa Shoten, 1988), 6:16. (M)

69 Katagami Noboru, "Sakusha to dokusha." This exact quotation and essay title are not found in his three-volume zenshū *Katagami Noboru zenshū* (Sunagoya shobō, 1939). A similar sentiment can be found in his "Tsūzoku shōsetsu no kako genzai oyobi shōrai," in *Katagami Noboru zenshū* (1939), 21–29.

70 Ozeki Iwaji, "Tsūzoku bungei no ichimen" (One aspect of popular literature), *Shinchō* (July 1925). (M)

71 Maedakō Hiroichirō, "Tsūzoku shōsetsu e no kōjō" (Advancing toward a popular novel), *Yomiuri*, 31 January–1 February 1925. (M)

72 Katō Kazuo, "Atarashiki tsūzoku shōsetsu" (A new popular novel), *Tokyo Asahi shimbun*, 4–6 May 1925. (M)

73 Aono, "Kikuchi Kan ron" (On Kikuchi Kan), in *Gendai Nihon bungaku zenshū*, vol. 27 (Chikumaban, 1934). (M)

74 Kikuchi Kan, "Zoku han jijoden," in *Nihon no bungaku* (Chūō Kōronsha, 1969), 32:461.

75 Ōya Sōichi, "Mikami Otokichi no insū bunkai" (Factoring Mikami Otokichi), in *Bungakuteki senjutsu ron* (Chūō Kōronsha, 1930). (M)

76 Kikuchi Kan, "Bungei to jinsei," in *Kikuchi Kan zenshū* (Bungei Shunjū, 1995), 22:277.

77 Kikuchi Kan, "Junan-bana," in *Kikuchi Kan zenshū* (Bungei Shunjū, 1994), 6:672–673.

78 Arishima Takeo (1878–1923), novelist. Known for his humanitarian idealism, Arishima was a member of the Shirakabaha (White Birch Society). Affluent and with an elite education, Arishima nevertheless expressed profound sympathies for the downtrodden, as revealed in his 1917 short story "Kain no matsuei" (Descendents of Cain), which dealt with the misery of tenant farmers, and his 1919 novel *Aru Onna* (A certain woman), a powerful portrait of the social pressures constricting modern Japanese women. His 1922 essay "Sengen hitotsu" (A manifesto) reveals the despair Arishima had begun to feel over not only the sharp inequities between himself and those at the lowest levels of society but his inability to effect any

change. The following year he committed a "love suicide" with Hatano Akiko, a married woman.

79 The following represents the reaction of a female reader to Arishima Takeo's love suicide: "Akiko was a victor in love, having battled alongside Mr. Arishima the slings and arrows of human sorrow. She was a woman who sought perfect happiness in that which was distanced from social conventions. . . . Arishima Takeo was *superior* [the word is written in English] to have given his life in an effort to live a life that was supremely human." Kida Yasuko, "Shikō no hito Hatano Akiko" (A woman of perfect happiness, Hatano Akiko), *Fujin kōron* (August 1923). (M)

80 Patricke Johns-Heine and Hans H. Gerth, "Value in Mass-periodical Fiction, 1921–1940," in *Mass Culture: The Popular Arts in America* ed. Bernard Rosenberg and Davis Manning White (Glencoe, Ill.: Free Press, 1957). (M)

81 American sociologist Hugh Dalziel Duncan identifies "make-believe" [*dairi taiken*] as one of the social functions of literature. In his analysis, Aono Suekichi reveals a close affinity with Duncan's argument, which is as follows: "If literature of make-believe is transformed by actual behavior, if it fosters experiences that are conscious and logical, then this creates distance between actual behavior, thus dispelling the many sentiments that threaten the preservation of the social system." [Translator's note: The above is a translation of Maeda's paraphrase from Duncan. The actual citation is as follows: "Make-believe literature, on the other hand, removes us from practical action by dissipating emotions which, if developed into actions (as in the use of magical art) or into conscious, rational experience (as in the use of great art), would be a threat to those in control of the society."] Hugh Dalziel Duncan, *Language and Literature in Society: A Sociological Essay on Theory and Method in the Interpretation of Linguistic Symbols with a Bibliographical Guide to the Sociology of Literature* (Chicago: University of Chicago Press, 1953), 42. (M)

82 Aono, "Josei no bungakuteki yōkyū," 331–333.

83 Oku Mumeo (1895–1997), feminist, social and political activist. Shinfujinkyōkai (New Women's Society) sought the reform of Article 5 of the Peace Preservation Law, which denied women the right to participate in political activities.

84 Yamakawa Kikue (1880–1980), essayist, feminist, social activist. Yamakawa is known for her work *Oboegaki: Bakumatsu no Mito-han* (Women of the Mito domain).

85 Kuwabara Takeo, *Bungaku nyūmon*, Iwanami shinsho, vol. 34 (Iwanami Shoten, 1950, reprinted 1963, 1970, 1989), ch. 3, "Taishū bungaku ni tsuite," 80. (M)

86 Okamoto Kanoko has the following to say about women's perceptions of life following the earthquake: "Because women's daily life grew more convenient, the longing for something new and different lost the irresistible energy that it had had during the Seitō era of the early twentieth century. Rather, this energy was spent on hairstyles and clothing. When women read women's magazines they invariably came across new and trendy terms, and thus assumed that by reading about

them, they too were new and fashionable. But this was not something that every woman would relate to. Women of this period were generally very utilitarian. They put the calculation of plusses and minuses ahead of their own feelings, so in this age, you rarely saw a woman who ignored this kind of calculation and who revealed the spark of her own innate passion." "Shinjidai josei mondō," *Shinchō* (September 1925). (M)

87 Fujimori Junzō, "Tsūzoku shōsetsu no sakusha ni atau," *Shinchō* (September 1925). (M)

88 Maeda's bracketing of "loan word" denotes the status of this terminology as more a neologism based on foreign words than a locution existing in the West.

89 Kamishima Jirō, *Kindai Nihon no seishin kōzō* (The structure of spirituality in modern Japan), (Iwanami Shoten, 1961), 197. (M)

90 In the article "Profile of a Modan Gāru," *Fujin kōron* (April 1925), Nii Itaru (1888–1951) pits the shakai fujin against the modan gāru, offering the following observations: "Shakai fujin had constructively united with one another, but the modan gāru threatened to collapse this union by marching off as an individual. The former was motivated by logic, the latter by passion, despite the fact that they were agreed in their opposition to preexisting ideas." (M)

91 "Shinjidai fujin no katei kan," *Fujin kōron* (January 1925). (M)

92 *Sandei mainichi*, 10 July 1922. (M)

93 *Asahi shimbun*, 15 February 1927. (M)

94 Sasaki Kuni, "Bunka mura no kigeki" in *Sasaki Kuni zenshū* (Kōdansha, 1980), 8:353.

95 For a more accomplished translation, refer to Anthony Chambers, *Naomi* (Tokyo: Charles E. Tuttle, 1986), 7–8: "The 'household' in modern Japan requires that every cabinet, brazier, and cushion be in its proper place; the chores of husband, wife, and maid are fastidiously distinguished; hard-to-please neighbors and relatives must be humored. None of this is pleasant or beneficial to a young office worker, as it requires a good deal of money and makes complicated and rigid what should be simple. In this respect, then, I considered my plan an inspiration of sorts."

96 *Chijin no ai* (Kaizōsha) was first published in July 1925. By September of that year it had gone through an astonishing fifty editions. (M)

97 Horiguchi Daigaku, "Shinjidai no josei ni taisuru kōsatsu," *Shinchō* (July 1925). (M)

98 Kume Masao, "Seibi," in *Kume Masao zenshū* (Hon no Tomosha, 1993), 4:495.

99 *Kami-fūsen* was a play written by Kishida Kunio (1890–1954) in 1925. Kishida, a student of French literature, lived in Paris for a number of years before returning to Japan and making his debut as a playwright. His bright and airy French-inspired plays challenged the dark Northern European and Russian dramas that were then popular in Japan. Kishida opened the Bungaku-za, along with fellow playwrights Kubota Mantarō and Iwata Toyoo, in 1937, a theater that was as

much opposed to popular stage entertainments as it was to proletarian dramas. The one-act *Kami-fūsen*, first staged in 1925, was Kishida's most popular play. It involves an unnamed man and woman who, bored one Sunday afternoon, fantasize lazily about what they might do. Their reverie is interrupted when a paper balloon drifts over their garden wall. Nothing happens in the play. Nevertheless, audiences were beguiled by this portrait of a perfectly happy couple. The translator is grateful for the assistance of Yasuko Sensui in helping to track down this reference.

7. From Communal Performance to Solitary Reading:

The Rise of the Modern Japanese Reader

(Ondoku kara mokudoku e: Kindai dokusha no seiritsu)

TRANSLATED BY JAMES A. FUJII

As in many of Maeda's best works, close attention to literary concerns pries open dimensions of social history that historians have hitherto missed. By foregrounding everyday practices of reading in the Meiji era, Maeda's essay radically revised the genealogy of the Japanese modern novel (*shōsetsu*)[1] as he simultaneously reworked the significance of such figures familiar in the study of the vernacular (*genbun'itchi*) novel such as Tsubouchi Shōyō and Yamada Bimyō. Varied practices of reading—from family performances to nation-building sermons and homosocial *shosei* (male higher school students) recitations in private academies, to name a few—are stitched together in Maeda's magisterial study that inaugurated the interrogation of the modern Japanese novel, which remains an area of vital research in Japanese literature today. Through a finely nuanced discussion of multiple practices of reading and of writing as performance, Maeda shows how they played key roles in the production of the modern prose narrative form (shōsetsu). At the same time, Maeda limns for us the middle decades of the Meiji era that opens up the nation to modernity as a moment of failed community, where solitary reading and privatization echo the silencing of not just reading, but of sociality that found brief expression in the Freedom and Popular Rights Movement (Jiyūminken undo).

1

Today we take for granted that the novel [*shōsetsu*] is something to be read alone in silence, but when by chance we encounter an elderly person's idiosyncratic intoning of a newspaper, we begin to realize that the habit of silent reading became widely established perhaps only with the last two or three generations of readers.[2] A look at the Meiji-era reader as he or she appears in such places as diaries and memoirs, moreover, reveals somewhat unexpectedly how vital and firmly rooted was the attachment to the pleasures of reading aloud.

In his autobiography written after the war, Ishikawa Sanshirō (1876–1957), one of the leading theorists of anarchism, records how deeply he was impressed by his mother's bedtime stories from *Records of Kusunoki* [*Kusunoki kōki*] and *Tales of Seidan* [*Ōoka seidan*].[3] He further relates with great interest touching scenes of his father and older brother reading aloud together about the storm clouds of civilization and enlightenment as they threatened the intellectual climate of the rural elite living along the Nakasendō corridor: "Father, too, enjoyed listening to my brother read various works, and I remember Father having him read for him *Han-Chu War Chronicles* [*Kanso Gundan*] and *Romance of the Three Kingdoms* [*Sangokushi*]. Sometime later, my father who went all the way to Tokyo to purchase Fukuzawa Yukichi's *An Encouragement of Learning* [*Gakumon no susume*], had him read it."[4]

Han-Chu War Chronicles and *Romance of the Three Kingdoms* may very well have been borrowed from a book rental store. In the earlier years of Meiji, families with their own copies of readers [*tokuhon*] and military chronicles [*gunki-mono*] were rare, so possession of such works borrowed from rental stores or friends was apparently occasion for group reading involving the whole family. In Yamakawa Hitoshi's (1880–1958) *Record of an Ordinary Person: The Biography of Yamakawa Hitoshi* [*Yamakawa Hitoshi jijoden: Aru bonjin no kiroku*] we find a similar account of reading practices of the time:

> When I was a youth, reading material was scarce . . . and in the countryside, after the demise of bookstores dealing in woodblock prints, there were not yet any new bookstores selling books printed with movable type. . . . When I was in grade school, a newspaper ad piqued my interest in a book on natural history and I took the trouble to order it from Fuzanbō of Tokyo. Unless it was an exceptional case, families did not have their own libraries, and in our home we just had some works along the lines of *The Analects of Confucius* [*Rongo*], *Mencius* [*Mōshi*], *Selected Tang Dynasty Poems* [*Tōshi sen*], and *The Unofficial History of Japan* [*Nihon gaishi*]. One winter I borrowed *The Eight Retainers of Satomi* [*Satomi Hakkenden*] from a friend whose family had a copy, and my father would give a nightly spirited reading. All of us in the family listened — mother mending clothes, my older sister knitting. Then, a year or two later, the urge hit our family again, so I went out to borrow the book and we resumed our nightly performances.[5]

In Higuchi Ichiyō's diary covering the period from 1891 to 1892, there are repeated entries in which we find Ichiyō reading novels to her mother, Takiko. It is also worth noting that March 1892 was the month that Ichiyō's maiden work, *Flowers at Dusk* [*Yamizakura*], appeared in the literary magazine *Musashino* on the recommendation of Nakarai Tōsui.[6]

16 September 1891: After sunset, I read *Gleanings from Yoshino* [*Yoshino shūi*] to my mother.

12 March 1892: Tonight I read some passages from a story for Mother.

18 March 1892: After a particularly spirited dinner, I read aloud from various works by the masters to my mother.

24 March 1892: After dark, I read a few stories to my mother.[7]

Ishikawa Sanshirō's father had served as the headman of Honjō, Yamakawa Hitoshi's had been responsible for overseeing storage charges as the warehouse superintendent under the shogunate vassalage, and Ichiyō's father was a government clerk for the Metropolitan Police—each figure, in other words, came from a middle-class family without intellectual pretensions. Even so, it appears that they all viewed the novel, not as something for private appreciation, but as the object for the whole family's edification and entertainment. Today, we are on the verge of forgetting how reading was very much a communal activity.

In my view, this communal practice linking reader to listener echoes the way life was lived by the Japanese family. To be more specific, this reading practice is associated with the absence of privacy that some time ago Lafcadio Hearn had identified as being the defining feature of the Japanese family: "And in this world of paper walls and sunshine, nobody is afraid or ashamed of fellow-men or fellow-women. Whatever is done is done, after a fashion, in public. Your personal habits, your idiosyncrasies (if you have any), your foibles, your likes and dislikes, your loves or your hates, must be known to everybody. Neither vice nor virtue can be hidden: there is absolutely nowhere to hide them."[8] Until quite recently, if not overtly critical about reading novels, more than a few families did not exactly welcome the practice. Might this reflect not so much concern with any ill effects the novel could exert on their readers as uneasiness with the idea of a reader shutting himself or herself away in the world of the novel and thereby threaten to undermine the sense of familial unity that Hearn saw in the Japanese family? In the early years of the Meiji era, when Confucian morality firmly held sway, the novel was dismissed as being little different from a plaything, and in fact, such genres as *kusazōshi* [illustrated storybooks] were treated as a kind of parlor game for the whole family. Hasegawa Shigure's (1879–1941) *Old News of*

Nihonbashi [*Kyūbun Nihonbashi*] is an interesting chronicle of the everyday life of middle-class downtown Tokyoites in the second decade (1870s-1880s) of the Meiji period.[9] It tells us that kusazōshi were read aloud after dinner in the recesses of the house warmed by a large brazier, where all the women in the house, the children, and the maids gathered around in a family circle to enjoy paper lantern shows, *kishago-hajiki*,[10] and needlework, with the grandmother taking the lead in song, and at other times delivering disquisitions on ethics [*shūshin-dan*]. Many who lived through the Meiji era remember with acute nostalgia their childhoods when grandmother, mother, or older sister unraveled the mysteries of the kusazōshi.

We must not overlook the connection between the practice of reading aloud and low literacy rates in this era, particularly in relation to women, children, and readers who belonged to the classes below the middle class. There is very little material that directly records writing and reading ability of the masses in the early years of Meiji. According to an 1888 survey tracking the educational attainment of young men in Ishikawa Prefecture, 1,869 out of 4,583, or roughly 41 percent, possessed the competency to read on their own as measured by their facility with texts widely used for basic instruction [*ōrai-mono*] in temple schools.[11] This relatively low literacy rate represents the level attained by the first cohort group of young men who had been educated under the new school system established in 1872. The level of education attained by women was even lower than that of their male counterparts; for example, school enrollment figures for 1887 show around a 60 percent rate for boys compared to 28 percent for girls. In her lifetime, Ishikawa Takuboku's mother, renowned as the most talented female student to attend the Senboku temple school at the end of the Tokugawa era, produced only forty-five letters written in *hiragana* [the simple, phonetic writing system],[12] and Ichiyō's mother, who was a farmer's daughter from Kōshū, could just manage bookkeeping in *kana*.[13] As illustrated by the scene in [Tsubouchi Shōyō's] *Tōsei shosei katagi* [The character of modern students] where the geisha Tanoji reads in a whisper the *Iroha Shimbun* [The A-B-C newspaper] that her friend has tossed away, it was common practice for a poorly educated woman or child reading alone to simply pick out the main points he or she could understand. Such limited literacy predisposes one to this simple if indirect method of comprehension—of listening to someone else's reading. Among those who frequented the book lenders in the early modern era [*kinsei*], particularly readers of *ninjōbon* [romantic stories], such methods were common. For example, in Tamenaga Shunsui's *Sweet Conversations* [*Eitai dango*] there is a scene in which Momiji Ofusa's lover Minejirō reads the ninjōbon *Sono kouta hiyoku no murasaki* [That little ballad, this adorable couple]

to her sisters under mosquito netting.[14] *Shungyō Hachiman kanen* depicts Fukagawa geisha whiling the afternoon away reading rental books,[15] and in *The
Maidens of the Seven Spring Flowers [Otome Nanakusa]* a young woman begs
her older sister, the proprietess of a pleasure boat, to read to her.[16] Ubiquitous
in Shunsui's work, such scenes not only faithfully portray the reader of ninjōbon, but also provide his readers with hints about how to read and enjoy his
work. They also hold one of the keys to unlocking the mystery of Shunsui's
writing style, which was designed to please the ear [*chōkaku-teki na sutairu*].[17]

The appeal of the prose narrative form called *gesaku* ["playful" prose narrative forms] that circulated widely through the book rental outlets during
the late Tokugawa era extended beyond the literate class [*shikijisha*] and began
to create a new, latent readership [*senzaiteki dokusha*]. In his distinctly suggestive way, Yanagita Kunio observed that the practice of listening to written
material borrows from the tradition of oral literature,[18] and in this case one
can say that such new readers begin to appear in the very process of a written literature spreading among the masses whose interest in the literary arts
has been nurtured by oral literary traditions. While this tradition provided
interest in and demand for reading material, the new reader was deficient in
both ability and desire to engage in independent reading, or, to put it more
bluntly, he or she was reluctant to read for private comprehension, prefer-
ring instead the pleasure of listening. As I see it, the modern literary genre
that contributed most spectacularly to the rise of this reader was the ninjōbon, with its primarily female readership. The ninjōbon reader was also the
audience who sought accessible, small-format reprints of such popular performance art forms as kabuki, *onkyoku* [samisen-accompanied songs], *hanashi*
[tales], and *kōdan* [historical narratives].[19] To borrow the words of Moriyama
Shigeo, this was a reader "whose foundation had been laid by prior visual
and auditory cultural traditions."[20] In the case of a form like ninjōbon, replete with elements of traditional popular performance arts, the relationship
between writer and reader is modeled on the theatrical setting of an on-stage
performer addressing an audience of listeners. Records show that Tamenaga
Shunsui would sit on stage with Kenkonbō Ryōsai and deliver oral recitations of his own work, *Colors of Spring: The Plum Calendar [Shunshoku umegoyomi, 1832–33]*,[21] giving credence to the view that Shunsui's works ought to be
considered not so much as *shōsetsu*[22] as something like Enchō's stenographic
notes [*kōen sokki*] for his oral performances.

The early years of Meiji, when the introduction of movable type print led
to an unprecedented increase in the production of inexpensive printed matter, was a time when the proportion of literati to an incipient mass reading
public would shift dramatically in favor of the latter. A society experiencing

the heady changes of "civilization and enlightenment" demanded that the masses consume an immense volume of information. Both the newspaper reading groups [*shinbun kaiwa kai*] that were led by public-spirited villagers who gathered their neighbors for reading sessions, and the "sermons" delivered to the masses by Buddhist and Shintō priests who used material from newspapers and "The Three Principles" ["Sanjō no kyōken"][23] to explain the ins and outs of civilization and enlightenment or the ideology of the imperial restoration [*ōken fukkō*] employed printed information supplemented by oral presentation. What gave birth to this new peculiar hybrid form of communication was the unsettled marketplace of communicative possibilities in a transitional period.

It was a time when newspapers were enlivened by moving anecdotes about parents who were inspired to subscribe to a newspaper after hearing their grade-school children read from them.[24] From around the late 1870s gesaku narratives from rental shops began to lose readers to serialized novels in the newspapers. The convenience of daily morning newspaper delivery reduced to a relic the rental book vendor who would make his rounds every three days with a large package of books on his back, wrapped in a *furoshiki* (cloth used for wrapping and carrying gifts). When "little newspapers" [*ko-shinbun*][25] began gaining acceptance into private households, they were read aloud for aural appreciation. In the following passage from *The Curious Fate of Hanaoka* [*Hanaoka kien-dan*], a merchant's daughter begs a young clerk to read to her from a serialized work: "When she beseeches him to leave the accounts for the evening and to come back [living quarters were typically set back from the storefront] and read her today's installment in the newspaper, Sannosuke refuses saying that since she only likes romantic and love-suicide stories and thus nothing of any worth, it is a waste of money to buy a newspaper."[26] In chapter 15 of *Tōsei Shosei Katagi* there is a similar passage, where the courtesan Kaodori has her guest, Yoshizumi, read from the *Yomiuri Shimbun*.

The scene of a family gathered together in a room reading and enjoying a novel is suggestive of the custom wherein the whole family sits together listening to the radio in the living room after dinner. By the mid-1950s, when portable transistor radios had been invented and the television set had become the center of entertainment in the living room, radio-centered communality broke down, and radios moved into private chambers and bedrooms for solitary listening. These changes brought transformations in the nature of radio broadcasts and the style of radio announcing; for example, late-night radio announcers began to address solitary listeners in hushed tones, temporarily creating a space for private communication. In contrast to the remarkable transformation in radio listening practices that lasted a decade beginning in the 1950s, the shift from communal to private reading practices took place at a much slower pace. Put differently, the novel was marked by the somewhat lengthy coexistence of both solitary reading and communal modes of reception.

2

The still prevalent practice in the early Meiji years of communal reading involving a single reader surrounded by several listeners reflected such conditions as the absence of privacy in the household, a low literacy rate, and the tradition of gesaku literature rooted in popular performative arts [*minshū engei*]. Although it cannot be denied that reading aloud was an effective means of communicating simultaneously to multiple listeners who each had their own expectations of the material being read, such practice was not something that necessarily signified an inner motivation at work that was strong enough to immediately stir up interest and admiration for the act of reading aloud in this reader-as-performer. Students educated at the level of temple schools, where language instruction was carried out through calligraphic practice using *ōraimono* [instructional readers] and *jitsugokyō* [a type of buddhist text], were clearly able to read texts aloud and be moved by their rhythms. Whether or not they developed the sensibilities to thoroughly appreciate the rhythms of writing or gained the capacity to read a text aloud and appreciate its aural qualities is linked to their experience with the Chinese classics through *sodoku*, where one reads only for sound without attending to meaning.

Let me clarify my discussion by sorting out *ondoku*, or reading texts aloud, into two types: the first might be characterized as a method of transmission, a recitation [*rōdoku*] that aids in the task of comprehension, the second type a performative recitation [*rōshō*] where the primary focus is on conveying the rhythms of a text through sonorous reading. The first type, rōdoku, embraced primarily by the masses, was suited for family-centered communal readings. Such literary styles as gesaku narratives, small newspaper serials, Meiji-style *gōkan* [bound volumes], and transcriptions of kōdan belong to this lineage. The second type, rōshō, came to be emblematic of the *shosei*, advanced students who had received instruction in reading Chinese classics aloud with no regard for understanding their meaning [sodoku, henceforth "sound-reading"]. Their ritualistic practice of intoning these classics helped give shape to a communitarian space for students whether at school, boardinghouse, dormitory, or political association. It was Chinese poetry, readers [*tokuhon*], editorials of the large newspapers, and political novels that corresponded to this second type of reading aloud. Let me briefly outline this second type, which I neglected in part 1.

Children of former samurai and the wealthy and powerful families in the provinces had begun sound-reading of the Chinese classics, in some cases by age 5 and at the latest by 10. Some examples from prominent figures whose childhood years spanned the late Tokugawa–early Meiji transition are:

> Ueki Emori (1857–1892): at age 11, enters the Domain academy for literary and military arts [*hankō bunbu kan*] and is instructed in the punctuation of the *Nine Chinese Classics*. (Ueki Emori den)
>
> Mori Ogai (1862–1922): at age 5 begins his studies with the *daimyō* scholar Yonehara Tsunae, sound-reading the Chinese classics, and in the following year enters the Tsuwano Domain School of the Elders.
>
> Tokutomi Sohō (1863–1957): at age 8, his maternal grandfather begins instruction through sound-reading of the Confucian *Analects*; prior to this, had been prepared by his mother with college reader of *Analects*. (Sohō jiden)
>
> Saganoya Omuro (1863–1947): at around age 5 receives instruction in the Four Chinese Classics through sound-reading by his father, and after the latter's imprisonment for his part in the Ueno Rebellion, his older brother and uncle take him through book 2 of *Mencius*. (Saganoya Omuro denbunsho)
>
> Kōda Rohan (1867–1947): begins sound-reading lessons with *The Book of Filial Piety* [*Kōkyō*] with a teacher of Chinese named Kaneda from Adachimachi at age 7, and continues after his enrollment in Ochanomizu Normal School. [*Shōnen jidai*]
>
> Masaoka Shiki (1867–1902): at age 6 begins sound-reading of *The Analects*, and when 8 or 9, sound-reads Mencius with maternal grandfather. [*Fude makase*]
>
> Taoka Reiun (1870–1912): around age 10, receives a grade school primer from his father, and soon thereafter begins commuting to a schoolteacher's house for sound-reading of *An Abbreviated History* [*Kokushiryaku*], *A History of Warrior Families* [*Nihon gaishi*], and *Jūhasshiryaku*. (From *Sūkiden*)[27]

Even after the new educational system was instituted in 1872, the study of Chinese was highly esteemed among fathers and older brothers, so that while young children were sent to grade school, it was apparently quite common for these children to learn the Chinese classics through sound-reading in their own homes and in private academies. Taoka Reiun recalls, "There was a competitive streak in the way [children] were sent to the private residences of teachers to receive extracurricular instruction in the Chinese classics."[28] Kōda Rohan's daily routine saw him rise while it was still dark and read aloud at the top of his lungs in candlelight, before running off to school. Through such strict discipline, Rohan tells us, "[I] turned the phrases into familiar expressions and memorized them all, so that except for the first two or three pages of the text, I didn't even bother to look at the words in the book [when reciting them later in the classroom]."[29]

The sound-reading of the Chinese classics—wherein repetition of the rhythms and the vibrations of the voiced words creates a kind of "spiritual language" [seishin no kotoba] that is radically different from everyday Japanese—represents a form of instruction that imprints the very form of Chinese language [kango no keishiki] on the souls of these youth. Even if comprehension of meaning remains beyond reach, the material qualities of the words, their resonance and rhythm, are fully mastered, and the understanding that is attained through reading, explication, and reading groups [rindoku] when the students have matured adequately supplements their grasp of these texts. These students whose thinking and literary sensibilities have been cultivated through largely uniform sound-reading instruction become a part of a community of intellectual elites whose shared interest overrides any geographic or class differences. Moreover, this practice of reciting Chinese literature aloud (an ability that presumes a common training that promotes the capacity to respond to the cadence and sounds of Chinese compounds) engenders and strengthens the feeling of community much as, for example, the use of a common regional dialect reinforces a sense of belonging among those from the same locale.

Many a youth who had flocked to Tokyo from all over Japan with dreams of rising in the world first enrolled in a private academy specializing in the study of the Chinese classics [kangaku juku]. "For entrance into a national university, the Army-Navy Military School, or law schools, the study of Chinese classics was essential."[30] Additionally, because boarding costs at these academies for the study of Chinese classics were low, many students used them as cheap alternatives to boardinghouses, commuting to their actual institutions of choice from these academies where they resided.[31] In *My Thirty Years in Tokyo* [*Tokyo no sanjūnen*][32] Tayama Katai reminisces about his youth as an apprentice and errand boy at the Yūrindō bookstore, when he was loitering outside the window of his older brother's private academy and listening with envy to the "voices of reading that spilled forth." In the 1870s and 1880s, Tokyo was teeming with these private academies—Nakamura Keiu's Dōjinsha, Mishima Chūshū's Nishō Gakusha, Sugiura Jūgō's Shōkō-juku,

Mukōyama Kison's Kison-juku, Oka Rokumon's Oka-juku, Yoshino Seikyō's Yoshino-juku, to name a few. "Voices spilled forth" not only from the *juku*, but from student boardinghouses. The following letter appeared in the 13 March 1877 edition of the *Yomiuri shimbun*:

> In contrast to the West, in Japan the practice has been to read material lacking grammatical rules, commas, semicolons, or full-stops, each reader freely adding one's own idiosyncratic tonalities—stretching out their syllables like the *dodoitsu*[33] master, Shijo-kotobuki, quoting the same attribution to an unofficial historian's account five times when one would do, adopting the voice of a pilgrim's vocalizations, calling out like a beggar, emitting sounds in the style of a Shinto funeral prayer, or in the manner of burlesque Buddhist scriptures, causing listeners to wonder if comic storytellers had arrived. And then there are some who sound like the calls of a bulletin vendor—all sounds that one can somehow still endure—but the students' voices booming from boardinghouses at night, just about the time people here and there have fallen asleep and keeping others from sleep is something we would like curbed, and, if I might add, to read properly one must punctuate it and speed it up a bit in the manner of the priests of the Shinshū Buddhist sect.

There is nothing surprising about the fact that among the forms of recreation favored by students was the recitation of memorized passages from Chinese-style prose and poetry [*kanshibun*] and the *yomihon* ["elevated" fiction] of Bakin. Ichijima Kenkichi, who had moved from Niigata to Tokyo and was preparing for university entrance, remembers those days this way: "It was all the rage among students to read Takizawa Bakin's *shōsetsu* such as *Tales of the Eight Retainers of Satomi* [*Nansō satomi hakkenden*, 1814–41], *Tales of the Crescent Moon* [*Chinsetsu Yumiharizuki*, 1807], and *Modern Chronicles of a Handsome Youth* [*Kinsei bishōnen roku*, 1829–32], and the dramatic scenes in *Tales of the Eight Retainers of Satomi* were memorized by many students. If you couldn't recite the separation scene of Shino Hamamichi in *Tales of the Eight Retainers of Satomi* you felt just a little second-rate."[34] Some years later, Masamune Hakuchō observed that when he was a child, "we felt affinity for the writing of Bakin and San'yō, and we read aloud passages from their works much as one might recite poetry."[35] Like Bakin's *yomihon*, the political novel, written in a sonorous simplified Chinese [*kanbun kuzushi*], was a literary form highly suited for oral recitation. It is already well-known that Tōkai Sanshi's *Chance Encounters with Beautiful Women* [*Kajin no kigū*, 1885–97], written in an elegant prose making liberal use of a splendid four-six syllabic meter, with Chinese poems inserted in key passages, was a favorite among students for reading aloud, and I hardly need to mention the memorable scene in [Toku-tomi Roka's] *Dark Eyes, Brown Eyes* [*Kuroi me to chairo no me*, 1914] depicting three hundred boarding students at Dōshisha who interrupt their studies to listen, transfixed by the recitations of Chinese poetry from *Chance Encounters with Beautiful Women*.[36] As Emi Suiin, who studied at the Sugiura Jūgō's Shōkō Academy, remembers it, the Chinese academy students who typically didn't pay any attention to cheap romances [*nanpa no shōsetsu*] were strongly drawn to the style of Tōkai Sanshi's *Chance Encounters with Beautiful Women* and Yano Ryūkei's *Inspiring Instances of Statesmenship* [*Keikoku bidan*, 1883], which they read aloud enthusiastically.[37] As I suggested earlier, in the case of those students who possessed a shared (trained) fondness for the rhythms of Sinified prose and poetry [*kanshi bun*], oral recitation held the power to stimulate feelings of communal belonging. The prototypes for these practices of reading and enjoyment predate the appearance of the political novels *Inspiring Instances of Statesmenship* and *Chance Encounters with Beautiful Women*, already mentioned. The manifesto exhorting "our 35 million brothers" in the form of a petition to the National Diet by Taoka Reiun, who spoke for a subsidiary branch of the Tosa People's Rights Movement, and village youth who celebrated by singing the "Song of the Fall of Poland" are examples of these communal performative occasions.[38] By promoting communal group reading in the inner sanctum of student communities like the school, dorm, boardinghouse, private academies, and associations, the political novel was able all the more effectively to serve as a catalyst in promoting sympathy for the People's Rights Movement. Such activity would begin to resemble the forms of reception accorded epic poetry that was recited aloud in public.

3

David Riesman, well-known as the author of *The Lonely Crowd*, identi-fies three stages in the development of culture in a work addressing the his-tory of communication.[39] Stage 1 might be designated as the culture of oral communication, stage 2 the era of print culture, and, stage 3 the moment of popular culture defined by such media as radio, film, and television. This work by Riesman focuses not so much on the relationship of print culture to inwardly directed subjects as on the trajectory of visual culture (movies and television) that helps gives rise to other-directed beings, but my intention here is to concentrate on the transitional period between stages 1 and 2, when print is employed together with oral communication as a means to reproduce or represent orality.

Riesman attempts to grasp the rise of the practice of silent reading in connection with Puritanism. Accordingly, the invention of printing in the fifteenth century inaugurates the preparatory stage for print culture and culminates in the spread of an inwardly focused, private reading practice that takes shape under Puritanism in the eighteenth century:

> Even after the appearance of Gutenberg, it took a long time before the current manner of reading became accepted practice. Texts continued to be read aloud even for private reading. In fact, before Dr. Samuel Johnson's dictionary helped create a uniform standard for spelling, each writer used his or her own phonetic renderings of words. But, befitting the severe restraint that we ascribe to the Puritans, they would read the written lines of text at an angle, their heads moving quickly like a shuttle traversing a loom, in unilluminated silence. Thus, it was only in relatively recent times that printed matter helped open the doors leading outwardly as well as to the inner reaches, inviting individuals away from the clamor and noise of others and into solitude.[40]

In addition to social scientists such as Riesman, literary historians concerned with readership have also observed that the age of silent reading was preceded by an era when the practice of reading aloud was gradually abandoned. Taking England for example, they note that in Elizabethan times not only poetry but even prose was written for oral performance. A radically different literary expression conceived strictly as a printed medium (i.e., the prose narrative form of the novel) begins to appear only with the advent of journalism in the early eighteenth century.[41] On the other hand, almost without exception, in the seventeenth century, "reading" signified oral recitation. Punctuation separated words and phrases to aid the proper delivery of words rather than to act as grammatical diacritics.[42] The depiction of domestic scenes with mothers or fathers reading aloud to their children was said to be a staple of eighteenth century popular art in Germany.[43]

In Japan, this period of reading aloud can be thought of as coinciding with the era of woodblock printing, which preceded the importation of movable type print. The early years of Meiji, when woodblock printing was giving way to movable type print, also witnessed the final stages in the transition from what Riesman calls oral communication [kōwa] to the written word. This was still an age when the printed word had not quite realized its function as an independent medium in its own right, and was seen partly as a means of presenting or reproducing oral communication. Put differently, this meant that while on the one hand, movable type print functioned as a form of private communication, it was also not uncommon for type print to be employed as a means for communication where the "reader" was a group or community—the family, local associations, and groups with shared interests such as the shosei—rather than a solitary individual. The family and its newspapers and gesaku fiction, local and regional associations and their news discussion groups, and communities of like-minded students and intellectuals and the political novel—each in its own way represents a unit of collective reader reception.

Tsubouchi Shōyō was one of those individuals who experienced and to some extent correctly understood the implications of this shift from reading aloud communally to private, silent reading. His essay "For the Purpose of Promoting Reading" ["Dokuhō o okosan to suru shui"], which appeared in the April 1891 issue of *Kokumin no tomo*, was written at a pivotal moment in his literary career, when his attention shifted from the task of reforming the novel to that of reformulating theater.[44] His ideas in that essay on the nature of literary reception merit special attention.

In the introduction to this piece, he notes that the very difficulty of disseminating writing back in antiquity when print technologies were absent and paper was a scarce commodity engendered the "necessity of oral recitation." Employing the work of Homer and Herodotus, Shōyō argues that the appearance of poetry and other rhythmic compositions in advance of "a-rhythmic" [*muchō*] or prose literature are related to this oral form of presentation. Making his points in the form of a soliloquy, Shōyō observes that in contrast to antiquity, at present, education has become widely available and print technology has developed to create "a world in which writing is immediately transformed into tens of thousands of pieces of printed matter that is silently read by a hundred million people at the same time. The ancients 'read' the work of others with their ears, while people today enjoy the benefit of reading with their eyes." That, he continues, transformed the practices of *gakushū*, or learning (which had formerly depended on oral recitation), into meaningless acts. Shōyō proceeds to advocate a "logical method" [*ronri-teki dokuhō*]—a new reading technique that applies to what he calls a new "method of studying life." Reading must follow the principle of "excavating the deep significance of the text, and criticism requires the reader to discern the nature of the author, or in the case of drama, its characters, while interpretation dictates that the reader be prepared to assume the position of that writer or his characters." Although not clear in relation to the practice of reading aloud [ondoku], Shōyō notes that these principles "must be followed for silent, private reading [*mokudoku*]." Following such guidelines provides the foundation for a kind of belletristic reading practice [*bidokuhō*], which emphasizes the process of representation [*hyōgen katei*]. Premised on the adoption of silent reading [*mokudoku*] as the new rule for reader reception, bidokuhō required the rejection of the established convention of rōdoku, or recitative reading, so that reading could be given new form in performative expression that was to be found in theater. That is, it had to "express the true will of the author enacted as recitation," and to that end, Shōyō identifies *gen-bun'itchi* and the scripts of dramatic masterpieces as the written forms suited for such belletristic reading, a practice that requires sensitivity to a tonality that can express emotions ranging from inspiration to sorrow, attentiveness to shifts in cadence and intonation for conveying proper emphases, and care in expressing the required tempo and pauses appropriate to the feelings conveyed by the writing.[45] Shōyō's prescription completely reverses the path of sodoku (recitation without concern for meaning comprehension), which presumes form to be the point of entry for grasping content.

Insofar as this "logical reading method" emphasizes not so much any aesthetic appreciation of writing as understanding its phenomenality, Shōyō's approach shows the reader the proper orientation for appreciating prose. Literary works that are adequate to such a reading method that require the reader to identify with the author or the characters and to relive their thoughts and feelings must, of course, also demand strict models for characters that have been realized by the author's exacting determination to express himself or herself. Without realizing it, Shōyō had outlined the provisions for reader reception of the modern shōsetsu. Let us now turn our attention to how, in fact, the development of literary modernization after the late 1880s intersected with transformations in reader reception.

4

The work that launched Ozaki Kōyō's career, *The Amorous Confessions of Two Nuns* [*Ninin bikuni irozange*], appeared in the April 1889 volume of *A Hundred New Literary Works* [*Shincho hyakushu*]. In May of the following year, under the name of Kyō Wakako a review appeared in the *Publisher's Monthly Review* [*Shuppan geppyō*]. "The reader appreciates more deeply with each reading the fecundity of the elegant prose," she wrote, but praise gives way to some criticism. "However, the preponderance of staccato sentences/phrases [*ku*] makes reading awkward, resulting in prose narrative that is neither *uta* [*noh* chant] nor *jōruri* [dramatic ballad]; I doubt it will please the reader when it is recited."[46] The impression she receives of a "preponderance of staccato sentences" must be criticism that was directed at Kōyō's experimental writing style, marked by short sentences following one another in rapid-fire succession. It is worth noting that her perspective presumes that the language of the shōsetsu must "please the reader when it is recited."

What is evident here is a literary sensibility that is inextricably linked to aural reader reception, wherein appreciation is sought through exclusive focus on the aesthetics of literary style. This orientation does not exactly lead to a practice of reading that seeks clear and swift understanding of rich and complex ideas as they take shape through writing. The sensibility articulated by Kyō Wakako is realized not through prosaic, transparent language, but in elevated, baroque, and florid poetic expression. In spite of Kyō Wakako's assertion that the shōsetsu is "neither uta nor jōruri," there is little doubt that her notion of prose narration is firmly rooted in the genealogy of these narrative-recitative forms [*katari-mono*]. Recast in the idiom prevailing in those days, these literary expectations corresponded to the flowing rhythms characteristic of Bakin's style.[47]

Like Kyō Wakako, who felt dissatisfied with *Amorous Confession*'s hybrid elegant-straightforward style of writing [*gazoku-setchūtai*], it is easy to imagine the antipathy felt by traditional readers toward literature written in the new colloquial language, absent the pleasing performative metrics and rhythms of an earlier-age literature. Yamada Bimyō, one of the leading advocates of the genbun'itchi movement, never missed an opportunity to rebut the simplistic reactions of such readers by raising issues related to the rhythm of language and focusing on, to use his terms, accent [*gochō*], tone [*seichō*], and euphony [*onchō*]. He argued his case on two grounds. Prose literature should not be assessed by standards developed from poetic conventions, and the rhythms of prose were fundamentally different from the rhythms of poetry. Bimyō's thesis on genbun'itchi was a theory of readership, shedding considerable light on the relationship of author to reader in the 1880s and 1890s.

In the preface to his story, "Fake Diamonds" ["Nise kongō-seki," 1887], Bimyō was already promoting a new set of standards for literary appreciation. The prevailing view that written Japanese was distinctly different from everyday speech, he said, was misguided. Accordingly, he exhorted his audience to read novels written in genbun'itchi as if it was spoken Japanese so that they might enjoy them more. More explicit arguments for the reform of orality-centered textual conventions were to follow in March 1888 in "Genbun'itchi ron gairyaku" [An outline of genbun'itchi].[48] The criticism of genbun'itchi proponents by those who denigrate the baseness of colloquial language in contrast to the elegance and tonality of classical writing, he said, was misguided, for it presumed Chinese and Japanese poetry to provide the standards for judgment, when in fact, syllabic rhythm [*onchō*] was not the most significant aspect of prose texts. Because "colloquial texts express language exactly as it is spoken," it naturally followed that they were to be "read as if one were reading everyday speech." Bimyō's concern for reforming widely held views on writing and literature would wend its way through his somewhat confusing explanations in "Bun to gochō" [Writing and rhythm][49] and develop into an affirmation of the difference in rhythms and cadences for prose and poetry.[50] This essay, which was written explicitly to challenge Mori Ōgai's "Thoughts on Genbun'itchi," provides thirteen principles of gen-bun'itchi writing: the last three, which specifically refer to the rhythms of prose, merit our attention:

> Principle 11: It is called stagnation [*jūtai*] when one recites prose and fal-ters [*shiburu*], thereby failing to convey its meaning. When one recites such prose smoothly (without hesitation) and successfully conveys its meaning, it can be designated "flowing" [*fujūtai*] in distinction from "musical" [*gakuchō*].
>
> Principle 12: Even if one successfully conveys the feelings expressed by this prose, and though it may be free-flowing and sincere, such voicing is not necessarily musical.
>
> Principle 13: The term that accurately describes the supreme achievement of prose recitation is "flowing" [fujūtai]. On the other hand, "musi-cal tonality" [gakuchō] best describes the sonorous quality of reciting verse.[51]

Bimyō attempts to identify the rhythms of prose in the very process of reader reception. In order for intention or meaning to be understood by and feelings to be aroused within the reader, what is required is the process of smooth, flowing recitation [*shō shite shiburazu*, literally "reading aloud without hesi-tation"]. Reading marked by hesitation clouds comprehension and prevents the reader from being moved by the words. For Bimyō, prose is marked by its flowing rhythm, evenness, and a uniform and regular cadence. In other words, he understands the rhythms of prose writing as something that serves as a filter (i.e., to clearly limn) the "meanings" and "emotions" conveyed by the words, rather than as something that (itself) conveys the subtle shifts in intentions/meanings and emotions found in writing.[52] This proclivity to view form and content as separate rather than integral also appears in a work that exerted considerable influence in reshaping the rules of Japanese poetry, Uchida Roan's *Japanese Poetry* [*Nihon inbun ron*]. Allowing for some mis-understanding on the part of both parties in this debate regarding poetry [*shi*] and verse [*inbun*], Uchida Roan is convincing when he states that even as Bimyō argues for poetic style [*seichō*] he does not recognize the presence of the thought or concept within poetry.[53] Roan's criticism pointedly reveals the incompleteness of Bimyō's poetic principles.

Even Mori Ōgai, who generally remained a bystander in the debates over genbun'itchi, had taken the position that "verse is created to be sung and re-cited and appeals to the ear, while prose is meant for reading, beckoning only to the eyes and the heart."[54] Ōgai had reached the understanding that, as a rule, prose was to be read silently, whereas Bimyō had not quite escaped the custom of reading out loud. Although what Bimyō called "reading" [*yomu*] was conceptualized in opposition to "recitation" [*ginzuru*], it is clear from his essay "Writing and Rhythm" ["Bun to gochō"] that he did not have silent reading in mind. For him, the rhythms of prose were conceived in terms of the reader's voice.

Only when genbun'itchi stopped being viewed as "writing that employs vernacular language" or "writing the spoken language exactly as it is," and was understood as language "written the way one speaks"—that is, genbun'itchi language was no longer seen as the transparent rendering of speech but rather as a vernacularized expression stamped by the author's subjectivity and his or her distinctive style—did it finally attain its status as the language of modern literature.[55] The writer freed himself or herself from such stylized adornments as rhythm and meter to address the reader in his or her own voice—a voice that is dictated by the writer's own self-awareness and impulses [*shōhaku*] rooted in his or her interiority. It is not surprising that the examination of prose writing coalesced not around the issue of reading [literally, the "readers' voice"] but on the "voice" assumed by the writer—the line of inquiry pursued by Shōyō and then Futabatei. It is one of the ironies of modern Japanese literary history that Futabatei's *Ukigumo* and *Aibiki* were more effective in urging on a revolution in reader reception than were the copious arguments found in Bimyō's essays urging reading reform.

5

> Back around 1892, Takase Bun'en was so helpful to me, and I remember how he used to tell me what a remarkable character Futabatei was. After telling me "you must meet Hasegawa [Futabatei], the likes of whom you will never find in Japan," he proceeded to recite from Part 3, "Miyako no hana" from *Ukigumo* in an entertaining, rhythmic narration.[56]

The passage is taken from Tayama Katai's reminiscence of Futabatei. In his *Thirty Years in Tokyo* Katai credits Bun'en as a figure "who provided surprisingly profound inspiration in literary matters."[57] Here, I wish to draw your attention to the fact that Bun'en had performed an entertaining rhythmic recitation of a passage from *Ukigumo* for Katai. Bun'en had observed in his "Views on Literature" ["Bungaku iken"]: "Is the prose narrative [*sanbun shō-*

setsu] just like the historical narrative [*kōdan*] delivered from a stage? Even when the intense emotions take expression in the form of prose or poetic voice, isn't it by its very nature unable to escape the characteristics of spoken language *dan'wa*]?"[58] It is said that Bun'en read aloud his 1893 novel, *New Leaves* [*Wakaba*], to Katai.

For those of us who are accustomed to reading *Ukigumo* alone and in silence today, this episode alerts us to its different historical context. Isn't *Ukigumo* a work that was originally intended to be heard much in the spirit of *ninjō-banashi* [traditional melodramas] as they were recited from the stage? Ought we not to at least once again acknowledge that the literary style of this work requires voiced delivery [*koe o tomonatta buntai*]? In his essay "*Ukigumo no sekai*" [The world of *Ukigumo*] Togawa Shinsuke points to three examples found in the first half of *Ukigumo* that illustrate a narrative style [*katari*] that follows the formal conventions of Enchō and other raconteurs: (1) the narrator itself appears in the text to make comments and judgments; (2) the writer himself greets the reader at the conclusion of the tale; (3) interjections are made to solicit the reader's sympathies.[59] In the first half of the work, the author remains a detached bystander and, accordingly, at times assumes the role of interlocutor [*tōjisha*], at times addressing the reader, adding commentary, or performing as the occasion demands.

Let me raise an aspect of *Ukigumo*'s narration that Togawa neglected to address: onomatopoeia [*giseigo*] and mimetic words [*gitaigo*]. For example, here is the passage in part one when Bunzō arrives at the Sonoda household.

> Takai otoko wa genkan o tōri-nukete engawa e tachi-deru to katawara no zashiki no shōji ga surari hiraite toshigoro jūhachiku no fujin no kubi chonbori to shita tsumamippana to, hinomaru no mon o somenuita muk-kuri to shita hō to de sono mochinushi no mibun ga shirareru to iu yatsu ga nutto deru.

> When the tall man slipped through the entryway and made his way to the hallway, the drawing room door adjacent to him slid open and out popped the head of a girl in her late teens. The little pinched button nose and the plump cheeks as red as the sun on the [Japanese] flag betrayed her rustic origins.[60]

Such mimetic expressions, we all know, borrow from spoken or voiced utterances [*onsei hyōshō*] to convey the essence of the targeted meaning by appealing to the senses. Generally, they are more effectively employed in spoken language than in writing. In the well-known climactic scene when the ghost of Otsuyu appears in Enchō's rendition of *The Tale of the Peony Garden Lantern*

Table 1. Use of Onomatopoeia in Selected Texts[1]

	Narrative Line #	Onomatopoeia Used	Onomatopoeia per 10 Lines
Ukigumo part 1	587	140	2.4
Ukigumo part 2	754	144	1.9
Ukigumo part 3	634	65	1.0
Musashino	148	7	0.5
Kochō	199	12	0.6
Botan dōrō 1–8	243	71	2.9

[1] Statistics compiled from Iwanami Bunko editions of these works. (M)

[*Kaidan botan dōrō*, 1884], the sound of the low clogs echoing as they hit the ground—*karan-koron*—very effectively evokes an atmosphere of otherworldliness. Although not as numerous as in *Kaidan botan dōrō*, compared to other genbun'itchi novels of the time, *Ukigumo* employs a large number of these "performing" words.

The decline in the use of onomatopoeia from part 1 to part 3 of *Ukigumo* corresponds to what Togawa Shinsuke calls the transformation of the writer's position from observer [*bōkansha*] to coparticipant [*kyōhansha*]. Even in part 3, their frequency far exceeds such contemporary works as Bimyō's *Musashino* and *Butterfly* [*Kochō*] (see Table 1).

In the preface to his second genbun'itchi work, *A Tune for the Organ* (*Fūkin shirabe no hitofushi*), Yamada Bimyō describes his own work like this: "In short, it is as if you embellished Enchō's notes for his ninjōbon."[61] And in his first genbun'itchi work, *Mockery and Reproof for a Braggart Novelist* [*Chōkai shōsetsu tengu*], one can observe a cartoon-like depiction of the novelist-character who is "either a raconteur-in-training or someone who hammers together some warmed over or imitation novel and butters up the publisher."[62] For example, in the following passage, which appears in *Musashino*, it is abundantly clear that his work is like "embellishing Enchō's own outlines for his ninjōbon": "Even if you close your eyes and quiet the mind and attempt to devote your full attention to reading the Darani Sutra (even though a voice issues forth from the mouth), there is no feeling that comes from the heart. 'Neither present nor absent, active nor quiet, red nor white . . .' these lines resemble the words spoken by Oshimo [in *Botandōrō*]."[63] The passage that resonates with this one is in part 8 of *Botan dōrō*: "After crawling under the mosquito netting he had hung, Hagiwara struggled to read the Darani Sutra. Nao bo ba gyaba tei ba zara da ra. sa gya ra niri gu sha ya. ta ta gya ta ya. ta ni ya ta on so ro bei. ban da ra ba chi. bō gya rei a sha rei a sha ha rei. It sounded like the rantings of a foreigner that made no sense to him."[64]

This reply corroborates the view that in forging new genbun'itchi writing, like Futabatei, he worked from the bare-bones transcriptions [*kōen sokki*] of Enchō's oral narrations, but in Bimyō's case, we cannot say that his writing assumes Enchō's performance, which was narrated to an audience from a stage. In the following sentence from chapter 2 of Futabatei's *Ukigumo*, we can observe the author-narrator's [*sakusha*] self-referential nod to the reader: "Before I launch into a charming little episode here, why don't we entertain a short biography of Magobei's eldest daughter, Osei."[65] Bimyō's work explicitly avoids such intrusions. This strategy seems to reflect the demands Bimyō placed on his readers to read his works "as one would read ordinary conversation." Accordingly, the vestiges of gesaku flavor found in the first part of *Ukigumo* are absent in Bimyō's *Kochō* and *Musashino*.

However, precisely because Futabatei strove to faithfully incorporate Enchō's manner of recitation, he was able to realize a highly nuanced depiction of interiority in the second half of *Ukigumo*. Togawa is somewhat critical of this gesaku-like style used in the first half of *Ukigumo*, but for Futabatei to achieve what he did in the second half, he first had to actively work through Enchō's narrative style.

Tsurumi Shunsuke identifies the characteristic of Enchō's style in "language as gesture"—"a practice that had disappeared from the world of written language after the Meiji Restoration."[66] For example, Tsurumi notes that in the scene where the masseur, Sōetsu, massages the shoulder of Fukami Shinzaemon in *The True Views of Kasanegafuchi* [*Shinkei kasane ga fuchi*, 1898], removed from their context, such plain expressions as *konna* ["this sort of"] and *kono hidari no kata* ["the left shoulder here"] don't add much in the way of explanation, but deftly employed in a specific context they exhibit their appeal by allowing the reader to experience the singular quality of that scene.[67] It was Tsurumi who observed as an example of "language as gesture" the hollow echoes—*karan-koron*—of the low clogs [*koma-geta*] hitting the pavement to evoke the sensation of ghostliness. And in *The Biography of Shiobara Tasuke* [*Shiobara Tasuke ichidaiki*, 1878], he asserts that it is precisely the tedious, repetitive ineffectiveness of his attempt at seduction in the parting scene between Tasuke and Ao that so effectively expresses the stark pathos of a protagonist with no companion in life and nowhere to go.

In *Language as Gesture*, R. P. Blackmur argues that the repetition of the words "to die, to sleep" that appears in Hamlet's well-known soliloquy works in tandem with the repetition of "to die," not so much to convey some literal meaning, but as itself a *gesture* to arouse dread and fear in the observer/reader [*kankyaku*].[68] This kind of language as gesture—what the materiality of words and language convey in such contexts as the scene from *Hamlet* or the passage in *Shiobara Tasuke ichidaiki*—appears in part 1, chapter 4 of *Ukigumo*:

> Soreyori ka mazu sashiatari *eeto* nan*dak*ke. . . . Sōsō, menshoku no koto o obanihanashite. . . . Sazo iyana kao o suru kottarōna. . . . Shikashi hana-sazu ni mo okarenai kara omoikitte konya ni mo oba ni hanashite. . . .
> *Daga* Osei no iru mae dewa. . . . *Cho*[tto] iru mae demo kamawan oba ni hanashite. . . . *Daga* moshi are no iru mae de kuchigitanaku demo iwa-reta ra. . . . *Cho*[tto] kamawan Osei ni hanashite *iya*. . . . Osei ja nai oba ni hanashite. . . . sazo. . . . Iyana kao. . . . Iya na kao o hanashite. . . kuchi. . . . Kuchigitanaku hanashi. . . . shite. . . . *Aa*, atama ga midareta. . . .[69]
> [Maeda's emphases]

> At any rate, what *was* it now. *um* . . . Oh yeah, I've got to tell my Aunt about losing my job. . . . She's not going to like this, I know. . . . Still, I've got no choice, so I'll bite the bullet and tell her tonight and. . . . *But*, in front of Osei. . . . *Well*, even if Osei is present, *okay*, I'll tell my Aunt and . . . . But, if she chastizes me in front of her. . . . *Wait*, okay, I'll tell Osei no *wait*. . . . *No*, I'll tell my aunt, not Osei. . . . But she'll . . . speak with her offensive face . . . say . . . say abusive things . . . her mouth . . . *ohh*, my head is splitting. . . .

His determination to disclose his unemployment to Osei and the fear of in-curring Osei's disdain are locked in struggle within Bunzō. This dissension is directly expressed by the repetition of words alternately addressing his aunt and Osei. The interrupted sentences that mirror the hesitation and indecision in Bunzō, the repetition of words expressing the desires and attachments he feels for the two, and finally, the transition from longer sentences to short broken phrases that illustrate a shift in the rapidity of Bunzō's thoughts—more like short, gasping breaths of thought at the end of the passage—these formal devices permit the reader to "experience" what is being described by the text. Rather than reproducing a psychological analysis of Bunzō's mind by employing concepts [*kannen*] and symbols, Futabatei is able to convey the doubts and hesitations in Bunzō's peripatetic inner state in a way that stimulates and resonates with the reader's own feelings by making extensive use of such immediate properties of language as tempo, rhythm, and other modulations—that is, by employing a method that fully exploits the qualities of language as "gesture." Among the works that helped to advance this approach were Hirotsu Ryūrō's genbun'itchi novel, *Early Winter Chrysanthemums* [*Zangiku*, 1889] and, in more dramatic fashion, the scene in Ozaki Kōyō's *The Gold Demon* [*Konjikiyasha*, *Yomiuri shimbun*, 1897–1903] at the seashore of Atami where Kan'ichi stubbornly repeats the famous soliloquy that begins *kongetsu kon'ya* . . . ["This month, tonight . . ."] might be viewed as an example of such language use. Accustomed to the practice of silent reading rather than reading aloud, our tendency is to eschew this kind of writing. Let me provide one other example of this style, this time from *Ukigumo*, part 1 chapter 9:

> Munen munen Bunzō wa chijoku o totta. Tsui chikagoro to itte ni-san nichi mae made wa, kantō ni chitobakari ni kōge wa aru tomo onaji ikka no kyokuin de, masari otori ga nakereba oshi mo osare mo shinakatta Noboru gotoki inujimono no tame ni chijoku o totta, shikari chijoku o totta. Shikashi nan no ikon ga atte, ika naru gen'in ga atte.
>
> Omou ni Bunzō, Noboru ni koso urami wa are, Noboru ni uramirareru oboe wa sara ni nai. Shikaru ni Noboru wa nan no dōri mo naku nan no riyū mo naku, atakamo hito o hazukashimeru tokken demo motte iru yōni, Bunzō o dokai no gotoku ni mikudashite, inu-neko no gotoku ni toriatsukatte, amatsusae oba ya Osei no iru mae de, chōshō shita bujoku shita.[70]

Damn it, Bunzō felt humiliated. Until a few days ago, even if they were not of identical rank, they had enjoyed close status as colleagues in the same office, and now because of that dog, Noboru, he was humiliated, just humiliated. What could have been the reason, why had Noboru felt such malice toward him?

Many were the reasons for Bunzō to resent Noboru, but why would Noboru detest him? Without rhyme or reason, it was as if Noboru had special license to insult people, looking down on him as worthless, laughing derisively and treating him as if he were a dog or a cat—and all this humiliation in front of his aunt and Osei.

In this passage, the narrator amplifies just how Noboru's affront effectively bottles up Bunzō's anger, which can only be refracted into an inner dialogue of anguished voices intoning repeatedly, "What could have been the reason," and "laughing derisively and insulting him." By interweaving Bunzō's inner voices with the narrator's teasing tone, Futabatei depicted the subtle reactions of the mind in the second half of *Ukigumo*. Just as Enchō was able to differentiate the social standing and character traits of different characters according to their narrative situations, Futabatei similarly portrayed the voices and the drama within Bunzō. The vivid depiction of dialogic confrontation between Noboru and Bunzō, Osei and Bunzō, which we find in part 2, is in fact achieved by Futabatei in his role as performer-entertainer [*engisha-teki yakuwari*].

At this point we are reminded of Futabatei's encounter with Nicholas Gray at the Foreign Language School.[71] Gray's recitations of Russian literature, writes Futabatei, "closely resembled dramatizations of gestures accompanied by vocalizations, hand and feet movement, the eyes gesturing and the head shaking."[72] It hardly needs reiteration how profoundly Futabatei's work was influenced by Gray's method of physically reenacting and bringing to life the characters in Russian literature. Deeply impressed by his oral recitation, Futabatei would borrow his books to take home to read the best passages to himself, but "perhaps because the novelty had worn off, at any rate they weren't as arresting as when the professor had recited them."[73] In the same essay, he notes how boring a poorly delivered *gidayū* recitation was, while the lively performance of a skilled chanter made all the difference. To Futabatei's ears, still reverberating with the voice of oral performance in the classroom, the inability to recapture that experience through silent, solitary reading must have left him unsatisfied. The "language as gesture" that Futabatei had learned from Enchō's narrative performances and put to such effective use in *Ukigumo* must have been stimulated by the remembrance of Gray's classroom orations. (Bimyō was never to experience a similar experience with literary orality.)

Bimyō, whose first genbun'itchi novel employed the copula *da*, switched to the more polite *desu* beginning with his short story collection, *Summer Grove* [*Natsu kodachi*, 1888]. Because the more abrupt da is used in speaking to someone of lower social standing, he tells us that he opted for desu with its associations to the middle class, but even if desu and *masu* fix the relative position of the narrator in relation to the reader, what is lost is the capacity to vividly and realistically reproduce the subtle shifts and gradations of the character's mind, for example, by mixing together the voices of the narrator and characters [as seen in the *Ukigumo* passage quoted above]. Bimyō failed to notice this limitation inherent in the use of a copula that erases such differentiation. It is also possible that because he was not particularly adept at realistic depiction of interiority, he chose a way of writing that sacrificed this capability.

What was the issue that was left to Futabatei to resolve? Both Gray's recitations and Enchō's oral tales were conceived for a group of listeners, and as Fukuda Tsuneari has stated, when *Ukigumo*, which had been influenced by these narrative forms, depicts the serious psychology of its characters, "in order to candidly narrate the tale while directly addressing the reader [listener], the author [narrator] is compelled to depart from realism and adopt a comic narrative vein."[74] This exaggerated narrative style, inflected by humor and dramatic flair, would be shunned in Futabatei's translation of Turgenev's *Rendezvous* [*Aibiki*, 1888].

6

In "My Favorite Reading" ["Yo no aidoku sho"] Futabatei makes the following observation: "Whenever I wanted to foreground prose rhythms in writing Japanese, I was almost overcome by the difficulty of the task." This prose rhythmicity [*bunchō*] differs from the vocalized rhythms [*seichō*], which, in his essay "Our Genbun'itchi Writing" ["Wareware no genbun'itchi-tai"], Bimyō noted, had closer affinities to the old grammar. For Futabatei, the rhythms of traditional Japanese writing (what Bimyō called the old grammar) "somehow lacked variation and seemed devoid of modulation and stops." Futabatei's understanding of and appreciation for prose rhythms came from Professor Gray's recitations of Goncharov's work. If Bimyō's oral rhythms [*seichō*] denoted a kind of extrinsic rhythm, what Futabatei sought was an intrinsic rhythm immanent in the author's poetic sensibilities; what Gray had displayed through dramatic recitation of Goncharov's work were concrete expressions of such prose rhythms. "Any writing has its own rhythms (the skill with which it is delivered aside) so that even if you read a passage silently to yourself and deliberately flatten out the reading, the rhythms are irrepressibly conveyed to the reader."[75]

It is not that oral reading for the first time reveals these rhythms; rather, it is that silent reading permits us to perceive and to feel the mysterious forms of prose rhythms. Futabatei saw in the very way such prose rhythms resonated in readers' minds solid clues regarding the form and very nature of literature. When he used Japanese writing [*Nihonbun*] to reproduce the rhythms of the Russian literature he translated, we can discern the pains he took in completing this task: "Enchantment [*enrei*] touched with loneliness, such is the poetic sensibility that informs Turgenev's writing. . . . Since his novels are infused with such sentiment, to translate his works without losing it demands writing as if one had become Turgenev, for otherwise one risks missing the rhythm of his prose which conveys that very sensibility. . . . When I translated his work, I conscientiously endeavored to retain this poetic sentiment [*shisō*] and to assimilate my own sensibilities to his."[76] Futabatei was able to accomplish his daring experiment to "assimilate his own sensibilities" to Turgenev's by managing the difficult task of applying Shōyō's "logical method" to a foreign literature, and in place of a Japanese literature he viewed as lacking diversity, metric variation, and shifts in tempo, he succeeded in forging a pliant and highly refined [*sensai na*] prose that could reproduce the rhythms of Turgenev's work. How were the results of his experimentation received by his contemporaries? Let us consider the question through Kanbara Ariake's comments on Futabatei's *The Rendezvous* [*Aibiki*, 1888]. For this young writer, *Ukigumo* was a work with a ponderous rhythm in contrast to the limpid and even musical *impression* [English in original] conveyed by *The Rendezvous*, which he found unforgettable: "In those days when I had just entered middle school and my still youthful powers of literary discernment saw me loudly reciting from *Chance Encounters with Beautiful Women*, the very idea of translated Russian by Turgenev seemed so mysterious. Whenever I began reading it, I was struck by the unusualness of colloquial language skillfully employed in a written text that seemed to murmur familiarly and ceaselessly right next to my ear. I felt an indefinable pleasurable sensation, and, at the same time, germinating somewhere deep within me, a feeling of resistance. I could not explain why I disliked being spoken to with such familiarity."[77] Ariake's description of a "continuous stream of words murmured with a presumed familiarity next to my ear" accurately mirrors Futabatei's intentions to produce "writing that even if read silently to oneself and deliberately flattened out, irrepressibly conveys its rhythms to the reader" so as to reproduce the modulations [bunchō] of writing inextricably tied to its poetic sensibilities. Ariake speaks to the mix of pleasurable shivering and a trace of resistance produced by this private exchange between writer and reader. In solitude, the reader comes face to face with the writer and listens to the hushed whisper of a tale told in confidence. The reader on whom was conferred the privilege of participating in this kind of mystery—is that not what we call the modern reader? Although Ariake does not refer to it in his reminiscence, it is worth adding that as an important condition for creating the sensation of erasing the psychological distance separating the writer from the reader, the use of the vantage point of peeping [*nozoki*]—the most emphatic and sensational of first-person perspectives—must be noted. What was devised was a point of view that assumed the role of co-conspirator gazing at the scene of clandestine activity along with the writer. In the earlier works written in colloquial language, first-person accounts frequently take the form of the writer directly narrating to the reader, but the artless and frank stance adopted in these confessional and life-story formulas such as Bimyō's *Crepe Wrap* [*Fukusazutsumi*, 1887–88], Saganoya Omuro's "First love" ["Hatsukoi," 1889], or Ryūrō's *Late Chrysanthemums* [*Zangiku*, 1889] are a far cry from the subtle renderings of the inner life found in Futabatei's work. For example, as illustrated by the direct-address interjection "Now, ladies and gentlemen" [*aah minasan*] that appears near the end of "First Love," the enunciative scene presumes a small group sitting fireside and listening to the nostalgic reminiscences of an elder. The narrative perspective assumed in *Aibiki*, in contrast, is conceived to address a silent, solitary reader.

The *Chance Encounters with Beautiful Women* that Ariake had enjoyed reading aloud as a young reader still lacking literary discernment had been delivered in the very form of oral recitation [*ginzuru*] that Bimyō had rejected. As we saw earlier, Roka's *Dark Eyes, Brown Eyes* provided a vivid account of how schools, boardinghouses, private academies, and political associations were close-knit communities [*seishin-teki kyōdōtai*] responsive to such works. The end of the Freedom and Popular Rights Movement [Jiyū minken undo] also spelled the demise of these sites of reading as collective activity, and the reading subject shifted to the household or the solitary reader. Bimyō's demands for the reader to read as if it were "ordinary speech" [tsūjō no hanashi-buri] was perhaps best represented by the new, "improved" gesaku that could meet "the demands of an entire family reading aloud from an open book," as suggested by Shōyō in *The Essence of the Novel* [*Shōsetsu shinzui*].[78] Its concrete realization was perhaps the literature of the Ken'yūsha [Friends of the Ink-pot], as well as in serialized newspaper fiction and domestic novels. In contrast to the large readership enjoyed by the neo-gesaku works by the stable of Ken'yūsha writers, the audience for *Aibiki* was small. Yet, the genealogy of the modern reader originates not with the students who were enraptured by the rhythms of splendid simplified Chinese prose [*kanbun-kuzushi*] that inflamed their political passions, nor with the Meiji-era families mesmerized by the patriarch's rhythmic oral recitations of the mixed classical-colloquial narratives [*gazoku-setchūtai*]. Rather, it can be traced to the few solitary readers of Futabatei's translation of Russian literature who responded to the poetic sensibilities and the rhythms of this prose by identifying with the writer or the characters in the work. If the reader of *Chance Encounters* can be represented by the Dōshisha 300 who rest their pens and interrupt their own studies mesmerized by its oration in the boardinghouse, the reader of *Aibiki* is to be captured in the solitary figure of a reader with a book tucked under his or her arm, wandering through the forest and listening to the soft sounds of nature. Let me end with the image of one other reader of *Aibiki*:

> I was never stricken by "unrequited love" as much as by "nomadic impulse," and in my experiences of the latter, I was taken by the remarkable portrayal of nature in *Aibiki*. The wondrous rendering of the sound of

footsteps just as you heard them in life itself, breathtaking description that could let you hear the hushed clarity of a whisper—this was the skill of no mere mortal. Wearing what was back then the rather bold mantle of "unrequited love," I remember roaming the woods adjoining the temple grounds just behind my middle school during lunch. Imagining myself a character in Turgenev's work, I was lost in reverie until the bell beckoned me back to the classroom.[79]

Notes

1 The term *shōsetsu* subsumes what, in the context of Western literary culture, would be such forms as the novel, novella, short story, and essay. Additionally, on occasion Maeda uses the term to denote premodern prose narrative forms. Because the primary object of interrogation in this essay is the modern novel, even though the word shōshetsu occasionally refers to some of these other forms, I use the word *novel* throughout this essay rather than the Japanese term, asking the reader to keep in mind this incommensurateness. However, when Maeda uses the term to reference a pre-Meiji work, I use the word shōsetsu.

2 This essay first appeared in *Kindai dokusha no seiritsu* (The rise of the modern Japanese reader), 1973. This is a translation of "Ondoku kara mokudoku e: Kindai dokusha no seiritsu" (From reading aloud to silent reading: the development of the modern reader), in *Maeda Ai Chosaku Shū 2, Kindai Dokusha no Seiritsu* (Collected Works of Maeda Ai 2: the development of the modern reader) (Chikuma shobō, 1989). Maeda had taken three earlier essays he had written—"Ondoku kara mokudoku e" (*Kokugo to kokubungaku*, 1962), "Kindai bungaku ni okeru sakusha to dokusha, Bimyō-Futabatei to sanbun rizumu no mondai" (The author and reader in modern literature: Bimyō, Futabatei and the issue of prose rhythm) (*Bungaku gogaku* 34, 1964), and "Kindai bungaku to rakugo: Enchō no 'miburi' to Futabatei" (Modern literature and *rakugo*: Enchō's "gestures" and Futabatei) (*Kokubungaku: Rinji zōkan*, March 1973)—and woven them into this extended piece, which first appeared in *Kindai dokusha no seiritsu* (Yūseidō, 1973). This translation is based on the version that appears in his *Maeda Ai Chosaku Shū 2, Kindai Dokusha no Seiritsu* (Chikuma Shobō, 1989).

3 *Kusunoki kōki*, or "Nankō-ki" is a record of a well-known defender of the imperial throne, and "Ōoka Seidan" are tales of the magistrate, Ooka Echizen no kami.

4 Ishikawa Sanshirō, *Jijoden: Seishun no henreki* (Autobiography: Youthful wanderings) (Rironsha, 1956), 31. (M)

5 *Yamakawa Hitoshi jiden: Aru bonjin no sonota* (Iwanami Shoten, 1961), 157–158. (M)

6 For an English-language account of Ichiyō's mentor, Tōsui, see Robert Lyons Danley, *In the Shade of Spring Leaves: The Life and Writings of Higuchi Ichiyō, a Woman of Letters in Meiji Japan* (New Haven: Yale University Press, 1981).

7 *Zen shaku Ichiyō nikki*, ed. Nishio Yoshihito (Ōfusha, 1976), 1:163 2:63, 66, 68. (M)

8 Lafcadio Hearn, *Glimpses of Unfamiliar Japan* (Boston: Houghton, Mifflin, 1894), 2:619. (M)

9 Hasegawa Shigure, *Kyūbun Nihonbashi* (Iwanami Shoten, 1983).

10 A game similar to marbles played with periwinkle hulls.

11 *Bun*, Ishikawa-ken tsūshin, 25 March 1889. (M)

12 Ishikawa Takuboku, *Nikki* (Seikai Hyōronsha, 1948–49). The entry is from 13 April 1909. (M)

13 Wada Yoshie, from *Ichiyō no nikki* (Chikuma Shobō, 1957), 2:203, 204. (M)

14 Mine: "I'll read this book to you in bed." Fusa: "Wonderful." Momi: "What book is it?" Mine: "A *ninjōbon* called *E hiyoku no murasaki* [The picture book of the purple chicks, here an imaginary pair of birds, each with one eye and one wing that always flies together]." Fusa: "Then, please read it from beginning to end." Momi: "Ha ha ha, Ofusa, even if you want that, aren't you going to fall asleep during the first volume?" From "Eitai dango" (Sweet conversations), section 8. Tamenaga Shunsui, "Eitai dango," in *Umegoyomi Part II* (1893; Iwanami Shoten, 1973), 65. (M)

15 "From a circle of women bound by their common labor of love sharing the inti- macies of their misery and happiness day and night, the scene upstairs is marked by a bevy of singular beauties. . . . They are washing their faces, fixing their hair, chatting as they ready themselves. . . . 'Oh, that's the one—come on and read the rest to us. It's my treat later on if you do.'

"'Yeah, I was listening too, and if you read it for us, I'll really give you a treat.'

"'What a fanatic young lady you are. Let me start then with the second in- stallment from "Ōgon Kiku" [The golden Kiku],' he says as he pulls out the middle section.

"'Why don't you read that big book there instead?'

"'All right . . . let me see now, how far had I read . . . ah, up to here.'" Tame- naga Shunsui, *Shungyō Hachiman kanen* (Tokyo Fukyūsha, 1932), 127. (M)

16 Otoyo: "Hey, that's one of those things they call a romance [*yomihon*], isn't it?" Oroku: "Un huh, it's a story called *Kōbun shiden* [The life of a learned warrior] by Tamenaga Shunsui. . . ." Otoyo: "It ought to be good then. Read a little to me." Oroku: "Okay, but only if you toast up some *kakimochi*." Otoyo: "Whatever you want." Oroku: "And some tea, too." Otoyo: "My, what an expensive fee. . . ." She laughs. Oroku: "Well, it's work to read aloud, and on top of that, whenever we get to romantic or suggestive scenes, right away you end up throwing yourself into it and bring it around to your own affairs. So unless I'm well rewarded it's not worth it." Tamenaga Shunsui, *Shunshoku enrei musume nanakusa* (The maid- ens of the seven spring flowers) (1836; Ninjōbon Kankō-kai, 1926), ch. 25, pp. 275–276. (M)

17 The style of Shunsui's ninjōbon, including his use of diacritics, is rooted in the practice of reading texts aloud. For example, in part 1 of his *Shunshoku umegoyomi* [Colors of spring: The plum calendar], there is a scene where Yonehachi visits

Tanjirō at his retreat: "I'm so. . . . My heart was beating so loudly, I was so worried that I'd be found out or something. I walked here so fast and whenever I'd get out of breath, I would beat my chest and keep going. . . ." Tamenaga Shunsui, *Shunshoku umegoyomi*, in *Nihon koten bungaku taikei* (Iwanami Shoten, 1973), 48. The periods here are not grammatical markers, but rather stops used to mimic the breathlessness of Yone's speech. (M)

18 "In former times, people would read books out loud. One person would read and many others would listen with pleasure so that even those who could not even read *hiragana* could join in the enjoyment of reading what we now call literature [*bungaku*]. People like myself see this as the vestige of the days before the era of mass literacy when memorized accounts were transmitted orally." Yanagita Kunio, "Josei seikatsu shi," part 4, in *Fujin kōron* (April 1941), *Yanagita Kunio zenshū* (Chikuma Shobō, 1990), 28:534. (M)

19 It is well-known that Sanba's *kokkeibon* have connections to Karaku's *rakugo*. See Honda Yasuo's "Kaiwatai no sharebon no seiritsu ni tsuite no shiron," *Kokugo to kokubungaku* (November 1959): 51–63. For the relationship between *gōkan* and *kabuki*, see Suzuki Jūzō, "Gōkanmono no daizai tenki to Tanehiko," *Kokugo to kokubungaku* (April 1961): 57–71. (M)

20 Moriyama Shigeo, "Edo shōsetsu no mondai ten," *Kokugo to kokubungaku* (April 1961): 20. (M)

21 In addition to the old man, Sekine recalls: "When I was a young man, I remember it to be the tenth month of 1840, at a booth in Shitaya Yamashita there was a sign announcing a split bill with Kenkonbō Ryōsai in the midst of a *sewa kōdan ninjō banashi* [narrative performance of soap operatic content] with Tamenaga Shunsui scheduled to perform at the end. Shunsui was not the clearest speaker to begin with and he was an old man of over 70, so he gave his delivery in a low voice that was not pleasant to the ears; on top of that, he further disappointed me by presenting something other than the promised reading from *Umegoyomi*." Harunoya Shujin, "Tamenaga Shunsui ryakuden," in *Chūō gakujutsu zasshi* 21 (1 February 1886, Dōkō-kai Hensan): 43–44. (M)

22 To preserve the historical particulars of the Japanese novel, I have retained the term *shōsetsu* in this case.

23 These were a set of edicts issued in 1872 by the Ministry of Education (Kyōbu-shō) that combined religious and rational thought, and were aimed at promoting nationalistic sentiment in the wake of clan abolition and the establishment of prefectures.

24 For example, see *Yomiuri shimbun*, 5 April 1877, and 23 April of the same year. (M)

25 An early Meiji-era incarnation of the *kawaraban* ("extras") "were printed on small sheets of paper, carried no editorials, included *furigana* . . . reported simple news in a conversational style and featured serialized novels." Kathryn Ann Ragsdale, "Serialized 'Domestic Novels' and the Retraditionalization of Women's Roles in Late Meiji Japan" (Ph.D. diss., University of Chicago, 1991), 50.

26 Okamoto Kisen, *Hanaoka kien-den*, second half, part 1, 1882, 2–3. (M)

27 *Kokushiryaku* is a five-volume history of Japan covering the age of the gods to the Yōzei emperor (876–884) written by Iwagaki Matsunae in 1826 (Iwagaki Matsunae, ed., Kokushiryaku, 5 vols. [Kyoto: Gosharō, 1877]). *Nihon gaishi* (1827) by Rai San'yō is a military history of Japan (1780–1832) focusing on the late eleventh century. *Jūhasshiryaku* is an anecdotal chronicle of Chinese history covering antiquity to the Song Dynasty.

28 Nishida Masaru, ed., *Taoka Reiun zenshū* (Hōsei Daigaku Shuppankyoku, 1969), 5:500.

29 Kōda Rohan, "Shōnen jidai," in *Rohan zenshū* (Iwanami Shoten, 1979), 29: 200. (M)

30 See Katayama Sen's *Jiden* (Autobiography) (1922; Iwanami Shoten, 1954), 97.

31 For detailed accounts of Chinese studies academies, see Katayama Sen, *Jiden* [Autobiography], Abe Iso'o, *Shakaishugisha to naru made: Abe Iso'o jijoden* [My path to socialism: the autobiography of Abe Iso'l] (Meizensha, 1947). and Shinoda Kōzō, *Meiji hyaku-wa* [A hundred tales of Meiji]. (M)

32 Translated into English by Kenneth G. Henshall as *Literary Life in Tokyo 1885–1915* (Leiden: E.J. Brill, 1987).

33 A popular Japanese song of the times with 7–7–7–5 syllabic metrics.

34 Ichijima Kenkichi, "Meiji bungaku shoki no tsuioku," *Waseda bungaku* (July 1925): 11. (M)

35 Masamune Hakuchō, "Mukashi no nikki," *Kindai bungaku*, no. 1 (1946): 14. (M)

36 Dōshisha School of English, originally the Kyoto Kyōshisha Eigakkō, established in 1875, would later become Dōshisha University, as it is known today.

37 Emi Suiin, *Jiko chūshin Meiji bundanshi* (Hakubunkan, 1927), 29. (M)

38 Taoka Reiun, "Sūkiden," in *Taoka Reiun zenshū* (Hōsei Daigaku Shuppankyoku, 1969), 5:510. (M)

39 David Riesman, *The Oral Tradition, Written Word, and the Screen Image* (Yellow Springs, Ohio: Antioch Press, 1955); "Books: Gunpowder of the Mind," *Atlantic Monthly* (February 1957). (M)

40 Riesman, *The Oral Tradition*, 12. In place of Riesman's text, I have retranslated Maeda's translation, which is close to the original but makes the salient points a bit clearer.

41 Ian Watt, *The Rise of the Novel* (Berkeley: University of California Press, 1957), 190. (M)

42 Q. D. Leavis, *Fiction and the Reading Public* (London: Chatto and Windus, 1932), 218. (M)

43 L. L. Schucking, *The Sociology of Literary Taste* (London: K. Paul, Trench, Trubner, 1945), 72. (M)

44 Tsubouchi Shōyō, "Dokuhō o okosan to suru shui" (For the encouragement of reading), *Kokumin no tomo*, no. 115 (Minyūsha, April 1891).

45 Ibid., 13, 16, 17.

46 Kyō Wakako, "Ninin bikuni irozange hihyō" (Review of the amorous confession of two nuns), in *Shuppan geppyō* (1889; Ryūkeishosha, 1983), 20:157–58.

47 Yamada Bimyō, "Bakin no bunsho ryakuhyō" (Brief comments on Bakin's writing), *Shinshōsetsu* (10 April 1889). (M)

48 Yamado Bimyō, "Genbun'itchi ron gairyaku" (An outline of genbun'itchi), *Gakkai no shinshin* (A guide to the world of knowledge), (March 1888): 2–21. (M)

49 In *Iratsume* (January 1889): 12–23. (M) *Iratsume* was begun as a women's magazine in 1894 to promote enlightenment values to women, but later, under Bimyō's editorship, became increasingly literary.

50 Yamada Taketarō [Bimyō's pen name], "Ware ware no genbun'itchi-tai" (Our genbun'itchi style), *Shigarami zōshi*, 8 (Shinseisha, 25 May 1890). (M)

51 Ibid., 12–13. (M)

52 "Rhythm is more profound than this. It is born, not with the words, but with the thought, and with whatever confluence of instincts and emotions the thought is accompanied. As the thought takes shape in the mind, it takes *a* shape." Herbert Read, *English Prose Style* (Boston: Beacon, 1961), 61. (M)

53 Uchida Roan, "Shiben: Bimyō ni atau" (Poetic discernment: for Yamada Bimyō), *Kokumin no tomo*, Minyūsha 105 (3 January 1891): 18. (M)

54 Mori Ōgai, "Genbunron," in *Ōgai zenshū* (Iwanami Shoten, 1973), 22:145. (M)

55 Based on the discussion by Sakakura Atsuyoshi, "'Hanasu yōni kaku' to iu koto" (What it means to write as one speaks), *Kokugo kokubun* (June 1957). (M)

56 Tayama Katai, "Futabatei Shimei-kun o omou" (Remembering Futabatei Shimei), in *Teihon Katai zenshū* (Kyoto: Rinkawa Shoen, 1937), 15:37. (M)

57 Tayama Katai, "Ueno no toshokan" (The library in Ueno), in *Tokyo no sanjūnen*, in *Teihon Katai zenshū* (Rinsen shoten, 1994), 15:489. The English-language translation by Kenneth Strong (with introduction by Kenneth G. Henshall) is *Literary Life in Tokyo 1885–1915: Tayama Katai's Memoirs (Thirty Years in Tokyo)* (Leiden: E.J. Brill, 1987).

58 Takase Bun'en, "Bungaku iken" (Views on literature), in *Yamada Bimyō, Ishibashi Ningetsu, and Takase Bunen shū*, *Meiji Bungaku Zenshū* (Chikuma Shobō, 1971), 23:360.

59 Togawa Shinsuke, "*Ukigumo* no sekai" (The world of *Drifting Clouds*), *Bungaku* (October 1965): 28–29. (M)

60 Futabatei Shimei, *Ukigumo*, in *Futabatei Shimei zenshū* (Chikuma Shobō, 1984), 10.

61 Yamada Bimyō, "Fūkin shirabe no hito fushi" (A tune for the organ), in *Iratsume* (1887; Fujishuppan, 1983), 15. (M)

62 Yamada Bimyō, "Chōkai shōsetsu tengu," in *Garakuta bunko, kappan hibaibon* (1886; Yumani Shobō, 1986), 9:13. (M)

63 Yamada Bimyō, *Yamada Bimyō, Hirotsu Ryūrō, Kawakami Bizan, Oguri Fūyō shū*, vol. 11 of *Nihon gendai bungaku zenshū* (Kōdansha, 1968), 11.

64 Yamada Bimyō, "Kaidan botan dōrō," in *Meiji kaikaki bungaku shū*, vol. 1 of *Nihon kindai bungaku taikei* (Kadokawa Shoten, 1970), 301.

65 Futabatei, *Ukigumo*, 16.

66 Tsurumi Shunsuke, "Enchō ni okeru miburi to shōchō" (Gesture and symbol in Enchō's work), *Bungaku* (July 1958): 1. (M)

67 Ibid., 4.

68 R. P. Blackmur, *Language as Gesture: Essays in Poetry* (New York: Harcourt, Brace, 1952), 15. (M)

69 Futabatei, *Ukigumo*, 31–32.

70 Ibid., part 1, ch. 9, 95–96.

71 For background information and accounts of the skilled classroom readings of Russian literature by this naturalized U.S. citizen from Russia at Gaigo Gakkō, see Marleigh Grayer Ryan, *Japan's First Modern Novel: Ukigumo of Futabatei Shimei* (New York: Columbia University Press, 1967), 26–28.

72 Gray's recitation corresponds to Shōyō's dictum in "Ronri-teki dokuhō" (Logical reading method) that "it must be read as if you yourself have assumed that author's or the character's feelings." (M) From Tsubouchi Shōyō, *Shōyō senshū* (Dai'ichi Shōbō, 1977), 11:262.

73 Futabatei Shimei, "Yo no aidoku sho," in *Futabatei Shimei zenshū* (Chikuma Shobō, 1985), 4:163.

74 Fukuda Tsuneari, *Hihyōka no techō* (A critic's notebook) (Shinchōsha, 1960), 151. (M)

75 Futabatei, "Yo no aidoku sho," 163–164.

76 Futabatei Shimei, "Yo ga honyaku no hyōjun" (My standards for translation), in *Futabatei Shimei zenshū*, 4:168. (M)

77 Kanbara Ariake, "*Aibiki* ni tsuite" (On *The Rendezvous*), in *Hiun sho* (Misfortunes) (Nihon Tosho Sentā, 1989), 219–220. (M)

78 Tsubouchi Shōyō, *Shōsetsu shinzui*, in *Shōyō zenshū* (Shun'yōdō, 1927), 3:120.

79 Aono Suekichi, "Meiji no bungaku seinen" (Meiji literary youth), in *Meiji bungaku nyūmon* (Kyoto: Zenkoku Shobō, 1948), 71. (M)

8. Modern Literature and the World of Printing

(Kindai bungaku to katsujiteki sekai)

TRANSLATED BY RICHARD OKADA

The following essay by Maeda Ai is his classic statement on the relations among the rise of modern Japanese literature, the technologies of printing, and the general tenor of the times and how they enable a reassessment of Tsubouchi Shōyō's *Shōsetsu shinzui* (Essence of the novel). An important moment in his lifelong interest in the production and reception of literature, the essay identifies the processes that led to a new paradigm that emerged in the way literary texts were produced and read. According to Maeda, a "visual revolution" occurred during the first few decades of the Meiji period that went hand in hand with the technological change from printing by woodblock to printing by movable type. He points out that as more emphasis was placed on the visual, the illustrations that had been an integral part of Edo-period books were replaced by visualized descriptions. In other words, the written text, which had heretofore emphasized dialogue, now bore the additional burden of providing visual description, which previously had been relegated to the illustrations. Also important is Maeda's discussion of how Shōyō handles two seemingly contradictory conceptions of art: art as idea versus art as mimesis. The wide-ranging essay includes discussions of Tsubouchi Shōyō, Ernest Fenollosa, Tamenaga Shunsui, Futabatei Shimei, and Mori Ōgai, as well as references to writers such as Raymond Williams, Zola, Stendhal, and Flaubert.

It is commonly believed that *Essence of the Novel* [*Shōsetsu shinzui*, 1885], by Tsubouchi Shōyō, valorized the earliest form of a concept that corresponds to realism in modern literature.[1] What Shōyō actually attempted to develop in *Essence of the Novel*, however, was a problematic broader than anything that can be contained within the framework of realism. Take the term *mosha* [copy], for example. We tend to understand the term as being interchangeable with *shajitsu* [realism], but in Shōyō's usage it seems to have been closer to a term used by Edo painters to mean the affixation of their names to their paintings; in other words, the characters for mosha,[2] when following a proper name, meant painted by so and so. When we discuss literature today we have at hand a received system of literary critical terms, but that was not the case for Shōyō, who had to create the very terms he used to discuss literature. We must be mindful of that situation when we read him.

In the same way, we find in *Essence of the Novel* many instances of the word *miru* [see]. One of Shōyō's favorites terms is *bōkan* [observe]. The characters for bōkan are often given the reading *okame* [observe; literally, "view from a hill"]. To think of bōkan as interchangeable with *kyakkanteki* [objective], as is often done, is to lose an important aspect of its meaning. In Ōgai's writings, for example, we find the term *bōkan kikan* [observing device], which the author takes to be equivalent to *nozoki karakuri* [peep show]. I would like to consider the term bōkan as it appears in *Essence of the Novel* in light of the hint gained from Ōgai's usage.

One of the famous precepts in *Essence of the Novel* is the following: "Fictional narratives [*shōsetsu*] are works of art [*bijutsu*]."[3] We today regard the term bijutsu to be interchangeable with *geijutsu* [i.e., the arts in general]. The term bijutsu for us has come to connote "fine arts," and by stating, "Fictional narratives are works of art," Shōyō seems to have been thinking of something close to what we today consider the fine arts, namely, painting, sculpture, and handicrafts.

Again, Shōyō writes in *Essence of the Novel* that fiction "makes visible that which is difficult to see." "That which is difficult to see" refers to what lies within the human heart, psychology or, to use Shōyō's language, human feelings [*ninjō*]. It is fiction that takes the invisible, that which is without form, and transforms it into the visible, or something that possesses form. Here we can begin to discern Shōyō's logic. Beginning with such terminological examples, I shall consider what has been called his mosha theory from the point of view of the act of seeing, or the division of such an act into the *person* who sees and the *object* that is seen.

In the history of modern literary studies, a common belief has been that the basis for literature lies in the effective combination of the self as the subject of expression and realism as the means of expression. That is the reason *Observations on the Novel* [*Shōsetsu sōron*], by Futabatei Shimei, who put forth in that text the idea of "borrowing the actual and conjuring up the fictional," is considered superior to *Essence of the Novel*.[4] The fact is, however, that the theory advanced in *Essence of the Novel*, at least concerning its privileging of sight, corresponds to what was happening in European literature at the same time and to the theory of naturalism. In other words, the industrialized societies of nineteenth-century Europe and the spirit of positivism that produced the literature of Flaubert and Zola had privileged sight as the most important of the human senses. Separating the seer from that which is seen means that what is seen becomes objectified and segmented. It is important to note that it is this analytical perspective, more than anything else, that forms the foundation of literary realism.

In the texts of European realism and naturalism, we can find any number of comments concerning the separation of the seer and the seen. In Stendhal's *The Red and the Black*, for example, we read, "Novels are like mirrors one takes along on a walk through the streets of a city."[5] And in Zola we find, "Novels are windows that open out on to nature to which a movie screen has been attached." We can see in both Stendhal and Zola that novels are understood through the use of decidedly visual metaphors. Furthermore, in a letter that Flaubert sent to Georges Sand on 6 February 1876, we read the following: "A writer must strictly refrain from having characters in a work express his personal opinions."[6]

The stance taken by Stendhal, Flaubert, and Zola—that is, to write novels from a visual perspective, to write as if everything is seen through the eyes, and to strictly suppress the writer's own personality and ego—was, needless to say, a reaction against romanticism. The authors wanted to curtail the almost limitless exposé of the ego that had existed in romanticism. Contrary to their avowed method of suppressing the ego, however, a paradox arose because Flaubertian and Stendhalian egos were, of course, apparent in their works. The fact remains, nevertheless, that their avowed purpose was to go to any lengths to erase all traces of the self.

Why, then, was Shōyō so preoccupied with sight, with separating the seer from the thing seen? I would argue that, rather than consider his text only within the bounds of literary discourse, it is easier to examine it within the context of cultural discourse as a whole. In other words, isn't the fact that *Essence of the Novel* is difficult for us to understand the result of our having situated it wholly within the discourse of literary theory? If, instead, we were to reconsider *Essence of the Novel* in terms both of literary theory and of its cultural context, wouldn't that resolve many of our problems? I shall now continue this essay under that assumption.

The period between the Meiji Restoration and the writing of *Essence of the Novel* in 1885 can be thought of as a time when a visual revolution was quietly in progress. For example, the Industrial Art School which was directly under the management of the Ministry of Public Works [Kōbushō] was established, and the Italians Antonio Fontanesi and Vincenzo Ragusa were invited to join its teaching staff. In this way, Western painting techniques take root in Japan. The year is 1876.

A year earlier, the Currency Division [Shiheiryō] of the Ministry of Finance, finding it necessary to import techniques for copperplate engraving and lithography in order to print paper money, hired another Italian, Eduardo Chiossone. In addition, copperplate engraving turned out to be crucial to map making, accurate maps being a sine qua non of the modern nation-state. It was about this time too that the Army Ministry [Rikugunshō] was actively adopting the same techniques and beginning to make detailed maps.

The year 1877 saw the opening of the First National Industrial Exhibition. Mounted on display were lithographs, copperplate engravings, and etchings by Japanese artists. Of course, traditional *ukiyo-e* and *nishiki-e* [polychrome prints] were also made in great numbers at this time, in even greater numbers, most likely, than had been made during the Edo period. Ukiyo-e and nishiki-e continued to enjoy popularity but were to be gradually overwhelmed by lithographs and copperplate engravings due to the ability of the latter to depict reality in greater detail. It was an age that saw the appearance of nontraditional artists like Kobayashi Kiyochika, known for his *Scenic Spots of Tokyo* [*Tōkyō meisho zu*]. Having begun his career as an ukiyo-e artist, Kobayashi went on to incorporate into his work the European realistic technique of lithography.

Behind the creation of *Essence of the Novel* a kind of visual revolution tied closely to a policy of industrial development was taking place. In an age of revolutionary change like the first years of the Meiji period, we can trace concomitant or parallel developments among various cultural phenomena. Rather than consider *Essence of the Novel* as an isolated problem of literary history, we need to rethink it within the context of the era of civilization and enlightenment in its totality.

The following is a passage from "Narrative Method," a chapter that appears toward the end of *Essence of the Novel*. It has not received very much attention in commentaries, essays, and criticism on the text, but I believe it is an extremely important passage:

> When describing the forms of things one should be as precise as possible. In the fictional works written in our country, detailed illustrations have been used to depict the forms of things and supplement what was lacking in the written text. Not a few authors thus naturally came to rely so much on the illustrations that many tended to be lax when it came to providing scenic descriptions. This is a grave mistake. The charm of fiction lies

not only in having a particular character act but also in having the whole world depicted on paper come alive with movement. To make the thunder roar, to make the waves pound wildly as if crashing down from the sky, to make a warbler burst out in song, to make plum blossoms proffer their scent, all these attest to the skill of the fiction writer. To depict only the attitude of characters without including the presence of nonhuman things is like painting a dragon rising to the heavens without including the clouds.[7]

Shōyō states, "In the fictional works written in our country, detailed illustrations have been used to depict the forms of things and supplement what was lacking in the written text." In his youth, Shōyō frequented a book-lending store called Daisō in Nagoya and read voluminously in *gesaku* [playful compositions] literature. Among the intellectuals who were attracted to European civilization during this period, Shōyō was a first-rate gesaku specialist. The statement just quoted, then, is extremely suggestive, coming as it did from a person with such a background.

We read works like *The Bathhouse of the Floating World* [*Ukiyoburo*, 1809–13], *The Barbershop of the Floating World* [*Ukiyodoko*, 1813–14], and Tamenaga Shunsui's *Spring Colors: The Plum Calendar* [*Shunshoku umegoyomi*, 1832–33] primarily through printed texts. Rarely do we see what the originals actually looked like. Aside from what specialists might do, we are accustomed to seeing *The Bathhouse of the Floating World* as a volume in a collected series like Iwanami's *Compendium of Classical Literature* [*Koten bungaku taikei*]. It doesn't mean that we haven't read *The Bathhouse of the Floating World* or *Spring Colors: The Plum Calendar* in those editions, but the reading experience is of a different order.

Edo-period fiction, as Shōyō notes, was inseparably tied to its illustrations. Writers had to possess painterly instincts to be successful. One can even go so far as to say that unless one had a modicum of skill as a book designer or illustrator, one could not become a writer. In other words, when writing fiction, outline sketches for the illustrations had to be drawn. There were even cases of writers who were extraordinarily gifted at drawing outline sketches: Santō Kyōden, for example, whose actual profession was that of an ukiyo-e artist, and Ryūtei Tanehiko, who drew exceptionally accurate sketches. An ukiyo-e specialist executed the final illustrations based on the author's sketches. It was the author, then, who determined the layout of the text.

Even today, it is not impossible to find writers who design the layout or draw the illustrations but, in general, I'm sure that such cases are few. The

Edo gesaku writer, on the other hand, was a book designer who was responsible for the total book-making process. This was especially true for *kusazōshi*, which closely resemble what we call *giga* [playful paintings] today. Edo-period books were made by woodblock print, which meant that, unlike our printed editions, discrepancies did not arise between the letters of the text and the illustrations. In terms of page layout, that familiar worm-like style of writing was a brilliant invention as it perfectly matched the illustrations.

Another important matter concerns the Edo reader, who read fiction not silently but out loud, a phenomenon that continues into the Meiji period. Even when they did not actually raise their voices when reading, readers were inwardly conscious of the sound of the voice. Modern print is uniform, which makes it easy to read, or at least the possibility of its being easily read is quite high. Letters carved in woodblock printing, however, look like worms and are quite difficult to read. Kusazōshi texts, moreover, are written only in *kana* (phonetic syllabry). Because they are difficult to read, one's reading speed slows down. Consequently, even though the voice may not be used, images of the linguistic sounds appear in the mind. In contrast, for modern readers used to reading silently, the speed at which one reads is much faster compared to readers in the past; the sound of the voice thus naturally disappears. Yet, even for us, there are occasions, reading poems slowly, for example, when we are implicitly aware of the sound of the voice. In fact, poets rely on devices — dividing poems into lines or using lots of *hiragana* (cursive syllabry) — as a means of allowing the reader to sense directly the sounds of the words. We usually forget, however, that during the Edo period fiction was read in close conjunction with the human voice.

Now let us turn to the method of punctuation in Edo fiction. We today use commas and periods to demarcate units of meaning. Although we do have punctuation to indicate the rhythms of breathing, meaning, as a rule, determines punctuation. Edo-period punctuation marks, however, were used in a manner quite the opposite of how they are used today. In other words, marks were inserted according to the rhythm of the voice, another indication that texts were read out loud. Bakin's works *Biography of Eight Dogs* [*Satomi Hakkenden*, 1814–41] and *Crescent Moon* [*Yumiharizuki*, 1806–10], for example, are called *yomihon* [reading books]. They were so called because, as the name states, they were "books read with the voice." Other works, like Shikitei Samba's *Bathhouse of the Floating World* and *The Barbershop of the Floating World*, were written in a manner that suggests the reproduction on paper of *rakugo* [comic monologue].

When we view the texts in that way, we come to understand why late Edo fiction contains very few descriptive passages and is written primarily in dia-

『春色辰巳園』三編巻之七

Figure 1. Illustration of Tanjirō, Yonehachi, and Adakichi. From *Spring Colors: The Southeast Garden* (*Shunshoku tatsumi no sono*, part 7, section 3, 1833–35) by Tamenaga Shunsui. Courtesy Chikuma Shobō, 1989

logue form. Readers could modulate their voices and add melodic inflections as they read. To have one person read the text while several others around him or her listened seems to have been a common way of reading fiction.

Earlier I noted this passage from *Essence of the Novel*: "In the fictional works written in our country, detailed illustrations have been used to depict the forms of things and supplement what was lacking in the written text." Let us now take the most appropriate example of it from a *ninjōbon* [stories of human feeling]. It is one of the illustrations found in *Spring Colors: The Southeast Garden* [*Shunshoku tatsumi no sono*, 1833–35], a text that portrays the willfulness and pride of a Fukagawa geisha written by Tamenaga Shunsui and considered to be one of his masterpieces (figure 1). On the left is the fold-out page [*mihiraki*]; the one-page portion on the right is the page that precedes it.

The figure on the far left is Tanjirō, a name that became synonymous with the amorous man. The figure leaning up against Tanjirō is Yonehachi. Beyond the *shōji* screens, just one page apart, is another Fukagawa geisha, Adakichi, whose pose suggests that she is eavesdropping. Tanjirō and Yonehachi are inside the screens engaged in amorous play. Yonehachi's speech is written as follows: "Nothing's wrong but I wonder if anyone's peeping in."[8] The reader, however, as he or she reads along, has not yet seen the next page. Adakichi is listening intently to the voices coming from the other side of the screen, as her heart, filled with indescribable emotion, is ready to burst. When the reader turns the page, there appears the amorous scene that Adakichi is peeping at or eavesdropping on. Given the layout of the text, there is no need for laborious verbal description. This is only one example, but it shows that, for Edo fiction, depictions of a visual nature were left to the illustrations and all the writer had to do was attach a brief passage, a comment to accompany the illustration. Similar depictions occurred frequently.

With the advent of the Meiji period this way of book making gradually declined. Woodblock-printed books continued to be produced, but the early years of Meiji marked an era of utilitarianism, led by Fukuzawa Yukichi's groundbreaking ideas, and economic concerns took precedence in book making as well. Up until around 1877, the cost of printing by movable type was clearly higher than printing by woodblock. The cost differential closed by 1882 or 1883, and from this time on the cost of movable-type printing began to undercut that of woodblock printing. Fictional texts, too, began to be published by movable type rather than by woodblock.

What, then, happened to the illustrations? The written text was printed with movable type and the illustrations were done by woodblock. Plates were made by fastening a woodblock inside the surface of a page, which had been type-printed. The result was a sense of awkwardness compared to pages that had been printed with a single carved wooden plate. We must remember that in the Edo period, even the texts called kusazōshi were produced at an extremely leisurely pace, perhaps two or three volumes a year, so that the woodblock carvers had the freedom to take great care with their work. In the Meiji period, the carving of blocks came to be done haphazardly in the hasty pursuit of newsworthy events, such as the case of the famous kusazōshi concerning Takahashi Oden, the famous Meiji murderess.

From about 1882 to 1883 the number of woodblock-printed gesaku texts, which had circulated primarily through lending bookstores, gradually declined, and in their place printed editions of older texts gained popularity. Seven versions of *Biography of Eight Dogs*, for example, appeared at the same time. The number of books published in these printed editions of old texts from 1882 to 1887 probably outnumbered severalfold the total output during the Edo period. In other words, we must consider Bakin's *Biography of Eight Dogs*, which Shōyō had made a target of his criticism, to be, unquestionably, a work of contemporary literature.

What we must not overlook, then, is that *Essence of the Novel*, as a work of literary criticism, was conceived at a crucial juncture when the technology of movable-type printing was beginning to displace that of woodblock-printed texts, which had been produced by hand and had achieved a high level of perfection as artistically crafted objects. Literary studies have heretofore tended to slight issues like publication, printing, and readership, but I feel that we must, when discussing the rise of modern literature, begin with a consideration of these institutions [*seido*] that existed beyond the confines of literature itself.

In Japan the period of woodblock printing that preceded movable-type printing was an extremely lengthy one. The age of orality or recitation did not immediately change to the age of print. Texts printed by woodblock are of course printed texts, but they preserved the oral and recitative tradition to a great degree. The printed words in those texts could be reconstituted back into the human voice and were actually read aloud.

Now, what about the style of the written characters used in woodblock printing? Authors themselves sometimes wrote the characters on the blocks or sometimes left the task to a scribe. In the latter case, a certain stylization occurred, but when there was a change of scribe, the style of the characters, depending on the text, changed ever so slightly. Traces of the human brush strokes, in other words, would remain. When we read Natsume Sōseki's *Botchan* [Young master], for example, only the rarest of souls among us would think of reading Sōseki's original manuscript itself or a reproduction of it. For us, fiction is to be read with printed words. Woodblock printing, on the other hand, preserves in some fashion traces of the human brush stroke, traces related to the sense of touch.

The person who pioneered the study of the reading audience is the English literature scholar Toyama Shigehiko. In *On Modern Readership* [*Kindai dokusharon*] he writes, "The medium of the printed text cannot serve as a channel for the human voice, at least for the author's voice. The reader frequently has to compensate in some manner for the fact of being unable to hear the authorial voice. The reader thus must strive on his or her own to reconstruct the world of the text as faithfully as possible. He or she cannot expect validation from the author's voice. In this way, author and reader, in the context of the printed word, become alienated from each other."[9]

Toyama goes on to compare the relation between author and reader in regard to printed texts to the case of the theater. For example, how were Kabuki and Shakespearean stages configured? In Shakespeare's time, the front section of the stage jutted out and, because, as a rule, there was no curtain, the audience and the actors could communicate intimately with each other. All you needed to do was pay for a ticket or, in the case of the nobility, watch the performance from the seats provided by the management that were placed directly on the stage. In the case of the Kabuki stage, a *hanamichi* (elevated runway) ran directly between the seats where the audience sat.

The Shakespearean stage, in which there was no distance between actors and audience, came over time to be fitted with a curtain that dropped down at the front of the stage, thereby cutting the audience off from the actors. The audience now looked into the stage as a kind of visionary space, and the theater became a kind of spectacle. Toyama's comments also apply to fictional texts because their being printed by movable type produced a similar distance between reader and author. Ian Watt, the well-known scholar of the eighteenth-century English novel, notes in his *Rise of the Novel* that the alphabet as represented by printed symbols does not possess the individual style apparent in handwritten drafts. Thus, one reads a text, as it were, automatically. Watt writes, "Ceasing to be conscious of the printed page before our eyes we surrender ourselves entirely to the world of illusion which the printed novel describes."[10] Let me add an anecdote here. During the first years of Meiji, readers accustomed to the style of characters in woodblock texts that retained traces of human brush strokes felt uncomfortable with the Ming Dynasty style of modern print. Toward the end of the second Meiji decade, the Ching Dynasty style, which was used in textbooks and which preserved a bit more of the human touch, came to be the heavily preferred style for printing fictional texts. Shōyō's *Essence of the Novel* and *Tōsei shosei katagi* [The character of modern students] were both printed in the Ching Dynasty style rather than the Ming style. Based on what we've observed thus far, woodblock-printed texts comprised a graphic style that involved a direct transfer of the author's or scribe's hand to the printing plate, a system of signs and marks that incorporated sounds, modulations, and rhythms and a skillful page layout calculated to take full advantage of the interrelations between the text and the illustrations. Such works can be thought of as a collection of crafted objects that constituted an extremely complex and organic system. As I noted before, texts printed in a uniform typeface, although they isolate the functions of text and illustration, are easier to read and can be read quickly, but that ease and speed result in an erasure of sound.

Compared to printed texts, the function of the "signifier" (i.e., the expressive signs) in woodblock printing was arguably greater than that of the "signified" (i.e., the content of the signs). In other words, the role the word played in all its materiality, whether in terms of its sound, the shape of the written letter, or other related matters, was great in the case of woodblock-printed texts. Books printed in movable type, however, owing to the uniformity of the printed letters, cast off the material aspects of the word. The surface of the letters became exceedingly transparent and the reader was able to grasp directly the ideas and signs that lay behind it. The passage from *Essence of the Novel* cited above must, I feel, be understood in this context.

In sum, the written text in Edo-period fiction depended to a large extent on the signifying power of the illustrations. As the relative role of the illustrations declined with the importation of movable-type printing, the written text had to take over the task of visual description that had been handled by the illustrations. Shōyō's mosha problematic must be viewed, then, as part of a literary theory that corresponds to the period of transition from woodblock printing to movable-type printing.

The phrase "Fiction is art" in *Essence of the Novel* may be considered in two ways. First, we must remember that at the First National Industrial Exhibition the Art Pavilion was located in a spot corresponding to the pivot point of a folding fan. Art, in other words, was thought to embody the essence of the "power of vision" that formed the fulcrum that would propel industrial production. Second, it is likely that Shōyō was greatly inspired by the concept of art found in *A True Account of the Fine Arts* written by Ernest Fenollosa, whose lectures Shōyō heard at Tokyo University.

Fenollosa's *True Account of the Fine Arts* appeared as one volume in 1882. It consisted of a shorthand transcription of a series of his lectures sponsored by the Dragon Lake Society [Ryūchi-kai]. It is well-known that a passage from *A True Account of the Fine Arts* is cited at the beginning of *Essence of the Novel*, but for some odd reason, Shōyō writes only that it is the theory of a certain person and does not cite Fenollosa's name. It certainly couldn't have been due to his resentment at not having received good marks in Fenollosa's class, but the fact that he erased the name of Fenollosa, his teacher, provides a clue to understanding the literary theory found in *Essence of the Novel*.

The passage from *A True Account of the Fine Arts* that Shōyō cites contains the following points. The various aspects of human life are divided by Fenollosa into two categories, "necessity and ornament" [*suyō to sōshoku*]. Necessity refers to need and "ornament" refers to what uplifts people's hearts or elevates their character. Art, then, is put into the category of ornament. Shōyō extended Fenollosa's claims and argued that the effects of fiction, too, lie in providing an ornament for life, uplifting people's hearts and elevating their character, and had no direct connection to actual life. Shōyō's criticism of Bakin's view of literature as based on the principles of encouraging good and castigating evil derives from Fenollosa's thinking.

When Fenollosa put art in the category of ornament, what did he see beyond the move itself? The answer is related to the actual position of the Art Pavilion at the First National Industrial Exhibition and to the position accorded art in Wagner's manifesto. Fenollosa aimed his incisive critical barbs at those who regarded art as a technological necessity for an industrial society. In *A True Account of the Fine Arts*, Fenollosa introduces three commonly held notions regarding the definition of art: first, it must display finely honed technique; second, it must give pleasure; third, it must take its forms from nature. He then proceeds to reject all three.

What, then, is the essence of art? The passage is difficult in Japanese translation, but Fenollosa states the following: "That which maintains the internal integrity of each of its elements and in which the elements constantly interact to produce a sense of total uniqueness — that is what we can call the marvelous conception [*myōsō*, glossed as *aijiya*, or 'idea'] of art."[11]

For example, say that various colors are scattered on the surface of a painting. Those colors must be unified by something. That something is what Fenollosa calls "marvelous conception" or "idea." In doing so he forges a theory in which the essence of art lies in its organic unity. Fenollosa had read deeply in Hegelian philosophy and we can see that the traces of Hegelian idealism are visible here.

In Fenollosa's view, European painting did not contain this marvelous conception. He felt that the European belief that the essence of art lay in the imitation [mosha] of real things was shallow and he argued that Japanese painting, even though it seemed at first glance to be far removed from imitation [mosha], was instead informed by the marvelous conception that did not exist in the realistic paintings of the West.

As readers well know, Fenollosa's authority at the time as a professor at Tokyo University was absolute; his comments on art, therefore, marked a turning point in the history of Japanese painting. From the time of his remarks until around 1887, Western-style painters found themselves in an extremely difficult position. Behind the art scene, Ōkubo Toshimichi's industrialization policies were in fact facing a time of crisis. The art academy under the aegis of the Ministry of Industrialization would soon be eliminated. At the same time, traditional Japanese painting, which had been struggling with great difficulty to remain viable, seized the opportunity for revitalization that Fenollosa's comments provided.

Now let's see what happens when we look at Fenollosa's remarks from a different point of view. Take the term *bijutsu*, deriving from the term "art" [*aato*]. In the West, the term art did not include what we understand to be the meaning of bijutsu. The English critic Raymond Williams, in *Culture and Society*, states that art [bijutsu], or Art with a capital A, appeared during the Industrial Revolution. This Art emerged as an antithetical response to the uniformity of mass production brought about by the Industrial Revolution. Until that time, art with a small a meant "craftsmanship" or "skill." The newer term Art came to signify works authenticated by the psychic interior of the artist who has turned his back on industrial society. Fenollosa's remarks, then, seem to designate the point of transition from art with a small a to Art with a capital A. The manufactured products on display at the First National Industrial Exhibition or the works designated as art in Wagner's manifesto were artworks necessary for industrial society, that is, art as craft. The role that Fenollosa's *True Account of the Fine Arts* played in the history of art during the Meiji period is the formulation, against the notion of art as craft, of a concept of Art with a capital A, cut off from utilitarian concerns—in other words, art as marvelous conception. Thus aided by the concept of Art with a capital A, Shōyō raised the status of fiction, which had been disparaged until then as gesaku, to a form that could withstand critical appreciation by all people, and positioned it at the head of the other literary genres. At the same time, he appropriated the theory of the copy [mosha] that Fenollosa had criticized, cleverly slipping into his discussion a notion of the visual that was closely linked to the technological aspects of industrial society. Isn't it possible, then, to find in the contradiction a reason for Shōyō's erasing Fenollosa's name when he cited the passage from "A True Account of the Fine Arts" in *Essence of the Novel*? The ambivalence constitutive of the thinking in *Essence of the Novel* results from the fusing of two elements that are foreign to each other: fiction as art, which offers an elevated form of entertainment for civil society, and fiction as imitation, which results from intense and repeated visual observations of the mores and conventions of the world. The position that conceives of art within a policy of industrial development as evidenced by the Industrial Exhibition and the position of Fenollosa, who rejected the utilitarian aspects of art, were completely at odds. Yet, in terms of an economic nationalism that sought to export Japanese products abroad, they were one and the same. The only difference lay in whether one gave preference to the importation of European methods or allowed traditional methods to be refined. In *Essence of the Novel* we can discern the attempt to create an art form that could rival European literature by modifying the already existing form of gesaku. The desire to modify is usually referred to as the spirit of reform [kairyōshugi]. In fact, it seems to be the case that Shōyō had internalized the prioritizing of national interests that authorized the policy of industrial development at this time.

The following passage appears in *Essence of the Novel*: "We must be tireless in our heroic attempt to continue to rectify and reform the immaturity of our fiction, of our popular tales, to make them complete and flawless works that can surpass those of the West, to turn them into great artistic works that deserve to be called the flowers of our nation."[12] We smile as we hear in the expression "great artistic works that deserve to be called the flowers of our nation" a conceit supremely appropriate for the age of "civilization and enlightenment."

As we have seen, Shōyō's *Essence of the Novel* incorporated a wide variety of aspects that cannot be addressed entirely within the framework of literary theory. By allowing the text to collide with the overall context of civilization and enlightenment during the early Meiji years, factors hitherto obscured become clear. I've hinted in various ways at those factors, but let me now offer a couple of examples of how the image of fiction as a representation of the visual world that Shōyō advocated in *Essence of the Novel* plays out in actual texts.

How does Shōyō's stance vis-à-vis the representation of the visual world manifest itself in the descriptions contained in his *Character of Modern Students [Tōsei shosei katagi]*, a work said to put into practice the theory formulated in *Essence of the Novel*? One example, from the first installment, is the following description of the appearance of the protagonist Komachida Sanji, who makes his debut in the flower-viewing scene on Asuka Hill [Asukayama]: "His coat was of an old-fashioned weave. Was it something redone from his mother's outer garment? The hem is a dead giveaway; quite frayed. Judging from his appearance, he doesn't seem to be the son of a good family; neither does he seem to be from the country. He's surely the son of a county official. In any case, he's without a mother. That's the author's own conclusion based on an observation of the hem of his pants."[13]

Actually, this is a passage that Yoshimoto Takaaki cites in his *Gengo ni totte bi to wa nanika* [Linguistically speaking, what is beauty?]. Yoshimoto states the following: "Compared to the type of description of the 'sun rises in the east and sets in the west' variety found in *Strange Tales of Beautiful Women [Kajin no kigū*, a representative piece of political fiction that appeared the same year as *Essence of the Novel*], Shōyō's way of being attentive to the hem of the coat being frayed shows that he has clearly realized the importance of the position of enunciation, which is connected, as we can ascertain from this admittedly primitive example, to a consciousness of the object originating in the visual judgment of the author."[14] The author does not state directly that the student has no mother. Rather, the author first presents the visual image of the frayed hem of the student's pants, then offers a judgment based on that image. Furthermore, the fact that Komachida Sanji has no mother is an important part of the overall plot of *Shosei katagi*. Yoshimoto Takaaki's statement regarding the "author's visual judgment" corresponds, then, to the "visual world" or "the spirit of natural history" found in *Essence of the Novel*.

Another example is the section in *Ukigumo*, near the beginning of part 1, where Utsumi Bunzō is about to confess his love to his cousin Osei: "Her features were actually no more beautiful than at any other time, but with her lovely oval face pale in the moonlight, and two or three loose strands of hair, stirred by the faint breeze from her fan, playing about her cheeks, there was a chilling quality to her that made Bunzō shudder."[15] The passage isn't exactly purple prose, but we do see Osei through Bunzō's eyes. The oval face slightly pale in the moonlight, streaked by two or three loose strands of hair—the description tells us that Bunzō is physically close to Osei and is staring at her. Of course, we can't simply conclude that such descriptions are solely the influence of *Essence of the Novel*; we must also consider the influence of Russian literature that Futabatei studied. Still, it exemplifies the visualization of description that Shōyō advocated.

A description of Osei's appearance follows the above passage: "Her cool, clearly shaped eyes suddenly began to move about . . . and met perfectly the stare of someone who was enthralled."[16] Next comes a slightly grotesque description: "She hid her smile, laughingly formed at her conch shell of a mouth, behind a fan that she carried in her fingers which were like five smelt lined up in a row attached to a slender-rooted white radish."[17]

Smelt attached to a slender-rooted radish makes for a genuinely grotesque image in which Osei doesn't appear to be a beauty at all, but it was a style that Futabatei arrived at only with great effort as he searched for a visual description that would supplant clichés of the type "a rhododendron when she stands, a peony when she sits."[18] In *Shosei katagi*, the author's judgments are based on visual phenomena, as stated in the line "That's the author's own conclusion based on an observation of the hem of his pants," whereas in the *Ukigumo* passage just quoted, any judgment about Osei herself is left up to the reader. The bringing together of the visual images of radish and fish is given over to the reader's imagination. Such examples show clearly the stance of the author as an observing persona, as discussed in *Essence of the Novel*.

Last, let us look at the description of Berlin in Mori Ōgai's "The Dancing Girl" ["Maihime"]:

> I had the vague hope of accomplishing great feats and was used to working hard under pressure. But suddenly here I was, standing in the middle of this most modern of European capitals. My eyes were dazzled by its brilliance, my mind was dazed by the riot of color. To translate Unter den Linden as "under the Bodhi tree" would suggest a quiet secluded spot. But just come and see the groups of men and women sauntering along the pavements that line each side of that great thoroughfare as it runs,

straight as a die, through the city. It was still in the days when Wilhelm I would come to his window and gaze down upon his capital. The tall, broad-shouldered officers in their colorful dress uniform, and the attractive girls, their hair made up in the Parisian style, were everywhere a delight to the eye. Carriages ran silently on asphalt roads. Just visible in the clear sky between the towering buildings were fountains cascading with the sound of heavy rain. Looking into the distance, one could see the statue of the goddess on the victory column. She seemed to be floating halfway to heaven from the midst of the green trees on the other side of the Brandenburg Gate. All these myriad sights were gathered so close at hand that it was quite bewildering for the newcomer. But I had promised myself that I would not be impressed by such captivating scenes of beauty and I continually closed my mind to these external objects that bore in on me.[19]

In the all too famous passage, Ōta Toyotarō, courageously engaged in his mission to take European learning back to the imperial nation in the East, is standing on Unter den Linden Avenue. It is a brief passage, but it is written with great precision. For example, in the "tall, broad-shouldered officers" walking proudly with shoulders squared to the wind, the author has skillfully incorporated the image of militarist Prussia, victorious in the Franco-Prussian War. And we can distinguish men and women among the throng of people walking along the road. For the women, we get the line "attractive girls, their hair made up in the Parisian style." It is true that Germany crushed France in the war, but in the ironic scene where we see young women dressed in the Parisian mode of a defeated France, walking nonchalantly along Unter den Linden, Ōgai has accurately summarized, in two or three lines, the atmosphere of post–Franco-Prussian War Berlin.

"Carriages ran silently on asphalt roads"; asphalt paving was used during the time of Napoleon III by Haussmann, the governor of Seine Province, as part of his urban renewal initiative for Paris. The use of asphalt had the concealed intent of preventing Parisians from making barricades out of the stones that had previously constituted the surface of the roads. Asphalt pavement was also imported into Germany. Such accurate details give the reader the impression of looking at a miniature painting engraved on a copperplate. It may be written on a small scale, but every element of detail is executed with extreme accuracy. The impression I get from the way "The Dancing Girl" is written is of the illustrations found in Kume Kunitake's *Beiō kairan jikki* [Record of a tour of the United States and Europe] with its finely detailed copperplate-engraved miniatures.

Additionally, I would point out that the passage from "The Dancing Girl" is the first example among works of modern Japanese fiction in which a city is described in a kind of vanishing point perspective. In other words, in the foreground we have Unter den Linden Avenue. Soldiers and young ladies wearing the latest Parisian fashion are walking along it and horse-drawn carriages are rumbling over the asphalt pavement. The next sentence, "Just visible in the clear sky between the towering buildings were fountains cascading with the sound of heavy rain," constitutes the middle ground. The whole landscape finally converges in the distance extending from the image of the Brandenburg Gate, which today forms the boundary between East and West Berlin, to the image represented by the line "Looking into the distance, one could see the statue of the goddess on the victory column."

In terms of perspective, which was developed during the Renaissance, a point in the painting serves as the focal point where all other lines meet. If we looked at it the other way around, a human subject who views the landscape must necessarily be posited on the viewer's side of the canvas. This is one of the fundamental structures of vision for modern times. It is often stated that "The Dancing Girl" depicted the awakening of a modern self. We can in fact read in Ōta Toyotarō's perspectively based line of sight the implicit structure of that self. And at a yet deeper level lies Ōgai's own stance of taking a long hard scientific look at the cities of Europe aided by insights gained from his knowledge of hygienics.

Notes

1 This essay first appeared in *Tosho* as "Kindai bungaku to katsujiteki sekai," serialized from August to October 1979. This is a translation of "Kindai bungaku to katsujiteki sekai," which appears in *Maeda Ai Chosaku Shū 2, Kindai Dokusha no Seiritsu* (Chikuma Shobō, 1989), 329–348.

2 Often the character *sha* by itself appears.

3 Tsubouchi Shōyō, *Shōsetsu shinzui*, in *Shōyō senshū* (Daiichi Shobō, 1977), 3:58.

4 Futabatei Shimei, *Shōsetsu sōron*, in *Futabatei Shimei zenshū* (Chikuma Shobō, 1985), 4:8.

5 Stendhal (Marie-Henri Beyle), *The Red and the Black*, trans. C. K. Scott Moncrieff (New York: Modern Library, 1953), 166.

6 *The Correspondence of Gustave Flaubert and Georges Sand: Flaubert-Sand*, trans. Francis Steegmuller and Barbara Bray (London: Harvill, 1999), 388.

7 Tsubouchi, *Shōsetsu shinzui*, 154–155.

8 Tamenaga Shunsui, *Shunshoku tatsumi no sono*, in *Nihon koten bungaku taikei* (Iwanami Shoten, 1973), 64:345.

9 Toyama Shigehiko, *Kindai dokusha ron* (Suisui Shobō, 1964), 20–21.

10 Ian Watt, *The Rise of the Novel* (Berkeley: University of California Press, 1967), 198.

11 Ernest Fenollosa, "Bijutsu shinsetsu," in *Meiji bunka zenshū* (Nihon Hyōronsha, 1928), 12:163.

12 Tsubouchi, *Shōyō senshū*, 75.

13 Tsubouchi Shōyō, *Tōsei shosei katagi*, in *Shōyō senshū* (Shunyōdō, 1927), 1:15.

14 Yoshimoto Takaaki, *Gengo ni totte bi to wa nanika* (Keisō Shobō, 1965), 2:172.

15 Futabatei Shimei, *Japan's First Modern Novel:* Ukigumo *of Futabatei Shimei*, trans. Marleigh Grayer Ryan (New York: Columbia University Press, 1965), 218.

16 Ibid.

17 Ibid. I have given a literal translation to bring out Maeda's point. Ryan's version is quite different: "Coquettishly, she hid the smile which filled her pouting lips with the fan she held in her five slender, delicate, white fingers."

18 A standard expression, possibly dating from the Edo period, of a beautiful woman: "A rhododendron when she stands, a peony when she sits; she's the figure of a lily when she walks."

19 Mori Ōgai, "Maihime" (The Dancing Girl), trans. Richard Bowring, *Monumenta Nipponica* 30, no. 2 (summer 1975): 152–153.

9. Ryūhoku in Paris

(Pari no Ryūhoku)

TRANSLATED BY MATTHEW FRALEIGH

This selection is a chapter from Maeda Ai's 1976 book-length critical biography of Narushima Ryūhoku (1837–1884), a former shogunal scholar who was also an important literary figure in the early Meiji period.[1] Maeda's pioneering studies on Ryūhoku, which include several articles in addition to the monograph, have been by far the most influential in informing contemporary views of this author, whose best-known works are the urban chronicles, poems, travelogues, and essays he composed in classical Chinese.

The focus of this piece is the travel diary *Diary of a Journey to the West* (*Kōsei nichijō*), which covers Ryūhoku's tour of the West from 1872 to 1873. In the aftermath of the bakufu's collapse in 1868, Ryūhoku declared himself a *muyō no hito* (useless man), refusing to serve in the new Meiji government. About one year after his return to Japan, he entered the world of journalism, first as the editor of the popular *Chōya shimbun* newspaper and later as the publisher of the literary journal *Journal of Moonlight and Blossoms* (*Kagetsu shinshi*). The travelogue that Maeda discusses here belongs to a very diverse and broadly defined genre of foreign travel records produced in mid-nineteenth-century Japan, several examples of which Maeda refers to in the piece. Perhaps the most famous of these documents is Kume Kunitake's *Record of a Tour of the United States and Europe* (*Beiō kairan jikki*), the official report of the Iwakura mission, a mammoth diplomatic tour of governmental, industrial, commercial, and cultural facilities in several Western countries undertaken between 1871 and 1873 by the new Meiji government. Taking advantage of the fact that both Ryūhoku and the Iwakura mission were in Paris at the same time, Maeda's chapter explores the contrast between their approaches to Paris. In its illuminating juxtaposition of Ryūhoku's vision of the city with the more "realistic" or pragmatic vision embraced by the Iwakura mission, the chapter enriches our understanding of the Restoration era by imagining "another 'modernity,'" however partially glimpsed. Maeda's reconstruction of a conflict in values and orientations in the chapter reveals the tensions of the early Meiji period and the diverse responses of intellectuals to them.

Among the works that Ryūhoku published in *Journal of Moonlight and Blossoms* [*Kagetsu shinshi*] was a piece entitled *Diary of a Journey to the West* [*Kōsei nichijō*]. *Diary of a Journey to the West* is the diary Ryūhoku kept while accompanying the abbot of Higashi Honganji temple on an 1872–73 tour of France, Italy, England, and the United States. Yet, because *Journal of Moonlight and Blossoms* ceased publication just before Ryūhoku's death, the serialization of the work was suspended just at the point in the diary where Ryūhoku, having crossed the Atlantic, gazes at the city of New York. About one month's worth of the diary, covering Ryūhoku's landing in the United States through his return to Yokohama, was apparently already missing in 1897, when Kishigami Shitsuken was engaged by Hakubunkan to edit Ryūhoku's collected works.

Diary of a Journey to the West is readily accessible to contemporary readers, having been reprinted in such anthologies as *Meiji bungaku zenshū* as well as the *Foreign Culture* volume of *Meiji bunka zenshū*. Along with *Kōsei nichijō*, the latter volume includes a memorandum entitled "Accounting record of Ryūhoku's 1872 journey to the West." Its first page begins "29 September (08.27) I received 500 *ryō* from the Abbot," showing how Rev. Gennyo had entrusted Ryūhoku with the responsibility of being the group's treasurer and liaison during its trip to the West. Given Ryūhoku's deep interest in numismatics, as well as his experience serving as vice minister of finance under the bakufu, he was considered well-suited for the responsibility of managing the vast sum of 13,000 ryō that the group needed for its foreign tour. Moreover, having participated in instruction at the French military training program in Yokohama during the Keiō period (1865–68), Ryūhoku was presumed proficient in foreign languages.

Rev. Gennyo, Ryūhoku, and the others in their five-member group boarded the French mail steamer *Godavéry* and departed Yokohama on 16 October (09.14.72). Aboard the *Godavéry* with them were eight young Meiji government officials who had originally been scheduled to accompany Minister of Justice Etō Shinpei in his examination of legal systems in Europe, but official duties ultimately prevented Etō himself from going through with the tour. The group included such men as Numa Morikazu, who had participated in the tripartite military training program in Yokohama, Kawaji Toshiyoshi, who would later flex his talents as the grand commissioner of the police, and Inoue Kowashi, who essentially drafted the Meiji Constitution during his tenure as head of the Law Office. Inoue was also the man who later created the circumstances leading to Ryūhoku's incarceration, but obviously Ryūhoku could not have foreseen the significance of this fateful connection.²

The Japanese passengers on the *Godavéry* transferred in Hong Kong to the *Mei Kong*, a ship that ran a regular route to Marseilles, stopping along the way in Saigon on 27 October (09.25). Having been annexed by France as a result of the 1862 Sino-French War (a conflict in which Chanoine and Dubousquet had fought), this land was the first French territory with which Ryūhoku came into contact.³

> At 11:00, I could make out a lighthouse and some houses in the distance, and I knew that we had drawn near the port of Saigon. At noon, we entered the mouth of the [river leading to the] port. On both banks were green trees and dense, deep grasses. The landscape was just like a painting. Here and there grew giant fern palms. I also saw a group of monkeys playing together. Around the houses, the ground was lush green with rice seedlings, like Japan in the fourth or fifth month. Though the river is a large one, the current is gentle and the water is murky. . . . At 4:00, we reached Saigon, the capital of Annam, which has recently become French territory. The people here are racially related to the Chinese. The men and women all have blackened teeth. I wonder if perhaps it is because they eat coconuts. The roof tiles on their houses and huts are all red. For the first time in my life, I saw a grove of palm trees. Today, the thermometer read 94°; apparently this port lies just 10°17′ from the equator. At night, when I lay down to sleep on board the ship, the drone of insects on either side of the river filled my ears as I watched fireflies flitting about chaotically. They were immense! There were lots of mosquitoes and ticks, too.

In 1884, twelve years after Ryūhoku's trip to the West, Mori Ōgai would pass through Saigon on his way to Germany. Ōgai arrived in Saigon on 7 September, in roughly the same season as had Ryūhoku, and recorded its scenery in his "Diary of a Western Journey" ("Kōsei nikki") as follows:

> 7 [September]. Morning. We went up the Saigon River. There were flat marshlands on both banks, and the foliage grew luxuriantly. Village huts were scattered here and there. *The landscape was just like a painting. I saw palm trees and fern palms* in between. They were giant. . . . At 2:00, we reached the port. . . . When I looked at the city, I saw that *all of the roof tiles were red. I tried a coconut for the first time.* It was shaped like a watermelon.

> 8 [September]. The natives are all fond of "shanzi."⁴ They cut a single nut into four pieces, and then they chew it with mugwort leaf and lime. For

this reason, *the men's and women's teeth alike are all black*. Shanzi is betel.
At night, I composed a poem as I was going to bed.

暮天雨霽人忘熱	At dusk, the rains clear, and I forget the heat
始覺舟中一枕安	Now at last I feel the peace of sleeping aboard ship
夜半房奴吹燭滅	At midnight, a deck hand comes to blow out the lamp
虫聲唧唧迫窓寒	*The drone of the insects* just outside my window brings a coolness to the air

I have heard that *there are many mosquitoes and ticks* in this land, but that
doesn't particularly seem to be the case now. *I checked the thermometer and
it read 85°.*[5]

Serialized installments of Ryūhoku's *Diary of a Journey to the West* appeared
in nearly every issue of *Journal of Moonlight and Blossoms* from no. 118 (30
November 1881) to no. 153 (8 August 1884). Its sudden termination came just
half a month before Ōgai left to study abroad.

As narrated in *Gan* [The wild goose] and *Wita sekusuarisu* [Vita sexualis],
Ōgai was an avid reader of *Journal of Moonlight and Blossoms* when he was a
young man. Kanda Takahira's translation *The Strange Case of the Esquire* [*Yongeru no kigoku*], selections of which were published in *Journal of Moonlight
and Blossoms*, was apparently the first Western novel Ōgai encountered.[6] On
receiving the order to go study in Germany, Ōgai may well have reread *Diary
of a Journey to the West* in *Journal of Moonlight and Blossoms* as a way to familiar-
ize himself with the journey ahead of time. Beyond the resemblance of Ōgai's
title to Ryūhoku's, there are several passages in "Diary of a Western Journey"
that suggest *Diary of a Journey to the West* may have been the model for its narrative style as well. At the very least, the selection of elements from Saigon's
scenery for narrative attention, such as the townscape of red-tiled roofs and
the custom of tooth blackening, indicates that Ōgai was consciously aware of
the account in *Diary of a Journey to the West*. Surely it is reasonable to assume
that the "Kōsei nikki" line "I have heard that there are many mosquitoes and
ticks in this land" was based on the *Diary of a Journey to the West* line reading
"There were lots of mosquitoes and ticks too."

In the scenery as one approached Saigon by boat, villages and rice paddies could be glimpsed through the spaces between the palm trees and fern
palms that lined the river's banks. It is worth noting that both Ryūhoku and
Ōgai summarized this scene with the phrase "the landscape is like a painting." If there was something common to the two men's perception of landscape, surely it was related to the fact that the aesthetic senses or sensitivi-

ties of each man were joined in a common linguistic domain: the *kanbun* style.

Japanese intellectuals who traveled overseas in the late Tokugawa and early Meiji periods left behind an extraordinary wealth of travelogues and accounts of conditions abroad. As in the case of Ryūhoku and Ōgai, the kanbun style was the language most of these men had mastered. Ichikawa Wataru's *A Confused Account of a Trip to Europe, Like a Fly on a Horse's Tail* [*Biyō ōkō manroku*, 1862], Murata Fumio's *Record of Things Seen and Heard in the West* [*Seiyō bunkenroku*, 1869], and Kurimoto Joun's "Addendum by the Window at Dawn" ("Gyōsō tsuiroku," 1869) are all good examples.[7] Originally, these travelogues were not written with any literary aim in mind, but were instead the products of a burning sense of mission to record precisely information about Western culture and institutions that might further the national interest. Nevertheless, the authors' vigorous curiosity ultimately lent a delightful tension to their prose: stopped in their tracks by each and every *object*, they would invariably launch into an unrelenting inquiry to determine the object's purpose and utility. Here was a fresh and indeed exciting encounter between the traditional world of kanbun on the one hand and European civilization on the other. Aided by the richness of Sino-Japanese vocabulary and the clarity of kanbun prose structure, they avoided becoming transfixed by the dazzling façade of nineteenth-century European civilization and were instead able to seize quite naturally on the very rationality that underlay it.

More than the members of *bakumatsu* diplomatic missions, Ōgai, who had been sent to study in Germany for the purpose of investigating the army's hygienic system and conducting research on military hygiene, felt a clearly defined responsibility compelling him "to grasp in detail the actual structure and function of Western civilization."[8] However, if we can detect in Ōgai's "Diary of a Western Journey" a literary posture that is nearly absent from late Tokugawa and early Meiji overseas travelogues, we can understand it as a projection of *bungaku shumi*: the "taste for literature" Ryūhoku advocated as editor of *Journal of Moonlight and Blossoms* in opposition to the high estimation of practical knowledge that was the era's prevailing spirit.

Although the kanbun style of *Diary of a Journey to the West* clearly captures the contours of *objects*, Ryūhoku does not attempt to inquire into and precisely pinpoint the purpose and utility of these *objects*. To the contrary, Ryūhoku was blessed with the rare opportunity to encounter Western civilization as an individual traveler with no particular purpose to speak of, and his observations would ultimately be the record of a sensibility befitting a "useless person." To take the entry from Saigon—"the plaintive drone of insects on either side of the river filled my ears as I watched fireflies flitting about chaotically"—as an example, we can glimpse here Ryūhoku's solitary spirit as he stares unblinking at the melancholy elicited by the natural features of a foreign land.

On 22 November (10.22), Ryūhoku's group passed through the Suez Canal, which had just been opened to traffic in 1869, arriving safely in Marseilles on 28 November. They entered Paris early in the morning of 1 December (11.01). After spending both 1 and 2 December at the Grand Hôtel on the Boulevard des Capucines, one of the finest in Paris, the group transferred to the Hôtel de Lord Byron on the Boulevard des Italiens, and then on 24 December they moved again to the Hôtel Corneille, on the Rue Corneille near the Jardin du Luxembourg. Until the group left Paris in April of the following year, they stayed at this hotel.[9] According to the 1874 edition of *Baedeker's* guide book, the cost of a room in the Grand Hôtel ranged from 20 to 30 francs a day (Ryūhoku's group paid 289 francs for their two-day stay), the Hôtel de Lord Byron charged 5 francs a day, and the Hôtel Corneille charged 30 to 60 francs a month.

The deep emotions that must have recurred to Ryūhoku's mind on the day of his arrival in Paris receive full expression in the following seven-character quatrain:

十載夢飛巴里城	In my dreams these past ten years, I have flown to the city of Paris
城中今日試閑行	Today I seized the chance for a leisurely stroll through the city
畫樓涵影淪漪水	Picturesque buildings cast their shadows on the rippling water
士女如花簇晚晴	Men and women in floral splendor gather in the clear evening air

The "ten years" here could be counted from the time that Ryūhoku began his Western studies in 1863, or from the time he began French cavalry training in 1866. In any case, the dreams of Paris that Ryūhoku had cherished continuously from the end of the Tokugawa period had now been realized: wavelets lapping the banks of the Seine, Parisiens strolling the Champs-Elysées at twilight. Ryūhoku visited scenic spots and places of historical interest in Paris on a daily basis and searched out the pleasures of evening with no sign of fatigue. To borrow a phrase from *Ryūkyō shinshi*, his was the vigorous taste for refined diversion of a man "unleashed one day to go wherever the spirit might lead him, like a wild crane flying out of its cage or a flood surging over a waterbreak; anyone can imagine his delight!"[10] Let us take a look at Ryūhoku's excursions about ten days after his arrival in Paris:

Sunday, 8 December (11.08). Very fine weather.
Shimaji Mokurai, Umegami Hironobu, and Sakata Kan'ichi also came over today.[11] Today, I went to the Bois de Boulogne public park with Andō and Ikeda. There is a waterfall there, and it is a lovely place, refreshing and secluded. We went for a drink at the Anglaise, where the food was exquisite. Buoyed by our tipsiness on the way back, we went to a brothel on the Rue d'Amboise. Yet we left only a wild swan's tracks in the mud.[12]

Monday, 9 December. Fine weather.
I went out for a stroll with Shimaji and the others. We toured the Palais-Royal inside and out, and we also went to see the "Panorama." The "Panorama" portrays scenes from the Franco-Prussian War, and although they use pictures, one can hardly believe that the images are not real. The show is a marvelous and enchanting spectacle; I have never seen such splendid sights in all of my life. . . .

Wednesday, 11 December. Overcast.
Today I visited Mr. Kurimoto with Shuntai. In the afternoon, there were powdery snow flurries. After dinner, I went to see the Valentino dance hall with Osada, Ikeda, and Andō. The majority of the hall's patrons were young playboys, and among the women, too, there were many unlicensed prostitutes.

Ryūhoku visited Paris when it was the *capital* of Europe, its appearance completely transformed thanks to the urban plans Prefect of the Seine Georges Eugène Haussmann had formulated at the request of Napoléon III. Haussmann, who called himself an "artiste démolisseur," relentlessly tore down the old streets of Paris and in their place constructed large straight boulevards that permitted four-directional movement and unobstructed lines of sight. Circular plazas decorated with fountains and marble statues were built in the boulevards' intersections. A stylish shopping district was completed in the bustling vicinity of the Palais Royal, where blue sky could be glimpsed through the arcade's glass ceiling by day and the bright light of gas lamps would illuminate the night. Laborers' houses were relocated from within the city center to the suburbs, and, in what was regarded as a compensatory gesture, the Buttes-Chaumont public park was planned as their place of respite.

In fact, this urban reconstruction project concealed an ulterior motive: the protection of the capital from internal discord. The new roads had the function of facilitating the rapid movement of military and police forces, and their efficacy was actually proven during the Paris Commune (the bitter experience of having roadway cobblestones appropriated as materials for barricades during the Revolution and afterward had led the Second Empire to hit on the idea of introducing asphalt pavement). Regardless of the reconstruction project's original purpose, however, the scenery of remodeled Paris was enough to dazzle the great numbers of tourists being brought in on rail, the transportation mode of the new era. Moreover, during the time between the Second Empire and the beginning of the Third Republic, Paris had in store for them a set of alluring pleasures, from sophisticated restaurant cuisine to Offenbach operettas, not to mention the high-class prostitutes known as the demimonde.

The "Boadoburon" that Ryūhoku describes as "a lovely place, refreshing and secluded," is of course the woods at Boulogne.[13] Ryūhoku appears to have been quite taken with the scenic beauty of the place, visiting it a total of four times during the course of his stay in Paris. The "Zangurei" restaurant is surely the Taverne Anglaise, located near the Boulevard des Italiens. There are multiple references in *Diary of a Journey to the West* to drinking engagements with old acquaintances at the "Yōroppa tei" [Dîner Européen] and other first-class Parisian restaurants. Having cultivated his palate in Yanagibashi drinking establishments, Ryūhoku was undoubtedly an able connoisseur of the dining culture developed under the Second Empire. During his trip to Italy in the second half of March, he notes that the flavor of the "dried buckwheat" (probably macaroni or spaghetti) is "extremely fine."

The visit to "a brothel on the Rue d'Amboise" (the Rue d'Amboise was on the opposite side of the Boulevard des Italiens from the Hôtel de Lord Byron) just one week after arriving in Paris hardly comes as a surprise considering that Ryūhoku was the author of *Ryūkyō shinshi*, but for some reason this is the only mention of excursions into the pleasure quarters.[14] Rather, it is his nimble dodge—"yet we left only a wild swan's tracks in the mud"—that seems suspicious. Perhaps insufficient language ability brought about an utter loss of face for the ostensibly savvy connoisseur. On his first visit to the Théâtre de l'Odéon on 6 January of the following year, Ryūhoku would note that he was unable to record an outline of the play's plot "because I could not understand the language." Having assumed Ryūhoku's language ability would be their lifeline, Gennyo also seems to have been at quite a loss over the miscalculation, for Ryūhoku's language skills would not actually be useful to them while abroad. Following their move to the Rue Corneille, Ryūhoku and the rest of the group invited a tutor to begin giving them French lessons.[15]

Inasmuch as it posed no particular linguistic difficulties, the "Valentino dance hall" that Ryūhoku visited on 11 November became one of his favorite haunts. Before leaving Paris, he patronized the establishment five times in all. Such "singing and dancing halls" or *bals* were one of the famed attractions of Paris at the time, with something of the atmosphere of tourist establishments catering to out-of-towners. There were, in general, two varieties—those open in summer and those open in winter—but the Valentino was in business year-round. According to *Baedeker's*, the Valentino was located on the Rue St. Honoré not far from the Place Vendôme, and charged an admission fee of 1 or 2 francs. Ryūhoku describes the sort of people who gathered at the Valentino as "young playboys" and "unlicensed prostitutes," but let us turn to Baudelaire's striking sketch for a glimpse of the scene:

> And now, opening their galleries filled with light and movement, appear the *Valentinos*, the Casinos, the Prados . . . the capharnaüms where idle youth gives free rein to its exuberance. Women who have exaggerated the latest trend until its grace is corrupted and its design destroyed are grandly sweeping the floors with the trains of their dresses and the points of their shawls. They go, they come, pass by and return, their eyes wide open like a startled animal's, appearing to see nothing, but in fact observing everything. Against a background of infernal light, or against a background of the aurora borealis, red, orange, sulfurous, pink . . . sometimes violet . . . , against these magical backgrounds, imitating in their various ways Bengali fireworks, appears the manifold image of the shadier type of beauty.[16]

The "shadier type of beauty" that rose up against these magical backgrounds was unmistakably a product of the impostor Napoléon III's Second Empire, but the performances Ryūhoku saw at the Gaîté or the Opéra were not so far removed from what emanated from the Valentino. Ryūhoku recorded his impression of the Opéra, for example, as: "There was an undersea scene during the performance. They had secretly strung up silver wires on which were suspended green water plants and bluish floating weeds. It was truly a dazzling sight to behold." For the Gaîté, he wrote "[Among the most wonderful sights was] the chorus of girls who danced the mayfly dance. It was quite similar to the butterfly dance of Japan, and surprised me with its beautiful allure." Ryūhoku also recorded a quite detailed summary of a play based on Alexandre Dumas fils's *La Dame aux camélias*, the pioneering work that first brought the mode of life of the demimonde under the lights of the stage.

The "Panorama" next to the Palais de l'Industrie that struck Ryūhoku as "a marvelous and enchanting spectacle" was already the subject of impressions recorded in Kurimoto Joun's "Gyōsō tsuiroku" as follows: "Between the stone gate [the Arc de Triomphe] and the stone pillar [the Obelisque de Louqsor] on the left is a show of wax pictures called the 'Panorama.' It apparently means to gaze from a distance at realistic pictures. The pictures are of the war that took place over ten years ago in which the French Empire fought alongside Italy. They are enclosed in a glass circular hall, and can be seen with the naked eye or with a telescope as one wishes. . . . It engages the viewer's mind, and although he only watches with his eyes, it is as if he is actually there, traversing the ground himself."[17]

In the beginning of 1871, following the Franco-Prussian War, the images of the Italian battle were changed to images of the defense of Paris. The aim was to make citizens recall the humiliation of defeat and to boost their morale. Memories of the city's siege two years earlier had been engraved with graphic vividness on the hearts of the Parisian people. Did Ryūhoku fail to see these images as anything more than well-crafted spectacles? Ryūhoku's stay in Paris from 1872 to 1873 corresponded to the very beginning of the Third Republic. Fresh from putting down the Paris Commune, Thiers was president, but the time was ripening for a royalist faction plotting to overthrow him in the hope of restoring the Louis monarchy. It was on 24 May 1873 that Marshal MacMahon, highly regarded for his distinguished military service in subduing the Commune, was elected president with the royalists' backing (by this time, Ryūhoku was aboard a ship crossing the Atlantic Ocean for the United States). As far as we can see in *Diary of a Journey to the West*, Ryūhoku expressed virtually no interest in these sorts of political developments. On spotting MacMahon by chance at the Trianon villa in Versailles, he did no more than simply record the marshal's appearance: "With his white hair and venerable expression, he is a sturdy and dignified man." Similarly, when Ryūhoku visited the Arc de Triomphe on the Champs-Elysées, there would still have been bullet holes visible from the Paris Commune gunfire, and yet there is no mention of this in *Diary of a Journey to the West* whatsoever.

Indifferent to the scars of the Paris Commune or the smoldering standoff between Thiers and the royalists, Ryūhoku seems to have pursued pleasure almost single-mindedly in Paris. His sole political interest was in Napoléon III, whose time had already passed. After visiting the tomb of Napoléon I at the Hôtel des Invalides on 9 January 1873, Ryūhoku returned to his hotel to receive the news that Napoléon III had died in his London exile. Ryūhoku concluded his entry for the day with "Today, Napoléon III died while sick in England. It was truly tragic." On 21 January he noted how "somber" he felt after acquiring a valedictory photograph of Napoléon III, and on 31 January he recorded a seven-character quatrain entitled "Lament for Napoléon III":

| 哭那破崙第三世 | Lament for Napoléon III |
| 勝敗何論鼠噛猫 | No point rehashing the battle's outcome; a rat will bite a cat if cornered |

英雄末路奈蕭條	Such a lonely demise awaited the hero at the road's end
判他獨逸新天子	We can be sure that over in Germany, the new Emperor
高枕而眠從此宵	Sleeps easily tonight with his pillow propped high

Though he was only reporting what he had heard from others, Kurimoto Joun described Louis Napoléon's features in the following fairly negative terms: "His appearance is unspectacular, and his speech rather halting, almost as though he cannot manage to bring the words out of his mouth."[18] For Ryūhoku, however, it probably did not really matter what sort of person Louis Napoléon actually was. Instead, Ryūhoku's admiration of Napoléon III simply acted as a means for him to affirm his own long-cherished feelings of loyalty toward the Tokugawa house. Threaded through this process was the logic of a bakufu loyalist who had studied military arts as head of the cavalry under the French army in the bakufu's last days. The fall of the Second Empire was superimposed on the collapse of the bakufu, and triumphant Prussia was likened to the domains of Satsuma and Chōshū. These stirrings in Ryūhoku's heart were perhaps already apparent in the emotional impact the earlier trip to Trianon had on him: "The inner garden of this palace bore a striking resemblance to the Fukiage garden [in the palace] of our old bakufu, and I found myself overcome with feelings of sorrow."

During Ryūhoku's stay in Paris, the Euro-American mission led by Ambassador Plenipotentiary Iwakura Tomomi arrived in Paris via Calais. They were received in a diplomatic lodge prepared by the French government near the Arc de Triomphe on 16 December (11.16). Among the mission members were several affiliates of the old bakufu with whom Ryūhoku had associated previously, such as Tanabe Renshū, Fukuchi Ōchi, Utsunomiya Saburō, and Kawaji Kandō (Tarō, the grandson of Kawaji Toshiakira).[19] In addition, the liaison for the French government was Captain Chanoine, with whom Ryūhoku had lived side by side at the Ōta base in Yokohama. At the same time, former French Academy student Osada Keitarō was working as a secretary under Japan's Minister to France Sameshima Naonobu, and Kurimoto Joun's adopted son, Teijirō, was also studying in Paris. Furthermore, the overseer of the Japanese students living in Paris, Irie Bunrō, had formerly been dispatched to serve as an interpreter for the corps of French military instructors while serving as a professors' assistant at the Institute for the Investigation of Barbarian Books. In other words, Ryūhoku had the opportunity while he was in Paris to rekindle old friendships with the remnants of the faction that had supported Franco-Japanese collaboration. Ryūhoku's adopted son, Ken-kichi, the biological younger brother of Osada Keitarō, also arrived in Paris on 7 April of the following year.

Ryūhoku visited Chanoine's house three times during the course of his stay in Paris. His first visit took place on 19 January 1873: "I visited my old acquaintance Mr. Chanoine to thank him for his friendliness years ago. I met his wife for the first time. He had the Japanese sword and the copy of *Illustrated Guide to the Famous Sites of Edo* [*Edo meisho zue*] that I had given him on display in his study. Moreover, he had placed a photograph of me with my wife in his photograph album. I was genuinely moved to see that he had not forgotten our old feelings for each other. When we Japanese people meet old acquaintances, many of us treat them like mere streetside passersby; how could I not feel ashamed?"

The "Japanese sword" that adorned Chanoine's study was a memento that Ryūhoku never let leave his side during his tenure in Yokohama (*Ryūhoku shishō* includes a long poem entitled *Kokenhen* [On an old sword] that Ryūhoku composed in 1871 in wistful recollection of the then faraway Chanoine).[20] Even more than Chanoine's faithful friendship, what stirred Ryūhoku's heart must have been unpleasant memories of the betrayal and heartlessness that were not at all uncommon among former shogunal retainers. For Ryūhoku, was this foreign tour ultimately a journey wherein he discovered, in the Western world, a positive sign of life's beauty?

Using Chanoine and Tanabe Renshū as intermediaries, Ryūhoku was able to enjoy himself to the fullest even among such former adversaries as Iwakura Tomomi and Itō Hirobumi. On 22 January, he accompanied Iwakura, Kido, Ōkubo, and the others on a tour of the observatory, superior court, and prison. The entry for this day in *Diary of a Journey to the West* runs to about twelve hundred characters,[21] exceptionally long considering how partial the diary is to conciseness, but several interesting issues emerge if one reads it alongside the entry contained in the Iwakura mission's official record, *Record of a Tour of the United States and Europe*.

To begin with, whereas *Record of a Tour of the United States and Europe* provides its most exhaustively detailed explanations about the organization of the superior court and the circumstances of the public hearing the group was able to sit in on, *Diary of a Journey to the West* by contrast concentrates on description of the prison. *Record of a Tour of the United States and Europe* is rounded off with such objective statements as "In total, the expenses utilized for this prison amount to 8 million francs annually."[22] Yet in its painstaking record of the inmates' daily routine, for example, *Diary of a Journey to the West* does not try to hide Ryūhoku's own emotions: "Everything has been organized and planned to the last detail; it is the pinnacle of strictness where strictness is called for and the height of mercy when mercy is in order. Truly one cannot help but marvel at it." Subtly revealed here, one might say, is the rift between the logic of the ruler and the logic of one who stood on the side of the ruled. In later years, Ryūhoku would be sentenced to four months' incarceration for mocking the Meiji government's press ordinance. The experience led him to author an essay entitled "Tales from the Slammer" ["Gokunaibanashi"], reporting on actual conditions in a Meiji jail, but perhaps he had already caught a glimpse of his own fate while touring the Paris prison.[23]

At the observatory, damage from the shelling during the Paris Commune was still fresh, drawing the attention of the whole tour group. The account in *Diary of a Journey to the West* is characteristically blasé, reading simply, "When we asked about it, they said that the damage was suffered during the recent uprising of a rebellious faction." The account in *Record of a Tour of the United States and Europe*, on the other hand, reads: "(The concave lens of a reflective telescope) hung on the wall, but back during the 'Commune' rebellion, the rebels fired at it with their rifles, ravaging and shattering it with bullets, turning it into the useless discard it is today. *Among recent disturbances in France, the damage from the 'Commune' far exceeded that wrought by the Prussian army. Even in a civilized nation, when it comes to the middle and lower classes, there is no immunity from benighted brutishness.* To claim that the nations of the West have fine public morals shared by high and low alike is a great fallacy."[24] Fully realized here is the necessary level of realism required on the side of the rulers: a realism that was consistent with the position of the Thiers administration, which had marshaled the overwhelming firepower and discipline of a regular army to crush the Commune's resistance. When the Iwakura mission visited the cemetery of Père-Lachaise, they did not overlook the fact that it had been the site of the Commune's last stand. Reading *Diary of a Journey to the West* alongside *Record of a Tour of the United States and Europe*, with the latter's accurate observation of postwar Paris as seen from the side of those who suppressed the Commune, one is struck by how Ryūhoku's stance, trying to understand 1871 in terms of the impact of Napoléon III's demise, seems almost anachronistic. This difference is something beyond a merely formalistic distinction between the official record of the Meiji government and the leisurely travelogue of a private individual; what we can extrapolate from it is the logic of the victors and the feelings of the vanquished in the Boshin War.

To reconfirm just how far apart *Diary of a Journey to the West* and *Record of a Tour of the United States and Europe* are in the way they took in the sights of Paris, let us turn to their respective entries for the week preceding 22 January,

Table 1

	Beiō kairan jikki [record of a tour of the United States and Europe]	Kōsei nichijō [Diary of a journey to the west]
15th	Toured an army officers' school [St-Cyr-l'Ecole] and the Palace at Versailles	Spent the whole day reading
16th	Toured the underground sewer system	Toured the Louvre museum, saw a play at the Théâtre de la Gaîté
17th	Toured the Fortress of Mont Valérien	Browsed at a minerals store on the bank of the Seine
18th	Toured the Château de Vincennes Artillery Depot	Saw a play at the Théâtre de la Gaîté
19th	Toured Fontainebleau	Visited Chanoine
20th	Toured an architecture school and a mining school [Ecole Supérieure des Mines]	Toured the church of St. Sulpice
21st	Toured the Banque de France, the Gobelins textile factory, and a chocolate factory	Obtained a photograph of Napoléon III

the day Ryūhoku joined the mission on its tour of the observatory, court-house, and prison (Table 1).

On the side of the Iwakura mission was the Paris of fortresses and facto-ries, while on Ryūhoku's side was the Paris of theaters and art galleries. To what extent did these men understand the almost symbolic significance that these two Parises thrust upon Meiji Japan? In accordance with the program of a "rich nation and a strong army," the Iwakura mission was busy enthu-siastically assimilating the items on its agenda, while Ryūhoku had still not realized that the world he had abandoned himself to was linked to another "modernity," one that was the reverse of the "rich nation and strong army." After returning to Japan, Ryūhoku expressed the perception he brought back from his tour in the following way: "Some narrow-minded scholars maintain that Western people are only interested in profit and utility, and that they never dare to show any interest in pleasant diversions and amorous foolishness. This is just nonsense. I once took a one-year journey, and after close observation, I realized that *our emotions and feelings correspond to theirs without the slightest difference whatsoever.*[25]

Though he had gone so far as to discover that "our emotions and feelings correspond to theirs," Ryūhoku was ultimately not destined to have the experience of deepening this as an internal drama. The early Meiji period that Ryūhoku lived through saw a movement away from simple praise of cannons, steamships, and other conveniences of civilization created by Western science and technology. The focus shifted instead to the cultural tradition—Christianity, literature, and the arts—that lay in the background. Just as Nakamura Keiu, for example, believed he had understood the Christian concept of "God" in terms of the Confucian concept of *tian* [heaven], there was an optimistic cognitive pattern here that sought above all to discover shared features of Eastern and Western culture.[26] Ryūhoku was no exception. The project of scrutinizing the discontinuities between East and West as an internalized drama, of unraveling the significance of this other "modernity" that Ryūhoku could only dimly glimpse, would be a problem left up to the generation of Ōgai, Sōseki, and Kafū.

Notes

1 For more information on Ryūhoku as well as a discussion of Maeda's contribution to Ryūhoku studies, please see my article "Ryūhoku" in *Modern Japanese Writers*, Jay Rubin, ed. (New York: Scribner, 2001), which contains a bibliography of additional critical works. In particular, Maeda's formulation of the "useful"/"useless" contrast in this chapter has greatly shaped subsequent readings of Ryūhoku, but as even Maeda hints in this piece, questions remain about the applicability of the label "useless." Recent scholarship by Inui Teruo and others, for example, has significantly revised and refined this characterization by giving greater attention to Ryūhoku's career as a journalist.

   First appearing as "Pari no Ryūhoku: *Kōsei nichijō* o megutte," in *Koten to kindai bungaku*, no. 13 (1972), this translation was taken from "Pari no Ryūhoku," chapter 7 of Maeda Ai's *Narushima Ryūhoku* (Asahi Shimbunsha, 1976), 173–192.

   I would like to express my gratitude to Fukui Tatsuhiko for answering my many questions and for generously sharing his thoughts about the nuances of phrasing in Maeda's text. All errors and shortcomings of the translation are of course my own responsibility. Thanks also to Atsuko Sakaki, Steve Hanna, and the Japanese United States Educational Commission (Fulbright) for their encouragement, suggestions, and support. I should note that all of the notes are mine.

2 Maeda is referring here to the conflicts Ryūhoku later had with the new regime

over the severe restrictions it imposed on newspapers in 1875. After spending four months in prison for his sarcastic criticism of the press laws, which included a thinly veiled attack on Inoue, Ryūhoku gradually drifted away from the world of newspaper journalism, spending the remainder of his life as the publisher of an early literary magazine, *Kagetsu shinshi* (1877–84).

3 Chanoine and Dubousquet were two of the fifteen French officers who served in the bakufu's military training program at Ōta in Yokohama beginning in 1867. The nature of this "tripartite" program (artillery, cavalry, and infantry) and Ryūhoku's service as a cavalry officer in it are the subjects of the preceding chapter in Maeda's monograph.

4 Ōgai seems to be using the characters *shanzi* as a term for the areca nut, which is combined with betel-pepper leaf and lime to make a "quid" of betel for chewing. He seems to be identifying it as a term in the local dialect, for he goes on to explain its meaning with the term *binglang* (J. *binrō*), which is still the word used in modern Japanese and Chinese. Perhaps Ryūhoku had the betel palm in mind with his postulation that eating "coconuts" (literally, the fruit of the palm) caused the natives' teeth to darken. Alternatively, there is good reason to think that the character for coconut 椰 in Ryūhoku's text was a misprint for the similar character for betel palm 檳.

5 Ōgai's original text is in kanbun, and the emphases here are Maeda's. Mori Ōgai, "Kōsei nikki," in *Ōgai zenshū* (Iwanami Shoten, 1975), 35–78.

6 The narrator of Mori Ōgai's novel *Gan* refers to *Kagetsu shinshi* in the following description of his friend Okada: "Okada's habit of browsing secondhand bookstores came from what we would today call a *bungaku shumi* [taste for literature]. This was a time, however, when the new novels and plays had not yet appeared, a time before lyrical poetry such as [Masaoka] Shiki's haiku and [Yosano] Tekkan's *waka* had been born, and so everyone read magazines like *Kagetsu shinshi*, printed on Chinese rice paper, or *Keirin isshi*, printed on white paper, finding [Mori] Kainan and [Ue] Mukō's *kōrentai* poems the most stylishly sophisticated. I too was an avid reader of *Diary of a Journey to the West* and so I remember it well. It was the magazine that first published a translation of a Western novel. As I recall, the story was something about a university student in the West who was murdered while returning to his hometown, and it was translated into a vernacular style by Kanda Kōhei [i.e., Takahira]. That was the first time I had ever read this thing called the Western novel. The times being what they were, Okada's taste for literature was nothing more than the pleasure he found in reading scholars of Chinese who wrote about some new event in the literary style." Mori Ōgai, *Ōgai zenshū*, 8:494. A direct reference to Ryūhoku's travelogue occurs in a conversation between the narrator and Okada toward the novel's end: "'I once read in *Kagetsu shinshi* that the idea of going abroad suddenly occurred to Narushima Ryūhoku in Yokohama, and that he immediately made up his mind and went aboard the ship.' 'Yes, I read that too. Ryūhoku apparently left without so much as a letter to his family, but I have explained my plans to my family in detail'"

(8:597). Similarly, in *Wita sekusuarisu*, the narrator recalls reading *Kagetsu shinshi* with his friend Bitō Eiichi while a teenager: "Eiichi . . . excelled at Chinese studies and was partial to Kikuchi Sankei. I read the copy of *Seiunrō shishō* that I had borrowed from him, and then moved on to *Honchō gusho shinshi*. And when he would tell me that something by Sankei was coming out, I too would go to Asakusa to buy *Kagetsu shinshi* and read it. We tried composing Chinese poems ourselves, and we also tried our hands at short pieces in kanbun. That was mainly how we would spend our leisure time" (5:127). The narrator goes on to mention Ryūhoku specifically later in the text: "In those days, there was something in the newspapers called the *zatsuroku* [miscellaneous column]. The *Chōya Shimbun* enjoyed good sales on the basis of Narushima Ryūhoku's zatsuroku. It was serious scholarship mixed with sophisticated wit, and the argument endeavored to be unique. You could glimpse the tight logic in the words, and occasionally an aphorism that appeared in the column would suddenly be on everyone's lips" (5:163). As for the translated novel that both Maeda and Ōgai allude to, Ryūhoku published a condensed version of Kanda Takahira's translation *Oranda biseiroku* under the title *Yongeru no kigoku* in *Kagetsu shinshi*. For Kanda's translation, Ryūhoku's condensed version, and a modern Japanese translation of this book, see Nishida Kōzō, *Nihon saisho no hon'yaku misuterī shōsetsu: Yoshida Sakuzō to Kanda Takahira* (Japan's first translated mystery novel: Yoshida Sakuzō and Kanda Takahira) (Kesennuma: Kōfūsha, 1997). A thoroughly annotated version of *Oranda biseiroku* has just been published as part of Iwanami's new Meiji anthology of classical Japanese literature; see Nakamaru Nobuaki et al., *Hon'yaku shōsetsu shū II*, vol. 15 of *Shin Nihon koten bungaku taikei: Meiji hen* (Iwanami Shoten, 2002). The original Dutch text was Jan Bastijaan Christemeijer's 1819 *Belangrijke tafereelen uit de geschiedenis der lijfstraffelikje regstspleging en merkwaardige bijzonderheden uit de levens van geheime misdadigen* (Important scenes from the history of the corporal punishmental judicature and curious peculiarities of the lives of secret criminals). Thanks to Sascha at Antiquariaat A.Kok and Zn. B.V., Amsterdam, and Marjan Boogert for their help in deciphering the Dutch title.

7 The three texts Maeda mentions are available in large anthologies and in some cases annotated modern Japanese or English translations. Ichikawa Wataru (Seiryū, b. 1824) traveled to Britain, France, and other European states in 1862 with the Takenouchi/Matsudaira mission. Most of his diary was published in a serialized English translation by British diplomat and Japanologist Ernest Satow from 1865 to 1866. After studying English in Nagasaki, Murata Fumio (1836–1891) managed to escape to England in 1864, where he studied for four years. He returned to Japan after the Restoration, working for several years as a civil service engineer before going on to found the *Maru Maru Chimbun*, a humorous magazine. As discussed in the previous chapter, "Gyōsō tsuiroku" is the travelogue Kurimoto Joun (1822–1897) composed about his 1867 travels in France.

8 Haga Tōru, *Taikun no shisetsu* (The shogun's missions) (Chūo Kōronsha, 1968).

9 Of course, during Ryūhoku's tour of Italy in March, they vacated the hotel.

10 This section of *Ryūkyō shinshi* refers to the lifting of the bakufu's ban on samurai patronage of the pleasure quarters. The original passage can be found in the following two annotated editions. With annotations by Maeda Ai, *Meiji kaikaki bungakushū*, vol. 1 of *Nihon kindai bungaku taikei* (Kadokawa Shoten, 1970), 220. With annotations by Hino Tatsuo, *Edo hanjōki Ryūkyō shinshi*, vol. 100 of *Shin Nihon koten bungaku taikei* (Iwanami Shoten, 1989), 389.

11 Shimaji Mokurai (1838–1911) and Umegami Hironobu (Takuyū, 1835–1907), both from Nishi Honganji, had set out to tour European religious institutions roughly half a year before Gennyo's Eastern Honganji group. The Nishi Honganji group originally numbered five in all; three students from the temple stayed with Shimaji and Umegami briefly in France before going on to take up their studies in England and Germany. Shimaji and Umegami met up with Ryūhoku, Ishikawa Shuntai (1842–1931), and the others from Eastern Honganji while in Paris, socializing with each other and with French acquaintances on several occasions. Sakata Kan'ichi (or Kan'ichirō, b. 1850) had traveled to France to pursue military studies in 1871 and seems to have assisted several Japanese visitors by acting as a translator and tour guide. The others mentioned in this sequence of entries include Andō Tadatsune (Tarō, 1846–1924), an old friend of Ryūhoku's who was traveling as a diplomat with the Iwakura mission, and Ikeda Masayoshi (Kanji, 1848–1881), a French teacher who was also accompanying the mission. As Maeda mentions later in this chapter, Joun's son Kurimoto Teijirō (1839–1881) was studying in Paris at the time, and Osada Keitarō (1849–1889), whose biological brother Kenkichi was Ryūhoku's adopted son, was working as a secretary for the Japanese legation in France.

12 Originally a general metaphor for impermanence, the phrase about leaving "a wild swan's tracks in the mud" came to refer more specifically to a traveler passing momentarily through a particular place, and by Ryūhoku's time seems to have been especially associated with a momentary foray into the pleasure quarters or a brief visit to a place of entertainment.

13 Though it is difficult to convey in translation what Maeda is doing when he explains the names of people and places that appear in *katakana* in Ryūhoku's diary, these identifications represent a sort of puzzle solving; it is not immediately obvious, for example, that "Zangurei" is the Taverne Anglaise.

14 In a later essay, Maeda went on to speculate that Ryūhoku did more visiting of the pleasure quarters than is immediately apparent in *Kōsei nichijō*. By comparing *Kōsei nichijō* to the diary kept by Ryūhoku's traveling companion Matsumoto Hakka, Maeda showed that several of the mysterious references to unidentified Westerners in the text are surely covert references to prostitutes. See Maeda Ai, "Ryūhoku *Kōsei nichijō* no genkei," in *Kindai Nihon no bungaku kūkan: Rekishi kotoba jōkyō* (Shin'yōsha, 1983), 69–87, esp. 81–82.

15 Ryūhoku's entry for 26 December actually suggests that the target language was English: "Beginning today, a female teacher named Raguran (Legrand?) will be coming over to teach our group English, and I will also study under her." There

are indications elsewhere in the diary that Ryūhoku had lessons from two teachers, one of whom may have taught him French. In any event, Ms. "Raguran" presumably taught Ryūhoku English using French, which would have been a sort of French practice.

16　The original text of this passage is Charles Baudelaire, "Le Peintre de la Vie Moderne," in *L'Art Romantique*, unnumbered volume of *Œuvres complètes de Charles Baudelaire*, ed. M. Jacques Crépet (Paris: Louis Conard, 1925), 49–110. For the translation here, I have relied mainly on the French text, while at the same time trying to preserve something of the structure, diction, and content of the Japanese translation by Satō Masaaki that is cited in Maeda's essay. I have also made use of several felicitous phrases from the English translation by P. E. Charvet, "The Painter of Modern Life," in *Selected Writings on Art and Literature* (London: Penguin, 1992), 390–435.

17　Kurimoto Joun, "Gyōsō tsuiroku," part of *Hōan jisshu*, in *Gaikoku bunka hen*, vol. 17 of *Meiji bunka zenshū* (Nihon Hyōronsha, 1992), 175. The paintings that Kurimoto describes were of the *Siege of Sevastopol* and the *Battle of Solferino*, scenes from the Crimean conflict in which Napoléon III went to war against Austria to expel it from Italy.

18　Kurimoto, "Gyōsō tsuiroku," 183.

19　Tanabe Taichi (Renshū, 1831–1915) was a career diplomat who was also an accomplished kanshi poet. Fukuchi Gen'ichirō (Ōchi, 1841–1906) was a journalist and playwright who had served as a translator on several earlier bakufu missions to Europe. Ryūhoku had been friendly with Utsunomiya Saburō (1834–1902) when he was a student of chemistry in the Katsuragawa salon; Utsunomiya went on to a career in industry and public works. Kawaji Tarō (Kandō, 1844–1927) had studied in England in the bakumatsu period and was accompanying the Iwakura mission as a translator; after a failed business career, he went on to teach English. One of the earliest Japanese students of French, Irie Bunrō (1834–1878), who sometimes pronounced his name Fumio, taught in the Kaiseijo and the Bansho Shirabesho, two of the bakufu's institutes for Western learning in Edo. As Maeda notes, at the same time that Irie was pursuing his own studies in Paris, he also had an important supervisory role among the other Japanese students in France.

20　The poem "Koenhen" is contained in Narushima, *Ryūhoku shishō*, 3:19–20. For an annotated version, see Hino, *Narushima Ryūhoku*, 130–134.

21　In English translation, at least in the present version of my English translation, this would be roughly 950 words.

22　Kume Kunitake, *Tokumei zenken taishi Beiō kairan jikki*, ed. Tanaka Akira (Iwanami Shoten, 1979), 3:146.

23　"Gokunaibanashi" is included in Narushima, *Ryūhoku ikō*, ed. Narushima Fukusaburō (Hakubunkan, 1892), 2:200–232.

24　Kume, *Tokumei zenken taishi Beiō kairan jikki*, 3:140–141.

25　In 1878, Ryūhoku wrote a brief foreword for *A Spring Tale of Flowers and Willows* (*Karyū shunwa*), Niwa Jun'ichirō's translation of Edward Bulwer Lytton's *Ernest*

Maltravers. The foreword can be found in *Meiji hon'yaku bungaku shū*, vol. 7 of *Meiji bungaku zenshū* (Chikuma Shobō, 1972), 3.

26 Nakamura Masanao (Keiu, 1832–1891) was a Confucian scholar who had studied in England during the bakumatsu period. He converted to Christianity early in the Meiji era. He is best known for his 1871 *Tales of Western Men of Ambition* (*Saikoku risshi hen*), a translation of Samuel Smiles's *Self-Help*. The book became a best-seller and was thought to epitomize the era's aggressive spirit of individual advancement. Nakamura also translated Mill's *On Liberty* and was an active educator and participant in the Meirokusha, on the "Meiji Six Society," organized by Fukuzawa Yūkichi and others eager to promote the spread of western ideas and knowledge.

10. Berlin 1888: Mori Ōgai's "Dancing Girl"

(Berlin: 1888)

TRANSLATED BY LESLIE PINCUS

Mori Ōgai first published "Maihime" (The dancing girl) in the January 1890 issue of *Kokumin no Tomo*. The story, inspired by the German *Ich Roman* form, provides Maeda Ai with a rich set of materials for his meticulously researched meditations on a newly interiorized subjectivity inscribed within the urban hybridity of late nineteenth-century Berlin. Ōta Toyotarō, the protagonist of "Maihime," has been sent by his fledgling Asian "empire state" to advance his knowledge of law and politics in the cultural and political capital of Germany; he is, however, soon lured away from his official duties into an all-consuming affair with a dancer from the Viktoria Theater. Unlike many an Ōgai scholar, Maeda resists the temptation to read the story as a biographical roman à clef. Instead, with a close-up focus on text and material history, Maeda skillfully retraces Toyotarō's narrative journey in at least two registers: first, as movement through the exterior space of cityspace, from the modern monumentality of Unter den Linden to the medieval labyrinth of Alt-Berlin and back again; second, as a passage through different aspects of the protagonist's subjectivity, from the visual mastery of the modern, rational subject to the unconscious stirrings of desire of a Romantic self. Maeda seems to be particularly fascinated by that transitional moment in history when older layers of urban topography are being degraded by precipitous modernization and newly modern forms stand out in all their astonishing, and disturbing, strangeness. Set within this transitional moment, Ōgai's short story of an affair across cultural and class boundaries has clearly found its most creative interpreter in Maeda Ai.

1

In the autumn of 1883, the year before Mori Ōgai left Japan to study abroad in Germany, Panorama Hall, a huge, oval-shaped building over 50 meters in length, made its appearance directly across from Alexanderplatz

Station.[1] The designers, Hermann Ende (1829–1907) and Wilhelm Böckmann (1832–1902),[2] were soon to be invited to Rokumeikan-era Japan, where they would design the government office district in magnificent baroque style. The builder of Panorama Hall, an artist specializing in historical subjects and known for his painting of *The Coronation Ceremony at Versaille*, was Anton von Werner (1843–1870).

The opening ceremony of Panorama Hall was held on the first day of September. On that same day, thirteen years earlier, Napoleon III, under siege at Sedan, surrendered to Wilhelm I of Prussia. The kaiser and Bismarck, invited by Werner to the opening ceremony as guests of honor, had the opportunity to savor once again, this time leisurely, the glory of that day at Sedan where they had played the leading roles. In each of the four great paintings displayed in Panorama Hall, a decisive moment of the victory at Sedan was exquisitely reproduced. The first painting depicted a scene of the open battle that en-sued when the French Seventh Army unit, seeking an escape route from en-circlement by the Prussian Army, launched a desperate attack; the time was two o'clock in the afternoon on the first day of September. At seven o'clock that same evening, a French military envoy presented a letter signed person-ally by Napoleon to the kaiser—this was the subject of the second painting. The third painting, set at twelve midnight, reproduced the scene of high-level Prussian staff officers surrounding Moltke as they deliberated on terms for the French surrender. The last of the four painted scenes is set at five the follow-ing morning with Bismarck on a magnificent mount, awaiting the carriage of Napoleon III as it approached along a tree-lined road. This panorama of the final battle and surrender at Sedan, further refining the technique of the dio-rama discovered by Louis Daguerre (1789–1851), relied on the magical effect of lighting to create a splendid display of the transformations wrought by each of the four times of day: high noon, dusk, midnight, and dawn. Werner's artisans also achieved unanticipated effects by gilding the soldiers' bayonets and the instruments of the military band in gold and silver leaf.[3]

The citizens of Berlin who came in droves to Panorama Hall in expec-tation of bloodstained scenes of close combat could hardly hide their dis-appointment when they first saw these more serene visualizations of battle. Nonetheless, the observation deck in the center of the building was perpetu-ally crowded to overflowing with a ceaseless stream of humanity. It seems Werner had to take repeated measures to limit the numbers of people ad-mitted. In the first-floor restaurant, its garish decor reminiscent of an expo-sition, an orchestra performed a continuous medley of light-hearted military songs while a flood of lights from incandescent and carbon arc lamps out-lined the huge dome of Panorama Hall in bold luminosity against the night sky. For the citizens of Berlin, the day of the opening ceremony could only have been an occasion for renewed public celebration of the already eternal memory of Sedan.

In Ōgai's "Doitsu nikki" [German diary] there is no direct reference to the Berlin Panorama. But while he was studying in Dresden, Ōgai did make a trip to Leipzig, and it was then that he stopped in Berlin to visit the Panorama. The date was 26 December 1885. Later, on 17 April 1887, just two days after he moved back to Berlin, Ōgai, along with fellow lodgers Taniguchi Ken and Nagura Kōsaku, climbed the Victory Tower to enjoy the live panorama of Berlin's city streets just before the onset of spring. Ōgai composed a journal entry to that effect: "Together with friends, I went to the Zoological Gardens (Tiergarten) and climbed the Victory Tower. In every direction, we saw thick smoke rising from people's homes. To the west of the tower lay the Botanical Garden where green buds were just visible on the trees. To the east, we observed the Kaiser's military carriage as it made its return to the palace."[4] Moreover, from Ōgai's second lodgings at 97 Kloster Street, Werner's Panorama Hall was a mere 200 meters away as the crow flies. Although a description of the Panorama is absent from "German Diary," Ōgai composed a detailed account after his return to Japan titled "The Pamphlet Someone Gave Me on the 'Panorama.'" This short piece strongly suggests that he did in fact see the Panorama Hall with his own eyes.

Ōgai clearly had an interest in the Panorama itself; but it is rather in his use of a *panoramic viewpoint* as a method for comprehending the landscape of the modern metropolis of Berlin that the reader recognizes the imprint of a unique, creative spirit at work. The surest evidence of this panoramic viewpoint is the description of Ōta Toyotarō, the hero of "The Dancing Girl," who arrives in Berlin burning with lofty ambitions:

> I had the vague hope of accomplishing great feats and was used to working hard under pressure. But suddenly here I was, standing in the middle of this most modern of European capitals. My eyes were dazzled by its brilliance, my mind was dazed by the riot of color. To translate Unter den Linden as "under the Bodhi tree" would suggest a quiet secluded spot. But just come and see the groups of men and women sauntering along the pavements that line each side of that great thoroughfare as it runs, straight as a die, through the city. It was still in the days when Wilhelm I would come to his window and gaze down upon his capital. The tall, broad-shouldered officers in their colorful dress uniform, and the attractive girls, their hair made up in the Parisian style, were everywhere a delight to the eye. Carriages ran silently on asphalt roads. Just visible in the

clear sky between the towering buildings were fountains cascading with the sound of heavy rain. Looking into the distance, one could see the statue of the goddess on the victory column. She seemed to be floating halfway to heaven from the midst of the green trees on the other side of the Brandenburg Gate. All these myriad sights were gathered so close at hand that it was quite bewildering for the newcomer.[5]

Rather than painting the entire scene in broad strokes, Ōgai prefers to bring each detail into full clarity. One might even say that the author has created a panorama in miniature. To put it in more concrete terms, Ōgai's images are like the copper engravings of each of the important sites inserted in Iwanami's recently published and highly readable edition of Kume Kunitake's *Tokumei zenken taishi: Beiō kairan jikki* [Record of a tour of the United States and Europe].[6] Such a rendering is well suited to the fictional representation of Berlin in "The Dancing Girl"—a representation of Berlin that Ōta Toyotarō, on a homebound ship as it anchors in Saigon port for the night, attempts to reconstruct as he collects his memories one by one.

No doubt, the impression of meticulously rendered, miniature copper engravings derives from Ōgai's distinctively analytic narrative style. Berlin's grand avenue, Unter den Linden, 198 feet wide, was divided into four lanes, each separated by a row of linden, or bodhi, trees: one for foot traffic, one for carriages, another for those on horseback, and the last for leisurely promenading. In the final decades of the nineteenth century, the only street in Tokyo divided by a row of trees would have been the brick-paved Ginza; its width was a mere seventy-two feet, roughly one-third the scale of Unter den Linden. The description of this grand avenue that runs "straight as a die" is an allusion to walking down the "Rakuyōdō," the title of a poem by Chinese scholar-official Chokōgi' (707–759?); it suggests the culture shock Ōgai must have experienced in his first encounter with the urban space of Europe as a young man who had spent his student years in the *bunmei-kaika* [civilization and enlightenment] setting of Tokyo invoked in his short story "Fushinchū," translated as "Under Reconstruction."[7] In his description of the scene of Unter den Linden, Ōgai chooses to divide the avenue between pedestrian lane and carriage lane and to represent the people going to and fro with the terms *shi* [military men] and *onna* [young girls in Paris fashion]. These were by no means arbitrarily chosen details, but rather an accurate representation of the new fashions that appeared in Berlin following the Franco-Prussian War.

The sight of "tall, broad-shouldered officers" publicly paying respect to the long-lived Emperor Wilhelm I was an integral part of the scene on Unter den Linden. The regular appearance of the emperor at the *Eckfenster* (a window in one corner of the palace) every day at high noon was duly noted in the *Baedeker* guides published during those years.[8] In *Berlin in the New Empire*, Henry Vizetelly's (1820–1894) voluminous impressions of Berlin published in 1879, there is a descriptive sketch of Prussian soldiers strutting down Unter den Linden: "To give life to the scene there should be plenty of soldiers, both on and off duty, including perhaps a squadron of the famous White Auirassiers, also helmeted officers, scintillating with decorations, driving about in droschken, ambling aides-de-camp, and orderlies, everlastingly on the trot, and young lieutenants clattering their sabers on the pavement; for at Berlin the military element dominates every other."[9]

As if a reflection of the bands of Prussian officers who crowded the grand boulevard of Unter den Linden, the monuments in the vicinity were conspicuously suffused with the ideology of Prussian militarism. The statue of the goddess on the Victory Tower, a memorial to the Prussian-Austrian and Franco-Prussian wars built in 1873, is no doubt the most striking example: atop a column of 150 feet, the awesome figure of the goddess, an idealization of the full-bodied and wholesome woman favored by the Prussians, rising up with her wings spread to their full width, is covered head to foot in brilliant gold leaf. At the base of the Victory Tower runs a corridor lined on both sides by columns, its walls adorned by mosaics depicting the prolonged conflict between France and Germany. The designer of this monument was the same Werner who created the Panorama Hall in Alexander-Platz. Walter Benjamin, who spent his childhood in Berlin a quarter-century before Ōgai's tour of study, recorded the rather morbid impression left by the Victory Tower: "With the defeat of the French people, world history seemed to sink deep into a glorious common grave. The Victory Tower memorial was its tombstone and Victory lane, the road that led to the graveyard."[10] Obviously, Ōgai did not view the Victory Tower with Benjamin's cynical eye. Nevertheless, it is worth noting that what was carved on the "towering buildings" that lined both sides of Unter den Linden was the history of the Prussian Empire. It is precisely because Ōgai understood the Victory Tower as a monumental consummation of that history that he has Ōta Toyotarō's line of sight converge on a single point: the statue of the goddess.

It was only at the end of the eighteenth century that the grand boulevard of Unter den Linden began to manifest a consistency of style as centripetally oriented, baroque space. Gathering in the vista offered by the long straight avenue, the Brandenburg Gate, supported by rows of thick Dorian columns, was completed in 1793, at the height of the French Revolution. On the orders of Napoleon, the gold-cast statues of war carriages and victory goddess crowning the Gate were moved to Paris, but in 1814, they were returned to their original place. In 1836, the same year the palace of Wilhelm I was completed, Unter den Linden underwent a complete renovation. In 1843, the Opera House was refurbished, and in 1851, the copper-cast statue of Frederick the Great was erected just opposite the Palace. This central avenue running from the Brandenburg Gate to the Victory Tower—a good eighty years in the making—became, upon its completion, a theatrical space symbolizing the military victories of the Hohenzollern line. Every day at high noon, the Home Guard would present itself in perfect formation. The protagonist of this drama was, of course, the aging emperor, who gazed down from his palace window on what Lewis Mumford has called "a classic building in motion."[11] In other words, this was a "living panorama," ultimately more effective at displaying the authority of Prussian militarism than Werner's panoramic recreation in four scenes of the decisive moments in the battle at Sedan.

To this otherwise baroque-style panoramic tableau, Ōgai adds a single discrepant element when he notes the presence on Unter den Linden of "attractive girls, their hair made up in the Parisian style."[12] The excerpt cited earlier from *Records of Travel to the United States and Europe* regarding "the German aristocracy's rapture over French culture"[13] attests to the cosmopolitan character of Berlin in contrast to Germany's more provincial cities. With the precipitous rise of national consciousness in the wake of the Franco-Prussian War, newspapers and magazines loudly proclaimed that the everyday life of Berliners had become less susceptible to the influence of things French; in point of fact, however, Paris fashion captivated the women of postwar Berlin even more than it had before the war. Here is Vizetelly's testimonial: "Berlin is not a lively nor even a particularly bustling city. It altogether lacks the gay, kaleidoscopic life of a great metropolis. None of the crowd of well-dressed loungers, encountered on the Paris boulevards or in our own Regent-street, throng its principal promenade, where, moreover, elegantly-attired women are rarely seen. As a rule, the Berlin belles seem to know as little how to dress as a large section of our own country-women, the same war of colour prevailing in their toilettes, which are for the most part extravagant caricatures of Paris fashions."[14] Although Vizetelly's observation is somewhat acerbic, it serves to illuminate the significance of Ōgai's allusion to fashion "in the Parisian style."

The streets and storefronts of postwar Berlin were inundated not only with French fashion, but also with French novels and photos of French actresses. The blockbusters in the popular theater were inevitably French spectacle-dramas. At the Viktoria Theater on the north side of Alexander-Platz (opened in 1859), *The White Cat*, a fantasy play by Porte San Martin, enjoyed an extremely long run; the novel idea of dressing young girls as sprites in flesh-colored tights made quite an impression.[15] The light and cheerful mood of France's Second Republic, given voice in Offenbach's operettas, produced forms of expression completely at odds with the solemnity of Berlin as a military capital. With this complex urban setting in mind, it is clear that in the plot design of "The Dancing Girl"—a design in which Ōta Toyotarō is progressively drawn to Elise, a dancing girl from the Viktoria Theater—Paris is smuggled into Berlin, as if to undercut the world of Prussian discipline and order.

2

The first person to analyze the significance of the scene of Unter den Linden in the opening pages of "The Dancing Girl" was J. J. Origas in his essay "Spider-leg Streets: One Aspect of Sōseki's Early Works" ["'Kumode' no machi: Sōseki shoki no sakuhin no ichi danmen"]. As the title suggests, Origas draws hints from "London Tower" and "Carlisle Museum" to illuminate Sōseki's "urban experience and aesthetic." But before taking up his main theme, Origas undertakes a thorough exposition of Berlin as it is invoked in "The Dancing Girl" by way of contrast with Sōseki's London experience:

> As the prose unfolds [in "The Dancing Girl"], it produces a kind of perspectival effect with each part taking its place in the whole. While this method of constructing the narrative is highly appropriate for representing nineteenth-century Europe, the final effect is rather pictorial. . . . Once all of the separate sketches are gathered together to form a general description, the text moves upward from the asphalt road to "the clear sky" and "the towering buildings," and, from there, "look[s] into the distance." With the end of each phrase, the author's eye gradually moves further out into the distance as he continues his investigation. The ultimate object of this investigation is the most conspicuous architectural structure in the city. In the effort of the first-person narrator to command the urban panorama in one single view, inevitably, his eyes fix upon the most conspicuous monuments among the more ordinary edifices. Rising high into the sky in front of him are the Brandenburg Gate and the Victory Tower. Even the broad avenue, Unter den Linden itself, extending straight from the Brandenburg Gate to the Palace, is a monument of sorts. These remarkable structures contribute to the well-regulated order of the city as they reign over its urban space.[16]

As Origas explains, from his position on Unter den Linden, Ōta Toyotarō commands a full view of the baroque space formed by multiple monuments:

the Brandenburg Gate, which now stands as the boundary between East and West Berlin, and the statue of the goddess atop the Victory Tower overlooking the northern corner of the Zoological Gardens, among others. Toyotarō's gaze travels slowly from the close-up view to the distant vista, ultimately fixing on the figure of the goddess. This is, no doubt, the first attempt in the modern Japanese novel to interject linear perspective into the interiority of a fictional character.

Nevertheless, Toyotarō does not initially comprehend the scene in terms of perspectival space. "My eyes were dazzled by its brilliance, my mind was dazed by the riot of color"; as this refrain makes clear, he is initially overwhelmed by the impression of a tremendous *force* pulsating in "the middle of this most modern of European capitals." According to Panovsky, because we see things not with a single fixed eye but with two ceaselessly moving eyes, our field of vision resembles a spherical surface.[17] But for Toyotarō, who has just arrived in this "most modern of European capitals" from his empire in the Far East, the scene of Unter den Linden appears in the form of a "panorama in the round" that envelops him. In this sense, Origas's observation—that the narrative description begins with color and light and only later draws clear shapes in lines and planes—is a highly suggestive one. This early passage in "The Dancing Girl" is structured around a subtle discrepancy, a textual shift from panoramic vision to linear perspective.

In "The Pamphlet Someone Gave Me on the 'Panorama,'" mentioned earlier, Ōgai writes the following: "In contrast to a painting where the viewing eye focuses in on a single point, in the 'Panorama' the focal point is dispersed in multiple directions." Whereas an ordinary oil painting is constructed with a single focal point according to the law of perspective, in the case of the panorama, the artist must create a design in which multiple vanishing points operate simultaneously. Although it is unclear whether Ōgai was cognizant of this principle at the time he was writing "The Dancing Girl," at least in its effects, the combination of a panoramic vision with the space of linear perspective offers us a transparent view into the interiority of Ōta Toyotarō's mind.

Ōkubo Takaki points out a telling discrepancy in the description of Unter den Linden: "Though the character is supposedly standing right in the middle of this urban avenue looking up at the surrounding scenery, in reality, the impression made upon the reader is rather that of a bird's-eye view, as if one were gazing down upon the city from a considerable height."[18] Clearly, the impression of a bird's-eye view overlaps with the structure of linear perspective; but even more significant, the subtle contradiction between the appearance of an upward gaze and the impression of a bird's-eye view is intimately related to recollection as the narrative mode of "The Dancing Girl." The text produces a layered effect, overlaying Ōta Toyotarō's impressions as he stands on a corner of Unter den Linden with his thoughts some five years later as he ruminates on the same events in Port Saigon. His impressions of this "modern metropolis" are reexamined, and the various motives and desires that had earlier begun their work in the depths of his consciousness are once again hauled out into the light. The spatial perspective, as it is rendered in this passage, works to give the reader a glimpse into another kind of perspective in the narrative, this one temporal.

Even while Ōta Toyotarō is filled with "hope of accomplishing great feats" and "was used to working hard under pressure," he finds himself face to face with the baroque space of this "most modern of European capitals." In expressive phrases such as "the towering buildings," "the clear sky" and the goddess who "seemed to be floating halfway to heaven," the reader can imagine the upward direction of a gaze turned toward the limpid sky above Berlin's terrestrial structures, and, at the source of the gaze, the proud figure of a brilliant young man spurred on by a sense of mission to bring the essence of European Civilization back to his empire in the East. The figure of a young man burning with ambition to rise to great heights set against the backdrop of the urban panorama—this structural motif would be taken up time and again in the modern novel. As just one example, the same motif appears at the conclusion of Balzac's *Père Goriot* (1834) in the scene of Père Goriot's burial at the cemetery of Père Lachèse. The young Rastignac, who has attended the funeral, "looked out over Paris and the windings of the Seine," where "the lamps were beginning to shine on either side of the river." Like many a provincial youth driven by dreams of rising in the world, Rastignac turned toward "that humming hive" and then "said magniloquently, 'Henceforth there is war between us.'"[19] Rastignac's defiant gaze reflects the Parisian cityscape in panoramic form, his ego brimming with energy and strength. In contrast, Toyotarō, even in his air of triumph, betrays a certain stiffness, almost as if he were in pain: something stops him in his tracks just as he is about to give himself over to the magnificent view of this "most modern of European capitals."

Ōgai concludes the Unter den Linden scene with Toyotarō's reconfirmation of his inner resolution: "But I had promised myself that I would not be impressed by such captivating scenes of beauty and I continually closed my mind to these external objects that bore in on me." Exposed in this resolution is the will to self-denial common to a generation of Meiji youth who were expected to make *risshin shusse* [rising in the world] the sole purpose of their life. It is this same drive that burns fiercely in Toyotarō's breast as he gazes upward toward the Berlin sky. Long before he left for Germany to pursue his medical studies, he was firmly convinced that he was "a man of talent." And even in the face of Berlin's urban landscape, he manages to retain his confidence that he has been specially chosen because of his abilities. Nevertheless, when he suddenly finds himself surrounded by the dazzling colors of Berlin's "myriad sights," the clear outlines of his "self" begin to lose their clarity, and he is seized with a presentiment of the unknown. His fear of "such captivating scenes of beauty" suggests that concealed behind this show of "working hard under pressure," hidden beneath the uncompromising persona he had assumed ever since he began his studies, is a gentle and receptive heart.[20]

Reassuring himself of the strength of the fortifications he has erected around himself, Toyotarō distances himself from the external world. Here we have a clear case of subject-object dualism as the character partitions reality: his "mind" versus "captivating scenes of beauty"; his "self" versus "external objects." To the degree that Toyotarō is able to reconstitute the firm boundaries of his self as a knowing subject, the lived space of Unter den Linden is reduced to a surface that conforms to the laws of perspective, represented in the form of a panorama as if seen from great heights.[21]

In this case, perspective is not merely a metaphor for a cognitive act, but rather an expression that inevitably summons up a set of terms: observer, perception, point of view, focal point, and horizon, among others. Although the analogy between *seeing* and *knowing* enjoys a long tradition, beginning with Plato's *Republic*, the Renaissance gave that tradition new life, refining it into a concrete and precise science with the discovery and development of linear perspective.[22] As a principle that condenses space along the line of sight, perspective serves, somewhat paradoxically, to bring the origin of the gaze—that is, the human being as cognitive subject—to the fore. Gathering all parallel lines into one point, the unifying order of perspective is linked to the structure of modern knowledge, a structure in which human beings, usurping the position once occupied by God, position themselves at the very center of the world. Nevertheless, the eye that "sees in perspective" freezes the vividness of a lively visual world into a fixed geometrical order. At a given moment, space is forever immobilized, the dynamic interaction between the seeing subject and the seen object reduced to a fixed standard.[23] In the words of Panovsky, "Exact perspectival construction is a systematic abstraction from the structure of this psychophysiological space. For it is not only the effect of perspectival construction, but indeed its intended purpose, to realize in the representation of space precisely that homogeneity and boundlessness foreign to the direct experience of that space. In a sense, perspective transforms psychophysiological space into mathematical space."[24]

The baroque avenue built to display the royal prerogative of an absolutist reign is a perfect representation of this "mathematical space" manifested on a monumental scale in an urban setting. In this baroque space, the image of ordinary street life where real people encounter one another is erased; in its place, a *remote* and *expansive* vista conducive to ceremonial processions and military reviews takes shape. The charming effects produced by narrow lanes and decorative windows must give way to the theatrical effect of the street as a whole. As Vizetelly explains, the sheer massiveness of "the towering buildings" and the Brandenburg Gate projects a grim solemnity that chills the spirit of people passing through the vicinity.

In March 1873, fifteen years before Mori Ōgai's tour of study abroad, the Iwakura mission entourage recorded their impressions of Unter den Linden on their arrival in Berlin: "From the castle gate of Furandenbuerukeru [Brandenburg], we passed along a wide, straight road; this is called 'Unterudenrinden,' the largest avenue in the city. In the center is a lane for light carriages, and on either side, trees have been planted to form a matching pair of elongated gardens, creating an area for strolling. On the near side is a road for large vehicles, as well as space for storage. A pedestrian lane runs in front of a row of textile shops. The avenue is completely paved, lined with large shops and grand houses. The market, fully furnished with goods and facilities, is bustling and prosperous."[25] Although this passage from *Record of a Tour of the United States and Europe* shares the restrained and objectively matter-of-fact style of the document as a whole, if we compare it with the subsequent description of Köllnische as "a district bustling with activity and alive with the crush of people," the distinctive texture of Unter den Linden comes through, however subdued. Nevertheless, the official document fails to capture the perspectival structure of baroque space. With the same scenery in view, Ōgai differs considerably from the author of *Record of a Tour of the United States and Europe* in the actual content of his perceptions.

Making the protagonist's point of view his own, Ōgai has Ōta Toyotarō discover the perspectival axis that draws together the baroque space of Berlin in tight geometrical formation. In theory, Toyotarō might have seen the panorama of Berlin as a kaleidoscope of ceaselessly flickering and changing visual impressions; instead, with the self situated as the center point, Berlin is neatly organized along the lines of a perspectival drawing. Renewing his pledge not to be "impressed by such captivating scenes of beauty" and to close his mind "to these external objects that bore in on [him]," Toyotarō does indeed reconfirm the Confucian ethos of self-denial that until this moment has acted as a restraint on his life. Yet, by refusing to allow himself a sympathetic response to the object world, he chooses, however unwittingly, the ideal of the modern epistemological subject—a subject that aims to reify and abstract all things. Or perhaps it might be more accurate to say that the disposition in the novella toward the European world is less an intimate embrace at the level of sensibility than intellectual understanding at a distance. In any case, Toyotarō's initial choice leads to his easy assimilation into a European intellectual world—a world that has brought scientific thought to a high level of development by attaching excessive importance to the visual function. Earlier, I suggested that the perspectival vision imposing strict control over the scene of Unter den Linden operates as a *retrospective gaze*; as such, it defines the direction of narrative time. Such being the case, it is imperative that our interpretation of the significance of the urban space of Berlin as it is depicted in "The Dancing Girl" be closely linked to the elucidation of the structure of Toyotarō's self projected against this urban scene.

3

For Toyotarō, who looks at the goddess atop the Victory Column from his distant vantage point at one end of Unter den Linden, the only phrase capable of summing up the capital of the Prussian empire was "this most modern of European capitals." These words breathe life into the feelings and views of Ōgai, himself a foreign student during Japan's Meiji era, on his first encounter with the European metropolis. To grasp the historical context for Berlin's effect on Ōgai as well as his protagonist, one need only imagine the pride and confidence of the German people after their spectacular victory in the Franco-Prussian War. In the 1870s, before Ōgai's trip to Germany, the catchphrase "Berlin wird Weltstadt" (Berlin, the new world capital) was in every mouth, echoed in every newspaper: "We have vanquished the modern Babylon. Paris is at our feet like the dragon beneath the lance of St. George. She was the capital of the world; she is fallen. Berlin will take her place. The mode of Paris will become that of Berlin. . . . We have already 800,000 inhabitants, next year we shall have 900,000 and the year after that a million. We have distanced St. Petersburg and Vienna, we shall soon pass before Constantinople, then Paris, and afterwards commence to compete with London." Such is the rhetorical tone of the *Kreuzzeitung* cited by Vizetelly.[26] But what truly transformed Berlin's urban landscape after the Franco-Prussian War were the enormous crowds that now thronged the city streets. The upscale restaurants in the city became accustomed to complaints from guests who had missed their reservations, and the crowded streets became an overused excuse for arriving late at meetings and gatherings: "It was the crowds; I could hardly move ahead 100 meters in my carriage" became a common refrain. The 1870s was a decade of great migrations from all over Germany to Berlin. Workers left their homes in Brandenburg, Pomerania, and Bosen, among other places, lured by the magic words "Let us go to Berlin, the *neue Weltstadt*."[27] In 1851, when the nineteenth century had just exceeded the halfway mark, Berlin still had a meager population of 400,000; by 1871, the population reached 820,000; by 1877, it increased to 1 million; and in 1888, when Ōgai was on his way home to Japan, the population hit 1.5 million. The novella "The Dancing Girl" is best understood as the story of a foreign youth who disappears into the welter of this new "world capital" bursting at the seams.

If we look at the pattern of streets and plazas in M. C. Branch's 1833 edition of copperplate prints of Berlin city maps, it is obvious that Berlin was divided into three distinct districts.[28] The first of these three included the Kölln quarters and Alt-Berlin (Old Berlin), facing one another on either side of the Spree River. In this oval-shaped district bounded by castle walls and canals, arcing avenues and roads radiating out in all directions interweave to form an intricate pattern. Within the larger district, each set of blocks spreads outward from the center in a fan shape. Preserving a relatively large stretch of open space, the district was blessed with good light and fresh air. The gracefully curving façades of the buildings made for a lovely view and lent the entire area an air of composure reminiscent of a medieval city. This district is the oldest layer of Berlin, its origins dating as far back as the thirteenth century (figure 1).

The second district—including the Friedrichstadt and the Dorotheenstadt areas, both on the left bank of the Spree River and extending out from Unter den Linden to the north and the south—was developed by Friedrich Wilhelm, the Great Elector, at the beginning of the eighteenth century. Here, the orderly grid pattern of the streets is impressive. The district begins at the southernmost end with Belle-Alliance Platz, radiating northward along three trunk roads: Lindenstrasse, Friedrichstrasse, and Wilhelmstrasse. Crossing Friedrichstrasse at right angles, the mile-long Unter den Linden serves as the northern border of the grid structure. The French and German churches are located in the center of the district, while Pariser Platz and Friedrich Platz lie on the outskirts. It is in this district that city planning in true baroque style was reproduced most faithfully, based primarily on French and Italian models.

The third district consisted of the Königstadt and Spandau quarters, both on the north side of the Spree River. The street pattern of this district is distinctive, different from the Alt-Berlin and Kölln quarters with their air of a medieval city, but different also from the baroque style of the Friedrichstadt and the Dorotheenstadt areas. The irregular streets radiating outward toward

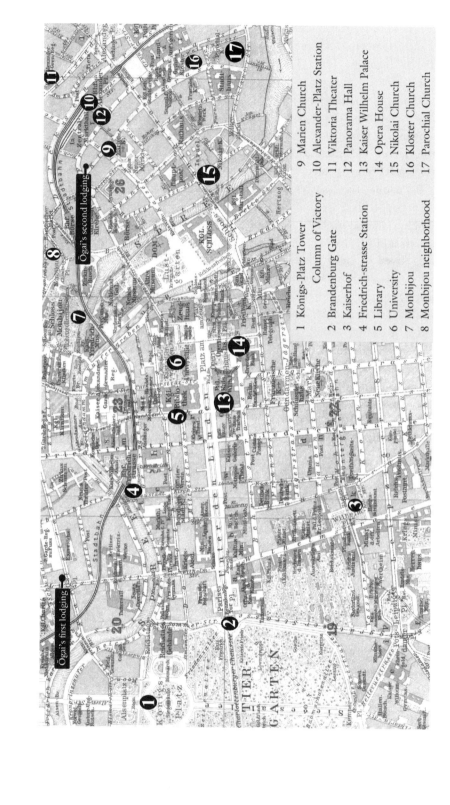

1 Königs-Platz Tower
  Column of Victory
2 Brandenburg Gate
3 Kaiserhof
4 Friedrich-strasse Station
5 Library
6 University
7 Monbijou
8 Monbijou neighborhood

9 Marien Church
10 Alexander-Platz Station
11 Viktoria Theater
12 Panorama Hall
13 Kaiser Wilhelm Palace
14 Opera House
15 Nikolai Church
16 Kloster Church
17 Parochial Church

Ōgai's first lodging

Ōgai's second lodging

the city margins lack any sense of logic or order. Viewed on a map from the period, this district reveals to the discerning eye all the signs of urban sprawl.

As late as the 1880s, the street patterns of these three districts had not undergone any fundamental change; nevertheless, within and around these basic patterns, transformations of urban space had already begun to take place at a dizzying pace. If we look at the map of Berlin in the 1885 edition of Baedeker's *Berlin and Its Environs*, there is no trace of the open spaces that once graced the city blocks of the Alt-Berlin and Kölln districts. The castle walls that used to mark the boundary between Alt-Berlin and the Königstadt-Spandau districts had been torn down, and the rails for the Ringbahn line had taken their place. (The castle walls were torn down in 1868; Ringbahn construction began in 1871.) The moat that once ran along the outside of these castle walls had been filled in. Expanding outward in a different direction, the Königstadt and Spandau districts had encroached heavily on the rural northern outskirts, now forming a vast urban area several times larger than the original castle town. If Königstadt was a suburban neighborhood of cheap lodgings, small merchants, and old-fashioned inns, Spandau had become Berlin's most densely populated district, inhabited primarily by laborers. In the factory district called Feuerland near the Oranienburg Gate, one of the barrier gates marking the outer castle perimeter, the city's huge steelyards producing boilers, steam engines, and steel girders for bridges were all concentrated.[29] Feuerland was in the very heart of the Spandau district.

In the 1860s, following the example of Haussmann's reconstruction plans for Paris,[30] Berlin's city officials initiated an urban redevelopment project, with one James Hobrecht (1825–1902) in charge. However, burgeoning population growth and the expansion of industrial zones exceeded all estimates, laying to waste Hobrecht's original plans. Ultimately, much of the city's development fell prey to speculative real estate developers who built expansive tracts of poor-quality housing on newly subdivided land. In particular, the living conditions in the blocks of tenement houses that now filled in the once undeveloped areas of the Spandau district and the open spaces of Alt-Berlin and Kölln districts were appalling enough to border on criminal. One had only to step through an archway leading from a main street into what had once been an open space to find a crowded maze of new residential struc-

(Opposite) Figure 1. Map of Berlin: area surrounding Unter den Linden. From Karl Baedeker, *Berlin and Its Environs: Handbook for Travellers*, 3d ed. (Leipzig: Karl Baedeker Publishers, 1908)

tures built flank to flank, two or three deep. The little open space that did remain was shrouded in a gloom that made one think of dank back alleys. As a matter of fact, sunlight was a rare commodity in these dark parts. To make matters worse, the tenements were home to numerous small factories and basement-level shoemakers and blacksmiths, all adding noise and waste to an already polluted environment. Berlin administrative regulations mandated a minimum standard of 28 square meters of open space per city block, but the regulations did nothing to assure adequate living space for local residents. Rather, they were intended primarily to allow sufficient room for Berlin's fire engines to pass through if necessary.[31] Engels's *Housing Question*, an incisive analysis of the urban housing crisis caused by rapid industrialization after the Franco-Prussian War, came out in 1873.[32] By the 1880s, the citizens of Berlin had no choice but to admit the fact that their "world capital" had Europe's worst industrial slums. Bismarck, who found himself at a loss when it came to urban problems and socialists, composed his own epigram for Berlin: "a desert of bricks and newspapers."

In the years surrounding the Franco-Prussian War, the extraordinary development of Berlin and the accompanying contradictions that plagued urban life found various forms of expression in the German literature of the period. As just one example, a story from Theodor Fontane's "Berlin novels" titled *Frau Jenny Treibel* (1892), an exposé in the form of a caricature of the hypocritical lifestyle of the new bourgeoisie in the late 1880s, has for its primary setting the grand residence of Councilor of Commerce Treibel built on the lowlands extending from Köpenickerstrasse toward the Spree River.[33] In the 1830s, this land was still beyond the boundaries of Berlin proper. Treibel had become discontent with his previous residence on Jakobstrasse adjacent to the old city, because, as the narrator put it, the neighborhood suffered from a dearth of both fresh air and good taste. Nevertheless, his new house on the banks of the Spree River, supposedly blessed with fresh air and good circulation, was subject, depending on prevailing winds, to great gusts of soot and smoke from the nearby factory district. As he sketches the setting for the novel, Fontane renders his indictment of the "agreeable life" of the bourgeoisie with painful irony.

From an entirely different angle, W. Raabe's (1831–1910) *Die Chronik der Sperlingsgasse* (1856) immediately comes to mind as a work that depicts in minute detail the lives of those who lived in the back streets of the old city. Sperlingsgasse was modeled after Spreegasse, which ran from the middle of Brüderstrasse cutting west along the bank of the Spree River. The poet himself lived at number 11 Spreegasse:

I love these old neighborhoods in big cities with their narrow, twisting, dark alleyways into which the sunlight dares to enter only furtively. I love these rows of gabled houses with their quaint eaves, these neighborhoods where old cannon are used in place of upright curbstones. I love these places, the heart of a time past, around which the large avenues and plazas demanded by a new way of life are creating orderly streets that move forward like a march in straight columns. Nor can I turn the corner onto my Sperlingsgasse without lovingly touching the barrel of that old cannon engraved with the year 1589. These twisting alleyways are home to a carefree breed who live their lives not so far from the more serious and industrious inhabitants of Berlin's modern districts. Here are the dark, smoke-filled offices of old and influential firms; and here is the true realm of basement rooms and attic dwellings.[34]

In this work, Raabe attempts to depict two distinct aspects of Berlin: one is the modern life of the newer, urban areas with broad avenues and plazas, orderly and systematic in its division of space; the other is the older part of the city, vestige of a former era, where densely twisting and weaving alleyways were perpetually cloaked in semidarkness. The somewhat idiosyncratic, but warmly humorous, portrait of the petit bourgeois who populate the back alleys in *Die Chronik der Sperlingsgasse* serves as a subtle form of resistance to those sunlit places in Berlin whose inhabitants applied themselves so assiduously to attaining the trappings of modern civilization.

The textual space of *Die Chronik der Sperlingsgasse* is structured in the form of a closed circle. Its center is occupied by a narrator (the recorder of a chronicle in diary form) who has settled comfortably into the unhurried time of his declining years; surrounding him are the people he meets in Sperlingsgasse. For the inhabitants of Berlin who live outside the bounds of this neighborhood, the novel reserves an unsympathetic, if not completely hostile, judgment. This is a text that clearly exemplifies Lottman's model of opposition between "we" [*uchi*/inside] and "they" [*soto*/outside].[35] Moreover, there are indications that Raabe himself was fully conscious of this textual structure. As "editor" of the work, he begins as follows: "The setting is limited in size, and the characters that appear on stage are few. Nevertheless, at least for this editor, the *Chronicle* reveals a world with its own intrinsic interest—an interest that dwells in the very fact that the work would be of no interest at all if it were to someday fall into the hands of an indifferent outsider."[36] For the "they" on the outside of the circle, it is a world with "absolutely no interest at all," but for the "we" on the inside, it is "a world with its own intrinsic interest." Here the text itself is understood as a set of signs that clearly discriminates between a familiar world and an alien world. Need-less to say, "they" and "we" can be substituted with the fundamental opposi-tion that structures the urban space of Berlin: new city versus old city. If we were to apply the same interpretive schema to Fontane's *Frau Jenny Treibel*, we would no doubt discover that the very act of estranging the world of the "they" produces a text in which that *other* world is negatively educed.

To be sure, Mori Ōgai's "Dancing Girl" is also a text structured by the opposing terms of uchi and soto. Unter den Linden, the grand avenue that captivates Ōta Toyotarō, constitutes a baroque theatrical space displaying the great power of Prussian militarism in all its glory. But what ultimately draws Ōta in is the garret room in Klosterstrasse where the love of the dancing girl, Elise, awaits his arrival. The history of Toyotarō's everyday life in Berlin leads from the open, externalized space of Unter den Linden to the closed-off and interiorized space of Klosterstrasse; it is a history marked by a momentous transformation that comes when Toyotarō crosses the boundary between the two spaces. Elise's garret room envelops Toyotarō's existence just as Raabe's Sperlingsgasse enfolds his characters: both are intimate places alienated from the "modern Berlin," and both border on Alt-Berlin, where the vestiges of a medieval cityscape are still conspicuous. The topography of "The Dancing Girl" stands out even more clearly if we shift the focal point from Toyotarō to Elise. In the end, the foreigner, Toyotarō, devastates Elise and returns once again to exterior space, creating a structure near mythic in its proportions.

4

Klosterstrasse, the street where Toyotarō encounters Elise, is identified as qualitatively different space from Unter den Linden. If the grand avenue Unter den Linden stands as monumental space, both *remote* and *expansive*, Klosterstrasse represents an erotic space that coils in on itself. This latter would be part of Alt-Berlin, once the center of Berlin; but with the end of the era of absolutist royal sovereignty, that honor was ceded to two districts stretching out to the west of the Spree River: Friedrichstadt and Dorotheen-stadt. Now a forsaken part of the city, Alt-Berlin preserved in solid form the memory of a distant medieval time, its surface fissured by the scars of his-tory. In stark contrast to the baroque space of Unter den Linden, a space that gave theatrical expression to the political strategy of the *Kaiserreich*, the dis-mal scenery of Alt-Berlin, a function of overpopulation and densely packed dwellings, allowed a glimpse from the underside into the structure of rule and oppression. Ōgai gave a surprising amount of thought to the setting for

"The Dancing Girl," particularly the Klosterstrasse, a quarter perpetually on the verge of night—a night into which Ōta Toyotarō slips . . .

> One evening I sauntered through the Tiergarten and then walked down Unter den Linden. On the way back to my lodgings in Monbijoustrasse, I came in front of the old church in Klosterstrasse. How many times, I wonder, had I passed through that sea of lights, entered this gloomy passage, and stood enraptured, gazing at the three-hundred-year-old church that lay set back from the road. Opposite stood some houses with the washing hanging out to dry on poles on the roofs, and a bar where an old Jew with long whiskers was standing idly by the door; there was also a tenement house with one flight of steps running directly to the upper rooms and another leading down to the home of a blacksmith who lived in the cellar.[37]

As with his description of Unter den Linden, here again, Ōgai selects just the right details to summon up Berlin's urban landscape. In his impressions of Berlin, Vizetelly notes that the basement abode, like that of the "blacksmith who lived in the cellar," was one of the street scenes that aroused the curiosity of visiting foreigners. These subterranean dwellings, ubiquitous on the streets of Berlin, were occupied primarily by small merchants: purveyors of milk, bread, meat, groceries, shoes, and furniture, among other things. Here and there, one would be remodeled as a beer hall from which merrymaking would occasionally spill over onto the main avenue.[38]

Contrary to Ōgai's representation, the real Klosterstrasse in Alt-Berlin counts among the bright and open avenues of Berlin. It is more likely that the actual site of the "gloomy passage" depicted in "The Dancing Girl" was one of the back streets still remaining in the vicinity of Klosterstrasse—Rosenstrasse, for example, the narrow alley that led northwest just across the street from the Marien Church, a prostitution quarter dating from medieval times; or Parochialstrasse, which intersected with Klosterstrasse at the Parochial Church. In this narrow back street (it would be more accurate to call it an "alley/*Gasse*" rather than a "street/*Strasse*") a number of shoemakers practiced their trade in cellar shops, and leftover scraps of leather littered the road.[39] Another of these narrow alleys that could well have served Ōgai's purposes was Krögelgasse, running from Molkenmarkt to the banks of the Spree River (figure 2). Until its renewal in 1934, Krögelgasse was known as the most medieval in flavor of Berlin's wretched backstreet neighborhoods. Katayama Koson documents this backstreet scene in his *Berurin* [*Berlin*] published in 1913:

Figure 2. Scene from
Krogel Alley. Courtesy
Chikuma Shobō, 1982

At the "gateway" marking the entry into the neighborhood, houses seemed to be gouged out of the wall. Inside the gateway, the houses were dyed with the dust and smoke of centuries. Leaning at an angle, three and four-story houses, their crumbling walls revealing bare brick, lined the alleyway. Built at a time when medieval architectural methods prevailed, the top floor, larger than those beneath it, jutted out into the alleyway, blocking the sky and limiting the entry of sunlight. Paved with stone as it was, the alley sloped down from the west side toward the center so that run-off water and sewage could flow down the middle. During the Middle Ages, all the filth of the neighborhood was dumped in the alley. Krögelgasse was now a slum-like warren for the poorest of artisans—coopers, bricklayers, junkmen, shoe-repair shops. Beneath the eaves, a cart lay on its side; above, dirty-looking laundry hung in rows; a few hens roamed the alleyway in search of garbage. Whenever a traveler came through, women of questionable character would look down from darkened second-floor windows with seeming curiosity.[40]

Though a good quarter-century separates Ōgai's "Dancing Girl" from Kata-yama Koson's *Berlin*, Koson's description of Krögelgasse could usefully function as a detailed footnote for Ōgai's "Kloster quarter." On 15 June 1887, the day Ōgai moved from Mariengasse to new lodgings at 95 Klosterstrasse, he wrote the following journal entry: "My new place is in the eastern end of the city, near the district called 'Alt-Berlin'; it is generally looked upon as a den for scoundrels and whores, but whereas the neighborhood doesn't merit a special trip, it certainly doesn't qualify as the dregs either."[41] Could it be that Ōgai intentionally recreated a fictionalized "Kloster quarter" to fit with this image of "a den for scoundrels and whores"? By placing the ruins of a three-hundred-year-old church in this impoverished neighborhood, he is able to evoke the atmosphere of a medieval city. Along the same lines, the Marien Church fronting on Kaiser Wilhelmstrasse serves as the model for the old church where Elise lingers; but the church that best fits Ōgai's description of a concave façade that "lay set back from the road" is the Kloster Church at the south end of Klosterstrasse. Here again, it is best to think of this fictional image as a composite created from a number of real churches.[42]

Rather than a term referring to a specific place, the Kloster quarter resembles an inlaid design within the text of "The Dancing Girl," an aggregate sign that symbolizes all the gloomy backstreet neighborhoods of Alt-Berlin. But even more crucially, the Kloster quarter must function as the *mark* of a world diametrically different from the baroque space of Unter den Linden.

Ōta Toyotarō's path, beginning from the Tiergarten, moving along Unter den Linden, and then turning into the maze of the Kloster quarter, is divided into two parts, the separation between them marked by the opposing phrases "pass[ing] through that sea of lights" and "enter[ing] this gloomy passage." Almost without thinking, we find ourselves superimposing the afterimage of Unter den Linden, with its brilliant glitter of lights, on the scene of the Kloster quarter wrapped in the deepening gloom of evening. If Unter den Linden, that grand avenue running "straight as a die," floats in the glitter of gas lamps and electric lights, the Kloster quarter is a labyrinthine space veiled in deep shadows.[43] If the former is peopled with "the tall, broad-shouldered officers" and "attractive girls" in "Paris style" who saunter down the pavement, the latter is assigned "an old Jew with long whiskers . . . standing idly by the door" of a bar—a symbol of marginal territory distanced from the center. On the one hand, we have the point of view from Unter den Linden, a perspectival composition that converges on the Victory Tower "floating halfway to heaven" as its vanishing point; on the other, we have the visual field of the Kloster quarter, where the eye is inevitably drawn to the door of the old church, with its concave façade "set back from the road." What attracts Toyotarō's gaze is the figure of Elise as she leans against "the closed door of the church"; Elise appears to form a paired image with the Goddess of Victory adorning the top of the Victory Tower. (This same motif is repeated in another of Ōgai's German stories, "Utakata no ki [A sad tale]," where the two figures, the young girl Marie and "the statue of the Goddess of Bavaria," are brought into correspondence.)[44] On the one hand, we have a viewing eye that extends, resolutely and without limit, straight ahead along a perspectival axis; on the other, an eye that wavers hesitantly among the twists and turns of a street contained within a closed-off space (manifested in images of hanging laundry and stairways). In the latter case, we might also say that the folds of the secretive and intimate space of the Kloster quarter completely enclose the "eye." This overarching visual regime operates to bind together various contrasts, clearly revealing two opposing and qualitatively different spatial structures.

The everyday space that surrounds Toyotarō before he meets Elise is organized primarily by the line that connects his lodgings at Monbijoustrasse with the university on the north side of Unter den Linden. Untroubled by doubts about his role and status as a government-sponsored student sent abroad from the Japanese Empire, Toyotarō lives his everyday reality within the systematic space of Berlin's central district—in the radiant embrace of Berlin's monumental space, symbol of the will and authority of the Kaiserstadt. The occasion for his liberation from the magical spell cast by this space comes when he begins to breathe in the air of Germany's free university; it is then that his eyes are first opened to his "real self, which had been lying dormant deep down." Nevertheless, Toyotarō's newly discovered "real self" disdains all contact with his fellow students from Japan, making no effort to open up to others: "Attributing the fact that I neither drank nor played billiards with them to apparent stubbornness and self-restraint on my part, they ridiculed and envied me."[45] The envy and suspicion of fellow students from Japan serve to drive him even further into isolation. With rare persistence, Toyotarō shuns both the gathering places of his confreres and the many pleasures offered up by the city; the Berlin he inhabits is a city marked by missing pages, a text filled with still blank pages. No doubt, this is why the Kloster quarter comes to represent a place of calm where Toyotarō recovers his identity. We catch a glimpse of him surrendering to a moment of ecstasy as he gazes up at the old church that dominates a corner of Klosterstrasse. This experience marks the process by which Toyotarō, already estranged from the center of Berlin and deviating from the norm, is gradually lured into the marginal parts of the city. But the experience also signifies that the boundary line separating the firm outlines of Toyotarō's consciousness of himself from his intimations of an encounter with an unconscious world on the other side is beginning to dissolve at the edges.

5

The "door of the [old] church" in the Kloster quarter, the site of Ōta Toyotarō's encounter, marks the limit of the world in which he has lived up until now. At the same time, that door represents an invitation from a still unknown world about to unfold on the other side. The scene in which Elise awaits Toyotarō's arrival is marked by inverse images of the tightly closed church door and the seductive invitation in Elise's eyes. These opposing images reveal the device that organizes the text: the labyrinth with its characteristically ambiguous structure, operating on the one hand to prevent trespass by involuting space and, on the other, to lure the human subject into a hidden center.

Startled by the sound of Toyotarō's footsteps, Elise turns around to look, and in her *gaze* is a mysterious power capable of stirring up the very depths of his being: "Her eyes were blue and clear, but filled with a wistful sadness. They were shaded by long eyelashes which half hid her tears. Why was it that in one glance over her shoulder she pierced the defenses of my heart?"[46] Up until this point, Toyotarō, oriented toward the baroque space of Unter den Linden, has taken its perspectival composition as the object of his gaze. Here, in a telling reversal, he becomes the object of Elise's gaze. Moved as he is by this *gaze*, Toyotarō recovers the capacity to look inward at himself with gentle acceptance. For Toyotarō, the "wistful sadness" in Elise's eyes was like a faint light in the darkness of his heart, a minute point of light that made the profundity of that darkness all the more perceptible. The riddle at the heart of the maze into which Toyotarō strays stands in inverse relation to the riddle posed by Elise's gaze; the labyrinth of narrow alleyways he enters with Elise as his guide can be read as a form of initiation that transmutes the process of descending to the deep unconscious into a spatial dimension. The ecstasy that comes on Toyotarō each time he lingers in that "gloomy passage" of the Kloster quarter prefigures his experience of the labyrinth—an experience anticipated not by the objectifying eye but by the dream gaze.

Elise serves a double role as the one who guides Toyotarō into the labyrinth and as the enigmatic female figure hidden in its secret center. Before Toyotarō is able to get a close-up look at Elise's "palid skin" with its "faint blush" in the lamplight of her garret room, he must cross one boundary after another, each marking the limits of another layer of convoluted space. From the door of the church and the large entranceway across the road, to the entrance of the Weigert home, and from there to the door of Elise's bedroom— Toyotarō follows Elise through a series of doorways, lured into the depths of a labyrinth turning in upon itself in the form of a spiral. Kobori Keiichirō observes that this particular part of the text "impresses the reader with a precision of detail that goes beyond the usual demands of literature," and creates "a sense that the author has used his pen to reclaim 'things German' as his own, to resurrect his remembrances of German life with words."[47] Although I agree with Kobori's views here, I would also propose that the subtlety of this descriptive passage is directly related to Ōgai's desire to reproduce the space of the labyrinth on paper. As one significant example, the final version reads, "Through a large door across the road from the church was a flight of old worn stone steps. Up these steps on the third floor was a door so small that one needed to bend down to enter."[48] In an early draft of the story, Ōgai described the way to Elise's rooms in slightly different terms: "Through a large door across the road from the church, in back of another house was a multistoried tenement, its walls blackened with soot; these walls surrounded an inner courtyard where a garbage bin stood in one corner. Still, considering the neighborhood, the courtyard was relatively clean. Up a flight of stone steps was a doorway that looked as if one would have to stoop down low to get through." Here we have a description that accurately captures the maze-like structure of these back-alley tenements. As Kobori explains, Ōgai ultimately cut this particular passage from the final draft because it was at odds with the idea of having Elise live in a fourth-floor attic room. Nevertheless, the early draft allows us to clearly decipher Ōgai's secret intent to hide this lovely young girl away in the depths of a space layered in upon itself. But whether we look at early drafts of the story, or at the meticulous account of the layout and furnishings of the three rooms in the description of Elise's home, the text seems to be getting at something that goes far beyond the restraints of realism. Rather, the descriptive detail appears to be a technique for revealing the vicissitudes of Toyotarō's interiority by working backward through a chain of glimmering lights along his path. Invited at last into Elise's room, Toyotarō describes the room in these terms: "[She] led me to an attic; it faced onto the street and had no real ceiling. The beams sloping down from the corners of the roof to the window were covered with paper, and below that, where there was only room enough to stoop, was a bed. On the table in the middle of the room was spread a beautiful woolen cloth on which were arranged two books, a photograph album, and a vase with a bunch of flowers. They seemed somehow too expensive for the place. Standing shyly beside the table was the girl."[49] The expensive vase that decorates this attic room might possibly be a sign of Elise's moral purity and aesthetic sensitivity. On the other hand, it could have been a gift from a frequent visitor to the backstage dressing rooms of the Viktoria Theater. In any case, there is something suspicious about that particular arrangement of elegant table covering, vase, books, and album. For Elise, whose only access to books had been the few novels brought by the "traveling book-lender," what could possibly be the meaning of these "two volumes" carefully placed upon "a beautiful woolen" cloth? The family photograph album, a replacement for the miniature portrait painting, was a petit bourgeois accoutrement that allowed for an illusory recovery of vanished family ties. As Benjamin describes in his "Little History of Photography," "[These albums] were most at home in the chilliest spots, on occasional tables or little stands in the drawing room—leather-bound tomes with repellent metal hasps and those gilt-edged pages as thick as your fingers."[50] Normally, next to the album there would be a vase with flowers serving as a humble memorial to the dead. This assemblage of *things* amounted to a dubious imitation patched together from the ruins of a petit bourgeois life, and it is this very *counterfeit* quality that makes the wretched poverty of Elise's attic room so glaringly conspicuous. No doubt, the hasty improvisation was staged specifically to receive the manager of the Viktoria Theater, whose single desire was to rob Elise of her virginity.[51]

Along the same lines, but even more horrifying, is the spatial configuration that juxtaposes the bed on which Elise was expected to yield her body to the manager—the bed beneath the attic beams—with another bed where the dead man has been laid out on a white sheet. And was it not in this place tainted by the smell of putrefying flesh that Elise anticipated sharing her bed with Toyotarō instead? Against the backdrop of this grotesque interior scene where sex and death intermingle, as Elise's fragile beauty becomes all the more radiant—here in this labyrinthine space, the most unfathomable of temptations lies in wait.

At this early stage, Toyotarō, offering a simple watch to stand as his personal guarantee, is still capable of evading temptation. He persuades himself to extend this service precisely because he sees himself as the "knight in shining armor" who has come to the rescue of a desperately wretched young girl. But what actually moves Toyotarō even more powerfully is a voice that comes from the depths of his heart—this heart of his already captivated by Elise's beguiling beauty. Just when we have decided that Elise is an innocent young girl seeking a savior, she appears in a different guise, reflected against the backdrop of the bed in the attic room, as a lovely young woman who casts a *look* of "irresistible appeal" in Toyotarō's direction. This vaguely enigmatic figure stands in direct relation to the rigidity and immaturity of Toyotarō himself, who possesses neither the courage to respond to the invitations of the women in the cafés "soliciting for customers" nor the freedom of spirit to open himself to the various pleasures promised by the city. The fear accompanying his first glimpse of strictly forbidden territory is superimposed upon the image of Elise, thus blurring the outlines of his object of desire. The mother who greets Elise on her return home is depicted as an old woman: "Although her hair was graying and her brow clearly showed the traces of poverty and suffering, it was not an evil face."[52] This slightly repugnant image, operating ambiguously as Elise's *shadow*, can be read as one more metaphor that serves to intensify the meaning of Toyotarō's labyrinthine experience. Elise's dwelling place, first rendered as a labyrinth that offers glimpses into the depths of Toyotarō's unconscious, is soon revealed to us in another form: as a refuge where his wounded being is enfolded in a soothing embrace. In a similar vein, Toyotarō first encounters Elise as an enigmatic, dreamlike woman who offers him salvation; but his image of her undergoes a transformation as she assumes the guise of a wholesome helpmate who contributes to their shared household.[53]

However, before Toyotarō can enter into a communal life with Elise, he must pass through a number of trials: the slander of his fellow countrymen; the humiliating dismissal from his official post; and, overlapping with these affronts, the news of his mother's death. For Toyotarō, the enticement of Elise's *gaze* was no different from the "evil fate" that drew him into the plot hatched by his fellow students; furthermore, his sexual liaison with Elise begins in the vaguest of circumstances: "The way she stood there, a picture of loveliness, her hair hanging loose—I was distraught by so much suffering and powerless in the face of such enchantment." In order for Toyotarō, who is fundamentally weak in character, to enter into a fully embodied relationship with Elise, he must "be distraught by . . . suffering."[54] The state of "enchantment" that renders him powerless corresponds on a formal level to the feverish state of illness into which he falls at the end of "The Dancing Girl." While Toyotarō lies unconscious in his sickbed, his friend, Aizawa Kenkichi, takes the liberty of settling his accounts with Elise.

As I mentioned earlier, the topography of "The Dancing Girl" can be summed up schematically as follows: Toyotarō moves from exterior into interior space; he passes through a period of cohabitation with Elise; he finally returns once again to exterior space. Following the implications of this schema, the series of crises that draws the protagonist progressively deeper into the seductive territory of the maze and the ambiguous circumstances under which he becomes sexually involved with Elise all function as signs indicating the boundary between exterior and interior space—a boundary he is compelled to cross. In contrast, the fever that overcomes Toyotarō in the end is clearly the sign of plot reversal marking the crossing of the boundary back once again from interior to exterior space. Though the direction is reversed, the state of suspension that Toyotarō must experience whenever he crosses the boundary demonstrates that the period he spent with Elise, when they "managed, even in the midst of all [their] troubles, to enjoy life," was, in fact, a time enclosed within a closed circle without exit. In Elise's home, the period during which the two lived together constituted a sealed world sublimated in an unreal dream time.

Toyotarō, who has found work as a foreign correspondent for a newspaper through the intercession of Aizawa Kenkichi, spends his time in a café on Königsstrasse in search of material for articles. Unlike the cafés on the main avenues where lively social exchange takes place, this particular café is a seedy establishment, a haunt for young men without regular work and old men living on pensions. Beholden to the dim light that seeps in from "an open skylight," Toyotarō leafs through the newspapers on hand at the café, jotting down excerpts from various articles. The cave-like image of the café "with its narrow frontage and its long deep interior" where Toyotarō spends his daytime hours can be taken as a slightly altered, metaphorical substitute for the image of Elise's dwelling. The attic room, where the precious nighttime hours belong to Toyotarō and Elise alone, is illuminated by warm lamplight: "When she came home from the theater, Elise would sit in a chair and sew, and I would write my articles on the table by her side using the faint light of the lamp hanging from the ceiling." This "lamp hanging from the ceiling" of the attic room, an image expressing the discreet love shared by these two in the shelter of her abode, is like a single crimson thread woven through the fabric of the text. On the day Elise sends Toyotarō off to Russia, however, the image of the lamp is suddenly transformed, and Elise is tormented by the "unaccustomed sadness of sitting alone by lamplight."[55] Bachelard claims that the lamp "is the center of a dwelling, of every dwelling."[56] If this is so, we might conclude that the lamp in the attic room, now drained of all warmth, suggests that Toyotarō's absence has infiltrated their dream-filled dwelling and penetrated the very core of Elise's being.

It is generally acknowledged in discussions of "The Dancing Girl" that the line "Then came the winter of 1888" signals the onset of another kind of temporality. It indicates the turning point in the narrative when the dream-like time that Toyotarō and Elise have passed together begins to unravel under the assault of a new temporality rooted in a harsh reality. Invisible fissures begin to weaken the domestic sphere that has sheltered the lives of these two from the outside world: "Then came the winter of 1888. They spread grit on the pavements of the main streets and shoveled the snow into piles. Although the ground in the Klosterstrasse area was bumpy and uneven, the surface became smooth with ice. It was sad to see the starved sparrows frozen to death on the ground when you opened the door in the mornings. We lit a fire in the stove to warm the room, but it was till unbearably cold. The north European winter penetrated the stone walls and pierced our cotton clothes."⁵⁷ The severe climate of northern Europe, pressing in on the interior space in which Toyotarō and Elise have secluded themselves, symbolizes an external space about to break through their protective perimeter. Once the external world is completely covered over with snow and ice, the interior of the dwelling should, by rights, become a self-contained universe—a welcome place of warmth and repose. Yet, it is precisely at this juncture, when Elise first discovers that she may be pregnant, that a letter from Aizawa Kenkichi arrives urging Toyotarō to come to the Kaiserhof to meet the count. Here the narrative structure operates with consummate precision and ingenuity: just at the moment when, for the sake of the child to be born, Elise has no choice but to spend her days *in confinement*, a force begins to operate that draws Toyotarō back toward the external world. When the droshky arrives to take Toyotarō to the Kaiserhof, Elise opens the ice-covered window, her undone hair blowing in the freezing wind; but as she sees her man off, his figure has already hardened into its official persona. Elise, on the other hand, has become the image of what Bachelard calls "the maternality of the dwelling." The window, the "eye" of the house, is superimposed on Elise's own gaze, her body shaken by an ominous presentiment that she is soon to be torn from Toyotarō's side.

In the late nineteenth century, the Kaiserhof, rising up on one side of Wilhelmplatz at the southernmost end of Unter den Linden, was Berlin's most elegant hotel. Toyotarō describes his entry into this imposing place: "I climbed the marble staircase. It had been a long time since I had last been there." As his own words suggest, as soon as he sets foot in the Kaiserhof, which stands as an extension of the monumental space of Unter den Linden, a conflict begins to mount in his heart. The contrast between the small stove in Elise's room and the "big tiled stove" that warmed the dining room of the Kaiserhof is a particularly pointed one, as is the contrast between Aizawa's cheerful candor and Toyotarō's meek hesitancy. The latter finds himself readily agreeing both to the translation assignment entrusted him by the count and to Aizawa's advice that he break off all relations with Elise; but it is only when he walks out of the hotel into a bracing wind that Toyotarō finally comes fully to his senses. As the early evening chill of a wintry Berlin pierces his thin overcoat, Toyotarō feels "a strange chill in [his] heart as well."⁵⁸ According to Takemori Tenyū, the movement between "a strange chill" and the "big tiled stove" symbolizes Toyotarō's attempt to fix his mind on the prospect of a secure and comfortable life as represented by Aizawa and the Kaiserhof.⁵⁹ On the other hand, if we think about the way the textual structure of "The

Dancing Girl" is divided into two distinct spatial registers, the same images can also be read as a portent of Toyotarō's fate to be cast out of the warmth of interior space into the cold of exterior space. Recognizing his superior capabilities, the count has entrusted him with a translation assignment; it should be noted, however, that Toyotarō has been given a second task: to accompany the count to the "ice palace" in St. Petersburg. He returns to Klosterstrasse on New Year's Day to find that "the snow on the road had frozen hard into ruts in the bitter cold and shone brightly in the sunlight."[60] About to step into the frigid embrace of a world of ice and snow, Toyotarō begins to distance himself, little by little, from the small world in which Elise has confined herself. Elise takes Toyotarō, just home from St. Petersburg, into their room. Picking up a baby diaper, she begins to talk about the future of the child soon to be born; Toyotarō utters not a single word in response. His only reaction is one of surprise at the sight of white cotton and lace heaped up on the table. Before Toyotarō's trip to Russia, Elise had been dismissed from the Viktoria Theater on the pretext that she had been absent for too long. As the narrative of the second half of "The Dancing Girl" unfolds, the expansion of Toyotarō's sphere of action and the narrowing of Elise's sphere of daily life each proceed with gathering speed; both movements stand out in clear outline against the urban topography drawn by the catastrophe that brings "The Dancing Girl" to an end. As Toyotarō staggers through the streets of Berlin delirious with fever, what appears before his eyes is an urban landscape fallen to pieces.

Having acceded to the count's order that he return to Japan in his employ, Toyotarō finds himself wandering through the darkened city, his mind falling ever deeper into "indescribable turmoil." The area of the city he covers in his wandering turns out to be exactly the same district he once looked out on with great ambitions burning in his breast: Unter den Linden and the Brandenburg Gate. But for Toyotarō, now tormented by his guilt over having betrayed Elise, the "sea of lights" has been reduced to a vacant landscape that has lost all definition. Interestingly, in this penultimate scene, Toyotarō retraces his steps beginning from the Tiergarten and ending at Klosterstrasse—the same route he took when he first encountered Elise. This doubling back of the text over the same ground suggests something more than mere coincidence; at the very least, the image of warm lamplight still burning in the Klosterstrasse attic room seems to call up from the depths of the past Elise's *gaze*, "blue and clear," as she lingered in the doorway of the church. "In the fourth-floor attic Elise was evidently not yet asleep, for a bright gleam of light shone out into the night sky. The falling snowflakes were like a flock of small white birds, and the light kept on disappearing and reappearing as if the plaything of the wind."[61] That "bright gleam of light" must have awakened in Toyotarō a now distant memory of how he had once been so stirred by the "wistful sadness" in Elise's expectant gaze. Her gaze, and the gleam of light that evokes its memory, is itself a sorrowful question, a poignant appeal, addressed to Toyotarō from Elise. But Toyotarō has already abandoned the warm comfort of the Klosterstrasse refuge in his firm resolve to return to the cold external world; he is no longer permitted to respond to Elise's question. Blown about by the snowy winds of a harsh winter, the flickering flame in the attic room stove is a sign that all traces of his existence are soon to disappear from the world of Berlin.

Notes

1 First appearing in *Bungaku*, September 1980, the text used for this translation is from Maeda Ai, *Toshi kūkan no naka no bungaku* (Chikuma Shobō, 1982), 213–249. I am indebted to Junko Matsuura, who demonstrated skill and perseverance in tracking down even the most arcane references for this translation.

2 Karl Baedeker, *Berlin and Its Environs: Handbook for Travellers*, 3d ed. (Leipzig: Karl Baedeker Publishers, 1885), 108. (M)

3 Dolf Sternberger, *Panorama of the 19th Century* (New York: Urizen Books, 1977), 7–16; translated from the original German, *Panorama oder Ansichten vom 19. Jahrhundert* (Hamburg, 1955). (M)

4 Mori Ōgai, "Doitsu nikki," *Ōgai zenshū* (Iwanami Shoten, 1975), 35:162.

5 Mori Ōgai, "Maihime: The Dancing Girl," trans. Richard Bowring, in *"Youth" and Other Stories*, ed. J. Thomas Rimer (Honolulu: University of Hawaii Press, 1994), 9.

6 Kume Kunitake, ed., *Tokumei zenken taishi: Beiō kairan jikki* (Record of travels to America and Europe by the Japanese envoy extraordinary and ambassador plenipotentiary), 5 vols (Iwanami Shoten, 1979); originally published by Hakubunsha, 1878. (M)

7 Mori Ōgai, "Fushinchū," in *Ōgai zenshū*, vol. 7 (Iwanami shoten, 1972), originally published in 1910; translated as "Under Reconstruction" by Ivan Morris in *Youth and Other Stories*, ed. J. Thomas Rimer (Honolulu: School of Hawaiian, Asian and Pacific Studies, University of Hawaii, 1994), 148–153.

8 In response to the advice of the royal physician that he give up this daily routine, the aging kaiser is said to have responded as follows: "As long as my daily appearance is recorded in Baedeker's *Handbook*, it wouldn't do for me to disappoint people's expectations." Alois Metz, *Berlin* (London, 1911), 34.

9 Henry Vizetelly, *Berlin under the New Empire* (New York: Greenwood, 1968), 1:179; originally published by Tinslex Bros., London, 1879, 2 vols. (M)

10 Walter Benjamin, *Berliner Kindheit um Neunzehnhundert* (Frankfurt am Main: Suhrkamp Verlag, 1950), 18–19. (M)

11 Lewis Mumford, *The City in History: Its Origins, Its Transformations, Its Prospects* (New York: Harcourt, Brace, and World, 1961), 370. (M)

12 Ōgai, "Maihime: The Dancing Girl" (hereafter "Maihime"), 9.

13 *The Iwakura Embassy 1871–73: A True Account of the Ambassador Extraordinary and Plenipotentiary's Journey of Observation through the United States of America and Europe*, comp. Kume Kunitake, ed. Graham Healey and Chushichi Tsuzuki, trans. Andrew Cobbing (Chiba: Japan Documents, 2002), 3:304.

14 Vizetelly, *Berlin under the New Empire*, 1:181–182. (M)

15 Ibid., 2:255. (M) [I have been unable to locate information on a play by Porte Saint Martin with a title approximating Maeda's rendition of the title as *Hakubyō* (The white cat); but the original story that provided material for this play may have been "La Chatte Blanche" by Madame d'Aulnoy (1650–1705).

16 Jean-Jacques Origas, "'Kumode' no machi," *Kikan geijutsu* 24 (1973). (M) Also in *Natsume Sōseki zenshū* (Kadokawa Shoten, 1975), 16:308–309.

17 Erwin Panovsky, *Perspective as Symbolic Form* (New York: Zone Books, 1991), translated by Kota Hajime as *Shōchō keishiki toshite no enkinhō* in *Gendai shisō* 4 (1974). (M)

18 Ōkubo Takaaki, *Yume to seijuku: Bungaku-teki seiyō-zō no henbō* (Kōdansha, 1979), 26. (M)

19 Honoré de Balzac, *The Works of Honoré de Balzac: Father Goriot (Le Père Goriot) and Other Stories*, trans. Ellen Marriage and James Waring (New York: Fred De-Fau, 1901), 285.

20 "Maihime," 9–11.

21 This analytic description of Unter den Linden from on high is not unrelated to Ōgai's practiced skill in the kind of thinking that captures urban structure from the perspective of public health. For example, in his "Outline for Urban Improvement" in *Kokumin no tomo* 73 (13 February 1880), Ōgai expounds on city streets as follows: "The street comprises a single unit accommodating a maximum number of vehicles, each vehicle width measured by its axle-length. In addition to this standard, [city planners] should ensure that the street receives ample natural light and circulation of fresh air. If the vertical height of buildings exceeds the width of the street, the resulting gloom will take a toll on the quality of life. As with light, air should circulate freely through the street. In the event that the street is wider than required by the above standards, even if it is paved or regularly washed down, the excess area simply becomes a source of dust and grime." (M)

22 Ernst B. Gilman, *The Curious Perspective* (New Haven: Yale University Press, 1978), 29. (M)

23 Gorgy Kepes, *Language of Vision* (Chicago: University of Chicago Press, 1944), 86. (M)

24 Panovsky, *Perspective as Symbolic Form*, 30–31. (M)

25 Kume Kunitake, ed., *Tokumei zenken taishi: Beiō kairan jikki* (Munetaka Shobō, 1975), 3:337.

26 Vizetelly, *Berlin under the New Empire*, 1:165. (M)

27 Ibid.

28 Melville C. Branch, *Comparative Urban Design: Rare Engravings, 1830–1843* (New York: Arno, 1978), 29. (M)

29 Vizetelly, *Berlin under the New Empire*, 2:224. (M)

30 Baron Georges Eugene Haussmann (1809–1891), French civic official and city planner who spent seventeen years (1853–70) transforming the face of Paris under Napoleon III.

31 Walter Henry Nelson, *The Berliners: Their Saga and Their City* (New York: P. Mckey, 1969), 84. (M)

32 Friedrich Engels, *The Housing Question* (New York: International Publishers, 1935).

33 Theodor Fontane, *Jenny Treibel*, trans. Ulf Zimmermann (New York: Frederick Ungar, 1976); originally published as *Frau Jenny Treibel*.

34 Wilhelm Karl Raabe, *Die Chronik der Sperlingsgasse* (Berlin: Grote, 1908), 8–10. Maeda relied on the Japanese translation by Itō Takeo. I, in turn, am indebted to my colleague in Germanic studies, Helmut Puff, for helping me to decipher the original German in gothic script.

35 Yuri M. Lotman, *Universe of the Mind: A Semiotic Theory of Culture*, trans. Ann Shukman (London: I. B. Tauris, 1990), 131.

36 Raabe, *Die Chronik der Sperlingsgasse*, 7–8.

37 "Maihime," 12.

38 Vizetelly, *Berlin under the New Empire*, 1:22. (M)

39 *Berliner Pflaster* (Berlin: W. Pauli), 1894, 26. In addition, in the passage from "The Dancing Girl" that reads "I collected up my things and locked the door on my way out, leaving the key with the cobbler who lived at the entrance in Maihime" (20), the description is suggestive of the Parochialstrasse area where cobblers' shops congregated. (M)

40 Katayama Koson, *Berurin: Tokai bunmei kyūgazu* (Hakubunkan, 1913), 29–30.

41 Ōgai, "Doitsu nikki," in *Ōgai zenshū* (Iwanami Shoten, 1975), 35:166.

42 Among those who have investigated the referent for "the old church in the Kloster district," Kobori Keiichi, in his *Wakaki hi no Mori Ōgai* (1969), identifies it as the Kloster Church, whereas Shinohara Seiei, in "Ōgai to Berurin," in *Ōgai* pp. 5, 6, 9 (May 1969, October 1970, June 1971) and Kawakami Toshiyuki, in "'Maihime' o meguru hochū-teki kōsatsu," *Ōgai* 18 (1976) argue that "the old Church" is actually the Marien Church. Based on the description of a church "that lay set back from the road," Kobori surmises that the reference is not to the Parochial Church, which is actually located on Klosterstrasse, but to the Kloster Church. Shinohara offers the counterargument that the "Kloster district" actually alludes to a neighborhood that would include Klosterstrasse, and that, judging from the order of streets traversed by Ōta Toyotarō, the Marien Church is the most likely reference. Reinforcing the latter explanation, Kawakami adds two further observations. First, at the time of Ōgai's study abroad in Germany, an iron fence running along the front of the Kloster Church would have prevented

outsiders from entering; second, the city streets surrounding the Marien Church took the shape of a U-shape enclosure that corresponds to Ōgai's description of a "church that lay set back from the road." There is no obvious counterargument to Kawakami's first point, but on the second point, Ōgai's phrase, taken at face value, clearly refers to the façade of the church. And if we observe the now war-damaged ruins of the Kloster Church, at the bottom of the stairway down from the level of the main road we can see a recessed rectangular garden in front of the church and, just behind, the entrance. Furthermore, the fact that the Marien Church, despite its location in Alt-Berlin, fronted on Kaiser Wilhelmstrasse, one of Berlin's more prosperous and busy streets, renders the argument in its favor less persuasive. In my view, the following passage from "Maihime" strengthens the case for the Kloster Church: "When Elise had rehearsals, she would call in [at the coffee shop on Königsstrasse at] about one o'clock on her way home." If we assume that Elise stopped at a resting point somewhere along Königsstrasse on her way home from rehearsal at the Viktoria Theater, it makes perfect sense that Elise's home where the two live together lies at the south end of Königs-strasse. (M)

43 One could also read the street patterns of Unter den Linden and Alt-Berlin as an opposition between the "cultural" layer of the city and an even deeper "natural" layer. E. Leach, relying on the analogy of the unifying linguistic function, op-poses "nature," defined as a collection of irregular curved lines, to "culture," iden-tified as a world constructed of geometric figures like straight lines, rectangles, triangles, and circles. Edmund Leach, *Culture and Communication* (Cambridge, England: Cambridge University Press, 1976), 51. (M)

44 Mori Ōgai, "Utakata no ki (A Sad Tale)," trans. Richard Bowring, in *"Youth" and Other Stories*, 27.

45 "Maihime," 10–11.

46 Ibid., 12.

47 Kobori Keiichirō, *Wakaki hi no Mori Ōgai* (Mori Ōgai's early years) (Daigaku Shuppankai, 1969), 501. (M)

48 "Maihime," 13.

49 Ibid.

50 Walter Benjamin, "Kleine Geschichte der Photographie," in *Angelus Novus: Aus-gewählte Schriften 2* (Suhrkamp Verlag, 1966), 244. Maeda used the translation by Nomura Osamu. Translated into English as "Little History of Photography" in *Walter Benjamin: Selected Writings*, vol. 2, *1927–1934*, ed. Michael W. Jennings, Howard Eiland, and Gary Smith (Cambridge, MA: Harvard University Press, 1999), 515.

51 Among those who take up the issue of Elise's prostitute-like role are Shimizu Shi-geru in his "Elise-zō e no ichi shikaku," *Nihon kindai bungaku* 13 (October 1970) and Kawazoe Kunimoto's "*Ki-naru men no Toyotarō*" in *Gendai sakka, sakuhin-ron*, Senuma Shigeki koki kinen ronbun-shū (Kawade Shobo Shinsha, 1974). (M)

52 "Maihime," 14, 11, 13.

53 "(In all cultures, the labyrinth has the meaning of an entangling and confusing representation of the world of matriarchal consciousness; it can be traversed only by those who are ready for a special initiation into the mysterious world of the collective unconscious.) Having overcome this danger, Theseus rescued Ariadne, a maiden in distress." Joseph Henderson in C. G. Jung, ed., *Man and His Symbols* (Garden City, N.Y.: Doubleday, 1971), 125. (M) Maeda used the translation by Kawai Hayao, *Ningen to Shōjō* (Kawade shobo, 1975), 1:197.

54 "Maihime," 15; Togawa Nobusuke, "Ōta Toyotarō no Yūtsu: Ushirometasa ni tsuite," *Bungaku* (November 1972). (M)

55 "Maihime," 16, 20.

56 Gaston Bachelard, *The Flame of a Candle*, trans. Joni Caldwell (Dallas: Dallas Institute, 1988), 11.

57 "Maihime," 17.

58 Ibid., 19.

59 Takemori Tenyū, "Meiji nijūichinen no fuyu: *Maihime* ron," *Kokugo to Kokubungaku* (April 1972): 19. (M)

60 "Maihime," 22.

61 Ibid., 23.

11. In the Recesses of the High City: On Sōseki's *Gate*

(Yamanote no oku)

TRANSLATED BY WILLIAM F. SIBLEY

Mon by Natsume Sōseki (1867–1916)—literally, *The Gate*, though neither the trans-lator of the existing English version nor most Anglophone writers on this text have chosen to call it anything but *Mon*—the main textual focus of this chapter, was first published serially in the *Asahi Shimbun* between March and June 1910. Accord-ing to a critical convention that has long since existed in Japan, *Mon* is averred to be the concluding work of a "trilogy" by Sōseki that begins with *Sanshirō* (1908), with *Sore kara* (*And Then*, as it has been translated) forming the middle volume. Although as far as I know Sōseki himself never used this designation, and though its near-universal usage by Japanese critics and literary historians runs counter in some basic ways to protocols observed by Euro-American criticism with re-spect to such designations, to many of those who have read all three works some solid justifications for the designation will be apparent, if not persuasive enough for others.

Maeda, without committing himself explicitly to the notion of the trilogy, does refer here with some frequency along the way to both *Sanshirō* and *Sore kara*. A curious circumstance surrounding the writing of *Mon*, which he does not men-tion here (though he does, briefly, in the posthumously published draft of a work entitled *Bungaku tekusuto nyūmon* [A primer on literary texts]), is that Sōseki him-self, being at the time too busy to supply in advance a title for his forthcoming work to be serialized in the *Asahi Shimbun*, directed a couple of his young asso-ciates (*deshi*, customarily rendered as "disciples," in a premodern usage that he eschewed) to concoct one, without giving them any idea of so much as a basic outline of the work; they chose *Mon*. The eponymous "Gate" is indeed brought in toward the end of the novel, in the episode where the protagonist Sōsuke makes a brief retreat to a Zen temple in Kamakura. Although, as can be seen below, Maeda somewhat brusquely disparages various critics who have expatiated on the sig-nificance of this finally futile retreat, he clearly does not do so on the basis of chalking the episode up to Sōseki's need to justify the title that his devotees had invented. Rather, it would seem, though readers of this essay should of course judge for themselves, that Maeda considers the rarefied atmosphere surrounding Zen too remote from the here and now, which in customary fashion he analyzes so acutely apropos this text, to be accessible to the likes of Sōsuke, who, like most of us, has no choice but to live through the vicissitudes of life in this mundane realm.[1]

1

Tayama Katai's *Thirty Years in Tokyo* [*Tōkyō no sanjūnen*] is a superb literary memoir that impressionistically chronicles the ebb and flow of power within the *bundan* [literary guild], between the high tide of the Ken'yūsha (Friends of the Inkpot) and the rise of naturalism. But in the background of the portraits of various writers, their careers now waxing, now waning, there emerges in clear relief the diverse neighborhoods of Tokyo that encompassed Katai's ceaseless struggles as an aspiring writer, and in particular a montage of the *yamanote* [the "High City" or uplands that form the western part of Tokyo, settled by the middle- and higher-ranking samurai during Tokugawa rule] as, inundated by successive waves of modernization, it underwent vertiginous changes. Katai's characteristic elegiac "tempus fugit" tone, and his customary sentimentality, are here transcended through the contrapuntal treatments of the "portraits" and the "place."

It was 1886 when, upon his brother Miyato's appointment to the Bureau of Historical Documents (the precursor of the *Shiryō hensanjo* at Tokyo University), Katai left his native Tatebayashi and moved his family to Tokyo, where they took up temporary lodgings at the former Aizu daimyo's residence in Ushigome Tomihisa-chō. Over the next twenty years or so, until he bought his first new house in Yoyogi San'ya, Katai moved repeatedly, while remaining throughout an inhabitant of the yamanote. With the exception of a brief residence in Yotsuya Naitō-machi, he stuck to Ushigome Ward (Tomihisa-chō, Nando-machi, Kōra-machi, Kikui-chō, Yakuōji-chō, Bentenchō, Yamabushi-chō, etc.). Or, to put it more precisely, through all the moves he remained located within a trapezoid whose four corners were formed by Kagurazaka, the Army Officers' Academy, the Ichigaya Penitentiary, and the Toyama Army Training Center. Around the time Katai first took up residence in the yamanote, that is, 1887, the environs of Ushigome Ward, which he describes as displaying a decaying, overgrown panorama—"though beginning to be developed, still retaining the old yamanote open fields and steep hills, with plenty of groves, forests, even sunken ponds in the midst of overgrown estates that no one knew about, and in the remote corners of Ushi-gome, nightly sightings of foxes and badgers"[2]—was in fact already being gradually built up around the district that extended from Waseda to Ōkubo as a new residential area designed for military officers and government offi-cials. Kagurazaka, with its festivals at the Bishamon shrine, was emerging as one of the few commercial and entertainment centers readily accessible to the inhabitants of Ushigome, in no small measure because of the convenient transportation afforded by the station on the Kōbu Line[3] that had opened here.

Katai sums up the contrast between the stagnant but stable lives of *shita-machi* [the "Low City"][4] dwellers, bogged down in their traditional commu-nal customs, and the unstable but dazzlingly novel lifestyles that were emerg-ing in the yamanote: "The yamanote is a giant whirlpool of lives led by men who have come from nowhere, lives fraught with unforeseeable difficulties but, surrounded by their cheerful wives and young families, full of great ex-pectations for the future. Witness the plethora of inexpensive furniture stores aimed at starter households, butcher shops selling beef by the slice, cheap Western-style eateries, and the like which abound in Ushigome."[5] This pic-ture of an urban lifestyle as at the same time rather frugal and slightly fancy,[6] no doubt represents a collage combining Katai's earliest observations of the yamanote, from the 1880s with those of the 1910s. But aside from such pano-ramas, Katai's account focuses, as on a distant mirage, on his own melancholy existence between adolescence and maturity as a long-suffering apprentice writer laboring under the stern rule of the literary guild. The rented house in Nando-machi consisted of three rooms, measuring two, six, and four-and-a-half tatami mats; the one in Kōra-machi, with two rooms, of six and eight mats, cost 7 yen a month—a serious burden, as his family had to subsist on whatever Katai's brother could spare from his meager wages. Their daily fare was a far cry from sliced beef: "mostly pickled radish and sliced ginger fin-ished off with coarse, scratchy rice," with occasional "treats" of bean curd, whether plain square "servant style" or deep-fat fried. As he pursued his pro-tracted apprenticeship in the midst of such penury, the sight of the elegant residences of army officers and high-ranking bureaucrats stretching out over the upper ridges of the yamanote, the sound of the *koto* plucked by their pretty young daughters, afforded Katai ample opportunities to feel both envy and shame. This resentment-tinted gaze at the city is a subtext in his story "Girl Crazy" [or perhaps "Nymphettomania"; "Shōjobyō"],[8] always cited as one of his most promising early works. *Thirty Years in Tokyo* presents a vivid pic-ture of the way the parallel microcosm of the shabby rental houses, cheek by jowl along the backstreets, gradually encroached on the world of sun-drenched mansions arrayed across the bucolic upper reaches of Tokyo's west-ern suburbs.

In the yamanote of the Meiji period Koishikawa Ward sustained the great-est growth in population; Ushigome came next. In the thirty years between 1883 and the end of Meiji, it has been calculated that the population of Koi-shikawa quadrupled.[8] This district had been full of daimyo mansions in the Edo period and was targeted right after the Restoration by the government's program to turn these areas over to the cultivation of mulberry trees (for seri-culture) and tea bushes. Along the Sengawa aqueduct, wedged between the Hongō and Koishikawa ridges, the vales that undulated from Yanagi-machi to Hakusan were for a time even covered with rice paddies. The Meishuya dis-trict, the setting for Higuchi Ichiyō's "Troubled Waters" ["Nigorie"], stood on filled-in paddies that had been newly "reclaimed" as part of the reurban-ization of this area that took place around 1892–93.

Meanwhile, the population growth in those parts of the yamanote that en-circled the old city center, particularly the residential areas along the western borders (Shinagawa, Ōsaki, Shibuya, Sendagaya, Yodobashi, Ōkubo-mura, Takada-mura, Tozuka-mura, etc., roughly arrayed around what was to be-come the Yamanote "Loop Line"), lagged somewhat behind that of Koishi-kawa and Ushigome. Not until the years around the Russo-Japanese War did these areas experience explosive growth, for example, 90 percent between 1903 and 1908, and another 70 percent over the next five years, into early Tai-shō (1912–26).[9] A major spur to such growth was of course the completion of a large-scale network of intraurban public transport: the city street railway that opened in 1903; the electrification of the Yamanote Loop Line in 1910; and the connection through to the city center provided by the Chūō Line, which opened between Shinjuku and Manseibashi in 1912. Next came the de-velopment of new streetcar lines that intersected with various stations along the Yamanote Line, such as, by 1910, those at Sugamo, Ōtsuka, Shinjuku, Shi-buya, Ebisu, and Meguro. As Katai sums up the diverse urban phenomena that were accelerated by the Tokyo street railways, "With the proliferation of streetcars, there was a gradual shift in the commercial and entertainment centers around the city. Suburbanites stopped shopping at their local mar-kets, instead taking the streetcars into the city center. Such former custom-made clothing stores as Shirokiya, Matsuya, etc. were then transformed into massive department stores. In particular, the junctures and terminals of these lines, where many passengers had to get off the streetcars, plundered, so to speak, the business of the old commercial centers, until the whole face of the city was changed."[10]

The kind of drastic changes in the spaces between the Yamanote Line and the western suburbs that were sketched out in *Thirty Years in Tokyo* can also be seen in such works as Kunikida Doppo's "Tragic Death" ["Kyūshi"], wherein the crushed body of a day laborer suffering from tuberculosis is found on the railroad tracks near Ōkubo, "where the broad fields glistened with young leaves and fresh grasses"; and his "Bamboo Gate" ["Take no kido"], which gives a memorable description of the progressive erosion of communal life in the outlying suburbs. Other examples could include Shirayanagi Shūko's (1884–1950) "Diary of a Station Worker," in which the coming of age of a young railway worker is interwoven with an impressionistic season-by-season sketching of the suburban scenery. But among contemporary writers, it was Natsume Sōseki who scrutinized most closely, even obsessively, the significance of the reconfigurations of yamanote space and of the different lifestyles that proceeded to develop there.

Through Sōseki's eyes, as through Katai's, one sees clearly the complex mosaic of the yamanote neighborhoods: the tranquil blocks of substantial dwellings over whose brick and stone walls waft the strains of koto and piano; the densely packed new development of cheap rental houses. Especially in the works beginning with the trilogy (viz., *Sanshirō*, *And Then* [*Sorekara*], and *The Gate* [*Mon*]) and ending with *Until after the Equinox* [*Higansugi made*], a firmly delineated drama ensues within the setting of the yamanote space, with contrasting roles played by the prosperous original inhabitants and the newcomers seeking to make their way in the world. Satomi Miyako in *Sanshirō* and Daisuke of *And Then* belong to the former category; Sanshirō in his student lodgings and Hiraoka (in *And Then*), who has quit his life in the provinces to return to Tokyo, to the latter. In the case of *Until after the Equinox*, there is the contrast between Sunaga, who lives an isolated life with his mother in an old-style house, surrounded by a wooden fence topped by the traditional axe cuts and jagged shards of glass, and Keitarō, that budding detective of urban space, whose future in the new middle-class elite has been assured by the backing of the businessman Taguchi. This novel can be read as a tale that, starting from the provincial Keitarō's surreptitious explorations of the yamanote surfaces, proceeds to examine the deep-rooted bonds in which its original inhabitants are enmeshed.

Up from Kyushu, Sanshirō is gradually inducted by his classmate Yotarō into a circle of yamanote intellectuals that includes Hirota Sensei, Nonomiya and his sister Miyako, and the painter Haraguchi. Their dwellings, understated but exuding a certain aura of refinement, are perfect examples of late Meiji yamanote domiciles. Take, for example, the house in the tenth block of Nishikata-machi to which Hirota Sensei moves, assisted by Sanshirō and others, on the Emperor's Birthday holiday (3 November): "In place of a *gen-*

kan [entryway], at the front protruded a Western-style room, joined at one corner to a Japanese-style sitting room, beyond which lay a dining room, and across from that a suite composed of kitchen and maid's room. There was also a second story. What the total square footage came to, he could not tell." A house of five or six rooms, then, with altogether around 800 square feet of living space—such was the rental house that a bachelor high school teacher had for 25 yen a month. This type of layout, a modest-size painted wooden Western-style room at the front with traditional Japanese-style rooms attached, was the latest thing in yamanote domestic architecture of this era. In particular, the inclusion of a study and a maid's room was, as we can see from the house of Kushami in "I Am a Cat" ["Wagahai wa neko de aru"], de rigueur: a kind of class badge for the Meiji bourgeoisie.

Miyako's house in Masago-chō is approached through a tile-roofed gate, down a path of some length, to a latticework door, complete with doorbell, to the entryway [genkan]. The Western-style room to which Sanshirō is first led has imposing wall decorations, a recessed fireplace, an oblong mirror, and a candelabrum. From somewhere deep inside the house a violin tune, played by Miyako, is faintly audible. Sanshirō's bewildered fascination with such novel accoutrements as the fireplace and the violin no doubt reflects a typical response by contemporary readers of newspapers to the type of lifestyle that was just then taking root in the yamanote.

Daisuke of *And Then* is entrusted by his father with a free-standing house located somewhere in the hollow formed by Fukuro-machi, off to the south side of hilly Kagurazaka; the main family residence is in Aoyama. Daisuke is not one to be intimidated about attending, in company with his older brother, a formal garden party at an Azabu mansion; when his father and brother arrange for a first meeting with a prospective bride for him, it takes place at the Kabukiza. In preparation for a trip, he thinks nothing of going off to Shiseidō on the Ginza to buy toothpaste and is quite blasé about inviting his sister-in-law to a "Western concert." In contrast to Daisuke's upper-class man-about-town lifestyle, that of the Hiraoka couple in their rented house in Sōji-machi [literally, "the Sweep-up" district] in Koishikawa appears teminally shabby. The Hiraokas' house presents a façade sufficiently shoddy to bear witness to more than a decade of escalating prices that pressed ever harder on the middle classes. Daisuke is appalled by it:

> It was barely twelve feet from the gate to the entranceway, and about the same around to the kitchen door. Behind and to both sides of the Hiraoka house stood identically cramped houses. They served as monuments to this version of the survival-of-the-fittest, in which bottom-

feeding capitalists, seizing the opportunity of Tokyo's explosive but severely underfunded growth, turned usurious profits of 20–30 percent on their meager investments in the cheapest, jerry-built housing. Tokyo was currently jammed with these shoddy structures, particularly out along the city outskirts. And they continued to multiply like clouds of fleas in the rainy season. Daisuke had some time ago termed this the progress of defeat, and seen it as a perfect emblem of contemporary Japan.[11]

This is a good example of Daisuke's characteristic way of elevating passing observations into a kind of cultural criticism, one that naturally ignores the point of view of such as Hiraoka, who is forced to dwell behind the "terminally shabby façade." No more than Hiraoka can understand Daisuke's "aesthetic life" can Daisuke empathize with the realities that Hiraoka must face on a daily basis. The chasm separating the two is inscribed in the passage where Daisuke gazes down from the high eminence of the Denzūin on the munitions factories with their belching smokestacks: "He looked down and reflected on the ugliness of these factories and their belabored exhalations, all for the sake of mere survival. In the murky depths of his consciousness he involuntarily yoked the Hiraokas, who lived down there somewhere, to the smokestacks."[12]

While fixing his gaze on the ugly cityscape of the "residential space" in which Michiyo was trapped with Hiraoka, Daisuke also conjures up the wider panorama of the "two parallel neighborhoods" divided by a fissure that ran straight through the yamanote. Daisuke's own house is located on Waradana Street at the very top of Jizō Hill, therefore adjacent to the impressive residences of Naka-machi: the same district where the adolescent Katai's fantasies had been aroused by glimpses of the pretty young girls who lived there. The twin poles of Daisuke's stylish house, paid for by his father, right next to Kagurazaka, which was then the yamanote's most thriving commercial and entertainment center, and the Hiraokas' rental house on the fringe of the working-class neighborhoods shaded by the tall smokestacks of munitions factory, with the deep folds traversing the valleys along the Edo River along which Daisuke and Michiyo commute back and forth—such is the yamanote topography that implicitly reinforces the structure of *And Then*.

2

In the trilogy's concluding work, *Mon*, Sōseki's acute sensitivity to place is put to work even more arrestingly than in *Sanshirō* and *And Then*. The trajectory of Sanshirō's regular walks encompasses the emerging "cultural center" of Hongō, with its chrysanthemum doll festival on Dangozaka, the branch of the Seiyōken restaurant[13] in Ueno, and performances of *Hamlet* at the Hongōza.[14] In *And Then*, the web of relationships in which Daisuke becomes more and more enmeshed is thrown into sharp relief by the particularities of the many places with which his activities intersect, in both yamanote and shitamachi, and here the narrative focus shifts to stress the steady transformation of the contemporary city into (in Daisuke's words) "a mere agglomeration of solitary individuals." When we come to *Mon*, we find that the approach of *Sanshirō* and *And Then*, which creates an ever-expanding panorama of a full range of urban phenomena, has been deliberately avoided. In Nonaka Sōsuke of *Mon*, there is no trace of Sanshirō's ceaseless perambulations of the city radiating out from his base in Hongō. For Sōsuke and his wife, "to live" is first and foremost to strive to maintain "their own home." Not the comparison of this place and that, nor any elaboration of the interrelatedness of diverse places, rather, the meanings of this one place where they have settled together are relentlessly interrogated. *Mon*'s structure consists, then, in a thorough excavation of the existential significance of the spaces in and around their dwelling place.

Oyone and Sōsuke's house is described as being "almost a twenty-minute walk from the last stop on a streetcar line, in the recesses of the yamanote." But where exactly is the location?[15] In *Sanshirō*, the title character lives in lodgings his prefectural association maintains in Hongō Komagome Oiwake-chō; Miyako in a house with a well-appointed Western-style drawing room in Masago-chō; Hirota Sensei, after his move, in the tenth block of Nishikata-machi. In *And Then*, as mentioned above, Daisuke's house is located in Fukuro-machi, at the top of Kagurazaka, and we may surmise that the Hiraokas' rental is somewhere around Koishikawa Omote-machi. In contrast to this precise situating of the characters' domiciles in the trilogy's first two works, there are no clues in the text of *Mon* with which to pinpoint on the map exactly where, "in the recesses of the yamanote," Sōsuke and his wife dwell. For such secondary characters as (Sōsuke's brother) Koroku and his cousin Yasunosuke, the places they are connected to are clearly specified: the former's boardinghouse in Hongō, the latter's factory in Tsukishima. Yet the narrative comes to an end without ever revealing the location of the house where Sōsuke and Oyone are joined together so closely as to warm each other's skins. This minor omission, overlooked in the previous critical literature, may nevertheless serve as a useful point of departure for exploring the meanings of the spatial structure of the microcosm presented by *Mon*.

According to Roland Barthes, among the signs that demarcate the city center from the peripheries are those that signify otherness and, conversely, those that point toward individual identity. The center is the site of meetings with strangers, a space where exchanges between self and other are constantly acted out through the ludic power with which it is suffused. Noncentral locales are by definition the preserve of all that does not partake of interaction with others: one's own family, one's home, one's individual identity.[16] This dualistic typology of city center versus outlying residential district[17] can be induced when reading *Mon* as well. That, as the narrative states, "for the two of them to be together was not only necessary but sufficient" dictates the choice of location for Sōsuke and Oyone's abode within the nether "recesses of the yamanote," an indispensable site for the forging of their mutual identity. Nor do they have the desire to give any significant part of their lives to that "city center" that enjoins interactions with others. For Sōsuke and his wife, who "inhabit the city while mountain fastnesses indwell in them," the urban macrocosm presents no more than a gestalt of concentric circles that appear ever more indistinct as they radiate outward from their home. *Mon* is so structured that from the perspective of their world centered on the circumferential "recesses of the yamanote," the actual city center is thrust back onto the periphery. Precisely because their home occupies the center, it cannot be situated along any precise exterior axes that define urban space: the place cannot be named.

If the exact location where the couple have settled cannot be pinpointed on a map, the details of its description are in complete accord with typical yamanote topography. For example, the two quarters are simply differentiated as Sakai's cliff-top house and Daisuke's house at the foot of the cliff:

> Past the fishmonger's, "Uokatsu," and turning into what was something between a sidestreet and an alley where this ended, one came to a high rocky outcrop at the foot of which, to either side, stood a row of four or five identical rental houses. Until recently this stretch of land had been occupied by a pleasantly weather-beaten domicile set back behind a sparse hedge of dwarf cryptomeria, which looked as though it had grown old housing generations of a shogunal retainer family [*gokenin*]. But then a man named Sakai who lived up above the outcrop had bought up the land, immediately razed the old thatch-roofed mansion, uprooted the hedge, and added more contemporary rental houses. Sōsuke's house stood at the left-most edge of the compound, at the end of the road, directly beneath the rocky outcrop. Rather dark and gloomy though its situation was, being the furthest removed from the road, it would no doubt be reasonably quiet, so Sōsuke had thought and, after consulting with Oyone, had chosen this house.[18]

Such are Sōseki's powers of description, to capture with a few brush strokes the transformation of the yamanote's surfaces. The "pleasantly weather-beaten domicile . . . as though it had grown old housing generations of shogunal retainers" conveys that this has been a samurai-class residential district, as indeed the modern history of Tokyo teaches us that the redevelopment of the yamanote most often took the form of subdividing former samurai properties. And how apt the detail of "the sparse hedge of dwarf cryptomeria" being replaced by "a fence of knotty wooden slats"[19] to describe a rental house on a newly redeveloped tract. It can be read as a sign of the erosion of warm neighborly communications—chats over a low evergreen hedge—in other words, as an entering wedge in the shift toward a culture of inter-action with strangers. As Daisuke in *And Then* expresses it, "In its natural state the earth extends itself uninterruptedly; put houses on it and it suddenly shatters into fragments." Thus, at the outset of *Mon*'s narrative, apart from paying the rent through the intermediary of their landlord's maid, there is no connection between Sōsuke's household and that of Sakai: "They might as well have been foreigners living up there, for Sōsuke and Oyone had no warm neighborly contact with them whatsoever."[20]

The landlord Sakai's status is described as that of "coming from the oldest family in the district, one that during the Tokugawa era bore the titular rank of Lord of Somewhere or Other." Though of shogunal retainer stock, Sakai had negotiated his way through the post-Restoration transition adroitly, and having had the wit to foresee the great demand for new real estate that would follow on the construction of street railways, bought up land and put up rental houses: a good example, minus the extreme rapaciousness, of Daisuke's observations in *And Then*, quoted above, on how "bottom-feeding capitalists seized the opportunity of Tokyo's explosive growth . . . to turn usurious profits."

Weighed down by the "discipline of the spirit exacted by his six-day work week," Sōsuke stands on the veranda beneath the outcrop gazing up at the Sakai estate and listening intently to the strains of piano music played by the eldest daughter. "They have nothing to do but amuse themselves," Oyone remarks of their close-but-distant neighbors. "With all these properties . . ." But when, after the burglary, Sōsuke comes to be on close terms with Sakai, he realizes that there is a whole discrete lifestyle enjoyed by their neighbors that conforms to the norm for the yamanote upper classes, characterized by a bright, cheerful atmosphere, such as suffuses Sakai's study, well illuminated by electric lights, comfortably warmed by a gas fire. It was in 1901 that gas heaters were first advertised in the newspapers, targeting banks, corporations, trading companies, and upper-class residences. Still, by 1910, when *Mon* was published, there were only a total of 308,000 accounts in all of Tokyo for gas fuel delivery. (In chapter 2, Sōsuke is described, while on his outing to Suru-gadai, as marveling at the streetcar advertisement for "gas stoves.")

Illumination in Sōsuke's house is supplied by oil lamps. Oyone and Sō-suke customarily keep a lamp burning, with the wick turned down, all night long in the alcove [*tokonoma*] of their bedroom, one of the few "luxuries" this couple, living on a rank-and-file bureaucrat's[21] salary allow themselves. Their heating devices consist of no more than a charcoal hand warmer in the sitting room, an oblong *kotatsu* [brazier] in the small dining room, and a portable kotatsu in Oyone's day room. The kotatsu does double duty as a dryer that Oyone uses on Sōsuke's wet shoes and trousers, in rainy weather a great boon to her husband, who has but a single pair of shoes. Such cumulative telling detail in the sketching out of the discrepancy between the lifestyles of the Sakais up above and the couple down below should not be overlooked.

Of the statement in the narrative that "with the paradisiacal spectacle of the Sakais' household before him, Sōsuke sometimes forgot his past; had his life unfolded smoothly, would he not have ended up the same sort of man?" Hiraoka Toshio acutely observes that Sakai is indeed the type that Sōsuke was meant to be.[22] This is one reason Sōsuke, far from being intimidated by the discrepancy in their lifestyles, comes to interact in a familiar manner with his landlord. The contrast between the lives lived above and below the rocky outcrop should be understood, not as a source of rancor in Sōsuke's consciousness, but as the juxtaposition of a bright painting and a dark one, or of a mirror image and the substance it reflects. The Sakai children, who make fleeting appearances only to vanish from sight, are described as "decorative accessories that lend a festive aura to the household." Sōsuke's household includes no children, "Oyone having gone and lost three already."[23]

These contrasting glimpses of the Sakais surrounded by numerous children afford only one of several qualifications one might wish to apply to Etō Jun's characterization of Sōsuke and Oyone as "paragons of conjugal love." By the same token, we should not fail to note the shadow that the narrative casts on Sakai, even as he presides over this apparent domestic bliss. At the slight-est sign of unpleasantness in his domain he seeks refuge in the "grotto" of his study, and is a man, we are told, who frequents the geisha demimonde: "He kept going back to such places, even though he had long since grown inured to their sensual stimuli; he was addicted, and would pay them any number of visits every month." In the polished little anecdote that Sakai relates about the wretched spectacle of frogs at the height of the mating season, crawling over the dead bodies of their fellows in the wetlands around Shimizu Vale and Benkei Bridge, we can see the cynicism of a man who makes no effort to find anything beyond the illusion he has managed to create of a happy family life. Let us also recall here the scene of Sōsuke's first meeting with the Sakais: "The husband sat facing Sōsuke over a low brazier finished with a warm gloss. The wife moved away from the brazier a few paces toward the veranda door, and likewise turned her gaze toward Sōsuke."[24] The two frozen figures of this tableau vivant cast a dark shadow across the bright picture conjured up when they are surrounded by their children.

3

The house where Sōsuke and his wife dwell "within the recesses of the yamanote" occupies the "left-most corner" of Sakai's rental compound at the end of a small street, "with a high rocky outcrop soaring up from the edge of the veranda, its steep face all but pressing down on the eaves of their house." The configuration of their living space, so cramped as to appear coiled in tightly upon itself, is recapitulated in Sōsuke's bizarre posture when he is first introduced in *Mon*'s opening pages, from the point of view of his wife as she looks through the glass door to the veranda: "lying there in a cramped posture that suggested a prawn, his knees oddly drawn up against his body."[25] In this reclining position Sōsuke cannot but reconfirm for himself the gap between "the tiny compass of the veranda" and the vastness of the early winter sky spread out above. To this extent have his living space and his very body language saturated each other.

The cramped microcosm to which Sōsuke is confined is shared by Oyone, and replete with the inconsequential *things* of their day-to-day life together. But if we perceive these "things" as not simply things, but signifiers of all that Oyone and Sōsuke share in common, we see how their home has been cumulatively created from the stuff of everyday life until it is packed full without an inch to spare. Along with the signifiers of these things that fill the house, we can adduce others, embedded in the same fixed context, which are enacted by the couple's body language and the looks in their eyes. As for the intermittent bits of conversation exchanged between Oyone and Sōsuke, these are no more than little replicated patterns showing through the interstices of the fixed context that is knit together from the other signifiers of everyday things, silent looks, gestures:

> That evening Sōsuke picked a pair of large banana leaves in back of the house and spread them out on the veranda next to the sitting room. He and Oyone sat there side by side, cooling themselves off and talking of Koroku.

After dinner they went out again onto the veranda where, the twin silhouettes of their figured white *yukata* showing through the darkness, they enjoyed the cool night and chatted about their days.

That night Sōsuke and Oyone went out to a street fair in progress at a local shrine and bought two potted plants of a manageable size. They brought them home, the husband carrying one, the wife the other; they decided the plants would benefit from a night's dew and, pushing back the storm shutters along the wall that faced the outcrop, set them side by side at the edge of the garden.[26]

A pair of banana leaves, twin silhouettes of white yukata, two matching potted plants. Such images show us how perfectly superimposed on each other are the areas to which Sōsuke and Oyone give meaning in their day-to-day lives. Their "talk of Koroku" and their "chat about their days" are completely subsumed under the category defined by these signs and devoid of any force that might take them outside the immediate reality of their everyday life together.

Fortified though they are by all these things dense with meaning, the collapse of the couple's recurring everyday life is foreshadowed in *Mon*'s first chapter, even as they are sharing the pleasure of the warm early winter sunlight. Having found himself suddenly unable to recall the Sino-Japanese character for "near" (近), Sōsuke stares at the traces of the ruler with which Oyone sketches it out for him and mutters, "Strange things, these characters. . . . Even the most basic ones can turn incomprehensible if you start to question them for so much as a moment. Recently it happened to me with the character for 'now' [今] as in 'nowadays'—I was completely stumped. I wrote down 今, without any mistake, on a piece of paper, but when I took a close look at it I got the feeling that it might be wrong. The longer I looked at it, the less it seemed like 'now.'"[27] Ruefully, Sōsuke bears witness here to that dislocating sensation that comes over us when we experience the metamorphosis of the familiar into the unfamiliar. A fissure has opened up between the signifier (here, a Sino-Japanese character) and the signified (its meaning), such that the signifier is reduced to nonsensical mere form. This passage offers us a metaphor for all that is unstable and unfathomable beneath the self-evident surface certainties on which our everyday lives depend. A severe fracturing of Sōsuke and Oyone's everyday world will ensue, it is implied, as the meanings attached to the things that surround them drop away and the forms of the things-in-themselves are exposed to the light. With the rending of the fixed context, the pattern of associations that so far has sutured together the things/signifiers, the anxiety lurking below the surface certainties of the couple's life will erupt.

P. L. Berger and T. Luchman, in their book *The Social Construction of Reality*, observe: "The reality of everyday life is organized around the 'here' of my body and the 'now' of my present. This 'here and now' is the focus of my attention to the reality of everyday life. What is 'here and now' presented to me in everyday life is the *realissimum* of my consciousness."[28] In the text of *Mon*, Berger and Luchman's "here and now" are shared by Sōsuke and Oyone. The particular temporal and spatial qualities of their common here and now are adumbrated in an unobtrusive but telling trope invoked in chapter 7, after Sōsuke has been plunged into anxiety by the resurfacing of his erstwhile friend Yasui from the past. It is contained in a single phrase apropos the couple's life together up to now: "United in a mutual embrace, they had come to describe a perfect closed circle." This trope of a closed circle refers not only to the spatial confines of the microcosm they inhabit, but to their temporal situation as well, cut off as they are from both past and future, living on in rhythms consonant with the cyclical patterns of the natural world.

Having forfeited the future, on the principle of "as ye sow, so shall ye reap," Oyone and Sōsuke have also sought to radically circumscribe the meaning of their lives within the sphere of the everyday, through a total repression of the dark past they share: "The sun slowly went down. Their neighborhood, where even by mid-day the traffic noise was quite subdued, grew utterly still. As was their habit, they went and sat by the lamp. It seemed to them that in all the wide world the only bright spot was here where they sat together. In the glowing lamplight Sōsuke was conscious only of Oyone, Oyone only of Sōsuke. Unilluminated by the lamp, the dark world of society was forgotten. Passing each and every evening in this way they had together found a new lease on life."[29] The sphere of their life together circumscribed by the lamplight, so vividly depicted in the passage, is constituted in temporal terms by the cycle of days and months that ceaselessly revolve around their nightly repetition of this interlude. Similarly, the constant repetitions of references to twilight and dawn, retiring and arising, set up a peculiar rhythm that punctuates the whole narrative flow. For example, "the fading light of another Sunday, his one day in seven," which closes the curtain on Sōsuke's brief respite; the vignette of Sōsuke and Oyone lying side by side in the study-cum-sitting-room, "waking up each morning while the dew still glistened, gazing up at the beautiful sun above the eaves." When Sōsuke awakens from a sleep made fitful by nightmares about the return of Yasui, "Oyone was as always crouched there at his bedside smiling at him." This cycle of day-to-day repe-

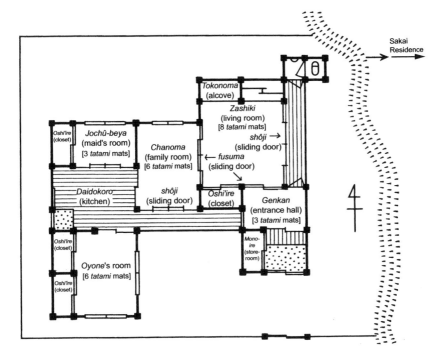

Figure 1. Residence of Sōsuke and his wife, Oyone. From *Mon* (The gate) by Natsume Sōseki. Courtesy Chikuma Shobō, 1982

titions also of course conforms to the couple's life of penance, performed to the inexorable rhythms of seasonal changes, as encapsulated in *Mon*'s closing lines: Oyone's "Thank goodness! Spring is here at last" and Sōsuke's "Yes, but winter won't be far behind."

Even more so than with this taut structure of cyclical temporality, the concentric spatial structure of the "here" of the couple's abode is worked out with great ingenuity, its contours etched still more deeply on the surface of the text. Moreover, the spatial configuration that emerges cumulatively amid the choreography of the couple's gestures and gazes serves to reinforce the traces of distinct temporal fault lines in their life.

The floorplan of Sōsuke and Oyone's house is centered on the six-mat dining room [*chanoma*, lit. "tea room"]. To the east side of this room is the *zashiki*,[30] complete with *tokonoma*, a room that serves as both a study for Sō-suke and the couple's bedroom; to the west, a suite of smaller rooms with the kitchen in the middle, flanked by the maid's room and Oyone's "day room" (figure 1). That Oyone can have a room of her own, as well as the inclusion of a maid's room, bespeaks a certain degree of comfort that could then be afforded by even a rank-and-file bureaucrat. Part and parcel with the husband and wife each having their own private space is the petit bourgeois tableau of their dining together in still another space, and at a proper table rather than off tray stands. This configuration of the couple's domestic space plays a supporting role, not "behind the scenes," but as the unobtrusive set for their daily enactment of their life's here and now. Another noteworthy spatial detail is to be found in the two verandas, one on the east side of the zashiki, the other on the south side of the dining room, which provide the points of contact for the constant interaction between their daily life and nature's seasonal progressions. These are the places where they sit on banana leaves and "gaze up at the shifting patterns in the narrow band of sky between the eaves and the rocky outcrop."

The solid structure of the "here" where Sōsuke and Oyone make their nest starts to turn creaky when Sōsuki's brother, Koroku, comes to live with them, having depleted his scholarship stipend. Oyone turns over the six-mat day room to him, thereby losing not only her own space, but the place where she has kept the portable heater for drying Sōsuke's clothes, which has to be moved to the zashiki. "'What's this thing doing in the middle of the room? Did something happen today?' asks Sōsuke. 'But it doesn't really matter, does it, since we won't be having any guests. Besides, with Koroku in the six-mat room, it would be a nuisance for him if we left it there.' This was the first news Sōsuke had of Koroku's arrival" (*Mon*, chap. 9).[31] As the woman of the house, Oyone was more grounded than Sōsuke in their domestic space and reacted with great sensitivity to realignments in this sphere (not that he was by any means oblivious to them). She is the kind of woman to go to great lengths to mitigate the distance between herself and her brother-in-law: in the novel's early pages we see her making sure to move the dining table into the zashiki in order to entertain the long-absent Koroku when he pays a rare visit; now that he has come to stay, she is solicitous enough to fuss over a lamp for him. In the same vein, her enlisting of her newly arrived brother-in-law in the repapering of the *shōji* can be seen as a subtle attempt to make him feel at home with the household routines.

It was Tada Michitarō who first took due note of the role played by Koroku as the "other" who intrudes on Oyone and Sōsuke's microcosm. As he points out, the already fixed framework of frequent descriptions of meals at the little dining table is used to bring home the full effect of Koroku's presence. The intimate tête-à-têtes that the couple enjoy at this table, and in general the happy state they have created for themselves in this refuge from the world at large, are swept away with savage swiftness by Koroku's intrusion. Brother/brother-in-law though he be, he is also a member of the conventional world that views their union as immoral, given its origins in the betrayal of Sōsuke's best friend. When she is required to share meals with this in-law while Sōsuke is away at work, Oyone's sense of constraint is exacerbated. For his part, Sōsuke must accustom himself to lingering forlornly over a solitary end-of-the-meal *o-chazuke* [the traditional pouring of tea over rice sticking to the bowl]. As his point of departure for this analysis, Tada offers the hypothesis that, not so much in the novel's plot or themes, but within the sphere of domestic living space and its material accoutrements, "the author's subconscious, even perhaps the collective unconscious of society and zeitgeist, has been deeply implanted."[32]

Tada's interpretation, in which the little scenes centered around the accoutrement of the dining table signal the collapse of the couple's everyday life, can be extended in terms of domestic configurations to Oyone's own room that she relinquishes to Koroku. Here special significance attaches to the small dressing table of mulberry wood that stands beneath the windowsill. It is Oyone's habit to retreat to her room, as if on cue, whenever her husband brings up the subject of children, and to sit gazing into the mirror on this dressing table: "When this topic came up she would often quietly slip off to the six-mat room and study her face in the mirror. It struck her that each time she looked at her reflected face her cheeks appeared still more hollow. For Oyone there was nothing in life so painful as to form any mental association between herself and children."[33] Just after it has been settled that Koroku is to quit his boardinghouse and move into his brother's house, Sōsuke catches a glimpse through the window of Oyone's reflection in the mirror, centered on one side of her face from the cheek down the neck to her collar. He is shocked at "the pallid appearance of this profile." As the day of Koroku's arrival approaches, Oyone spends more and more time shut up in her room: "Even after the sound of brush against hair ceased, she lingered on and on there; when Sōsuke went to check on her he would find her sitting there as if half-frozen at the dressing table." The closet of this room that served Oyone as both dressing room and place of refuge contained such things as "an old pock-marked chest of drawers," "a Chinese suitcase," and a "willow-wicker hamper" which were relics of the couple's life in the provinces. When the long rains came, it was always this room that started to leak first.

As the repository of reminders of their burdensome past, Oyone's room is, then, the dark sinkhole of the couple's abode. As the temporal fault line of memories conjured up about the three children she had lost, it contains the subconscious depths to which, when she retreats there, she commits herself, a place where even Sōsuke dare not enter. (That Oyone resolves to offer her own room to Koroku is precisely because she is aware of it as the repository of her shameful past.) But these same, only fleetingly visible signs of the burdensome past centered on Oyone's room are, from another point of view, bound up with deep-rooted parts of their life that sustain the surrounding domestic space. Just as their shared dark past in general acts as a strong impetus to their love for one another, so do such particularly ominous shadows over the stability of their day-to-day life constantly serve to renew the couple's here and now.

Koroku's cohabitation is a violation of the unconsciously constructed domestic sphere of Oyone and Sōsuke. The illness that Oyone contracts at year's end, after 20 December, as it is specified, stems most immediately from her mental stress at the "extraordinary solicitousness shown by her husband and Koroku." At a deeper level, the pathogen is the usurpation of her six-mat room, the locus of her dark past. The hidden power of this space is not accessible to Sōsuke, neither is Oyone conscious of it, yet its disruption assaults her very physical being, and within the existential context of their dwelling place, Sōsuke is if anything more affected by this power.

No sooner does Oyone recover than a second peril arrives, so threatening as to drive Sōsuke to seek refuge in Zen. Sōsuke's long-standing dread of the prospect that "one day, in one form or another, a terrifying drama would unfold and engulf his domestic life" has come to pass. If Koroku's intrusion is to be interpreted as a violation of the "here" where Sōsuke and Oyone are joined together, the imminent reappearance on the scene of their erstwhile friend Yasui, first announced by Sakai, must be viewed as a serious attack on the "now" of their everyday life. As Oyone's illness can be read as a metaphorical, psychosomatic reaction to the loss of order and balance in her living space, so too can Sōsuke's fear and trembling be seen as the consequence of a temporal hallucination brought on by the return of the repressed past in the form of Yasui's reappearance. In the same way as Oyone keeps locked inside herself the pain caused by Koroku's intrusion, Sōsuke takes no steps to divulge to her the deep foreboding that has taken hold of him. On the very night that Yasui is due to call on the Sakais, Sōsuke is panicked into the uncharacteristic conduct of staying away from home, drinking and nibbling on a beef stew:

> When at last he made his way home, Sōsuke took note of Oyone and Koroku, both of whom appeared *perfectly normal*, of the dining room and zashiki in their *normal state*, likewise the lamp and chest of drawers in

their *usual* positions, and it came to him that he alone had spent the past four or five hours in an abnormal condition. There was a small pot on the brazier from whose lid steam was rising. Next to the brazier, at his usual seat a cushion had been laid, with a proper place setting before it. Staring at his bowl with the lid turned upside down, the wooden chopsticks that for these past few years he had held in his hands morning and night, he said, "I won't be eating anything now."[34]

The significance of this passage is underscored by the repetition of "normal," "usual," "morning and night." In the intense gaze of Sōsuke on returning home, the exteriors of this everyday world, the things packed into his domestic living space, all appear in their normal guise. But in fact these things have become no more than their outward forms wrenched from the context of everyday life and robbed of meaning. Now ensnared in the web of an accursed past and thus rendered "in an abnormal state," he is utterly cut off from these signs of the here and now that have filled his abode, and totally alienated. This sensation naturally results as well in a distancing from Oyone, who lives for this home. At the very moment when the contentment of his everyday life has slipped from his grasp, he can only realize as never before what an irreplaceable blessing it has been.

Sōsuke's resorting to Zen is above all a flight from the hallucinatory return of the past that has come to haunt him. Yet this transitory excursion into the extraordinary in the end comes to nothing but an opportunity to reaffirm the importance of his ordinary everyday life: "'That's the way it is with vacations—when you're back home you start to feel a little fatigued. But you, my dear, look an awful old wreck. For goodness' sake please get some rest . . . go take a bath and have yourself a shave.' So saying, Oyone took a small mirror from the drawer and held it up to him to prove her point. These words from Oyone give Sōsuke the sensation that the lingering aura of the monastic hut had suddenly been blown away as if by a gust of wind. No sooner had he left the temple and come home than he reverted to his old self."[35]

If we mark well the import of this passage in which, with but a few words, Oyone eases Sōsuke back into their everyday realm, we will realize that all the critical interpretations that have been elaborated over the years about Sōsuke's resorting to Zen come to only so much empty intellectual gamesmanship.

Finally, though, even after the two crises that have befallen the couple have been resolved, with Yasui's return to Manchuria and Koroku's being taken in by the Sakais, it is doubtful that the fissures that have opened up in Sōsuke and Oyone's here and now will ever be fully repaired. For at the center of the text of *Mon*, as we have construed it, is a drama wherein each of them has experienced deeply a betrayal of their everyday life, Oyone in the realm of the "here," Sōsuke in that of the "now."

Notes

1 There is an English translation of *Mon*, so titled, by Francis Mathy published concurrently by Peter Owen of London and Charles E. Tuttle of Tokyo in 1972. First appearing as "Sōseki to yamate kūkan: *Mon* o chūshin ni," in *Kōza Natsume Sōseki 4: Sōseki no jidai to shakai* (Yūhikaku, 1982), the text used for this translation is from Maeda Ai, *Toshi kūkan no naka no bungaku* (Chikuma Shobō, 1982), 339–362.

2 Tayama Katai, "Return to Tōkyō" (Futatabi Tokyo e), in *Thirty Years in Tōkyō* (*Tōkyō no sanjūnen*), trans. with full annotations and an introduction by Kenneth G. Henshall (New York: E.J. Brill, 1987), 53.

3 The Kōbu Line, established in 1889, would later be renamed the Chūō Line.

4 *Shitamachi* is the other term in the binary naming of the two not-very-equal "halves" of Tokyo that just as easily might have been designated East End versus Westside, for example.

5 Katai, "Out in the Western Suburbs" (Yamanote no kūki) in *Thirty Years in Tōkyō*, 93. (M)

6 Maeda uses *haikara* (from "high collar") in the much invoked Meiji coinage.

7 Tayama Katai, "Shōjobyō," written in 1907. Kenneth Henshall translates the short story "Girl Watching," in *The Quilt and Other Stories by Tayama Katai* (University of Tokyo Press, 1981).

8 Ishizuka Hiromichi, *Tokyo no shakai keizaishi* (Kinokuniya Shoten, 1977). (M)

9 Okui Fukutarō, "Toshi kōgai ron," in *Toshi no seishin* (Nihon Hōsō Shuppan Kyōkai, 1975). (M)

10 Katai, "The Development of Tōkyō," in *Thirty Years in Tōkyō*, 229.

11 Natsume Sōseki, *Sore kara*, in *Sōseki zenshū* (Iwanami Shoten, 1975), 4:393–394.

12 Ibid., 4:430.

13 The Seiyōken was a Western-style restaurant first established in 1874, with a mainly foreign resident clientele; a branch was opened in Ueno in 1907, which proved particularly popular with Japanese customers.

14 E.g., the first performance of an "adaptation" (*hon' an*) of *Hamlet* by Kawakami Otojirō was given in 1903; of Tsubouchi Shōyō's translation in 1907.

15 In *Mon*, Sōsuke's commute to his office in Marunouchi involves a transfer at the Surugadai Station to the Sotobori ["Outer Moat"] Line. The other lines that come into Surugadai from the High City traveled these routes before reaching the station: (1) Tsunohazu-Hanzōmon-Kudan, (2) Ichigaya Mitsuke-Kudan, (3) Edogawabashi-Iidabashi-Kudanshita. Of these three, the line coming in from Edogawabashi would seem to supply the most appropriate location for the nar-

rative's "in the (further) recesses of the High City." And it is outside this same Edogawabashi terminus where, in *Until after the Equinox* [*Higansugi made*], Keitarō loses sight of the "gentleman with the mole" (Matsumoto) while executing the detective work that is the business Taguchi has assigned him. (M)

16　Roland Barthes, "Semiotics and a Theory of the City," trans. Shinoda Kōichirō as "Kigōgaku to toshi no riron" in *Gendai shisō* (October 1975). (M)

17　"Outlying residential areas" is my cumbersome gloss for Maeda's *kōgai*, frequently rendered as "suburb," which is, however, confusing for American readers, given the strictly defined American usage to mean an adjacent town or village with its own administrative autonomy. Maeda uses kōgai to designate various High City neighborhoods that are nevertheless administratively under the control of the Tokyo-shi (later Tokyo-to). For readers accustomed to British and Australian usages of "suburb," this cumbersome gloss would not be required.

18　Natsume Sōseki, *Mon*, in *Sōseki zenshū* (Iwanami Shoten, 1966), 4:638–639.

19　This new fence of "knotty wood" is not mentioned in the previously cited passage, neither in Maeda's quotation of it nor in this passage in the edition of *Mon* cited above. No doubt this detail occurs elsewhere in the novel, but I have been unable to locate it.

20　Sōseki, *Mon*, 4:726.

21　The pithy expression *koshiben*, rendered here as "rank-and-file bureaucrat," translates more literally as "lunchbox brigade."

22　Hiraoka Toshio, "*Mon* no kōzō," in *Sōseki josetsu* (Hanawa Shobō, 1976). (M)

23　The perhaps too folksy-sounding "gone and lost" is an attempt to convey the tone of the original's *shinasete iru*: a normal causative usage, admitting of either "caused to die" or "permitted to die," but in either case not without a chilly connotation of the mother's bearing some responsibility for the children's death at or before birth.

24　Sōseki, *Mon*, 4:758.

25　Ibid., 4:626.

26　Ibid., 4:668, 674, 677.

27　Concerning this passage, Yoshikawa Toyoko has observed, "Here the author is posing a question to the reader: 'Has it not happened to you that once your consciousness has been awakened from its habitual perception of life in the here-and-now and you look around yourself, the more you look the more unstable become the forms that meet your eye?'" Yoshikawa Toyoko, "Mon oboegaki," in *Sakuhinron: Sōseki*, ed. Uchida Michio and Kubota Mantarō (Sōbinsha, 1976). (M)

28　Translated by Yamaguchi Sadao as *Nichijō sekai no kōsei*. (M) I have quoted from the original: Peter L. Berger and Thomas Luckmann, *The Social Construction of Reality* (New York: Anchor Books, 1966), 22.

29　Sōseki, *Mon*, 4:689.

30　Denotes a multipurpose room (as indeed are most ground-floor rooms in traditional Japanese houses) of relatively ample proportions, such that, whatever other uses it may be put to, it may serve as a "reception" room for guests.

31 Sōseki, *Mon*, 4:727–728.

32 Tada Michitarō, "Mukashi chabudai to iu mono ga atta," in *Fūzokugaku* (Chikuma Shobō, 1987), 68. (M)

33 Sōseki, *Mon*, 4:683.

34 Ibid., 4:823 [emphasis Maeda's].

35 Ibid., 4:855.

We were privileged at the University of Chicago to have Mr. Maeda Ai as a guest professor in the spring quarter of 1981, and I to have the pleasure of being one of his hosts. Only half a dozen years later, all of us were shocked and saddened to learn of his death.

For myself, as I believe for many colleagues and students at Chicago and elsewhere in this country, the shock and sorrow were not only a normal response to the loss of someone whom we had come to admire during those months, who had been generous with the great gift of his quite distinctive insights into Japanese literature and cultural history in general. There was the wrenching feeling that came from a recognition that truly inimitable work-in-progress had been abruptly arrested.

We had been especially fortunate in that his weekly three-hour seminar for us coincided with the penultimate stages of his work on *Literature in Urban Space* (*Toshi kūkan no naka no bungaku*, 1982), undoubtedly one of the major books of his prolific career, selected chapters of which, in translation, make up a goodly portion of this volume. We were able then to hear (each of us understanding as best he or she could) his readings aloud from his draft versions of chapters on such diverse writers as Tōkai Sanshi (what a contrast, for some of us, with the "classic," mocking, though admittedly amusing synopsis of this work in George Sansom's *Japan and the Western world*!), Mori Ōgai, Natsume Sōseki, Nagai Kafū, Yokomitsu Riichi, and others. While he held forth in this fashion, reading from a carefully prepared text, which is not the norm for courses styled as seminars here, Mr. Maeda remained attentive to his small audience, interrupting his recitation here and there to self-gloss, elaborate in simpler language where he sensed some degree of incomprehension, and at the end would patiently entertain all manner of questions from among us, some of them no doubt fairly obtuse.

An afterword is normally an occasion where whoever undertakes it is afforded the license, if not the obligation, to indulge in personal reminiscences about the author. And here, as ample critical discussions of Maeda's works contained in this volume, as well as certain others, are presented in the preface and introduction, there is all the more reason to be somewhat personal in my remarks. Yet I find this is not possible. While he was with us at Chicago Mr. Maeda was very busy, in a way that I soon came to perceive was a normal state of affairs for him. (Simply to peruse his *nempu*, the chronology of his life and career, and the catalogue of his published works appended to the posthumously published *Maeda Ai chosakushū* [1990, vol. 6, 469–537] is, for the likes of me, exhausting.) During his stay with us he was naturally much in demand at other U.S. institutions, and did travel quite a bit, but still spent most of his nonteaching time in the library working on the aforementioned manuscript. It was my impression that when he did find a little free time he would wander off on his own around Chicago, no doubt in part out of his ingrained habit of seeking to map out for himself the cultural geography of any city he happened to inhabit for a while. Although I did not inquire much into the destination of his wanderings, somehow I do not think they were targeted to such specifically literary sites as the station where Dreiser's Sister Carrrie made her fateful entrance into Chicago, the all but obliterated remnants of Upton Sinclair's "jungle," the turf of James T. Farrell's Studs Lonigan (all within a two-mile radius of our campus), or even any of the still recognizable haunts of some of Bellow's antiheroes. Widely read though Mr. Maeda certainly was, and eclectic in his tastes, I doubt that they extended to American naturalism and its more intellectualized offshoots.

Nevertheless, at one point he did express an interest in making a literary pilgrimage of sorts, to Kalamazoo, Michigan, where Nagai Kafū spent the better part of one year in the early 1900s. Fortunately we were accompanied on this day's roundtrip by Mitsuko Iriye, a longtime scholar and translator of Kafū. Unfortunately, in driving Mr. Maeda, of all people, partly distracted by straining to catch the interesting chats that he was having with Ms. Iriye, partly because the interstate system around Chicago had recently been reorganized, I made a serious wrong turn at one juncture, and for an embarrassing number of miles proceeded back westward toward the sprawling south suburbs instead of eastward toward the fabled Kalamazoo ("The sins of Kalamazoo are gray," wrote Carl Sandburg in perhaps one of his better lines). When I realized my mistake and got off then back on the interstate in the right direction, Mr. Maeda commented quietly, and not at all acerbically, "Mr. Sibley . . . you are someone who often makes such mistakes." All too true. Having already visited Kalamazoo College some years previously, from the other direction and in the company of another distinguished Kafū scholar, Edward Seidensticker, I was not surprised at the slimness of the pickings when we arrived, though Mr. Maeda did not seem terribly disappointed. (Subsequently, so I gathered, as Japan rushed forward into the boom years and tourists arrived in ever greater numbers, people at this fine liberal arts college seem to have realized that there were needs and opportunities here not to be neglected and established what was described to me as a "Kafū Corner" in the library.)

Yet because I really did not get to know the man very well at all, I would prefer to use this occasion to say a little bit about some of his writings done, for the most part, after he was with us, which is to say in the all too brief six years before his untimely death: some of them published in his lifetime, others, including the one I wish to focus on, only posthumously, but in either case all contained in volume 6 of *The Collected Works of Maeda Ai* (*Maeda Ai chosakushū*, 6 volumes, 1989–90) mentioned above.

The editors gave volume 6 of *The Collected Works* the general title *The Utopia of Texts* (*Tekusuto no yūtopia*) and, as they set forth in their afterword, have placed in it a variety of texts that, with several exceptions (mostly involving posthumously published writing), have in common a central preoccupation with literary theory, as opposed to many other works throughout the other volumes of *The Collected Works* where, though literary theory may play an important role in Maeda's critical approach to this or that body of works of fiction and other types of writing, that role is supportive, not predominant. To be sure, it is often a fine distinction, but the editors have conscientiously striven to make it. Perhaps nowhere so boldly as in having removed what was originally the introductory chapter to the first published version of *Literature in Urban Space* (*Toshi kūkan no naka no bungaku*, 1982) entitled "The Texts of Space, the Space of Texts" ("Kūkan no tekusto tekusto no kūkan") and put it instead at the beginning of this sixth, "theory" volume. Not having been able, after several tries, to understand this essay, the main thrust of which is cast in terms of topology—quite simply, I could not do the math—I obviously cannot say anything about it. (For those who might be interested, there is a critique of this essay by Joseph Murphy contained in his forthcoming volume, *The Metaphorical Circuit: Negotiations between Literature and Science in Twentieth-century Japan* [Cornell East Asian Series], a first draft of which I read some years ago, and though likewise failed to understand, had the impression that it was clearly argued in a knowledgeable-sounding fashion.)

The single longest and, for me, most interesting work contained in *The Utopia of Texts* is entitled "A Primer on Literary Texts" (hereafter "Primer"; "Bungaku tekusuto no nyūmon"; it appears from the afterword that this had been previously published, though, as with the version that I have consulted, also posthumously, as "Chikuma Ribararii # 9," in 1988. Again, the editors of *The Collected Works* are to be congratulated for having collated the "Primer" from what I gather were a set of audiotapes recorded by Maeda at the outset of this project together with an unspecified amount of (re-) written manuscript, though one can roughly judge the proportion of each from the unusual combination of spoken style (so-called *desu/masu* style, along with distinctly un-Maedaesque *keigo* [honorifics]) and his more characteristic somewhat densely written prose. They not only collated it, but figured out what seemed to them the most natural order into which to place the various constituent parts, something that, presumably because Mr. Maeda was already seriously ailing at the time, he had not been able to decide on for himself.

The general purpose of the "Primer" (which, for varying reasons, was not included in the present anthology of translations), as the title announces, appears at first to be that of an introduction to critical theories about literary texts accompanied by concrete examples of literary—and eventually other, nonliterary, or at any rate nonbelletristic—texts for a relatively neophyte audience. And indeed it begins with a chapter entitled "The Utopia of Reading" that takes as its point of departure the amusing episode in Natsume Sōseki's *Kusamakura* (translated many decades ago by Alan Tourney as *The Three-Cornered World*), in which the wandering Tokyo intellectual–would-be painter narrator enters into a bantering conversation with a mysterious local woman named O-Nami, somewhere in the provinces, about how fictional narratives should be read. This first chapter title, with its emphasis on "Reading," along with the general title centered on "Primer," would indeed seem to suggest that the main purpose here is to instruct a relatively neophyte audience on how to approach the reading of literature, principally fiction, in a manner partly informed by theoretical insights that, though not necessarily in a condescending fashion, are to be presented with a certain degree of clarity that might require some kinds of simplifying, or, as the case might be, amplifying, on Maeda's part.

Maeda's opening quotation from the narrator's little chat with O-Nami about reading, in the course of which the wandering painter demonstrates his own preferred method by opening at random a volume in English (it happens to be George Meredith's *Beauchamp's Career*) and reads aloud a stray passage, simultaneously translating it for her, appears to further confirm that, whatever else may ensue in the "Primer," there will be some emphasis on not only an enlarging, but a liberating, even a playful approach to reading for the implied semineophyte. "To read wherever I please just as I please [ii-kagen na tokoro o ii-kagen ni yomu]" is how the narrator sums up his method. The

woman, who is by no means portrayed throughout this narrative as an ingenue, here responds with the commonsensical objection that in reading this
way one would never be able to tell "what happens" in the story.

Not surprisingly, given the long trajectory of Maeda's career as a critic and
as a theroretician of literature of a predominantly structuralist persuasion, as
it soon emerges in the following pages, readers are not simply to be left to
their own devices, no more than they are in fact encouraged by even this least
emplotted of Sōseki's texts, not to mention by those yet to come, to let their
imaginations soar off in one direction or another. Indeed, as it turns out, this
uncompleted "introduction" (nyūmon) by Maeda takes on a shape that is all
but impossible to reconcile with anything one might normally associate with
the word "primer."

In the initial chapter of the "Primer," in any case as rearranged by the
editors, for a while the focus does remain on the reader with a brief excursion into the beginnings of reader-reponse (a.k.a. reception) theory through
a reference to the pioneer in this field, Alfred Thibaudet, and his distinction
between the ordinary, looking-for-a-good-read *lecteurs* and the more serious
liseurs (glossed here as those who are conscious of "the privilege of seeking
out the humanity" in literary texts). After commenting that later theorists in
this area have gone beyond this distinctly elitist distinction, he pretty much
leaves reader-response theory aside for most of the remaining portion, that is
to say the bulk of his "Primer."

Maeda shifts instead to an overwhelming focus on theories of writing,
with pronounced emphasis on those from the realms of semiotics and narratology. Yet, although not nearly to the degree of the major essays and books
published in his lifetime, in widely varying measure, he does not on the whole
fail to link his presentation of this or that theory with at least one or two specific fictional texts, such that, at least in this respect, the ostensible purpose
of his "Primer" is served by acquainting his readers with how these theories
may be applied. This shift of focus suggests another motivation for producing
this "Primer": that of rethinking for himself the very broad range of theoretical insights he has developed through his extensive reading over the years, a
purpose that is inevitably often at odds with that of introducing presump-
tively semineophyte—or what used to be called "common"—readers to critical theory in order to broaden their horizons, for few if any of them could
be expected to absorb his insights in the often foreshortened, encapsulated
fashion in which they are presented. Passing references to and less frequent
but still numerous quotations from or paraphrases of major critics and theo-
reticians of the previous half-century, and then some, fly quite thick and fast
through these pages: from back as far as the aforementioned Thibaudet (he

goes back far enough, as I happened to note somewhere recently, to have actually met Proust!), Henry James, E. M. Forster, I. A. Richard, R. P. Blackmur, and others down to a preponderance of more recent (and mostly francophone) figures such as Saussure, Roland Barthes, of course, Kristeva, Baudrillard, Derrida, Todorov, and others, with the Russian formalists in between, so to speak, fulfilling eventually an important role. These comprise but a small sampling, for the total count, which I did not make, would come to quite a few dozen. Let it be added that Maeda does not snobbishly exclude Japanese critics of some stature and originality, nor toilers in the more traditional subfields of *kokubungaku* (i.e., academic studies of Japanese literature). Still, the sheer number of these passing sort of references to such critics-theoreticians, as opposed to those where he pauses to encapsulate for the reader with some clarity the relevant insights for his argument, is likely to be daunting for the reader of a "primer."

There is in addition a third underlying, if quite intermittent, focus that emerges, one where Maeda appears to move toward constructing a new periodization of "modern" Japanese literature (again, essentially fictional narrative) in the broadest sense, that is, new attempts to divide up the cultural-intellectual continuum that he, along with many other influential cultural historians, had hitherto agreed on as existing from some point in the so-called *kinsei* period (generally accepted as encompassing most of the Tokugawa or Edo period in general historical terms; though there is no such explicit consensus, it would seem to mean from the Genroku era onward) through *kindai*, that is, from the Meiji period on down to the by definition constantly shifting "Gendai" (i.e., more or less contemporary times), though here again there is no general agreement about what to do with the post–World War II era, the possibility of creating some cut-off point between "the modern" and the putative "postmodern" having proved irresistible for some—not for Maeda, I think, though there are considerable ambiguities here that will be referred to below. He also appears in this work ambivalent toward other aspects of history, and at times historicism itself, in ways to which I likewise recur briefly later on.

The rest of the "Primer" is organized (or again, reorganized by the assiduous editors) into five chapters, but perhaps more significantly into various subchapter headings, not a few of which, while not being entirely arbitrary, could have been put into some other chapter as well. In no regular order, then, I will speak briefly of a few of these subcategories of particular interest to me. In general terms, Maeda seems to emphasize, subsumed under the three apparent purposes of his "Primer" as outlined above, three fundamental, overlapping categories: the relationship between language and literary texts; the roles of story and plot in narrative, for which, despite his sometimes alarming proclivity for foreign words transcribed in *katakana* script, by and large he mercifully uses the quite ancient word *monogatari* (often rendered in English as "tale"); and certain aspects of his evident, if sporadic, project, as mentioned above, of a reperiodization of all of early modern-contemporary Japanese fiction. Underlying, or overarching, these three categories is his loud and clear call, somewhere in the middle of the "Primer," for a "decentered" (*datsu-chūshinteki*) reading of texts. I dwell here on these three broad categories, along with his general encouragement of decentered readings of literary texts.

Where "language and literature" is concerned, it soon becomes clear in the "Primer," as indeed it has been throughout many major writings in his lifetime oeuvre, that Maeda is, if not necessarily hostile toward, then disinclined to endorse fully the claims of *genbun'itchi* (the movement, extending from the mid-1880s to the mid-1890s, that sought to create a new written language that, as he astutely points out, whatever the intentions of its architects, finally did not so much result in making the written word accord precisely with the spoken, as in creating a form of writing in which an author could "write in a manner as if speaking")—to endorse its claims for the illusionist effects of making the written language "transparent." This point of view is proclaimed early on by the subheading "Bungaku wa gengo nari," that is, literally, "Literature Is Language," but this dictum is delivered with a good deal of stress by virtue of the copular being put into the premodern inflection of the verb "to be."

The corollary of this point of view is Maeda's privileging, in this "Primer" as so often in his prolific completed publications, of early modern texts, from the second half of the Edo period into the pre-genbun'itchi Meiji; of those aspects of "mainstream" post-genbun'itchi texts by such major figures as Ōgai, Sōseki, Kafū, and Yokomitsu which escape from, so to speak, or transcend the illusions of transparent language; and, as far as I know, a relatively new interest for him here, a number of quite recent texts by the likes of Murakami Haruki and the by and large anonymous authors of advertising copy and "pop" song lyricists (only one is mentioned here, under the name of "Kō Chinka," which surely has a non-Japanese antecedent pronunciation, Chinese/Taiwanese, I would suspect, though it could be Korean, perhaps).

It is surely not the least admirably quixotic facet of this "Primer," as of a good deal of Maeda's previous work, that he wishes here to stimulate interest—and in my view succeeds very persuasively in doing so—in both late Edo and "transitional" early Meiji writings, by such as Santō Kyōden and

Tamenaga Shunsui down to Narushima Ryūhoku, Kanagaki Robun, and, a figure new to me (though perhaps prominently present in Maeda's previous extensive oeuvre, amid which I could easily have missed it), namely, the fascinating-sounding Saitō Ryoku'u. Yet, even granted the still possibly very impressive—in comparison to contemporary U.S. standards, which would not seem to be very high—literary curiosity of Japanese readers and their willingness to go to considerable lengths to satisfy it, how many presumptive readers of his text could be expected to read such writings, with their formidable language difficulties (if they could even locate them in the first place)? It simply does not, I think, matter to him, passionate as he so palpably is about such texts. For semineophyte contemporary Japanese readers of the "Primer" it would be roughly comparable, where Kyōden or Ryūhoku are concerned, to the challenge of decoding, for imaginary Anglophone counterparts, some language intermediate between medieval Latin and Chaucerian English, if such ever existed, which it did not. It is puzzling, then, that neither here nor in his previous writings on specifically early Meiji "transitional" figures like Ryūkoku, Robun, and, latterly, Ryoku'u, does Maeda make any explicit mention whatsoever of their, some might say, obstinately "retrograde" insistence on a *kanbun-kakikudashi* (a "Chinese" writing reordered to Japanese syntax) style of language. Maybe he considered this protest-through-language too obvious to comment on.

Closely yoked to matters of "literature equals language," through various more or less plausible theoretical interventions, is the subsection related to literary texts and the Body. This line of inquiry would seem to proceed from certain strains of French, of all sources, haute critique, in the wake of semiotics, and so on in general; and for some of us contemporary Americans, of all people, at least the common readers among us, can only appear at the same time obvious and strange as a topic to elucidate as earnestly as many besides Maeda have done over the past quarter century or so. In these passages he does set forth in an appropriate primer-like fashion undeniable general, long-range historical truths about the body versus mind/soul dichotomy in Western high culture from Plato to the significantly neo-Platonized Christian patristic-to-scholastic view of human nature, subsequently renewed in a semisecularized, philosophical form by Descartes (i.e., without the "soul") in the same era when, on the other hand, stress on this dualism was redoubled by certain major theological tendencies, though by no means all of them, of the Protestant Reformation.

This very broad intellectual-historical overview of Western culture becomes, in turn, in a related context, an explanation, though ambiguously qualified on a few points, for modern Japanese analogues to the prevalence of "logocentrism" over "phonocentrism," in Derridean terms. Yet nowhere in these discussions does Maeda mention what would seem to be conceptions somewhat similar to the Western body-mind dualism (with or without the "soul") to be found, most immediately, in the neo-Confucian dichotomy between *li* and *qi*; nor, less surprisingly, back beyond that, the mainstream Mahayana (i.e., pre-Amidist and pre-Zen, though some exceptions no doubt have to be made as well for the antecedent Mantrayana and Tantrism) equal negation of both body and mind as delusive constituents of the unenlightened "natural person." To be sure, the Taoistic element, partly through Chan/Zen Buddhism, in the neo-Confucian synthesis contributed an abiding impetus to overcome li/qi dualism and sowed the seeds of the Wang Yang-Ming school's efforts to transcend it through meditation.

But steeped as Maeda has been from early on in his career in the non-elite culture of the Edo-period *chōnin* (mercantile) class and that of the mostly well-educated bourgeois Meiji-Taisho writers he focuses on, I can only conjecture that, far-ranging as his purview has always been, in his estimation such religiophilosophical issues do not have much bearing on the earlier texts he takes up, while, as set forth in the "Primer," in their Western inflections they do where his mid-Meiji on texts are concerned. That he chooses to invoke in a general way Platonic, patristic-to-scholastic Christian, then the semi-secularized Cartesian body-mind split suggests that in his view, these imported Western models of human nature had much more of an effect (e.g., in the context of his brief treatment of the well-known so-called *botsu-risō* [on the presence or absence of latent ideals/Ideas] debate between Shōyō and Ōgai, conducted, as he points out, often at cross-purposes) on his modern writers than anything in orthodox, or even heterodox, Japanese philosophies did on either the early modern (kinsei) or modern (kindai) texts that he treats.

Coming as this does from such a broadly synthesizing cultural historian (though with a certain ambivalence, to which I recur at the end of this afterword) as Maeda, with his deep understanding of the townspeople (chōnin), nonelite literary representations of the later Edo and early Meiji periods, this on the whole unqualified if tacit ascribing of an underlying, deeply formative acceptance by Japanese authors of the modern texts that he treats of major movements in post-Renaissance Western thought and increasingly secularized religion, however popularized or vulgarized their versions of it may have been, is striking and, I would agree, not far from the mark.

But to return to his recurring focus on body-mind dualism and the related phenomenon of the Derridean phonocentric-logocentric antitheses, it still puzzles me why he seems to resort in his argument chiefly to recent French critical preoccupations with these matters, without drawing on his deep knowledge of Japanese early modern and transitional texts or Edo-period philosophical worldviews—again, however "vulgarized." Above, I indulged on this general topic in what may have sounded like American chauvinistic or, conversely, francophobic remarks which, though at this moment of writing may in some quarters be quite au courant, I of course do not intend in any such spirit. Although these remarks are but a transitional argument on my part to raising questions about Maeda's apparent indifference, or at least a curious ambivalence, where various traditional Japanese models of human nature are concerned, I should pause a moment to clarify them as succinctly as possible. To this end, I quote here a few lines from Walt Whitman, from among countless others in his "Leaves of Grass" that could be cited on the same point, these from "Crossing the Brooklyn Ferry" (1856): "I too had receiv'd identity by my body;/That I was, I knew was of my body—and what I should/be, I knew should be of my body."[1] Whitman was, of course, as many good poets are, ahead of his time in expressing certain traits of the genius, for good and for ill, of a particular nation or collectivity and prefiguring later widespread manifestations of these traits. Unquestionably, the United States was at that time still, as far as the elite ideology was concerned, in the grips of a haltingly post-Puritanical ethos that was far from embracing such utterances (witness Emerson's odd mix of high praise and raised eyebrows in his famous response to the early sections of "Leaves of Grass"). Yet this was far from the case with the late Edo to early Meiji chōnin writers of *gesaku* fiction (literally, and significantly, "playful works") and related genres that Maeda knew so well, and from whose work, in the context of "the Body," he could have extracted any number of expressions of a pithy, earthy, body-centered experience of life. (He does at least mention a few, e.g., apropos texts by Santō Kyōden, Tamenaga Shunsui, and Shikitei Samba, to which there are passing references—if no doubt for sound reasons he omits any reference to Hiraga Gennai, whose works display much ambivalence toward the body, in a way remarkably similar to those of Jonathan Swift, where, as with Gennai, bodily functions are often invoked to the end of scatological satire of this or that prevailing ideology rather than in any celebratory fashion.)

Another new note (I believe) sounded by Maeda in the "Primer" is his startling positioning of *jōruri* (normally rendered as "puppet drama") and the, textually speaking, closely related kabuki as the central modes of chōnin cultural representations throughout the Edo period, of which all the gesaku fiction he has previously focused on, along with principal modes of visual representation in wood-block prints and the like, are declared by him to be derivative. In my efforts here to conjecture "Wither Maeda?" as opposed to "Whence Maeda?"—to which question all of the preceding volume here bears far less tentative witness—this new positioning of jōruri/kabuki is, along with a few other areas highlighted in the "Primer," a major innovation in relation to his previous work. What a gift it would have been for us had he been able to elaborate in his customary thorough fashion on this obiter dictum. In perusing the aforementioned nempu (chronology of his life), I noted with interest his early, at least from college years on, involvement in theatrical productions, and can only wonder why this experience at an impressionable age of the clearly corpocentric arena of the theater (both as an actor and in backstage roles, apparently) appears to have vanished from his major writings—at least up to this new valorization of jōruri/kabuki. Here, at least, to invoke the privilege of the personal-impressionistic granted by the occasion, I would recall Mr. Maeda's own physical presence, tall, slim, graceful in his movements, all of which conveyed the impression of someone at home in his own body.

Given, then, his new privileging of jōruri/kabuki, in the performances of which the body (the corporeality perhaps paradoxically accentuated by the "characters" being elaborately—by three supposedly "invisible" puppeteers—manipulated simulacra of human bodies) and his own early experience of the theater, not to mention his amply displayed intimacy with the multiform sensuality of gesaku fiction, why must French theory be invoked to legitimize this category of critical analysis? One can only speculate that, as with the comparable U.S. case, there is some sort of sense of cultural inferiority (what the Australians pithily call "the cultural cringe") at work here, in that already deeply rooted modes of representation in cultures perceived by European or Eurocentric intellectuals at the end of the nineteenth century, of course, but well beyond the mid–twentieth century as well, as exotic or marginal, as both those of Japan and the United States have been, still need to be interpreted and validated by Western European critical thought, with the French and German versions, in historically varying proportions, at the epicenter.

As a sequel or sub-subcategory of this theoretical focus on the Body, and as a reminder that a "decentered reading" can also include the ec-centric, which is of course not a bad thing, at this point the "Primer" introduces the topic of "The Supine Position [*Yokotawaru shisei*]." It begins with a succinct discussion of a story by Miki Taku entitled "The Floor," included in his collection *Kurumi* (Walnuts, 1980), in which the sun-stroked narrator, reclining on the floor of a friend's house, has a faintly erotic/flirtatious encounter with the friend's sister that would have been impossible, Maeda judges, had he not been discovered by her in this position, then moves on to cite examples, both from literature and purportedly true-life accounts, of various supine figures, including Sensei in the opening scene of Sōseki's *Kokoro*, floating on his back in the sea when first encountered by the young narrator; then, rather amusingly, a biographical reference to Saigo Takamori, according to which this martial hero/martyr of the Restoration preferred to entertain his guests, Roman-like, lying down, and insisted that his guests assume the same position. (In contrast, Maeda evokes here another major figure of the Restoration era, Okubo Toshimichi, who is portrayed as stiff and hyper-Westernized in his insistence on entertaining guests while seated in the still unfamiliar and uncomfortable chairs placed on exotic rugs.)

Now this subcategorical line of inquiry, whether or not it seems entirely appropriate to a "primer," is in fact slightly provocative and potentially entertaining, such as to lead readers, if they have read a certain range of fictional or other texts, regardless of being theoretically neophytes or not, to free-associate about all kinds of comparable instances of the supine figure: perhaps the Second Princess, the one who is the widow of Kashiwagi, much importuned by Yugiri's advances in *The Tale of Genji*, who is always flopping down and consequently "matting her bangs"; Mme Récamier on her chaise-longue; the lecher-hero of Katai's *Futon*, swooning on the eponymous article still redolent of the schoolgirl who has spurned him; and, for good measure, a few lines from the inimitable Edgar Allan Poe (another example of a non-European writer who was sufficiently vetted by the French to have been taken seriously by some Americans and not a few Japanese): "Sadly, I know/I am shorn of my strength/And no muscle I move/As I lie at full length—/But no matter—I feel/I am better at length" (from his poem entitled "Prone").

Maeda does end up making an interesting cultural-historical point here to the effect that the all-but-overnight imposition of even superficial forms of a Westernized lifestyle proved highly constricting, if not downright tortuous, for many upwardly mobile Japanese; then goes on to another clearly related category, that of "the Oppressed Body" (*kin'astsu sareta shintai*), in which he discusses acutely the contrastive roles of descriptions of clothing in Edo-period gesaku (e.g., Shunsui) as a kind of "second skin," both sensual and status marking, and those in mid-Meiji fiction (e.g., the Ken'yūsha writers), where the status-marking functions have taken over, with the inevitable attendant discomfort, all of which is capped by a reference, not to Tanizaki's unforgettable treatment of such matters somewhat later in his *Naomi*, but to Roland Barthes's on "the system of fashion." One cannot then help wondering why in this "Primer" he dwells, even to this extent and in this manner, on matters that he has so much more elegantly and naturally discussed in many of his earlier writings on texts from those of Narushima Ryūhoku and Higuchi Ichiyō to those of Sōseki and Kafū. No doubt it has to do in part with the inversion of the priorities that inform most of his lifetime writings, according to which fictional texts serve as the organizing principle, with critical theory then brought in to help elucidate the texts, into those of critical theory presented first then buttressed by brief references to literary and other types of texts.

But in Maeda's discussion of the Body and related subtopics, he seems to have toppled to one of the weirder manifestations of critical theory (here, chiefly francophone). In having quoted Whitman's prescient lines from "Crossing Brooklyn Ferry," I naturally intended to point toward the unmistakable fact that both contemporary American life and various forms of both popular and "high" culture, and much that bridges or lies between these artificial categories, are awash in body awareness and representations of the body and its functions. Not having spent much time in Japan, and ignorant as I am of all but a few recent cultural representations created there, whether "popular" or otherwise, I cannot comment with any assurance, yet still wonder if something of the sort could not be said about the contemporary Japanese case—or even the French, for that matter. In other words, I am not sure how urgent a need exists today to encourage common readers to tease out of close readings of texts this or that form of body consciousness, though to make the point that there is historical interest in finding in older texts quite different forms from those that saturate contemporary life and culture is, of course, worthwhile.

That the section devoted to the Body is followed, in the editors' reconstruction of the "Primer," by one on issues concerning compound predications and, only in passing, the structure of metaphor, largely based on the concepts of Saussure and those who have drawn on his work, might be experienced by some common reads as a plunge from something quite readily accessible into terra incognita. As the editors comment in their afterword, this is perhaps an area to which Maeda intended to return, and to revise, in the final version that unfortunately could not be realized. It is clearly the place where one of his three major lines of argument in this work, that about the relationship between language and literature (perhaps especially with respect to metaphor and metonymy), was to come into play, but because of its incompleteness must be passed over here.

To go on, then, to another of the main categories of the "Primer," the narratological focus on story/plot, suffice it to say that in the end, which is where the editors have chosen to put it in their reconstruction, Maeda does a good job of making reasonably clear the sharp distinction first drawn by the Russian formalists between story and plot, though on the whole he seems to prefer the terms "pretext" and "text." This distinction has of course been a vexed issue in narratology and has been modified, qualified, and complicated ad infinitum. Maeda's concise discussion of this issue is as good as, or better than, most I have seen. But prior to this concluding argument in the text we have (though as the editors themselves observe, it is perhaps precisely not on this particular treatment of narratology that Maeda would have been content to end), there have been various other subheadings under which he has addressed narratological, also thematic, matters that strike me as potentially more helpful to the common reader.

More helpful in a "primer" because some of these other subsections deal with basic matters related to how the great majority of readers, whether exactly "common" or not, in fact read various forms of narrative, whereas the subject versus plot issue finally is a challenge, however consciously at work, for writers. Most readers simply do not care how a given writer may have struggled to translate his "subject" (in Jamesian terms, the "donnée," "pretext" in Maeda's preferred term) into a plot so long as it simply "bumps them along," in E. M. Forster's well-known pithy phrase, in a way that makes the narrative not only readable but reasonably compelling.

To mention only a couple of these subcategories, there is one on "Titles" that is not only indeed primeresque, but helpful even to readers who may not think of themselves as complete neophytes. It is perhaps a good example of how effective in the hands of a Maeda the semiotic approach can be at times: in contrast to elucidating the obvious, as has sometimes been said against it (not without justification in certain cases), rather by focusing on things "under your nose" that nevertheless any of us may have overlooked. Here he invokes three or so examples of titles as one of his "signposts" (or, in a less happy designation that he uses here, in phonetic transcription, "vectors") which lead readers from the opening page toward shaping their expectations of the text: Stendhal's *Le Rouge et le Noire*, a good choice for making his point; then the contrasting examples of Mori Ōgai's *Gan* (The wild goose), which during its intermittent five-year serialization, did not bear this title, which was only conferred on its publication in book form, and Sōseki's *Mon* (The gate), which title was chosen, at his behest but with no guidelines, at random, by a couple of his young devotees before the text itself had even been begun. Yet, as Maeda points out, in both of his Japanese examples, despite their opposite modes of selection, the titles equally evoke climactic (in the case of *Gan*) or penultimate (in *Mon*) events that drive the reader on to these *yama* (literally, "peaks") in an inexorable fashion, whereas Stendhal's title prefigures for the reader, not only the protagonist's conflicting dual career choices, but the divided, ambitious soul of Julien Sorel as well.

This is the sort of category on which one imagines Maeda may have expanded in a revised, completed version of the "Primer," in the absence of which there is the temptation, again, to expand on one's own part. I will restrain myself here to the observation that the title-as-signifier obviously cannot apply to the many texts, in various literatures, that bear the title of an eponymous protagonist or a fictitious place-name, which can only remain opaque until the reader has got fairly well along in the narrative. This seems more common in the case of English fiction (e.g., the novels of George Eliot and Thomas Harding) than the Japanese, where a number of major modern writers such as Izumi Kyōka, Tanizaki, and Kawabata never chose titles of this sort. (And because I cannot resist, there is also that class of narratives whose titles seem not to do them justice; in the Japanese case, Tokuda Shūsei's *Shukuzu* comes to mind: literally, "A Reduced Map/Graphic Image," at best, more freely and idiomatically rendered as something like "A World in Miniature," but in either case, as in the Japanese original title, not at all evocative of the considerable richness of this, I believe, now generally unread and underrated major work, perhaps so in some measure because of the unfortunate title. In the case of more recent American fiction, one might mention the estimable novels of Anne Tyler, the titles of which point only toward the depressing aspect of these narratives: *Dinner at the Homesick Restaurant*, *The Accidental Tourist*, *Breathing Lessons*, etc.—an aspect that to be sure is never lacking, but there is also a good deal in them of something truly amusing that is not merely "gallows humor," which is not captured by these titles.) In any case, with the advantageous proliferation of paperback books (in Japanese, *bunkobon*), the old adage of not judging a book by its cover (or binding, etc.) has been rendered moot. But the common reader still will make some judgment, and perhaps a purchase as well, based on a title.

Another of these more apt-seeming, primeresque subheadings is "On Authors' Names," where Maeda addresses what is perhaps a particularly pronounced phenomenon in the climate of Japanese general readership. Contrary to what one might have expected here, this does not have to do with the interesting persistence into the early Shōwa era of, by Western standards, the somewhat archaic practice of writers adopting pen names, whether mock-self-deprecatory or aesthetically evocative, such as had prevailed throughout the Edo period (e.g., Ōgai, Sōseki, Kafū, the nuances of which space does not allow, nor Maeda's approach here encourage, any further discussion of). The main point he makes here is that within the cultural environment of, not simply soaring basic literacy, but broad-based forms of, to some degree, real literateness, fostered both by the system of universal education and by the impressive literateness of major daily newspapers and mass-circulation journals in early twentieth-century Japan, the names of prominent authors were known to ever growing numbers of people, though many of them may have read only excerpts in textbooks or a few installments, when they had time, of fiction serialized in these periodicals (it would apply to poetry as well). In any case, this resulted in widely circulated images triggered by the mere mention of various authors' names, some of them no doubt verging on caricature but that nevertheless achieved considerable currency. One telling example Maeda cites here is the association of Akutagawa and Mishima with suicide (he does not mention Arishima or Kawabata in this context, though both ended up suicides). Regrettably, he does not expand at all on this point, thus leaving some of us perhaps to worry that he thinks readers drawn to these authors' works may themselves have suicidal tendencies. (Mishima's lifetime works contain relatively little of the self-destructive, on the whole, rather of the self-aggrandizing, as opposed to the brief, by definition posthumously published, suicide note; Akutagawa's late, short work "Haguruma" [Cogwheels], on the other hand, one would not want to recommend to any reader perceived as unstable, presenting as it does a searing picture of a mind in the process of disintegration—partly, in fact, as a palpable result of excessive reading.) The general point here is well taken. Although there may still be in the United States not a few people who, say, at the mere mention of the name Hemingway or Fitzgerald reflexively conjure up "the Lost Generation," this authorial "name recognition" seems, for good or for ill, more widespread in Japan down to today.

If these two subcategories are examples of plausibly primer-like types of discussion he engages in, the next one, though in one sense equally so, raises some interesting questions and is more revealing of the complexities, reflecting the aforementioned perhaps conflicting aims, of this unfinished work: that of the signpost (or, as these categories are alternately called, "reading code") of "the Protagonist." From this rather brief section one can deduce, indirectly, some insights into Maeda's chosen purview of and perspective on "mainstream" post-genbun'itchi modern Japanese literature, which therefore impinges significantly on his intermittent attempts to create the new periodization of all of late-Edo-to-1980s texts that I referred to previously. The Protagonist, and as Maeda allows, other main characters as well, is without question a major sign/signifier through which common readers make their way in any narrative since, as Maeda puts it in a somewhat Puckish fashion, Stone Age viewers strove to make sense of the figures depicted in the Altamira cave paintings. Yet from this primordial observation he leaps to what he sees as a late twentieth-century impetus in Japan (for the first half of the century, he implies, it exists mainly in some "high modernist" Western texts) to subvert and simply escape from any distinctive individuality or centrality of the protagonist and other main characters, at the same time acknowledging that main-character-as-anchor is an ineluctable mode of cognition that common readers cannot or will not themselves seek to give up.

There is hereabouts a brief detour into, again, the challenging area of the topological, in which the protagonist of Kawabata's *Snow Country*, Shimamura, is discussed in terms of a figure who can move himself from the outer rim of the "sphere" (diegesis?) to inside the sphere (in nonmathematical terms this could, I suppose, be described as a "liminal" figure). He then moves on to the unassailable point that the reader needs to discriminate those protagonists whose point of view essentially coincides with that of the narrator of the text, though here citing as his sole example, perhaps somewhat problematically, Sōseki's *Sanshirō*, in which it seems to me that there is some considerable, indeed crucial to the richly ironic effects of this novel centered on an ingenue protagonist, distance between the narrators and Sanshirō that owes a good deal to the strategies of what are now known as "free indirect discourse"—a narratological area that Maeda does not enter into but that, I think, is precisely where some of the most interesting and subtle "tricks of the trade" are brought to bear, much enabled by certain characteristics of both pre- and post-genbun'itchi written Japanese, in narratives from those of Higuchi Ichiyō, through Sōseki's, on down to, of course, Tanizaki's.

Maeda then goes on to make another unassailable point, though one that might be literally disillusioning for the common reader: That, as he rightly comments, even as early as Sartre, that is, presemiotics per se, francophone theory has insisted on the point that fictional characters are no more, ontologically speaking, than the words (later, "signifiers") spun out to invent the illusion of them. Yet Maeda admirably, without a trace of condescension, allows that it is the readers' prerogative, even perhaps duty, to use their imagination to "animate," give provisional life to these illusionary concatenations of words/signifiers—a perspective that is a good deal more permissive than the more doctrinaire of poststructuralists would consent to.

It is at this juncture that he makes a rare reference to what for much of the twentieth century, by general critical consensus, passed for the canonical mainstream of so-called pure fiction (*jun bungaku*) in modern Japanese fiction, that is, the *watakushi shōsetsu* (often literally, if misleadingly, rendered as "the I-novel," something like "personal fiction" is better, in my opinion), the main thrust of whose narratives is to portray some portion of a single character's life, with ever growing emphasis on the interior life, with the protagonist's point of view assumed by professional and common readers alike to coincide with that of the narrator, whether the text is narrated in the first or the third person. This personal fiction is what historically lies, in Maeda's decentered readings of modern texts, at the center (detractors, of whom there are not a few more outspoken than Maeda ever has been, might say the dead center) canon of Japanese fiction as accepted for at least the first six decades or so of the twentieth century.

It is not surprising that he touches on the canonized central modern tradition of personal fiction under the aegis of the Protagonist rather than in various, collectively predominant subsections related to issues of language and literature and narratology (or, as mentioned above, more often refreshingly called simply *monogatari*). For the watakushi shōsetsu has naturally been the fictional subgenre par excellence where assumptions about and attempts to achieve something approaching transparency of language as a communicative mode are most evident, and where, conversely, preoccupation with the task of emplotting the seminal story in any well-constructed fashion is often most conspicuous by its absence. Here, though, under the signpost or "reading code" of the Protagonist, the hitherto omitted, innumerable texts of personal fiction could not be avoided. Having previously made considerable allowance, as mentioned above, for the common reader's need—and natural desire—to give provisional life to the ontologically illusory stuff that characters are made of, he then proceeds to make a startling, if highly ambiguous, declaration that if in the case of a Tokitō Kensaku, after reading Shiga Naoya's *An'ya kōro* (A dark night's passing), of which he is the protagonist, Kensaku may remain "etched in our memories," where such post-WWII characters as those of Abe Kōbō and Murakami Haruki are concerned, there are none like this whom we could remember or with whom we could identify. Such characters, he concludes, "today have come to strike us as a distant myth." Although a declaration like this might suggest that Maeda's sporadic, underlying project of reperiodization in the "Primer" also involves to some extent a revalorization of the canonical texts of personal fiction in the first half or so of the twentieth century, as we shall see, such is really not the case.

In conclusion, then, concerning Maeda's reperiodization of the kinsei-kindai-gendai (early modern–modern–contemporary) continuum alluded to above, however much he simply avoids what has passed for the mainstream of the kindai (modern) that is basically mid-Meiji to immediately postwar canonized texts, as has been pointed out before here, both in terms of his decentered readings of what are bona fide canonized texts (i.e., certain works by Ōgai, Sōseki, and Kafū) and his brief but provocative references to personal fiction, neither has he made attempts in the "Primer" to establish any explicit "anticanon" for this period. What Maeda has done in these pages is to make a bold move by asserting that from 1970 onward—he is quite specific about this date—in many cases basic traits of "texts," and here he broadens out his definition of what constitutes a text in a way that will be familiar to anyone slightly acquainted with critical theory of the past quarter century (whatever the common reader might make of it), revert to analogous traits in the late-Edo and early Meiji fictional narratives that have loomed so large in his life-time work: succinctly put, those of a foregrounding of language of a kind not designed to appear "transparent," indeed not even conceived as a mode of direct communication to the reader, and of characters whose constitutive signifiers do not aim at the creation of any illusion of distinct individuality, even with the intervention of the reader's imagination.

Reperiodization, as the awkward term itself conveys, can often come down to tedious matters of quibbling over details of chronology or mere tinkering with averred breaks or watersheds in the ever elusive zeitgeist. But the process also can point, as I believe it does here, to fundamental conceptions of what is at stake in cultural history and, as stated before, historicism itself. It is hard if not impossible to evaluate in a general fashion Maeda's astonishing move in this context, in large measure because his examples of the post-1970 side of the equation are so sparse in relation to those from the late Edo- to early Meiji periods. I hasten to add that nowhere in the "Primer" (at least according to my reading notes) does he conjure up explicitly the endlessly vexed, nebulous, and in many cases downright deceptive category of the Postmodern. Yet in some ambient but unmistakable way, that is in fact the category that hovers around this striking comparison he has chosen to make between more or less pre-1890 (Higuchi Ichiyō, an author of abiding interest to Maeda throughout his career, is here a transitional figure whose works came slightly over this line) and post-1970 texts. That Maeda chooses to emphasize a post-1970 recursion to pre-1890 modes of narrative representation, as opposed to a pre-1890 prefiguring of the post-1970 texts, does not, as far as I can see, make much difference. His insistent analogy is still closely akin to all those that have been made by mostly Western cultural critics over the past two or three decades in which they have managed to discover in various forms of premodern and early modern aspects of Japanese literary, visual, and performance artistic representations that prefigure those of the Postmodern.

This pronounced trend on the part of various Western critical theorists has of course been much influenced by Roland Barthes's *Empire of Signs*. There is in fact a kind of sub-subsection in the "Primer" devoted to this work in which Maeda, truly amazingly, endorses it without reservation (even pausing to make a derogatory remark about Donald Keene's putatively mocking observation on it, though without any specific citation, as "a fortnight's wonder," apparently with reference to the amount of time Barthes spent in Japan, which is of course, in those terms alone, a silly thing to say; but perhaps

Keene had more to say). Maeda's endorsement could of course be chalked up to his having been for some time under the sway of this most prominent of semioticians. But there is in the "Primer" a brief remark on his part, concerning one of Barthes's most notable excursions into literary narrative per se, *S/Z*, which Maeda characterizes as "a somewhat arbitrary and dizzying performance"—a description that would seem to suggest he was no longer, if he ever was, totally in Barthes's thrall. But then why does he give such a blanket endorsement to this whimsical exercise in a kind of neo-*Nihonjinron* (roughly translatable as "Japanese exceptionalism")? What could a Maeda, in particular given his aforementioned new privileging of jōruri, possibly make of Barthes's blithe characterization of the chanted narration of these plays as simply one of various "texts," auditory and visual, one that serves only to contribute to the creation of "surplus meaning" yet in itself is but another concatenation of opaque, if not outright "empty" signifiers? Of course, the narration is either opaque or "empty" for Barthes, who does not pretend to understand the words; but this can hardly be the case with Maeda. The theoretical concept of "surplus meaning" arising from the juxtaposition of somewhat out-of-synch texts is indeed quite useful when approaching jōruri (or the Noh theater, for that matter). But before the audience for these plays move on to surplus meaning, should they not extract, and enjoy as best they can, the significance of the various texts involved that in themselves do, in fact, have some meaning?

To return to the two basic grounds for making this comparison, the first, the foregrounding of "nontransparent" language, is surely an ineluctable matter where his pre-1890 writers are concerned. Before genbun'itchi had sunk down firm roots, and certainly in the late Edo period, there simply was no single uniform format for writing Japanese, rather, a rich but bewildering array of discrete, truly separate languages that could not very easily be synthesized, though that is precisely what many authors of all kinds of texts had to do: varying degrees of reinvented or "neoclassical" Japanese; straight classical "Chinese" (if to contemporary Chinese eyes this language appeared as archaic and stilted to the point of incomprehensibility); a whole range of heavily Sinified, so-called kakikudashi styles of what I suppose should be called Sino-Japanese; and the diverse attempts by the writers of certain fictional subgenres, collectively known as gesaku, to recreate on paper some semblance of the spoken language. Whatever form it took, writing in some synthesis of these quite distinct languages could never, even if the authors so chose, achieve any illusion of "transparency."

As for the creation of individualized, inward-looking characters, for the roughly speaking pre-1890 authors (leaving aside here the "precocious" Futabatei Shimei), again, there was little choice but to create fictional creatures who were essentially, to be sure, stereotypical caricatures drawn from one or another level of this still highly class-bound society, though there were other, nonfictional genres by writers mainly belonging to the elite (principally, of course, the *shizoku* or samurai class, but also of chōnin or "kulak" [*gōnō* in Japanese]) origin, whether philosophical or autobiographical (i.e., diaries) in which undeniable forms of individual self-consciousness were represented. Still, inevitably the epistemological revolution required to conceive of representing on a broad scale, and in fiction, discrete individuals with their own sense of their selves lagged behind the rapid development of various technological innovations in such areas as textile and weapons manufacture, shipbuilding, and the like. Although I do not believe that the particular view of human nature that emphasizes the inviolable—or inescapable—individuality of a single person was the exclusive product of the well-worn "Western Civ course" progression from the Renaissance through the Reformation followed by the Enlightenment and the rise of the mercantile and the industrialized bourgeoisie, the sheer scale of a deep resonance of this progression in the minds of many people does seem unprecedented in world-historical terms. As we have seen in the discussion of Maeda's subcategories related to the Body, he implicitly ascribes to all of his post-1890 authors a basic understanding of the results of this major shift in basic views of human nature as in due time they made themselves felt in post-Restoration Japan. The direct analogy, then, between the avoidance, or simply the absence, of any emphasis on palpably individualized characterization on the part of his pre-1890 and post-1970 cohort thus appears to disregard certain fundamental intellectual and cultural-historical realities.

To put it another way, I would argue that the fiction and other cultural products of the pre-1890 cohort were created under the twin signs of some form of alienation and of sporadically harsh, naked oppression—those of the post-1970 cohort under the twin signs of alienation, though presumably of a different form, and rampant consumerist commodification. Between the institutionalized oppression of the overwhelmingly chōnin (merchant) class of cultural producers of the late Edo and early Meiji periods and the consumerist commodification surrounding the post-1970 producers, with its much analyzed psychosocial peril but remunerative opportunities as well, there is quite a gap.

It should be mentioned that Maeda does more or less explicitly invoke some form of alienation for the post-1970 cohort by reminding us that this was the year the widespread ideological and political tumult that accompanied the drawn-out protest movement against the renewal of the Japan-U.S.

Security Treaty came to an end, with the renewal of this treaty in spite of the broad-based opposition to it. (Still, one cannot but wonder if various intellectual and emotional effects of this movement, with all its many ramifications, did not linger on in the consciousness of many Japanese, if not necessarily the postmodernish creators of texts he chooses to discuss, though only quite briefly.) Concerning the "sign" of alienation shared, under that very loose rubric, by the two cohorts who figure in Maeda's reperiodizing comparison, there are no doubt many distinctions, both broad and fine, that should be made, proceeding, to start with, from the several quite distinct definitions of alienation itself that could draw from Hegel, Marx, Sartre, and other existentialists. But I have neither the space nor the competence to do this here.

Finally, Maeda's severely curtailed discussion of the post-1970 producers of fictional texts (that of his "exhibit A," a single novel by Murakami, *Kaze no uta o kike* [Listen to the wind's song, precisely from 1970]) and those of pop song lyrics and advertising slogans from recent, at the time of writing, campaigns (e.g., "Don't Look at [the] Naked, Get Naked" and, accompanied by a glossy photo of a young woman in a bathing suit, "Because it's summer . . . this is what I've turned into") does not allow for much further examination of the terms of his striking analogy. Even if amplified by a reading of a separate essay on Murakami, suggestively entitled "The Binary World of 'I' (Boku) and 'Rat'" (with reference to the two chief characters of the aforementioned *Kaze no uta o kike*), which contains some passing reference also to Murakami's *Pinball* (1972), as it has been translated, it is hard for me to figure out if this new excursion by Maeda into relatively recent fiction can be viewed as presaging a possible sustained interest in post-1970 texts or simply, so to speak, a form of casual slumming on his part—a view that might be suggested to some readers by his juxtaposition of Murakami's works with pop song lyrics, openly declared by Maeda to be "nonsensical," and what he characterizes as the virtually aleatory, deliberate noncommunicativeness of advertising copy. At any rate, both quantitatively and qualitatively, the incommensurability of his treatment of the pre-1890 and post-1970 cultural products that he has brought into direct comparison is overwhelming.

Concerning Maeda's approach to history, and again, to historicism itself, with reference to the "literary texts" announced as the subject of his "Primer," on the basis of this regrettably uncompleted and unrevised (by Maeda himself, that is) text, it is not possible to know where he might have gone with his partial but nonetheless palpable intention here, not simply to reperiodize modern Japanese literature, but to engage in a broadly based reconception of both literary and cultural history. Unfinished though it is, this posthumously published "Primer" contains much of interest, sometimes couched in terms that are in fact accessible to the common reader, at other points, seemingly not so.

In spite of the likely challenges posed here to common readers, a patronizing-sounding category that is, however, conjured up by the very title of Maeda's "Primer" and from which I certainly do not exclude myself, I must say unequivocally that it was both a very admirable and a promising project that, even in its unfinished form, will continue to be, as no doubt it has been already for some readers, an entree into any number of ways, some old, some new, to approaching the life-enhancing experience of exploring all manner of texts, including, but by no means limited to, those of the merely belletristic canon. To have dwelled as much as I have over the past few pages on issues related to reperiodization but beyond that, more general matters of the complex relationship between history and literature (encompassing, by extension, other forms of cultural representation) to be found in this *spätwerk* by Maeda has probably not been in some basic way fair. He did, after all, call this a "Primer," not a "History" of literary texts.

To have read here and there in Maeda's extensive lifetime work is to realize full well that he hardly lacked a sense of history. To say that his sense of history most compellingly reveals itself in the localized contexts of particular literary texts that his own sensibility has led him to analyze first and foremost in terms of both space and place is no criticism. The detailed spatial analyses that distinguish his work are of course at some odds with the most general kind of historical, therefore to some degree also ideological, concerns. At the same time, his passion for places, in addition to his interest in space—for there is a sharp distinction to be made—ineluctably led him to engage, though far more evidently in his lifetime work than the posthumously published "Primer," in localized historical contextualizations. If his increasingly elaborate and abstract ideas about space (largely fictionalized space, of course) drove his ever more graphic, geometrical, even topological analyses of texts, his abiding preoccupation with places that, even in often semifictionalized form could not fail to evoke specific temporal, therefore, in the most basic way, historical associations, inevitably drew him to historical discussions of a quite concrete nature: in the end, one might say, to a wonderfully distinct inflection of that old Japanese, in fact common-readerly, hobby of the *bungaku sampo* (literally, "the literary stroll").

Note

1 *The Portable Walt Whitman* (New York: Viking, 1945), 197.

REBECCA COPELAND is Associate Professor of Japanese Language and Literature at Washington University in St. Louis. Her publications include *The Sound of the Wind: The Life and Works of Uno Chiyo*, *Lost Leaves: Women Writers of Meiji Japan*, and *The Father-Daughter Plot:Japanese Literary Women and the Law of the Father*, which she coedited with Esperanza Ramirez-Christensen.

EDWARD FOWLER teaches and writes about Japanese literature and film at the University of California, Irvine.

MATTHEW FRALEIGH is a Ph.D. candidate in the Department of East Asian Languages and Civilizations at Harvard University, where he is focusing on early modern Japanese literature. His main research interests are in *kanshi* and *kanbun* texts from the early modern period, and his dissertation focuses especially on the work of Narushima Ryūhoku. He contributed an essay on Ryūhoku to *Modern Japanese Writers*, and his more recent work on Ryūhoku's travel diaries has been published in *Kyoto Daigaku Kokubungaku Ronsō* and *Kokugo Kokubun*.

JAMES A. FUJII teaches Japanese literature and culture at the University of California, Irvine. His current project addresses the culture of Japanese metropolitan railways in the first half of the twentieth century.

SEIJI M. LIPPIT is Associate Professor of Modern Japanese Literature at the University of California, Los Angeles. He is the author of *Topographies of Japanese Modernism* and the editor of *The Essential Akutagawa*.

H. RICHARD OKADA teaches Japanese literature and culture at Princeton University. He has written on both premodern and modern topics and is currently working on Heian poetics and postwar Zainichi writers.

LESLIE PINCUS teaches in the History Department at the University of Michigan. She is the author of *Authenticating Culture in Imperial Japan: Kuki Shuzo and the Rise of National Aesthetics* and guest editor of a 2002 issue of *positions* titled *Open to the*

Public: Studies in Japan's Recent Past. Her new project explores linked genealogies of cultural theory and social movements in twentieth-century Japan.

WILLIAM F. SIBLEY is Associate Professor Emeritus of Japanese Literature at the University of Chicago and continues to take an interest in both literature and cultural history of Japan from the Kamakura period to the Showa era, mainly of the years down to 1970.

HENRY D. SMITH II is Professor of Japanese History at Columbia University. His research focuses on the social and cultural history of nineteenth-century Japan, particularly the visual culture of the city of Edo-Tokyo. He has written books on the prints of Hiroshige, Hokusai, and Kiyochika.

Bentham, Jeremy, 29, 35, 40; panoptic prison of, 27–29

Berger, P. L. and Luchman, T.: *The Social Construction of Reality*, 342

Berlin, 13, 296, 297, 299, 300, 303, 307, 309, 311, 313, 316, 323, 324; as cosmopolitan, 300; and fashion, 298; and Ōgai, 306; Origas on, 301; regulation of space in, 310; representation of, 298; as world capital, 310

Bijutsu, 266

Binary opposition, 104

Blackmur, R. P.: *Language as Gesture*, 242–43

Body (*shintai*), 5, 60, 363; and urban space, 5

Bōkan (observe), 256

Book making: movable type and, 262; woodblock printing and, 262

Book rental, 228

Booth, Charles: *Life and Labour of the People in London*, 45–46

Booth, William: *In Darkest England and the Way Out*, 46

Boshin War, 287

Bourgeoisie, 310

Boy's literature (*shōnen bungaku*): *Jugendschrift*, 113

Brandenburg Gate, 299, 300, 301, 302

Brombert, Victor, 29

Buber, Martin, 60

Bundan (literary guild), 164, 165, 166, 196, 330; and popular novel, 189; and print journalism, 179

Bunka (culture), 204–9

Bunmei kaika. *See* Civilization and enlightenment

Bunyan, John: *The Pilgrim's Progress*, 115

Byron, George Gordon (lord), 56–58

Caillois, Roger, 132

Campanella: *The City of the Sun*, 22

Captain Chanoine, 285, 286

Carnochan, W. B.: *Confinement and Flight*, 23

Carroll, Lewis: *Alice in Wonderland*, 110, 111

Casino Folies, 146, 147, 148, 150, 152, 153, 154

Champs-Elysées, 280

Chiba Kameo: "The Line between High-class Art and the Popular Novel" ("Kōkyūgeijutsu to tsūzoku shōsetsu tono issen"), 188

Chicago, 13

Children: as future adults, 110; of Meiji, 110

Chinsekai ("strange world"), 150

Cholera, 45

Chōya shimbun: and Narushima Ryū-hoku, 39, 40

Christianity, 289

Chūō kōron, 165, 167, 174, 175

Chūō Line, 332

City: baroque, 307; center, 337; colonial city, xiv; literary descriptions of, 73; medieval, 307, 312; as text, 87

Cityspace, xiii, xiv; in panoramic form, 303; texts and, xv

Civilization and enlightenment (*bunmei kaika*), 67, 79, 81, 82, 85, 101, 104, 228, 258, 268, 298; catalogue of, 81; and darkness, 56, 92, 95; in "The Fox," 94; and Ginza Brick District, 4; and imprisonment, 31; new scenes of, 99; panorama of, 69; and rationalism, 103; *things* as symbols of, 80, 81

Civilization and nature, 104

Cock's Fair (*Tori no ichi*), 131, 133, 135

Commodification: fetishism and, 82, 86

Communal life, 126

Confinement, 287, 322; and imagination, 22; liberation and, 21, 22, 23, 25, 29, 30, 35, 60; Yoshida Shōin on, 30

Constitution: and Imperial Rescript on Education, 112, 115, 116

The Crimson Gang of Asakusa (Asakusa Kurenaidan): as photographic negative of Tokyo, 156. *See also* Kawabata Yasunari

Daguerre, Louis Jacques Mandé, 72, 296

Daigaku (Great learning), 115

Daionjimae, 116, 118–21, 124, 129, 130; children, 126, 128, 129, 131, 136; neighborhood, 133; streets of, 121

Dangozaka, 336

Darkness (*yami*), 56, 92, 95, 101; and civilization, 45–48; in "The Fox," 94; and self-consciousness in Tōkoku, 58

Dentsūin, 102

de Sade, Marquis, 22, 29

Diorama, 296

Dorotheenstadt, 307

Dōshisha, 233, 248

Dumas, Alexander: *Ange Pitou*, 54

Edo, 71, 72, 103; *bakumatsu*, 99; as a city of water, 71, 72; guidebooks and, 74, 75; Inari shrine, 103; plan of, 75; as premodern, xiii; as space, 74, 75, 77, 78, 101, 104; in Tokyo, 101

Edo fiction, 259, 260, 260–61; and illustrations, 261, 265; period books, 260; visual nature of, 262

Edogawa Rampo, xv, 151, 157

Edo guidebook, 73, 74

Edo meisho zue (Illustrated Guide to the Famous Sites of Edo), 286

Edo reader, 260

Edo River, 335

Education: and literacy, 169–72

Emi Suiin, 233

Empson, William: *Some Versions of Pastoral*, 110

Engels, Friedrich: *Housing Question*, 310

Enlightenment Tokyo, 67

Enomoto Ken'ichi ("Enoken"), 147, 152

Enpon (one-yen books), 164

Ethnography: as method, xiii; premodern, xv

Etō Jun, 5, 339

Etō Shinpei, 276

Everyday (*nichijō*): and non-everyday space (*hi-nichijō*), 76, 77

Everyday life, 341, 342, 346, 347, 348; life of Berliners, 300

Exhibition: First National Industrial, 258, 265, 267

Family: and reading, 225, 235

Fenollosa, Ernest: *A True Account of the Fine Arts*, 265, 267

Fiction, 259; as art, 267; as imitation, 267

First National Bank (of Japan), 65–67, 68, 70, 72, 80–82, 101

Flâneur: Maeda Ai as, xv; Walter Benjamin and, 2, 14

Flaubert, 257

Fontane, Theodor (*Frau Jenny Treibel*), 310

Foster Sisters (Chikyōdai), 180

Foucault, Michael, 7; *Madness and Civilization*, 23; on prison, 28–29, 61 n.9; on ranking, 34–35

Franco-Prussian War, 270, 284, 298, 299, 300, 306, 310

Freedom and Popular Rights Movement, 30, 48, 54–56, 58, 59, 233, 248

French Revolution, 299

Friedrichstadt, 307

Fujimori Terunobu, 43

Fujin gahō (Woman's Pictorial), 176

Fujin kōron (Woman's Review), 167, 170–72, 176, 177, 199, 200; on women and society, 196–98

Fujin kurabu (Woman's Club), 174, 176, 178

Origas, J. J., 302; "Spider-leg Streets: One Aspect of Sōseki's Early Works" ("Kumode' no machi: Sōseki shoki no sakuhin no ichi danmen"), 301

Osaka Asahi shimbun, 165, 190

Osaka Mainichi shimbun, 165, 175, 178, 181, 184, 190

Ōtori Shrine, 120, 124, 135

Ōya Masao, 59, 61

Ōya Sōichi, 5, 172; on *bundan*, 165; on female readership, 166; "The Era of the Dissolution of the Bundan Guild" ("Bundan girudo no kaitaiki"), 164; "The Sudden Rise in Women's Magazines" ("Fujin zasshi no kyūgeki naru hatten"), 166

Ozaki Kōyō: *The Amorous Confessions of Two Nuns* (*Ninin bikuni irozange*), 236; *The Gold Demon* (*Konjikiyasha*), 244

Palais-Royal, 281

Panopticon, 40; and *Prison Regulations*, 35–36

Panorama, 73, 283, 304; and diorama, 72, 73; literature and, 73; and prisons, 28–29; of the Prussian military, 300; and realistic perspective, 72, 73; scenes from Franco-Prussian War, 281; urban, 301; viewpoint of, 297

Panoramakan (Panorama Hall), 149, 150

Panovsky, 302, 304

Paris, 280, 282, 284, 286, 306; capital of Europe, 281; of fortresses and factories, 288; Haussmann's, 309; of theaters and galleries, 288

Paris Commune, 281, 284, 287

Pascal, Blaise: *Pensées*, 24

People's Rights Movement. *See* Freedom and Popular Rights Movement

Perspective: bird's-eye view, 74, 302; and composition, 317; focal point,

302; laws of, 304; linear, 302, 304; multiple vanishing points, 302; Renaissance, 271; single point, 302; spatial, 303; in urban space, 316; vanishing point, 271; as vision, 306

Piranesi, Giovanni Battista, 29, 57; *Carceri d'invenzione*, 24, 25, 27, 28; *Prima Parte*, 27; "prison fantasies," 57, 58

Plato: *Republic*, 304

Play (*asobi*), 10; children and, 114, 118, 129, 131, 133; and daily life, 78; and festivity (*hare*), 78; and ordinary (*ke*), 78; Rokku, 149; space of, 118; in Yoshiwara and theater district, 77

Plaza, 281, 311; at Ryōgoku Bridge, 73

Pleasure quarters, 13, 282

Political novel (*seiji shōsetsu*), 31, 113, 268; *Admirable Tales of Statecraft* (*Keikoku bidan*) and *Chance Encounters with Beautiful Women* (*Kajin no kigū*), 113; and imprisonment, 30–31; as literature of the prison, 53. *See also* Kitamura Tōkoku; Miyazaki Muryū

Popular fiction, 165–66, 175, 178, 188, 194, 198, 200

Poulet, Georges: *Metamorphoses of the Circle*, 23; on Piranesi's *Carceri*, 58; on *Vathek*, 57

Print: modern, 260

Prison, 35, 286; as fantasy, 22; Ichigaya Penitentiary, 330; Kajibashi, 37, 39, 40; (map), 55; Meiji jail, 287; as metaphor, 56; and Narushima Ryūhoku, 30; and the nation-state, 21, 22–28; Paris, 287; reform of, 27–29; and sanitation, 45; structure of, 32, 33; Tenmachō, 31, 32, 53; and utopia, 21; utopia of, 33; of Western nations, 44; Western style, 40

Prison literature. *See* Political novel

Prison Regulations (*Kangokusoku*), 31–40

Proletarian literature, 157, 188, 189–90

Prosperity: tales of, 73

Prostitutes, 85, 281, 283; in literature, 181; Memorandum of Agreement, 135

Raabe, W.: *Die Chronik der Sperlings-gasse*, 310–11

Railroad, 8, 282, 332

Rakugo (comic monologue), 260

Reader (*dokusha*), 166, 173, 184, 188, 195, 226, 227, 228, 235, 239, 242, 246, 247, 269; and author, 263, 264; Edo, 260; female, 7, 180–81, 186, 197–99, 204, 207, 227; and imagination, 269; middle class, 189, 209; modern, 260; reception, 236–37; and text, 245–46, 263; of women's magazines, 165, 166, 171–72, 173–74, 197–98, 207, 208

Reading: and alienation, 263; aloud, 260; communal, 225, 230, 232, 233, 234–35; in education, 226; group, 234–35; printed words, 263; recitation and, 263; *rōdoku* (recitation), 229; *rōshō* (performative recitation), 229; silent (*mokudoku*), 235; *sodoku* (sound-reading), 229, 236; solitary, 225, 229, 235, 244, 248

Realism: beyond, 318; European, 257; in modern literature, 255; *shajitsu* as, 256

Riesman, David, 115; *The Lonely Crowd*, 233–34

Rindoku (reading groups), 231

Risshin shusse (personal advancement), 111, 116, 117, 203, 303

Rokku. *See* Asakusa

Rokumeikan Hall, 50, 55, 93, 296

Romanticism, 23, 257; imagination of, 29; self-consciousness, 27

Rousseau, Jean-Jacques: *Reveries of the Solitary Walker*, 23

Rue d'Amboise, 281

Russian revolutionaries, 55

Russo-Japanese War, 332

Ryōgoku, 71, 72, 77; summer fireworks at, 78

Ryōsai kenbo (good wife/wise mother), 170

Ryūsenji-chō, 121, 124

Ryūsenji-mura, 121

Ryūtei Tanehiko, 259

Sacred space, 102, 103; vs. secular space, 103

Saganoya Omuro, 230; "First Love" ("Hatsukoi"), 247

Saitō Gesshin: *Illustrations of the Famous Places of Edo* (*Edo meisho zue*), 74, 75, 76, 77

Sakai Tadayasu, 67

Sakurada Taiga: *Records of Exploration in the World of Dire Poverty, Hunger, and Suffering* (*Hin tenchi dai kikan kutsu tanken ki*), 45

Salvation Army, 46

Sameshima Naonobu, 285

Samurai, 55, 76, 95, 102, 230

Santama, 61

Santō Kyōden, 259

Sanyūtei Enchō, 227, 240, 241, 245; and oral narration, 242; *The Tale of the Peony Garden Lantern* (*Kaidan botan dōrō*), 240–41, 241–42

Sasaki Kuni, 174, 177; *Comedy at Culture Village* (Bunka mura no kigeki), 206

Satō Hachirō, 148

Satō Haruo, 166; "On the Livelihood of the Writer" ("Bungeika no seikatsu o ronzu"), 164

Satomi Ton, 179

Satsuma: and Chōshū, 285

Second Empire, 285

Seiji shōsetsu. *See* Political novel

Seiyōken, 336

Self, 5, 271, 316, 347; expression of, 256;
as knowing subject, 304; and other,
337
Senju, 78, 124
Sensōji Kannon Hall, 146
Sensōji, 78, 148, 149
Senuma Shigeki, 5; on domestic fiction
(*katei shōsetsu*), 175
Senzoku, 124
Senzoku-mura, 121
Senzoku Shrine, 125, 128, 133
Shakespeare, 263
Shanghai, 13; and Yokomitsu, xiii
Shiba Kōkan: *View of Ryōgoku Bridge*
(*Ryōgokubashi zu*), 73
Shikitei Samba: *The Barbershop of the
Floating World* (*Ukiyodoko*), 259, 260;
The Bathhouse of the Floating World
(*Ukiyoburo*), 259, 260
Shinagawa, 78
Shinbashi Station, 44, 70, 80, 81, 83
Shinjuku, 12, 332
Shintai. *See* Body
Shirayanagi Shūko: "Diary of a Station
Worker," 333
Shirokiya, 332
Shiseidō, 334
Shitamachi (Low City), 99, 101, 116,
117, 121, 125, 331; central, 99; and
yamanote, 336. *See also* Asakusa;
Slums
Shōsetsu (Japanese novel), 7, 227, 239–
40, 256, 257; communal reading of,
228, 229; and darkness (*see* Dark-
ness); and freedom and people's
rights movement, 30–31, 48, 54–
56, 58, 59; and *genbun'itchi*, 245–47;
and imprisonment, 21–23, 29–32;
and reading, 223; solitary reading
and, 229; and uneven development,
45–53; utopia and, 21–27. *See also*
Political novel

Shufu no tomo (*Housewife's Friend*), 166,
171, 173–74, 174, 176, 177, 178, 200;
and domestic concerns, 197–98
Shūyō (self-cultivation), 173, 202–5
Signifier: and signified, 264, 304, 341;
and things, 342
Sim, George: *How the Poor Live and
Horrible London*, 45
Slums, 10, 44, 103; Samegahashi, 128;
Shiba Shin'amichō, 49; Shin'ami-chō,
128; Yotsuya Samegahashi district,
49, 52
Smiles, Samuel: *Self-Help*, 111, 114, 115
Soganoya Gokurō, 146
Space, 2; *akusho* as, 7; Asakusa as, 148;
baroque, 299, 301, 303, 305, 316, 317;
chaotic, 97; class consciousness and,
116–17, 118–21, 125–30; colonization
of, xiii; as culture, 3; culture and, xii;
domestic, 344, 346; dwelling, 336;
and sight, 304; as dwelling place, 320;
of Edo, 74, 77, 78; Edo as, 71, 72;
in Edo guidebooks, 74, 75; everyday, 316; of evil, 7; expansion of, 30;
experience of, 304; forbidden, 131;
inside (*uchi*)/outside (*soto*), 311–12;
interior and exterior, 320–21, 322–24;
labyrinth, 318, 319; layer of, 317; and
light and shadows, 71; lived, 9, 304;
living, 334, 340, 346; mathematical,
304, 305; monumental, 322; as myth,
75; of non-everyday (*hi-nichijō*), 76;
perspectival, 302; play and, 149; private, 8, 344; public, 12; sacred, 149;
textual, 311; thesis on, 6
Spectacle: dramas, 300; theater as, 264
Stanley, Henry M.: *In Darkest Africa*,
46–49
Stendhal (Marie-Henri Beyle): *The Red
and the Black*, 257
Stepniak, Sergei: *Underground Russia*, 55

LIBRARY OF CONGRESS CATALOGING-IN-PUBLICATION DATA

Text and the city : essays on Japanese modernity / by Maeda Ai ;

with an introduction by James A. Fujii.

p. cm. — (Asia-Pacific)

Includes index.

ISBN 0-8223-3334-1 (cloth : alk. paper)

ISBN 0-8223-3346-5 (pbk. : alk. paper)

1. Japanese literature—1868—History and criticism.   2. Cities and

towns in literature.   3. Space and time in literature.

I. Maeda Ai.   II. Fujii, James A.   III. Title.   IV. Series.

PL726.57.C5T48   2004

895.6'09321732—dc22   2003022708